Cognitive and Soft Computing Techniques for the Analysis of Healthcare Data

Intelligent Data-Centric Systems: Sensor Collected Intelligence

Cognitive and Soft Computing Techniques for the Analysis of Healthcare Data

Edited by

Akash Kumar Bhoi
Department of Computer Science and Engineering,
Sikkim Manipal Institute of Technology,
Sikkim Manipal University, Majitar, Sikkim, India

Victor Hugo C. de Albuquerque
Department of Teleinformatics Engineering, Federal University of
Ceará, Fortaleza, Fortaleza/CE, Brazil

Parvathaneni Naga Srinivasu
Department of Computer Science and Engineering, GIT, GITAM
(Deemed to be University), Visakhapatnam, Andhra Pradesh, India

Gonçalo Marques
Polytechnic of Coimbra, ESTGOH, Rua General Santos Costa,
Oliveira do Hospital, Portugal;
University of Maia - ISMAI, Av. Carlos de Oliveira Campos,
Maia, Portugal

Series Editor

Fatos Xhafa

ACADEMIC PRESS
An imprint of Elsevier

ELSEVIER

Academic Press is an imprint of Elsevier
125 London Wall, London EC2Y 5AS, United Kingdom
525 B Street, Suite 1650, San Diego, CA 92101, United States
50 Hampshire Street, 5th Floor, Cambridge, MA 02139, United States
The Boulevard, Langford Lane, Kidlington, Oxford OX5 1GB, United Kingdom

Notices
Knowledge and best practice in this field are constantly changing. As new research and experience broaden our
understanding, changes in research methods, professional practices, or medical treatment may become
necessary.

Practitioners and researchers must always rely on their own experience and knowledge in evaluating and using
any information, methods, compounds, or experiments described herein. In using such information or
methods they should be mindful of their own safety and the safety of others, including parties for whom they
have a professional responsibility.

To the fullest extent of the law, neither the Publisher nor the authors, contributors, or editors, assume any
liability for any injury and/or damage to persons or property as a matter of products liability, negligence or
otherwise, or from any use or operation of any methods, products, instructions, or ideas contained in the
material herein.

Library of Congress Cataloging-in-Publication Data
A catalog record for this book is available from the Library of Congress

British Library Cataloguing-in-Publication Data
A catalogue record for this book is available from the British Library

ISBN: 978-0-323-85751-2

For information on all Academic Press publications visit our
website at https://www.elsevier.com/books-and-journals

Publisher: Mara Conner
Acquisitions Editor: Sonnini R. Yura
Editorial Project Manager: Isabella C. Silva
Production Project Manager: Maria Bernard
Cover Designer: Mark Rogers

Typeset by TNQ Technologies

Contents

CHAPTER 7   Comparisons among different stochastic selections of activation layers for convolutional neural networks for health care 151

Loris Nanni, Alessandra Lumini, Stefano Ghidoni and Gianluca Maguolo

CHAPTER 8   Natural computing and unsupervised learning methods in smart healthcare data-centric operations 165

Joseph Bamidele Awotunde, Abidemi Emmanuel Adeniyi, Sunday Adeola Ajagbe and Alfonso González-Briones

CHAPTER 11   Probabilistic approaches for minimizing the healthcare diagnosis cost through data-centric operations 221

Akhilesh Kumar Sharma, Sachit Bhardwaj, Devesh Kumar Srivastava, Nguyen Ha Huy Cuong and Shamik Tiwari

CHAPTER 12   Effects of EEG-sleep irregularities and its behavioral aspects: review and analysis 239

Santosh Satapathy, D. Loganathan, Akash Kumar Bhoi and Paolo Barsocchi

Contributors

Abidemi Emmanuel Adeniyi
Department of Computer Science, Landmark University, Omu-Aran, Kwara, Nigeria

Surabhi Adhikari
Department of Computer Science and Engineering, Delhi Technological University, Rohini, Delhi, India

Sunday Adeola Ajagbe
Department of Computer Engineering, Ladoke Akintola University of Technology, Ogbomoso, Oyo, Nigeria

Joseph Bamidele Awotunde
Department of Computer Science, University of Ilorin, Ilorin, Kwara, Nigeria

Paolo Barsocchi
Institute of Information Science and Technologies, National Research Council, Pisa, Italy

Sachit Bhardwaj
Manipal University Jaipur, Jaipur, Rajasthan, India

Akash Kumar Bhoi
Department of Computer Science and Engineering, Sikkim Manipal Institute of Technology, Sikkim Manipal University, Majitar, Sikkim, India; Institute of Information Science and Technologies, National Research Council, Pisa, Italy

Nguyen Ha Huy Cuong
University of Danang, College of Information Technology, Hai Chau, Da Nang, Vietnam

P. Deepalakshmi
School of Computing, Department of Computer Science and Engineering, Kalasalingam Academy of Research and Education, Krishnankoil, India

Simon James Fong
University of Macau (UM), Macau, Macau SAR, China

M. Ganeshkumar
Center for Computational Engineering and Networking (CEN), Amrita School of Engineering, Amrita Vishwa Vidyapeetham, Coimbatore, Tamil Nadu, India

Stefano Ghidoni
DEI, University of Padua, Padua, Italy

Awishkar Ghimire
Department of Computer Science and Engineering, Delhi Technological University, Rohini, Delhi, India

Francisco Nauber Bernardo Gois
Escola de Saúde Pública (ESP), Fortaleza, Brazil

Alfonso González-Briones
Research Group on Agent-Based, Social and Interdisciplinary Applications (GRASIA), Complutense University of Madrid, Madrid, Spain; BISITE Research Group, University of Salamanca, Salamanca, Spain; Air Institute, IoT Digital Innovation Hub, Salamanca, Spain

E.A. Gopalakrishnan
Center for Computational Engineering and Networking (CEN), Amrita School of Engineering, Amrita Vishwa Vidyapeetham, Coimbatore, Tamil Nadu, India

Pratiyush Guleria
NIELIT, Shimla, Himachal Pradesh, India

Muhammad Fazal Ijaz
Department of Intelligent Mechatronics Engineering, Sejong University, Seoul, South Korea

Ivan Izonin
Department of Artificial Intelligence, Lviv Polytechnic National University, Lviv, Ukraine

Vishalteja Kosana
Department of Electrical Engineering, National Institute of Technology Andhra Pradesh, Tadepalligudem, India

Tengyue Li
University of Macau (UM), Macau, Macau SAR, China

D. Loganathan
Department of Computer Science and Engineering, Pondicherry Engineering College, Puducherry, India

Alessandra Lumini
DISI, Università di Bologna, Cesena, Italy

Gianluca Maguolo
DEI, University of Padua, Padua, Italy

João Alexandre Lôbo Marques
University of Saint Joseph (USJ), Macau, Macau SAR, China

P. Nagaraj
School of Computing, Department of Computer Science and Engineering, Kalasalingam Academy of Research and Education, Krishnankoil, India

Loris Nanni
DEI, University of Padua, Padua, Italy

Abu ul Hassan S. Rana
Department of Intelligent Mechatronics Engineering, Sejong University, Seoul, Gyeonggi, Korea

Santosh Satapathy
Department of Computer Science and Engineering, Pondicherry Engineering College, Puducherry, India

Akhilesh Kumar Sharma
Manipal University Jaipur, Jaipur, Rajasthan, India

Jarbas Aryel Nunes da Silveira
Federal University of Ceará (UFC), Fortaleza, Brazil

K.P. Soman
Center for Computational Engineering and Networking (CEN), Amrita School of Engineering, Amrita Vishwa Vidyapeetham, Coimbatore, Tamil Nadu, India

Manu Sood
Department of Computer Science, Himachal Pradesh University, Shimla, Himachal Pradesh, India

V. Sowmya
Center for Computational Engineering and Networking (CEN), Amrita School of Engineering, Amrita Vishwa Vidyapeetham, Coimbatore, Tamil Nadu, India

Devesh Kumar Srivastava
Manipal University Jaipur, Jaipur, Rajasthan, India

Kiran Teeparthi
Department of Electrical Engineering, National Institute of Technology Andhra Pradesh, Tadepalligudem, India

Surendrabikram Thapa
Department of Computer Science and Engineering, Delhi Technological University, Rohini, Delhi, India

Shamik Tiwari
UPES, Dehradun, Uttarakhand, India

Roman Tkachenko
Department of Publishing Information Technologies, Lviv Polytechnic National University, Lviv, Ukraine

João Paulo do Vale Madeiro
Federal University of Ceará (UFC), Fortaleza, Ceará, Brazil

Preface

Cognitive and soft computing approaches in data processing for healthcare systems have been apparent for the past few years. They have brought about remarkable changes in the process of healthcare data acquisition, context processing, data transformation, data training, data pipelining, and data analytics. Information summarization would assist in faster decision-making on medication procedures, surgical planning, and the prediction of illness in advance, resulting in lowered risk of disease. Cognitive technology in the healthcare industry would empower work mechanisms and facilitate thinking identical to humans in solving real-time challenges. Generally, healthcare data is continuous. It can be from various sources such as real-time data, machine-dependent data, spatiotemporal data, open data, big data and structured, semistructured, and unstructured data from divergent sources. In such a context, advanced intelligent mechanisms like evolutionary computing, machine learning, artificial neural networks, fuzzy logic, nature-inspired optimization algorithms, big data in healthcare, and expert systems can efficiently handle considerable data in solving complex real-time tasks. The data are rendered from various sources such as transactional data from business expert systems, sensor data network components, temporal data from a real-time system that includes the date and time, web data from the Internet, and operational data. The data need to be analyzed through the features extracted alongside the feature scaling to perform descriptive, predictive, and prescriptive analysis. In data analysis and evaluation, many intermittent tasks are performed using supervised, semisupervised, or unsupervised mechanisms. It includes data exploration, data classification, model building, model deployment, model management, and prediction for generating the summarized outcome, followed by error analysis. In this book, the chapters are categorized across five sections: cognitive technology for processing healthcare data; artificial intelligence approaches for the healthcare industry; evolutionary algorithms for healthcare data analysis; computational intelligence; and soft computing models in processing the data related to the healthcare industry.

Chapter 1 investigates study of the machine learning classifiers and the evaluation metrics over various diabetes data sets, giving an insight into the working procedures and efficiencies of various models. The authors propose an ensemble model through the boosted trees and bagged trees algorithms to predict diabetes. The opportunities and challenges of artificial intelligence in the healthcare sector and various phases of data analytics in the healthcare domain are discussed in the introductory section, followed by the implementation architecture of the proposed model and statistical analysis of the experimental results. The experimental outcome concludes that the smart healthcare framework would perform better than conventional approaches.

Chapter 2 presents the cognitive technology for the personalized seizure, and a future perspective model through the neural network models and natural language processing is presented. The authors present the Internet of Things (IoT)-driven sensor-driven data analysis using cognitive technology for seizure detection. The role of various sensors in the data acquisition process in the IoT architecture is presented with a detailed architecture of the neural network-based model for monitoring, interpreting, and maintaining healthcare records. The performance of the proposed model is statistically analyzed using various evaluation metrics.

Chapter 3 describes the computation intelligence models for mental well-being. The authors introduce the computer vision for early diagnosis of mental disorders using MRI and a natural language processing-based diagnostic system. They present various machine learning models across divergent data sets to predict diseases like Alzheimer's and Parkinson's, and compare them with a normal control. The future scope of computation intelligence for well-being and the role of wearable devices outline the scope for further study in the healthcare field.

Chapter 4 aims at the artificial neural networks in disease diagnosis. The authors elaborate on the challenges involved in computer-aided diagnosis models and how they propose neural networks address those challenges. The authors also present on the performance of the proposed diagnosis model through various evaluation metrics. The authors also describe various types of neural networks with a better understanding of the underlying technology along with the layered architecture. The experimental studies on various medical imaging technologies and their efficiencies are presented in this chapter.

In Chapter 5, case studies based on the deep learning techniques for processing the massive amount of patient-centric data that assist in clinical decisions and statistical analysis of the proposed model are described. The authors present clinical decision support systems and knowledge-based systems to process and manage patient-centric data. The recent advancements in big data and AI for CDSS are presented along with real-time case studies and performance evaluation.

Chapter 6 implements the regression modeling of a small data set using the universal interensemble model that can effectively handle situations where the data for diagnosis, prevention, or treatment are scarce. The authors present the ensemble model over the support vector regression, general regression neural network, and RBF neural network, along with the architectures in the current study. Statistical analysis of the performances of various neural network models across various evaluation parameters is presented.

Chapter 7 focuses on the stochastic selection of activation layers for convolutional neural networks for health care, where various versions of activation functions are discussed. The study is carried out using ResNet50 as the backbone architecture for classification. The authors also present the statistical analysis of performance among the convolutional neural network models and various ensembles of the classifier over the medical imaging data sets.

Chapter 8 investigates the natural computing and unsupervised learning methods in smart health care for cardiovascular disease prediction. The authors also give a survey of various natural computing algorithms broadly used in the healthcare domain to predict and forecast diseases. The roles of unsupervised learning algorithms and data-centric intelligence in the healthcare system are discussed.

Chapter 9 deliberates on an optimized adaptive tree seed Kalman filter for an insulin recommendation system, and the authors present the mathematical model of the proposed system. The study demonstrates the various existing models for insulin recommendation systems. The proposed model combines the adaptive Kalman filtering (AKF) technique and the tree seeding optimization algorithm that has yielded a promising performance for insulin recommendation.

In Chapter 10, deep learning-based intracranial hemorrhage diagnoses from computed tomography images are presented. The authors present detailed information about the various existing models and evaluation metrics to assess the model's accuracy. The deep learning model called PCA-Net is used in intracranial hemorrhage identification. The detailed architecture of PCA-Net is presented, along with a performance evaluation of the proposed model.

Chapter 11 describes the probabilistic approaches for minimizing the healthcare diagnosis cost. The authors present the breast cancer diagnosis model using Bayesian neural network and statistical analysis of the model's performance concerning hyperparameters and weights association.

Chapter 12 presents an EEG-based analytical model for the study of sleep irregularities and their behavioral aspects. The authors offer a visual scoring procedure through various waveforms to determine sleep disorders. The existing classification models for sleep irregularities and associated input and feature extraction details are presented. The proposed ensemble learning stacking model for classification and the statistical analysis of the performances on choosing the various parameters are presented.

This book aims to extend the cognizance among academicians and researchers about the insight of data-processing applications in various domains through soft computing techniques and the enormous advancements in the field. This book focuses on data-centric operations in the healthcare industry, and it incorporates various data-processing models through cognitive learning. A wide range of soft computing approaches address the real-time challenges and suitable case studies in the healthcare industry are described.

Artificial intelligence and machine learning for the healthcare sector: performing predictions and metrics evaluation of ML classifiers on a diabetic diseases data set

Pratiyush Guleria[1] and Manu Sood[2]

[1]NIELIT, Shimla, Himachal Pradesh, India; [2]Department of Computer Science, Himachal Pradesh University, Shimla, Himachal Pradesh, India

1. Introduction

Machine learning is a program that learns to perform a task and make decisions from the data rather than being explicitly programmed to do so. Machine learning (ML) and big data techniques work in close relation to each other to mine a huge amount of unstructured data to obtain refined and meaningful information [1]. Machine learning techniques are a boon to the healthcare industry and help in identifying and diagnosing diseases that are difficult to diagnose. ML helps in analyzing the data and shows its applicability in areas such as identifying cancerous tumors, skin cancers, pattern recognition, image processing, etc. Machine learning techniques are mainly of two types: supervised and unsupervised learning. ML supervised learning helps in the classification of patients' diseases, whereas unsupervised learning identifies the patterns in the data.

ML has contributed a great deal to epidemiologists in helping to identify the risks of infectious diseases. ML applications have also transformed electronic health systems [2]. A major challenge in the healthcare industry is selecting the most appropriate ML model for handling the diagnostics [3]. The ML technique and big data analytics are used for value-based healthcare and supply chain pharmaceutical optimization. Deep learning is an emerging area derived from AI, with deep learning algorithms being helpful for personalized healthcare services. Deep cognitive computing tools are used in the healthcare industry for effective and timely diagnosis. The real-time, deep personalized value-based healthcare tools are also useful from an analytic perspective. Deep learning techniques have shown their efficacy in computer vision, natural language processing (NLP), etc. The NLP applications are a point of discussion in electronic health record data [4]. Personalized health care is also one of the greatest advantages of the ML field. Personalized health care involves electronic healthcare record maintenance, integrating health data, and computer-enabled diagnostics [5]. Machine learning helps in the development of a trained model, which learns from data to predict patients' diseases. ML techniques help to recognize patterns from voluminous data and can predict a patient's prognosis using ML algorithms [6]. ML techniques use data-mining algorithms for early disease detection and diagnosis. Researchers [7] have proposed a framework for a secure healthcare information system using ML and security mechanisms to protect patient data. DM techniques have been explored to construct predictive models using chronic kidney data sets, and the performance of algorithms has been compared for predicting diseases [8]. The Naive Bayes classification techniques have been implemented by researchers for disease prediction. The naive Bayes approach is suitable for performing an experimental approach on huge data sets, that is, big data [9]. According to these authors [10], expert systems developed using AI and ML are helpful for patient disease diagnostics. Others [11] have proposed a disease prediction method using fuzzy-based techniques. The unsupervised machine learning techniques are implemented on social media messages and perform sentiment analysis.

Herein, a smart healthcare framework is proposed in Section 2 followed by data analytics on health care in Section 3. The results and discussions are provided in Section 4. Finally, Section 5 concludes this chapter.

1.1 Artificial intelligence and health care

AI has many applications in the healthcare sector and is used for fixing problems related to the healthcare sector using machine learning techniques. Artificial intelligence (AI) involves discovering genetic codes, and using robots for surgical activities to achieve efficiency and accuracy. AI is efficiently providing support for diagnosing and reducing human errors, such as incomplete medical histories and unstructured data format. Research and development are using AI and machine learning techniques to cure deadly diseases. AI is also providing support for an intelligent symptom checker that uses an algorithm to diagnose and treat illness. Deep learning is the promising field of AI providing support for radiology diagnoses. Deep learning algorithms analyze unstructured medical data. The unstructured data include data in the form of lab tests, radiology images, patients' past medical history, etc. AI techniques are used for diagnosing blood-related diseases and also for image analysis, providing clinical decision support. Drug design and development is another area of AI where research and development are increasing to identify and develop new medicines. The major area of AI in drug development is helpful for immunology and neuroscience. AI is also used to track patients' characteristics for clinical trials and to extract information related to medical sciences using deep learning.

AI is a data science with a service on the cloud for integrating already-existing healthcare applications. Another application of AI is telemedicine, by which face-to-face consultations with doctors is possible. AI uses ML techniques for diagnosing patients, clinical decision support, predictive analytics, etc. Google's Deep Mind and Watson platforms use ML and data-mining techniques for accurate patient diagnosis. With the help of AI, virtual reality-enabled techniques have been implemented for performing surgical assistance using robots. The work carried out in the healthcare sector using ML techniques over the past 5 years by different authors is illustrated in Table 1.1.

Table 1.1 Machine learning work performed in the healthcare Sector.		
Authors	**Technique implemented**	**Work done in health care using ML techniques**
H. Harutyunyan, et al. [12]	ML classification	The authors proposed clinical prediction benchmarks. The task includes (1) modeling risk of mortality, (2) detecting physiologic decline, and (3) phenotype classification
W. Weng and P. Szolovits [13]	Machine learning	Information analysis of the data from electronic health records into the appropriate data format is done to improve clinical machine learning tasks
N.G. Maity and S. Das [14]	Artificial neural network	These authors performed classification of cell images to determine the advancement and severity of breast cancer using aartificial nnetwork. In addition, the authors studied and demonstrated use of the Bayesian ML technique for diagnosing Alzheimer disease
P. Kaur, et al. [7]	Smart healthcare information system using ML	An experimental approach is followed by the authors to analyze the role of big data in the healthcare industry. They proposed a novel design of smart and secure HIS using ML, handling big data from the medical industry
S. Vyas, et al. [15]	BlockChain and ML	Authors have proposed the convergence of blockchain and machine learning for achieving accurate results in the healthcare sector and decision making.
M. Chen, et al. [16]	CNN-based algorithm	An ML algorithm is implemented for the effective prediction of a chronic disease outbreak. The authors proposed a new CNN-based model for disease risk prediction algorithms using structured and unstructured data
G. Manogaran and D. Lopez [17]	Big data analytics	ML algorithms for processing big data in health care are discussed based on the study of the already-published big data architectures
A. Abdelaziz, et al. [18]	Cloud-enabled environment	A new model is proposed for healthcare services based on a cloud environment using parallel particle swarm optimization to optimize the virtual machine selection. In addition, a new model for chronic kidney disease diagnosis and prediction is proposed
J. Wiens and E.S. Shenoy [2]	ML tools and techniques	The authors reviewed ML techniques, and their applications to transform patient risk stratification in the medical field. ML techniques are reviewed, especially for healthcare epidemiologists and to reduce the spread of healthcare-associated pathogens
A. Qayyum et al. [19]		The authors used ML techniques for the prediction of cardiac arrest from 1-D heart signals with computer-aided diagnosis using multidimensional medical images
P.H.C. Chen, et al. [20]	ML model for image segmentation	ML model principles are discussed for clinical applications such as image segmentation for radiation therapy planning and measuring cardiac parameters from echocardiography

AI techniques help in developing wearable devices that provide data-driven mental health therapy. The sensors in devices measure changes in heart rate, temperature, and movement. AI and psychological fields are working together in research and development to achieve personalized health care and to provide accurate treatment for patients. AI algorithms and psychological data help to detect and study the emotions collected by the emotion sensors. Researchers [21] have adopted AI techniques for analyzing diagnostics images, which is helpful for radiologists, whereas others [22] have extracted phenotypic attributes using AI techniques to achieve diagnostic accuracy in the study of congenital disorders. ML techniques help in analyzing patient data and accordingly cluster the patient's information. ML clustering techniques also help in deriving the probability of a patient's disease outcomes [23]. AI techniques are often used for stroke-related studies and, with the help of AI techniques, the following can be achieved: (1) disease prediction, (2) diagnosis, (3) treatment, (4) prediction, and (5) prognosis evaluation. NLP is a technique that works closely with machine learning for extracting useful information from unstructured data. The information derived is helpful for already-available structured medical information. NLP techniques, along with ML, also result in semantic web ontological medical data analysis, clinical decision support, and electronic health record maintenance. NLP consists of two main components, that is, text processing and classification. NLP helps in identifying disease-related keywords from the meta-data and historical events [24].

Researchers [25] have combined IBM Watson as a reliable AI system for cancer diagnostics, whereas others have analyzed clinical images to identify skin cancer [26]. In Ref. [27], the authors devised an AI-based system for controlling the movement of patients suffering from quadriplegia. AI-based applications have also been used to diagnose heart diseases using cardiac images [28]. Movement-detecting devices for early stroke detection have been developed [29], and other researchers [30] have proposed wearable devices for stroke detection and prediction. Researchers have used the support vector machine (SVM) technique for disease evaluation, that is, neuroimaging techniques for stroke diagnosis. The SVM techniques have been used by authors to identify the imaging biomarkers of neurological and psychiatric diseases [31]. Naïve Bayes classification has been used also to identify stroke [32], whereas others [33] have reviewed the use of SVM in cancer diagnostics and early detection of Alzheimer disease [34].

1.2 Opportunities and challenges of AI and ML in the healthcare sector

AI and ML techniques optimize decisions in hospitals in real-time, with clinical support, and also improve the quality of and simplify healthcare operations. ML techniques are used for identifying clinical and meaningful patterns. The tasks performed using ML and deep learning involve imaging data, image segmentation, classification, generation of data, feature selection, and prediction of clinical data sets, etc. The availability of electronic health records in large amounts is a major opportunity in health care for drug discovery and improving medical care with the help of ML techniques, as ML techniques can handle large data sets. Wearable devices, including smartphones, have been developed using AI techniques targeting the safety and fitness of patients, and protecting them from life-threatening risks. AI helps in clinical decision support and pattern recognition of complications related to diseases. AI-based apps are being developed and deployed in wearable devices like wristwatches. With the help of AI apps, the following are achieved for accurate clinical decisions and preventing incorrect diagnoses: (1) users get notifications of their irregular heartbeats, (2) image analysis of diabetic retinopathy, (3) real-time analysis of MRI images using advance machine learning algorithms, (4) medical diagnostic tools have been developed for radiologists and physicians, as these tools are strong predictors of cardiac failure, brain stroke, etc., (5) speech therapy using AI and NLP techniques, and (6) ML algorithms have been developed for the detection of eye diseases. Telemedicine is another area of AI which is helpful for the comfort of patients. Patients are advised through smartphones, arranging appointments online, and allowing blood tests at the doorstep. AI techniques integrated with mobile-enabled apps help diagnose minor problems. In addition, many applications are integrated into cloud-based environments which helps to identify and explore treatment options. AI techniques are using ML algorithms for pattern discovery, which is a complex task for humans. This saves time and speeds up the drug-discovery process.

The challenges to AI in the healthcare sector include: (1) customization of AI architecture, (2) privacy and information security, (3) data reliability, (4) feature selection, and (5) data set quality for experimentation purposes. The major challenge to AI is data privacy and the security of sensitive, vital information. There are security issues related to wireless sensor networks in healthcare applications. Security related to the coordination of varied sensors in healthcare applications is a major concern. Another security gap is between the existing WSN design and the requirements of medical equipment [35].

2. Smart healthcare system

Technologies like the internet of Things (IoT), AI, and data science convergence are desired for smart health care. Humans have benefitted a great deal from ML learning in the healthcare sector. The applications of ML in health care involve personalized health care, electronic health records, disease prediction, medical imaging diagnostics, and risk identification. Machine learning primarily has two learning techniques: supervised and unsupervised learning. Supervised learning techniques include classification and regression techniques.

The example of classification techniques involves support vector machines, naive Bayes, nearest neighbor, ensembling methods, and discriminant analysis. The healthcare framework is outlined in Fig. 1.1. In the initial stage, the patient is enquired about the symptoms at the registration desk. The IoT helps in connecting to patients proactively and monitoring their health remotely with alerts. The IoT is also helpful in the device for analyzing data stream automation and enabling remote equipment configuration. In the proposed framework, the patient's data are collected from wearable devices through the connected sensors. The data collected are stored in the cloud for data storage and analytical processing. The patient health reports can be obtained from the cloud and submitted to the healthcare practitioner for early detection of diseases and diagnostics. The machine learning classification and clustering algorithms can be used for data analysis of the patient data to obtain the trained model for future predictions. Another aspect of AI, ML involves NLP and web ontology. The use of

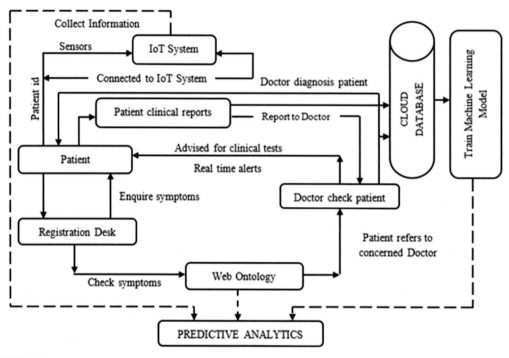

FIGURE 1.1

Proposed framework for a smart healthcare system.

NLP and web ontology is to derive meaningful information from medicinal prescriptions, terms, and historical events of the patient. The NLP and web ontology help in extracting information with similar meaning, content, and medical prescriptions diagnosed by doctors in the past. The patient's symptoms using NLP and the web ontology system are collated and the patient is referred to the relevant doctor. The doctor, after diagnostic analysis, refers the patient for lab tests. The patient's lab tests are recorded and the history of events is maintained. After the final diagnosis from the doctor the patient is issued with a patient ID which is connected to the IoT devices for future prognosis. The data and events associated with the patient's ID are stored on the cloud database and the ML models trained on the patient's data set enable the generation of predictive results.

3. Machine learning example of data analytics in health care

Machine learning consists of supervised and unsupervised learning techniques. Supervised learning techniques consist of precategorized data. This mainly consists of classification and regression

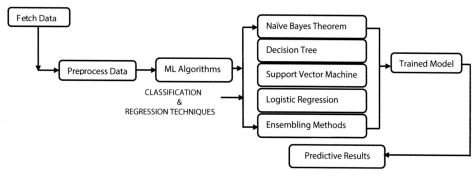

FIGURE 1.2

ML workflow for predictive analytics.

techniques. The objective of the supervised learning technique is to perform predictions and create predictive models. The supervised machine learning algorithms for continuous data are regression, decision trees, and random forest whereas, for categorical data, the classification algorithms are KNN, trees, logistic regression, naive Bayes, and SVM. In the unsupervised learning technique, the data are unlabeled and used for data analysis. The algorithms implemented by unsupervised learning are clustering, association, dimensionality reduction, etc. The objective of unsupervised learning is mainly pattern and structure recognition. Examples of clustering and dimensionality reduction algorithms are PCA, K-means, etc. and the algorithms for categorical data involve association analysis and hidden Markov model. The examples of association analysis are the a priori algorithm and FP growth.

3.1 Data classification

Data classification is performed using a supervised learning approach. In Fig. 1.2, the ML workflow is shown for performing predictions, in which, logistic regression, decision trees, naïve Bayes, SVM, and ensembling methods are implemented for training of a model. The model, once trained, is implemented for performing predictive analysis on the new test data. The classification and regression techniques are achieved using these algorithms. Here, experimentation is performed on Weka Software 3.8.5 and MATLAB R2021a.

3.1.1 Data collection

In the first stage, the data set is collected from the public domain, that is, UCI Machine Learning Repository (https://archive.ics.uci.edu/ml/datasets/Early%20stage%20diabetes%20risk%20prediction %20dataset). The data set used in the experiment is related to the prediction of early-stage diabetes risk. The data set is recent and contains the signs and symptoms of newly diabetic or would-be diabetic patients. The data set comprises 520 cases and the number of attributes is 17. The data set characteristics are of multivariate type. The sample data set is shown in Table 1.2.

Table 1.2 Sample data set.

Age	Gender	Polyuria	Polydipsia	Sudden weight loss	Weakness	Polyphagia	Genital thrush	Visual blurring	Itching	Irritability	Delayed healing	Partial paresis	Muscle stiffness	Alopecia	Obesity	Class
40	Male	No	Yes	No	Yes	No	No	No	Yes	No	Yes	No	Yes	Yes	Yes	Positive
58	Male	No	No	No	Yes	No	No	Yes	No	No	No	Yes	No	Yes	No	Positive
41	Male	Yes	No	No	Yes	Yes	No	No	Yes	No	Yes	No	Yes	Yes	No	Positive
45	Male	No	No	Yes	Yes	Yes	Yes	No	Yes	No	Yes	No	No	No	No	Positive
60	Male	Yes	Yes	Yes	Yes	Yes	No	Yes	Yes	Yes	Yes	Yes	Yes	Yes	Yes	Positive
55	Male	Yes	Yes	No	Yes	Yes	No	Yes	Yes	No	Yes	No	Yes	Yes	Yes	Positive

3.1.2 Data preprocessing

After data collection, the major challenge is to preprocess the data. In data preprocessing, the collected data consist of missing values, and therefore, for achieving better classification results, outliers need to be removed. The outliers are detected and missing values are removed, to boost the performance of the ML algorithms.

3.1.3 ML algorithms applied

In the third phase, the clean and preprocessed data consisting of categorical values are converted into numerical form to achieve accurate results. SVM, naïve Bayes, logistic regression, J48 decision trees, and ensembling algorithms, that is, boosted and bagged trees, are applied to the data set.

3.1.3.1 Logistic regression

Logistic regression is used to ascertain the probability of an event and estimates the probabilities of events as functions of independent variables. It uses the logistic function to model a binary-dependent variable [36], as shown in Eq. (1.1). It considers a dependent variable, such as, the outcome variable with two values, either 0 or 1. The logistic regression model is used to predict diseases related to the heart and diabetes based on attributes of patients including age, sex, body mass index, etc. [37,38].

$$y_i = \beta_0 + \beta_1 x_i + \varepsilon_i \tag{1.1}$$

Here, y_i is the dependent variable, x_i is the independent variable, and ε_i is the random error term.

3.1.3.2 Support vector machines

An SVM is a supervised machine learning model that analyzes data for performing classification, including regression analysis, also called support vector networks [39]. In a given set of training data sets of n points of the form $(\propto_1, \beta_1), \ldots\ldots, (\propto_n, \beta_n)$. β_n is either 1 or -1, with each indicating the class to which the points $\propto_i$ belong. Here, the maximum-margin hyperplane is obtained that divides the group point $\propto_i$ for which $\beta_i = 1$ from the group of points, such that the distance between the hyperplane and the nearest point $\propto_i$ from either group is maximized. A hyperplane separates the two classes of data, to increase the distance between them. A hyperplane for a linearly separable training data set is shown by Eqs. (1.2) and (1.3).

$$w^t \propto -b = 1 \tag{1.2}$$

$$w^t \propto -b = -1 \tag{1.3}$$

Here, $\propto$ is the set of points, and Eqs. (1.2) and (1.3) represent that anything on or above this boundary is of one class and anything on or below this boundary is of the other class with label -1. Here, w is the normal vector to the hyperplane. The distance between these two hyperplanes is represented by the parameter $\frac{b}{w}$ and the vector w is minimized to maximize the distance between the planes.

3.1.3.3 Boosted and bagged trees

The boosting method combines individual decision trees. In the boosting technique, the weak learners are combined and boosted to achieve a strong learner iteratively. This is a machine learning technique that produces a prediction model in the form of an ensemble of weak prediction models, that is, decision trees [40,41]. In boosting, for the observed value y_i, $\hat{y}_i$ is the predicted value by model $f(x)$ for n number of samples in y. The model predicts the value in the form of $\hat{y} = f(x)$ by minimizing the mean square error (MSE), that is, $\frac{1}{n}\sum_i (\hat{y}_i - y_i)^2$, where i is the index over the training set of size n of the actual value of the output variable y. The boosting algorithm performs in j stages. At each stage j in boosting, the weak model f_j is improved in every iteration by adding some new estimators $h_j(x)$, that is, new learners to build a strong model. Eq. (1.4) becomes,

$$f_{j+1}(x) = f_j(x) + h_j(x) = y \tag{1.4}$$

Bagging combines many decision trees to create an ensemble. Bagging was also described as bootstrap aggregation by Breiman [42]. It is an ensembling technique an ensemble of trees fits the bootstrap sampler.

3.1.3.4 Naïve Bayes

Naïve Bayesian classification is a supervised learning technique and a statistical classification method. Bayes theorem is used in decision-making and uses the knowledge of prior events to predict future events.

$$P(i|j) = P(j|i) * P(i)/P(j) \tag{1.5}$$

Eq. (1.5) states that the probability of i given j equals the probability of j given i times the probability of i, divided by the probability of j. In Eq. (1.5), i is the hypothesis to be tested and j is the evidence associated with i.

3.1.3.5 Decision tree

The decision tree is a supervised ML algorithm for data classification and regression. In a decision tree, if-then rules are applied to the data set to form a tree-like structure with decision nodes and leaf nodes. In a decision tree, the input features and target class are there to achieve the probability of an event. The information gained is calculated for each node of the tree to split further and to achieve the best possible result and perform predictions with the feature having the highest information gain. The entropy calculation is an important factor for building the decision tree. The equation for finding the entropy for building the decision tree is shown in Eq. (1.6), and the equation for finding the information gain metric is shown in Eq. (1.7).

$$e(s)(\text{attr}) = \sum_{j=1}^{n} -p_j \log_2 p_j \tag{1.6}$$

Here $e(s)$ is the entropy of the attribute for sample set s, and p_j is the probability of an input feature.

$$\text{infogain}(s, \text{attr}_i) = e(s) - \sum_{v \in \text{Values}(\text{attr}_i)} p(\text{attr}_i = v)e(s_v) \tag{1.7}$$

The information gain (infogain) calculated for a particular attribute (attr_i) gives the knowledge about the target function, given the value of that attribute, that is, conditional entropy.

3.1.4 Training and testing

In this phase, the data set is split into training and testing phases to avoid the chances of overfitting or underfitting of the results. The data set is split into training and testing data so that the ML model performs well on training data rather than performing on hidden and unseen data [43]. In the training phase, the machine is learned on the data set using ML algorithms to obtain the trained model and perform the right predictions whereas, in the testing phase, the input labels and target classes are predefined. In the testing phase, the ML model is verified to assess whether the correct prediction is achieved or not.

3.2 Clustering techniques

Another example of the ML technique which can be implemented in the healthcare sector is use of the clustering technique. This is an unsupervised learning technique and, in this technique, the input label and outcome values are not provided as in supervised learning techniques. Unlike classification and prediction, which analyze class-labeled data objects, clustering analyzes data objects without a known class label. The class labels are not present in the training data and clustering can be used to generate such labels. The clusters are formed in such a way that objects within a cluster have high similarity to one another, but are very dissimilar to objects in other clusters. The k-means clustering algorithm is an iterative, data-partitioning algorithm and uses the squared Euclidean distance for cluster center initialization. Here, k initial cluster centroids are chosen and x observations are assigned by an algorithm to exactly one of the k clusters defined by the centroids. The next step is to compute the point-to-cluster-centroid distances of all observations to each centroid [44]. The formula of the default squared Euclidean distance is shown in Eq. (1.8). In the equation, d is a distance metric, x is an observation, and c is a centroid. Each centroid is the mean of the points in that cluster k [45].

$$d(x, c) = (x - c)(x - c)' \tag{1.8}$$

The k-means clustering technique is one of the techniques that can be implemented to cluster diabetic patients, that is, diabetic or nondiabetic patients. The scatterplots of the positive and negative class diabetic patients for predictors, that is, "age" and "obesity" using decision tree, Gaussian naïve Bayes, logistic regression, SVM, and ensembling methods, such as, boosted and bagged trees are shown in Figs. 1.3A–F The result for the predictors "Age" and "Obesity" shows that people above age 30 and who have an obesity problem are more prone to be diabetic.

The predictions of the diabetic patients for predictors "age" and "polyuria" by decision tree, Gaussian naïve Bayes, logistic regression, SVM, and ensemblers, that is, boosted and bagged trees, are

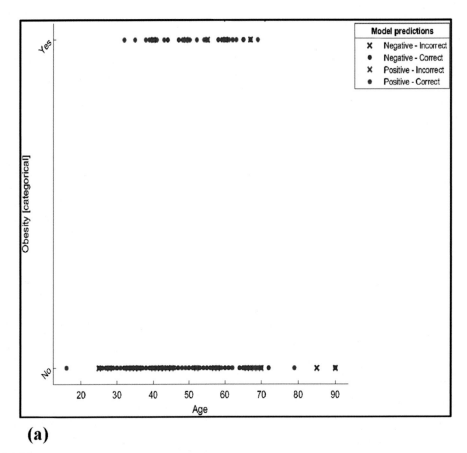

(a)

FIGURE 1.3A

Decision tree predictions: "age" versus "obesity."

shown in Figs. 1.4A–F. The decision tree shown in Fig. 1.5 shows that "polyuria" is the attribute at the root node which attains the highest information gain. The subtrees shown in Fig. 1.5 are decided based on the "polyuria" predictor. It shows that "polyuria" is an indicator for the patient being diabetic. It is also derived from the model predictions for predictors "age" and "polyuria," that, those with signs of polyuria are more likely to be diabetic compared to those with no signs of polyuria.

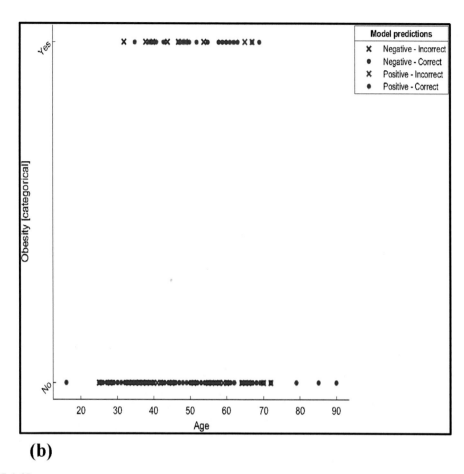

(b)

FIGURE 1.3B

Naïve Bayes predictions: "age" versus "obesity."

4. Experimental results

The data set is classified using ML classifiers, and the confusion matrix generated for the classification models along with their accuracy and training time is shown in Table 1.3. The classifier model obtained using the J48 decision tree is shown in Table 1.4 and the classification metrics showing the true positive

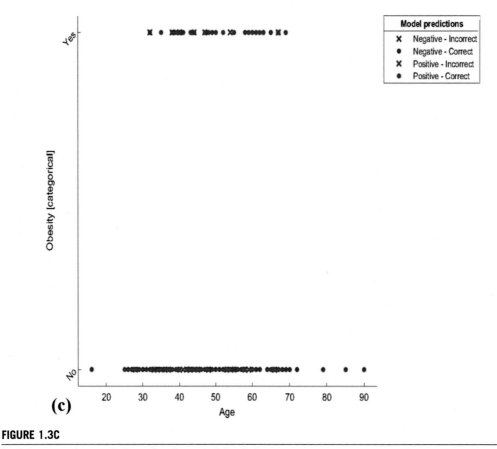

FIGURE 1.3C

Logistic regression predictions: "age" versus "obesity."

rate, true negative rate, F-measure, precision, and recall values of ML classifiers are shown in Table 1.5. The decision tree for the diabetic data set shown in Table 1.2 is displayed in Fig. 1.5. The decision tree shows that "polyuria" is the root node and the outcome classes after if-then analysis are shown as the leaf node. The root node is the node having maximal information gain. Information gain is one of the metrics used by the ID3, J48 tree-generation algorithms. It is the concept of entropy that is a common method to measure the impurity and when the entropy is higher, that means the information content is greater. Information gain measure is used in the J48 algorithm to select the test attribute at each node in the tree. The attribute having maximal information gain is selected as the test attribute for

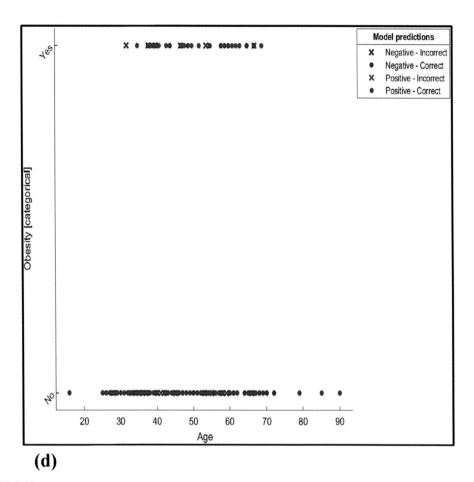

(d)

FIGURE 1.3D

SVM predictions: "age" versus "obesity."

the current node. The information gain measures how much information a feature provides about the class. It is a primary key accepted by the decision tree algorithm to build a tree.

The accuracies obtained by boosted and bagged trees for correctly classifying the instances were 97.3% and 97.1%, which are higher than for other ML classifiers. The results after comparison of the ML classifiers show that the ensembling methods performed better in comparison to the other ML algorithms in performing predictions for the diabetic patients. The true positive rate (TPR) is also called sensitivity. The formula for TPR is shown in Eq. (1.9). Sensitivity defines that the model has

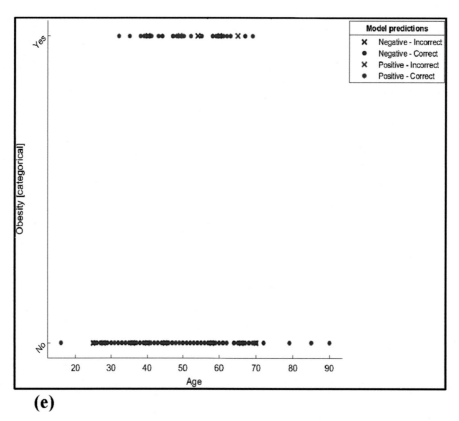

(e)

FIGURE 1.3E

Boosted tree predictions: "age" versus "obesity."

correctly identified a person with a disease and the specificity term means that the model has correctly identified a person without disease. The sensitivity and specificity percentages achieved by boosted trees were 97.5% and 97% whereas the sensitivity and specificity percentages achieved by bagged trees were 97.1% and 97%, respectively.

$$tpr = tp/(tp + fn) \qquad (1.9)$$

Here tp means "true positive" and fn means "false negative." The other term is called "specificity," also called the true negative rate (TNR). The formula for TNR is shown in Eq. (1.10).

$$tnr = tn/(tn + fp) \qquad (1.10)$$

Here tn means "true negative" and fp means "false positive."

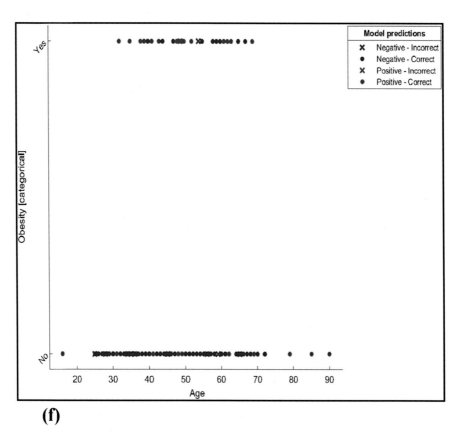

(f)

FIGURE 1.3F

Bagged tree predictions: "age" versus "obesity."

The accuracy and F-measure values of the models are calculated using the formulas shown in Eqs. (1.11) and (1.12).

$$\text{accuracy} = (tp + tn)/(tp + tn + fp + fn) \tag{1.11}$$

$$f - \text{measure} = 2 * ((ppv * tpr)/(ppv + tpr)) \tag{1.12}$$

The false positive rate (FPR) and false negative rate (FNR) are formulated in Eqs. (1.13) and (1.14).

$$fpr = fp/(fp + tn) \tag{1.13}$$

$$fnr = fn/(fn + tp) \tag{1.14}$$

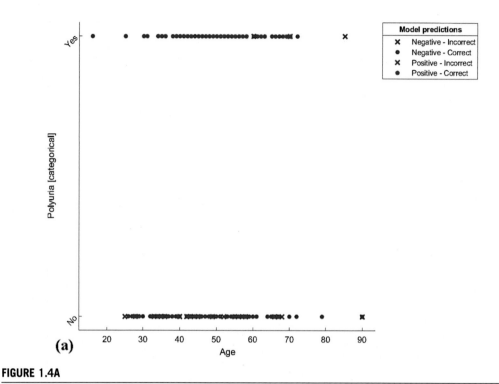

FIGURE 1.4A

Decision tree predictions: "age" versus "polyuria."

The negative predictive value (NPV) and positive predictive value (PPV), also called precision, are shown in Eqs. (1.15) and (1.16). The PPV values of predicting the patients with diabetes by ensemblers, that is, boosted and bagged trees, are the same, at, 98.1%.

$$npv = tn/(tn+fn) \qquad (1.15)$$

$$ppv = tp/(tp+fp) \qquad (1.16)$$

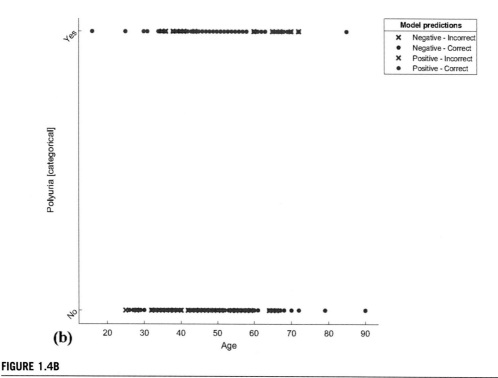

FIGURE 1.4B

Naïve Bayes predictions: "age" versus "polyuria."

The performance evaluation of the ML classifiers is visualized in Fig. 1.6. From Fig. 1.6, it can be seen that the ensembling methods performed better than the other ML classifiers.

5. Conclusion

AI and ML technologies working in close partnership with each other. AI helps in extracting meaningful information from large unstructured data, whereas ML algorithms enable the machine to learn complex relationships, forming patterns for effective decision-making. Both AI and ML are already being used in different sectors, but their introduction into the healthcare sector is aiding clinical support for patients and maintaining electronic health records. In this chapter, the authors have proposed a smart healthcare framework using emergent technologies. The convergence of IoT, cloud

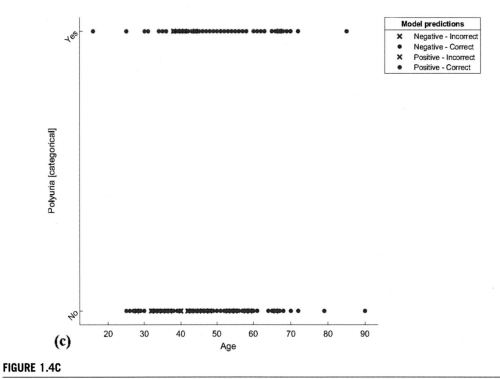

FIGURE 1.4C

Logistic regression predictions: "age" versus "polyuria."

computing, along with AI and ML is discussed for a smart healthcare system to provide clinical aid at the doorsteps of patients. ML classification algorithms are implemented and their performance metrics are evaluated on a diabetic patients data set for the early detection of diabetic patients. ML techniques can further be implemented on similar data sets of patients for developing trained models to perform accurate predictions to deliver care to patients and transform traditional health care into smart health care.

Abbreviations

AI	Artificial intelligence
CNN	Convolutional neural network
DM	Data mining

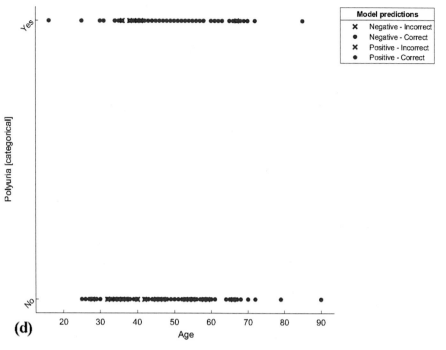

FIGURE 1.4D

SVM predictions: "age" versus "polyuria."

FN	False negative
FNR	False negative rate
FP	False positive
FPR	False positive rate
IoT	Internet of Things
KNN	K-nearest neighbor
LR	Logistic regression
ML	Machine learning
NLP	Natural language processing
NPV	Negative predictive value
PCA	Principal component analysis

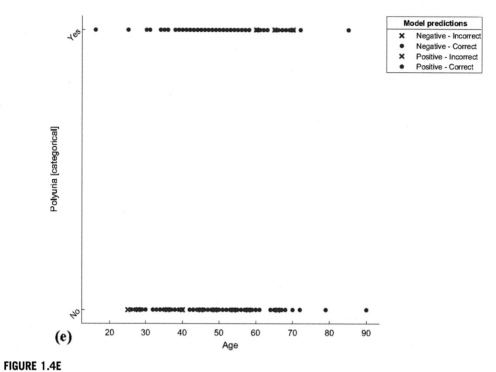

FIGURE 1.4E

Boosted trees predictions: "age" versus "polyuria."

PPV	Positive predictive value
SVM	Support vector machines
TN	True negative
TNR	True negative rate
TP	True positive
TPR	True positive rate
WEKA	Waikato Environment for Knowledge Analysis
WSN	Wireless sensor networks

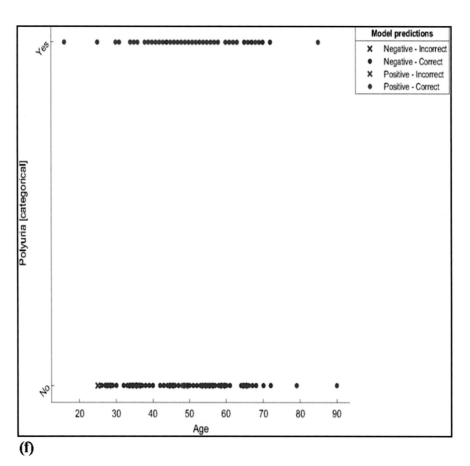

(f)

FIGURE 1.4F

Bagged trees predictions: "age" versus "polyuria."

Table 1.3 ML classifiers confusion matrix, accuracy, and training time.

ML model	Accuracy	TN (true negative)	FP (false positive)	FN (false negative)	TP (true positive)	Training time (s)
Logistic regression	92.9	184	16	21	299	6.22
Decision tree	93.5	185	15	19	301	6.52
Naïve Bayes	87.3	180	20	46	274	1.91
SVM	92.9	187	13	24	299	1.89
Boosted trees	97.3	194	06	08	312	4.10
Bagged trees	97.1	194	06	09	311	3.79

Table 1.4 Classifier model decision tree.

```
J48 pruned tree
------------------
Polyuria = No
|   Polydipsia = Yes
|   |   Irritability = No
|   |   |   Itching = Yes
|   |   |   |   Gender = Male
|   |   |   |   |   Alopecia = Yes: Positive (5.0/1.0)
|   |   |   |   |   Alopecia = No: Negative (7.0)
|   |   |   |   Gender = Female: Positive (4.0)
|   |   |   Itching = No: Positive (6.0)
|   |   Irritability = Yes: Positive (18.0)
|   Polydipsia = No
|   |   Gender = Male
|   |   |   Irritability = No
|   |   |   |   delayed healing = Yes
|   |   |   |   |   Age <= 40: Positive (3.0)
|   |   |   |   |   Age > 40: Negative (53.0/1.0)
|   |   |   |   delayed healing = No: Negative (97.0/2.0)
|   |   |   Irritability = Yes
|   |   |   |   Genital thrush = No
|   |   |   |   |   Age <= 42: Positive (3.0/1.0)
|   |   |   |   |   Age > 42: Negative (10.0)
|   |   |   |   Genital thrush = Yes: Positive (5.0)
|   |   Gender = Female
|   |   |   Alopecia = Yes: Negative (14.0/1.0)
|   |   |   Alopecia = No
|   |   |   |   visual blurring = No
|   |   |   |   |   Age <= 34: Negative (5.0)
|   |   |   |   |   Age > 34: Positive (16.0/1.0)
|   |   |   |   visual blurring = Yes: Positive (16.0)
Polyuria = Yes
|   Polydipsia = Yes: Positive (193.0)
|   Polydipsia = No
|   |   Itching = Yes
|   |   |   delayed healing = Yes
|   |   |   |   Alopecia = Yes
|   |   |   |   |   Gender = Male
|   |   |   |   |   |   Age <= 42: Positive (2.0)
|   |   |   |   |   |   Age > 42: Negative (15.0)
|   |   |   |   |   Gender = Female: Positive (2.0)
|   |   |   |   Alopecia = No: Positive (5.0)
|   |   |   delayed healing = No: Positive (11.0)
|   |   Itching = No: Positive (30.0)

Number of leave nodes:   22
Size of the tree:   43
```

Table 1.5 ML classifier metrics.

ML model	TPR (true positive rate)	FPR (false positive rate)	NPV (negative predictive value)	TNR (true negative rate)	PPV (positive predictive value)	FNR (false negative rate)	F-measure
Logistic regression	93.4	8	89.7	92	94.9	6.56	94.14
Decision tree	94.06	7.5	90.6	92.5	95.2	5.93	94.63
Naïve Bayes	85.6	10	79.6	90	93.1	14.37	89.19
SVM	92.5	6.5	88.6	93.5	95.8	7.43	94.12
Boosted trees	97.5	3	96.03	97	98.1	2.5	97.8
Bagged trees	97.1	3	95.5	97	98.1	2.8	97.6

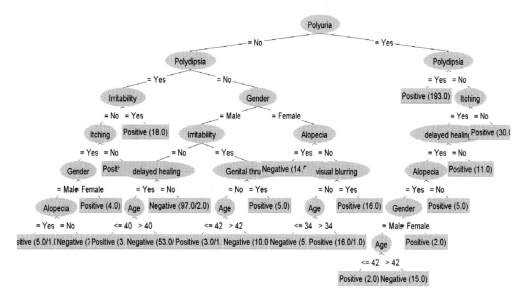

FIGURE 1.5

Decision Tree

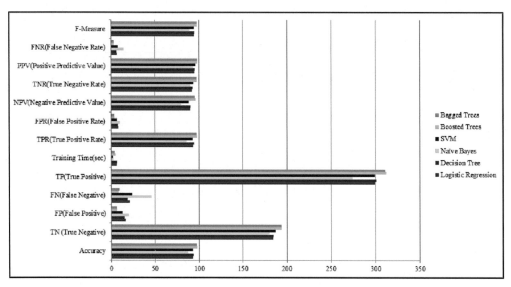

FIGURE 1.6

Metric Evaluation of ML Classifiers

References

[1] A.L. Beam, I.S. Kohane, Big data and machine learning in health care, JAMA 319 (13) (2018) 1317−1318.

[2] J. Wiens, E.S. Shenoy, Machine learning for healthcare: on the verge of a major shift in healthcare epidemiology, Clin. Infect. Dis. 66 (1) (2018) 149−153.

[3] M.A. Ahmad, C. Eckert, A. Teredesai, Interpretable machine learning in healthcare, in: Proceedings of the 2018 ACM International Conference on Bioinformatics, Computational Biology, and Health Informatics, 2018, pp. 559−560.

[4] A. Esteva, A. Robicquet, B. Ramsundar, V. Kuleshov, M. DePristo, K. Chou, J. Dean, A guide to deep learning in healthcare, Nat. Med. 25 (1) (2019) 24−29.

[5] P. Chowriappa, S. Dua, Y. Todorov, Introduction to machine learning in healthcare informatics, in: Machine Learning in Healthcare Informatics, Springer, Berlin, Heidelberg, 2014, pp. 1−23.

[6] A. Dhillon, A. Singh, Machine learning in healthcare data analysis: a survey, J. Biol. Today's World 8 (6) (2019) 1−10.

[7] P. Kaur, M. Sharma, M. Mittal, Big data and machine learning-based secure healthcare framework, Proc. Comput. Sci. 132 (2018) 1049−1059.

[8] A. Charleonnan, T. Fufaung, T. Niyomwong, W. Chokchueypattanakit, S. Suwannawach, N. Ninchawee, Predictive analytics for chronic kidney disease using machine learning techniques, in: 2016 Management and Innovation Technology International Conference (MITicon), IEEE, 2016, October, pp. MIT−80.

[9] R. Venkatesh, C. Balasubramanian, M. Kaliappan, Development of big data predictive analytics model for disease prediction using machine learning technique, J. Med. Syst. 43 (8) (2019) 1−8.

[10] I. Kononenko, Machine learning for medical diagnosis: history, state of the art, and perspective, Artif. Intell. Med. 23 (1) (2001) 89−109.

[11] M. Nilashi, O. bin Ibrahim, H. Ahmadi, L. Shahmoradi, An analytical method for diseases prediction using machine learning techniques, Comput. Chem. Eng. 106 (2017) 212−223.

[12] H. Harutyunyan, H. Khachatrian, D.C. Kale, A. Galstyan, Multitask learning and benchmarking with clinical time series data, Sci. Data 6 (2019).

[13] W. Weng, P. Szolovits, Representation Learning for Electronic Health Records, ArXiv, 2019 abs/1909.09248.

[14] N.G. Maity, S. Das, March). Machine learning for improved diagnosis and prognosis in healthcare, in: 2017 IEEE Aerospace Conference, IEEE, 2017, pp. 1−9.

[15] S. Vyas, M. Gupta, R. Yadav, Converging blockchain and machine learning for healthcare, in: 2019 Amity International Conference on Artificial Intelligence (AICAI), IEEE, 2019, pp. 709−711.

[16] M. Chen, Y. Hao, K. Hwang, L. Wang, L. Wang, Disease prediction by machine learning over big data from healthcare communities, IEEE Access 5 (2017) 8869−8879.

[17] G. Manogaran, D. Lopez, A survey of big data architectures and machine learning algorithms in healthcare, Int. J. Biomed. Eng. Technol. 25 (2−4) (2017) 182−211.

[18] A. Abdelaziz, M. Elhoseny, A.S. Salama, A.M. Riad, A machine learning model for improving healthcare services on cloud computing environment, Measurement 119 (2018) 117−128.

[19] A. Qayyum, J. Qadir, M. Bilal, A. Al-Fuqaha, Secure and Robust Machine Learning for Healthcare: A Survey, arXiv, 2020. Preprint arXiv:2001.08103.

[20] P.H.C. Chen, Y. Liu, L. Peng, How to develop machine learning models for healthcare, Nat. Mater. 18 (5) (2019) 410.

[21] R.J. Gillies, P.E. Kinahan, H. Hricak, Radiomics: images are more than pictures, they are data, Radiology 278 (2) (2016) 563−577.

[22] G. Karakülah, O. Dicle, Ö. Kosaner, A. Suner, Ç.C. Birant, T. Berber, S. Canbek, Computer based extraction of phenotypic features of human congenital anomalies from the digital literature with natural language processing techniques, in: MIE, 2014, pp. 570−574.

[23] A.M. Darcy, A.K. Louie, L.W. Roberts, Machine learning and the profession of medicine, JAMA 315 (6) (2016) 551−552.

[24] F. Jiang, Y. Jiang, H. Zhi, Y. Dong, H. Li, S. Ma, Y. Wang, Artificial intelligence in healthcare: past, present and future, Stroke Vasc. Neurol. 2 (4) (2017) 230−243.

[25] S.P. Somashekhar, R. Kumarc, A. Rauthan, K.R. Arun, P. Patil, Y.E. Ramya, Abstract S6-07: Double Blinded Validation Study to Assess Performance of IBM Artificial Intelligence Platform, Watson for Oncology in Comparison with Manipal Multidisciplinary Tumour Board−First Study of 638 Breast Cancer Cases, 2017.

[26] A. Esteva, B. Kuprel, R.A. Novoa, J. Ko, S.M. Swetter, H.M. Blau, S. Thrun, Dermatologist-level classification of skin cancer with deep neural networks, Nature 542 (7639) (2017) 115−118.

[27] C.E. Bouton, A. Shaikhouni, N.V. Annetta, M.A. Bockbrader, D.A. Friedenberg, D.M. Nielson, A.G. Morgan, Restoring cortical control of functional movement in a human with quadriplegia, Nature 533 (7602) (2016) 247−250.

[28] S.E. Dilsizian, E.L. Siegel, Artificial intelligence in medicine and cardiac imaging: harnessing big data and advanced computing to provide personalized medical diagnosis and treatment, Curr. Cardiol. Rep. 16 (1) (2014) 441.

[29] J.R. Villar, S. González, J. Sedano, C. Chira, J.M. Trejo-Gabriel-Galan, Improving human activity recognition and its application in early stroke diagnosis, Int. J. Neural Syst. 25 (04) (2015) 1450036.

[30] A. Mannini, D. Trojaniello, A. Cereatti, A.M. Sabatini, A machine learning framework for gait classification using inertial sensors: application to elderly, post-stroke and huntington's disease patients, Sensors 16 (1) (2016) 134.

[31] G. Orru, W. Pettersson-Yeo, A.F. Marquand, G. Sartori, A. Mechelli, Using support vector machine to identify imaging biomarkers of neurological and psychiatric disease: a critical review, Neurosci. Biobehav. Rev. 36 (4) (2012) 1140−1152.

[32] J.C. Griffis, J.B. Allendorfer, J.P. Szaflarski, Voxel-based Gaussian naïve Bayes classification of ischemic stroke lesions in individual T1-weighted MRI scans, J. Neurosci. Methods 257 (2016) 97−108.

[33] N.H. Sweilam, A.A. Tharwat, N.A. Moniem, Support vector machine for diagnosis cancer disease: a comparative study, Egypt. Inform. J. 11 (2) (2010) 81−92.

[34] L. Khedher, J. Ramírez, J.M. Górriz, A. Brahim, F. Segovia, Alzheimer's Disease Neuroimaging Initiative, Early diagnosis of Alzheimer's disease based on partial least squares, principal component analysis and support vector machine using segmented MRI images, Neurocomputing 151 (2015) 139−150.

[35] H.S. Ng, M.L. Sim, C.M. Tan, Security issues of wireless sensor networks in healthcare applications, BT Technol. J. 24 (2) (2006) 138−144.

[36] https://towardsdatascience.com/how-are-logistic-regression-ordinary-least-squares-regression-related-1deab32d79f5.

[37] D.A. Freedman, Statistical Models: Theory and Practice, Cambridge University Press, 2009.

[38] J. Truett, J. Cornfield, W. Kannel, A multivariate analysis of the risk of coronary heart disease in Framingham, J. Chron. Dis. 20 (7) (1967) 511−524.

[39] C. Cortes, V. Vapnik, Support-vector networks, Mach. Learn. 20 (3) (1995) 273−297.

[40] S.M. Piryonesi, T.E. El-Diraby, Data analytics in asset management: cost-effective prediction of the pavement condition index, J. Infrastruct. Syst. 26 (1) (2020) 04019036.

[41] T. Hastie, R. Tibshirani, J. Friedman, Boosting and additive trees, in: The Elements of Statistical Learning, Springer, New York, NY, 2009, pp. 337−387.

[42] L. Breiman, Bagging predictors, Mach. Learn. 24 (2) (1996) 123−140.

[43] https://datascience.foundation/sciencewhitepaper/underfitting-and-overfitting-in-machine-learning.

[44] S. Lloyd, Least squares quantization in PCM, IEEE Trans. Inf. Theor. 28 (2) (1982) 129−137.

[45] https://www.mathworks.com/help/stats/kmeans.html#d123e492036.

Cognitive technology for a personalized seizure predictive and healthcare analytic device

Vishalteja Kosana[1], Kiran Teeparthi[1] and Abu ul Hassan S. Rana[2]
[1]Department of Electrical Engineering, National Institute of Technology Andhra Pradesh, Tadepalligudem, India;
[2]Department of Intelligent Mechatronics Engineering, Sejong University, Seoul, Gyeonggi, Korea

1. Introduction

Today we are living in the era of a smart world where everything is connected via the Internet. Actions are carried out by intelligent devices with minimal involvement of humans as there is extensive growth of technologies such as cognitive technology, the Internet of Things (IoT), and artificial intelligence. The presence of smart devices and smart homes has made our lives easier and more comfortable. Technology connecting through the Internet of Things (IoT) [1]. The IoT has become an integral part of our daily lives through smart TVs, smartwatches, and smart streetlights. The IoT is also witnessing a massive growth in the healthcare systems through a health-monitoring system for sick persons, predicting a sudden rise in vital parameters such as blood pressure, pulse rate, etc. [2]. However, the IoT alone is not sufficiently productive and efficient. It must be associated with an external intelligent source to become more efficient and productive. This external source can be filled by artificial intelligence (AI). A new intelligent layer added to the existing IoT is known as the cognitive IoT [3]. The convergence of the IoT with AI gives rise to the cognitive development of the IoT (CIoT), which is more engaging, more efficient, and more intelligent. The cognitive computing technological inclusion with the IoT allows the timely accumulation of sensor-driven data. The application of artificial neural networks helps to provide a fully synthesized, efficient, and time-sensitive predictive model [4]. This integration turns the IoT into an intelligent system.

Around 65 million people have epilepsy worldwide, with around 10 million in India alone [5]. Epilepsy is one of the most commonly occurring neurological conditions in the world. It is a chronic noncommunicable disease that occurs due to the sudden onset of uncontrollable electrical disturbances in the brain, known as epileptic seizures. Therefore, an automated device that predicts the abrupt outcome of seizures and monitors the person's health parameters is urgently needed.

This chapter deals with a low-cost multifunctional framework device that protects the individual, alerts, monitors the individual, and engages with the individual throughout their life. The device is based on the CIoT. It is an automated voice-controlled device that predicts and monitors the individual's health state. The device is a powerful automated voice-controlled device that assists users and keeps them updated with their health conditions all the time. The device understands the health condition, analyzes it, communicates, and predicts the risk of the individual being subjected to unexpected health-hazardous risks.

It collects several corporal parameters from the individual and is analyzed using an artificial neural network to predict seizures. The device can predict three different types of seizures: atonic seizures, myoclonic seizures, and simple focal seizures. The collected and analyzed data are continuously uploaded to the cloud, allowing monitoring of the individual. Data analysis takes place using the artificial neural network (ANN) deep learning model. A mobile application also has been developed, allowing remote monitoring of the person and emergency warnings of sudden crises. In addition, the mobile application can display the individual's current health status, the live location of the individual, and all the individual's health information, which plays an essential role in future medication.

The rest of this chapter is organized as follows. The following section deals with epilepsy and types of seizures. Section 3 explores cognitive computing and its application in various domains, whereas Section 4 deals with the basics of the Internet of Things (IoT) and the significant changes it brings to human lives. Next, Section 5 discusses how the IoT and artificial intelligence are correlated and what the CIoT is. Next, Section 6 describes natural language processing and elaborates on models available in it. Then, Section 7 addresses the problem statement, and Sections 8 and 9 explore the approach for predicting epileptic seizures and remote health monitoring and health analysis of the individual. Finally, Section 10 explores the simulation results and discussions, while, finally, Section 11 concludes the chapter.

2. Epilepsy and seizures

Epilepsy is a neurological disorder. It occurs due to repeated seizures, in which a seizure is a condition where there is a sudden activation of ungovernable electrical disturbances in the brain [6]. It is a chronic noncommunicable disorder. Epilepsy can occur in all age groups and both genders. The seizure causes a sudden rise in anxiety levels of the body and leads to uncontrollable movements of the hands and legs, that is, convulsions, which can even result in sudden unexpected death. People with epilepsy are more prone to premature death, at a level which is around three times higher than for the rest of the population. The characteristics of the seizure and its impact on the individual depend upon various factors such as the location of electrical disturbances, how it spreads, and how long it takes place for.

2.1 Quick statistics

1. Around 65 million people have epilepsy around the world [7].
2. One in 20 people has a one-off epileptic seizure at any point in their life, although they do not have epilepsy [8].
3. Over 13% of people in India have epilepsy, with 12% of them are losing their lives because of the sudden occurrence of seizures, which is also called sudden unexpected death from epilepsy (SUDEP).
4. About 10 million people in India are living with epilepsy.
5. Between 4 and 10 out of every 1000 people have epilepsy at some time in their life.
6. Sixty percent of people with epilepsy do not know the cause of their epilepsy.

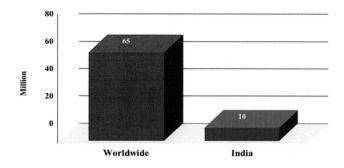

FIGURE 2.1

Comparison of levels of epilepsy in India and globally.

7. Around 87 people are diagnosed daily with epilepsy.
8. According to the WHO, of the 65 million people with epilepsy, 80% reside in developing countries.
9. A comparison of the number of epilepsy cases in India and globally is shown in Fig. 2.1.

2.2 Types of seizures

There are two major groups of seizures:

• Generalized-onset seizures;
• Focal-onset seizures.

2.2.1 Generalized-onset seizures

Seizures involving all brain areas during a seizure are called generalized-onset seizures [9], as shown in Fig. 2.2. However, they are also classified into different types, as shown in Table 2.1.

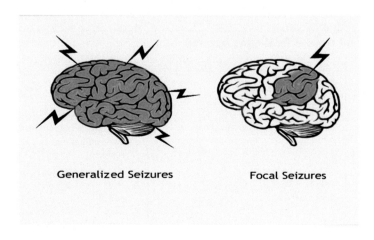

FIGURE 2.2

Schematic representation of generalized and focal seizures.

Table 2.1 Different types of generalized-onset seizures.

S. no	Type	Characteristics
1	Absence seizures	**a.** Also called petit mal seizures **b.** Occur in children **c.** Characterized by body movements such as eye blinking and lip-smacking **d.** Cause a loss of awareness
2	Tonic seizures	**a.** Cause stiffening of muscles **b.** Affect the back, arms, and leg muscles, leading to the person falling
3	Atonic seizures	**a.** Also called drop seizures **b.** Cause a lack of muscle control and may lead to the person collapsing to the ground
4	Myoclonic seizures	**a.** Appear as sudden small jerks in the arms and legs
5	Tonic-clonic seizures	**a.** Also known as grand mal seizures **b.** Most dangerous seizures **c.** Can cause sudden loss of consciousness, body shaking, and stiffening of the body
6	Clonic seizures	**a.** Cause repeated movements of muscles **b.** Affect the neck, arms, and face.

2.2.2 Focal-onset seizures

Seizures limited to only one area of the brain are called focal-onset seizures [10], as shown in Fig. 2.2. However, they are also classified into two different types, as shown in Table 2.2.

3. Cognitive technology

The term cognition indicates the mental ability to learn from experience, mistakes, etc. Cognitive technology refers to the technology that helps machines to possess mental ability to mimic humans [11].

Table 2.2 Different types of focal-onset seizures.

S. no	Type	Characteristics
1	Focal-onset seizures with impaired awareness	**a.** Involve a loss of consciousness or awareness **b.** No response to the external environment **c.** Performs repetitive hand rubbing, chewing, and swallowing, etc., during the seizure session
2	Focal-onset seizures without loss of consciousness	**a.** Alters the emotions **b.** Alters certain factors like smell, taste, and sound **c.** There is no loss of consciousness **d.** Involuntary jerking movements of arms and legs **e.** Symptoms such as dizziness, tingling, etc.

Table 2.3 Principles and characteristics of cognitive technology.

S. no	Principle	Characteristics
1	Interprets	• Understands data received from various sensors • Utilizes technologies such as computer vision, natural language processing to understand data
2	Learning	• Mimics human behavior of learning strange things and iterates multiple times to make correlations and patterns in the data
3	Prediction	• Predicts problems and learns from mistakes, and improves its working efficiency for better results. Technologies like deep learning, machine learning, and statistical reinforcement learning can detect anomalies and patterns to predict future problems

The purpose of cognitive technology is to infuse intelligence into the already prevailing nonintelligent machines. It is the evolution of devices into cognitive, that is, intelligent devices. It mimics human behavior and learns in a similar way to how humans evolve from childhood to adulthood based on experiences, mistakes, and different scenarios.

Similarly, applying cognition to devices helps them to think, analyze, and make decisions. Cognitive technology can be termed as a limited addition of artificial intelligence [12]. It can be understood in a better way through the following principles. Table 2.3 describes the principles and their characteristics of cognitive technology.

- **Application of Cognitive Technology in Healthcare Systems**
  a. Cognitive technology is used to develop a personalized healthcare system.
  b. It is used to develop a *remote patient monitoring system* [13]. The advantages of the remote health monitoring system are:
     - Improved patient management;
     - Predicts and prevents sudden deaths;
     - More reliable and cost-effective;
     - Better standard of health care;
     - Better rate of accountability.
  c. The healthcare system captures the corporal parameters of patients from various sensors or devices attached to the patient. Then, it analyzes the data, understands the patterns in the data, and predicts sudden health-hazardous problems.
  d. Patients lose their lives due to inadequate manual monitoring in emergencies. In contrast, this system saves lives and protects patients from sudden deaths and emergencies due to its highly effective system.
  e. The system also keeps all the patient's medical records collected and classifies the data, which can be helpful for the patient's future medication.

- **Advantages of Cognitive Technology**
  a. Greater efficiency;
  b. More reliability;
  c. The emergence of e-medicine or tele-medicine;
  d. Development of digital communication between patients and health professionals;
  e. Protection and monitoring all the time, proactively; helps in decreasing the number of sudden deaths.

4. Internet of Things

The Internet of Things (IoT) is a vast network of physical devices connected across the Internet. It is embedded with sensors, devices, and software for the transmission of data over the Internet. At present, there are nearly 10 billion IoT devices worldwide, and they are forecast to grow to 25 billion by 2022. The IoT makes tasks more accessible and simpler, with very minimal involvement of humans. Nowadays, everything is connected across the Internet; from a smartwatch, smart TV, smart fridge, smart lights, to critical control systems, everything is connected to the IoT. More straightforwardly, whatever is connected through the Internet, transmits data through the Internet and is described as an IoT product.

4.1 Why do we need the IoT?

a. Simplified and better decisions:
   - The data are collected from various sensors attached to the devices, and those sensors collect data and transmit them through the Internet.
   - For example: Let us suppose we have a smart refrigerator. It stores different varieties of vegetables, fruits, and food items. The data collected through sensors indicate which items are going out of date and how much energy has been spent.
   - It allows adjusting temperature and humidity to keep food fresh, if possible, and conserves energy as it consumes 30%–40% less power than a standard refrigerator.
   - More cost-effective and easy to use.
   - Thus, the IoT is the leading technology in the market.
b. Smart healthcare system:
   - Healthcare and health monitoring systems in hospitals have observed significant growth due to the emerging market technologies. The IoT is one such emerging technology.
   - The IoT facilitates face-to-face operations with remote locations and enables telemedicine to be used in hospitals.
   - For example: Let us consider a sick person. Sick people should be monitored carefully all the time, which is a complex process.
   - However, with the application of the IoT, they can be easily monitored proactively [14]. Moreover, the corporal parameters such as temperature, pulse rate, etc., can also be tracked using various sensors. Finally, the status can be shown in a portal that can be accessed by health professionals and contacts of that person.
   - Hence, IoT applications make the monitoring and tracking of people quick and simple.
   - Henceforth, innovative healthcare systems have been emerging regularly.
c. Automation:
   - The IoT helps in the automation of our daily tasks, decreasing the involvement of humans and making it convenient and straightforward.

- For example, let us take a smart room where lights, fans, and other equipment are automated using the IoT. It helps to decrease power consumption as the sensors are activated only when there is a need. For example, smart lights turn on only if there are people within a specific range. Air conditioning adjusts the temperature according to the temperature in the room.
  - The convenience factor and flexibility are enormous with automated devices.
  - It maximizes home security and increases energy efficiency.
d. Improved quality of life
  - In the end, all the benefits of automation, tracking, and monitoring and better decisions enable a better quality of life.
  - It decreases stress.
  - Tasks are simplified and made easy for humans.

4.2 Working principle

The IoT has a wide range of applications all around the world. As a result, the specifications may vary from one application to another. However, all the applications share a typical IoT architecture. The IoT architecture integrates four different components [15], which are tabulated in Table 2.4.

S. no	Component	Characteristics
		Table 2.4 Description of the components of the IoT.
1	Sensors/devices	• Sensors are used to collect data from the external environment
		• Collected data range from simple to the most complex data, such as full video feed
		• Multiple sensors are bundled together to collect several features and process the first step of the operation
2	Connectivity	• Once the data are collected from the external environment, it must transmit data to the cloud
		• The transmission requires a medium
		• The medium can be Wi-Fi, Bluetooth, satellite networks, wide-area networks (WAN), cellular networks.
		• Depending upon the bandwidth and specification of the application, the best medium is chosen
3	Data processing	• Once the data are transferred to the cloud, it is necessary to process them. The data processing can be done using several techniques such as machine learning, computer vision
		• After the data processing, the result made is sent again to the device to make appropriate decisions
4	User interface	• Users must have an interface to monitor the device proactively
		• The user makes certain decisions to adjust the device
		• An example can be the user portal used to adjust the temperature of an air conditioner proactively
		• It is the end part of the IoT working process

IoT technology is known for its wide range of applications around the world. Earlier, we stated that the IoT's main purpose is to connect everything through the Internet. But how? It is done through the automation of every device. Electronic device automation to develop smart devices, smart homes, and smart society is possible due to the IoT technology. Considering all these advantages of the IoT, industries are showing increased interest in adopting the IoT. The intelligence of the IoT (technically not intelligence but knowledge) connects different things and devices reliably and adequately through the appropriate channels. It depends on human involvement, however artificial intelligence makes the system think like a human, take decisions like a human, and act like a human. Without human involvement, the AI system's decision-making behavior can be much more reliable and accurate. Technically, the IoT's driving point is "connecting things," whereas it is the "intelligence" in artificial intelligence.

5. Cognitive IoT and neural networks

As discussed earlier, the IoT is a system that only makes appropriate connections with devices across the Internet. It cannot make decisions like humans. Hence, we can say that the IoT requires intelligence to get the best form from it. The IoT's initial applications cannot include decision-making, making applications unable to perform to their full potential. The addition of the intelligence layer to the IoT makes the system more engaging and more efficient. It allows the system to make its own decisions, train from the data, learn from mistakes [16], and automatically analyze it without human involvement. Human involvement becomes very minimal as the IoT no longer requires intelligence because AI acts as the brain for the existing IoT architecture.

The IoT consists of various sensors and devices which ultimately produce a vast set of data. As the data gets on increasing day by day, it leads to vast and huge sets of data. This massive data set makes the analysis an arduous task that increases the operating cost and increases the system's complexity. Ultimately, the efficiency and reliability of the system decrease. Therefore, the additional layer of intelligence makes the system capable of carrying out operations more efficiently and smoothly. The AI carries out critical analysis, classifies data, predicts futuristic problems, and triggers alerts in emergencies without human intervention. This makes the IoT system a more robust and efficient system. This convergence of intelligence with the IoT gives rise to the CIoT.

CIoT is defined as adding a layer of intelligence to the existing IoT architecture to develop a more engaging and more intelligent system. CIoT enables the system to learn from the data collected from various connected sensors, devices, and machines to make appropriate decisions and analyses [17].

Advantages of CIoT include:

- Increases reliability and efficiency;
- Enhances user experience;
- Creates patterns from the data, learns from it, and classifies the data automatically;
- Useful for future predictions and anomaly detection.

5.1 Deep neural networks

Have you ever wondered how the translation of web pages takes place in a fraction of seconds? Have you ever thought about how the face unlocking of a mobile works? All of these are the applications of deep learning (DL). In this section, we understand deep learning in a better way. DL is the subset of machine learning which in turn is the subset of artificial intelligence. Deep learning inspired by the human brain structure aims to develop a neural network that mimics the human brain's working. However, many machine learning algorithms, such as regression algorithms and classification algorithms, can process the data and learn and make decisions. However, it becomes an arduous and tedious task for the algorithms for increasingly complex data. Deep learning techniques are developed to handle highly complex data as they hierarchically possess many deep hidden layers. Now let us have a closer look at deep learning.

- *Neuron*
  Biologically, a neuron is the basic unit of the brain. It consists of dendrites and axons. The dendrites act as a signal receiver to a neuron. The axons are known as the transmitters of the signal for the neuron [18]. Individually a neuron is not powerful, but a large group of neurons can form a robust neural network. Now the question is how this neuron helps in the development of the neural network. We are moving away from neuroscience and moving into technology. Let us consider a network with three input neurons and one output neuron. The output neuron can represent a value that can be binary, continuous, and categorical. The input neurons help in the processing of the input signal. The inputs received are passed through the synapse, and the weights in the neural networks imply the strength of the synaptic connections. The synapses are assigned with some weights, which indicate the strength of the synaptic connection. Weights are crucial to artificial neural network functioning because neural networks learn by adjusting the weights; the neural network decides which signal is essential or which signal should be processed to further neurons [19].
- *Hidden layer*
  A group of neurons together forms a neural network layer. At the same time, the hidden layer is the layer present between the input and output nodes in the neural networks. These layers perform nonlinear transformations of the input data through activation functions [20]. The number of hidden layers present in the neural networks is greater than or equal to zero. As the number of hidden layers increases, the neural network's complexity increases, and hidden layers help to identify different types of features present in the inputs, improving efficiency.

  Three steps take place in the hidden layer of the neural network.

1. Summation of the weights:
    - All the weights are multiplied by their corresponding input value and added together. Thus, the value of the summed weights is shown in Eq. (2.1).
    - The summed value is then passed to the activation function.

$$a = \sum_{i=1}^{n} w_i x_i \tag{2.1}$$

2. Activation function:
    - This decides whether the given input is relevant or not. It can be useful, like a yes or no switch. The different types of activation functions are described in the literature.

3. Passing the value to the next corresponding node in the neural network.

- *How do neural networks learn?*

There are fundamentally two different approaches to a program to do what you want it to do. They are:

1. Hard-coded coding, where we define specific rules in the program to deal with all possible situations.

2. Neural networks where we provide inputs, and the outputs for those inputs. We also create a facility to let the program deal with all the possible outcomes.

The main aim is to develop a neural network that learns and predicts the possible outcomes. Let us suppose a single-layered feedforward neural network in Fig. 2.3. It is also called perceptron. There are two values present at the output node. The first is the actual output, and the other is the predicted output value. We follow a series of steps to calculate the appropriate weights for the neural network.

1. After the forward propagation with the given input features is completed, the neural network predicts the output. Finally, the output value is predicted using a primary network compared with the actual output value.

2. During the comparison, the cost function denoted by "C" is calculated.

3. The value of "C" decreases with an increase in accuracy value.

4. The "C" value is fed back to the neural network again, and the weights are updated.

5. The weights are adjusted, and the input is fed again to the network.

6. This process is continued until there is a minimal cost function value.

7. The cost function minimization is done using different methods such as stochastic gradient method, batch gradient descent, and mini-batch gradient descent method.

8. When there is a very minimal value of "C," it implies maximum accuracy. Thus, the adjusted weights are the final weights of the synaptic connections of the network [21].

9. This approach is known as the *backpropagation approach.*

- *Minimization of the cost function*

Achieving the optimal weights of the layers is critical. To achieve optimal weights, the cost function is minimized. The most common approach is the brute force approach [22]. However, if we use the brute force approach to minimize the cost function, the complexity increases drastically. Ultimately the curse of dimensionality arises. Therefore, we should make use of alternative

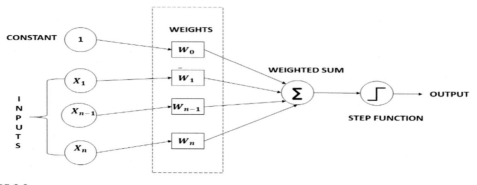

FIGURE 2.3

Representation of a perceptron.

approaches. The minimization of the cost function can be achieved using three different methods: the stochastic gradient method, batch gradient descent, and mini-batch gradient descent method [23].

- **Gradient descent method**

This is the process that occurs in backpropagation. This method aims to calculate the global minimum of the cost function through various mathematical techniques such as differentiation, global minimum, and the slope of the function. It adjusts the parameters so that the output deviation is minimized, that is, finding the global minimum of the cost function. The backpropagation method is depicted in Fig. 2.4. The number of samples provided to the network for every iteration is classified into three types.

a. *Batch gradient method:* All the available weights are injected into the network at once. In this gradient method, adjustment of weights is made only after the completion of all iterations. The complexity of this method is high.
b. *Stochastic gradient method*: In this method, the weights are updated for every row, that is, for each iteration, the weights are updated. This is faster than the batch gradient method.
c. *Mini-batch gradient method*: In this method, the adjustment and updating of the weight are made after batches of rows. It is the combination of both batch and stochastic gradient methods. It is the most used technique in backpropagation.

5.2 Steps to construct an artificial neural network or deep neural network

Step 1: Initialize the weights to minimal random numbers that are close to 0.
Step 2: Inject the observation of the data set in the input layer so that one feature is injected into one input node.
Step 3: Forward propagation is done using hidden layers to get the output Y's predicted value.
Step 4: Comparison of the predicted output Y with the actual output Y'. Compute the error generated.
Step 5: Backpropagation: feedback of the generated error to the network to adjust the weights accordingly.

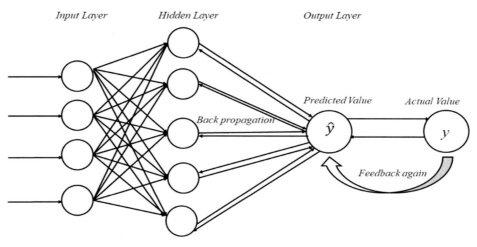

FIGURE 2.4

Illustration of the backpropagation in a neural network.

Step 6: Repeat the steps from step 1 to step 5 and update the weights using any gradient methods until the error generated is minimal.

Step 7: The artificial neural network model is ready.

6. Natural language processing

Have you ever thought about how chatbots such as Google assistant and Siri work? They are the outcomes of natural language processing (NLP). NLP is a subset of artificial intelligence that decreases the gap between machines and humans. Some of the successful NLP applications are Google translation, Google assistant, Alexa, and Microsoft Word, which find out the grammatical mistakes in sentences. First, let us discuss some examples of the natural language processing models. Before that, it is essential to know two types of models present: the classical NLP model and deep learning NLP models.

6.1 Classical models

1. If-else rules for chatbots: In these models, every question and answer is inbuilt into the program itself [24]. It has many limitations, such as if the question is different from inbuilt questions, the model fails to provide an answer.
2. Audio frequency component analysis (speech recognition): This is a nondeep learning model [25]. In this model, frequencies of the real-time audio of human speech are built into the model. The input is compared with the preexisting inbuilt frequencies, and matched words are recognized. Then, a mathematical frequency analysis is done to find out the result.
3. Back of words model: This is one of the most used models for classification and language modeling. It is beneficial in the applications of review systems [26].

6.2 Deep learning models

1. CNN for text recognition: This is also a classification model. A convolutional neural network is a powerful model in image identification [27]. Similarly, it can also be used to classify texts with the first step as embedding words. The remainder of the steps are the same as in the case of image classification.
2. Seq2Seq model: This is the end-to-end deep learning model [28]. Therefore, it is called a DNLP model, i.e., deep natural language processing model. It is the most potent encoder−decoder based mode in which two recurrent neural networks are used.

6.3 Applications of natural language processing

1. Chatbots: Recently, there has been a considerable increase in the development of chatbots on websites and mobile applications.
2. Sentimental analysis: This helps message services and stock market predictions.
3. Review systems: These help to decide the ratings of a product in applications such as Amazon, Flipkart, and Bookmyshow.

7. Problem statement

The inclusion of cognitive technology in healthcare systems resulted in many highly technical healthcare devices. However, there is always an omission in developing personalized healthcare devices to tackle diseases such as epilepsy. As discussed in Section 2, a seizure is a condition where there is a sudden activation of ungovernable electrical disturbances in the brain. Hence, we can say that it occurs suddenly and can cause sudden death. Therefore, persons with epilepsy must be monitored and protected to save their lives because seizures do not follow a particular date and time to occur. Therefore, epileptic individuals should constantly be monitored to avoid sudden death due to seizures.

Epilepsy is not a curable disease. However, it needs to be predicted before its occurrence to avoid sudden deaths. Thus, there is a need for a personalized monitoring device for epileptic persons to protect them. The device should monitor an individual's vital parameters such as temperature, pulse rate, and blood pressure. Furthermore, the device needs to predict seizures before they occur. Therefore, a device is required that protects an epileptic person, like a caretaker. We discuss a device based on CIoT in this section. It is a multifunctional device that protects the individual, and alerts, monitors, and engages the individual throughout their life. It is an automated voice-controlled device that predicts and monitors the health state of the individual.

8. Methodology

This section discusses the cognitive system methodology for developing a device to protect individuals from SUDEP. The device is based on CIoT technology. As already discussed, the IoT combined with artificial intelligence gives rise to a more intelligent and more interactive system, called the CIoT. We utilized CIoT technology to develop a smart healthcare system that always takes complete care of the individual. We demonstrate the system based on cognitive technology for the prediction of seizures and for constant monitoring of epileptic people. The following are the key technologies involved in the proposed system:

a. Internet of Things;
b. Deep neural networks;
c. Deep natural language processing;
d. Mobile application.

a. Internet of Things

In this first stage, we discuss the role of the Internet of Things in the system. The IoT system comprises various devices and sensors that collect vital parameters from the user and transmits them to the cloud. Table 2.5 provides a detailed description of each sensor.

Different sensors and modules are attached to the Raspberry Pi. It acts as an interface between the cloud and the user. The sensors are also attached to the user. These sensors collect vital parameters such as temperature, pulse rate, vibration levels, user orientation, that is, the coordinates of the hands and legs, sound frequency of the user, and location from the user, and transmit the collected data to the Pi module [29]. The Pi module acts as a processing device and processes the data sent to a deep neural network model. This model analyzes the data and predicts the sudden anomalies of the user.

b. Deep neural networks

This section discusses the deep neural network's role in analyzing the data collected through various sensors. First, the data are analyzed using an ANN, and it predicts the occurrence of sudden seizures. As discussed in Section 2, a seizure is a condition where there is a sudden activation of

Table 2.5 Description of various sensors and modules.

S. no	Type of sensor	Description
1	Temperature sensor	• The temperature sensor is used for obtaining the body temperature value
		• The LM35 model is appropriate for the system with a range of $-55°C$ to $+120°C$
2	Pulse sensor	• The pulse sensor provides the output in analog format
		• The Raspberry Pi does not have an analog input pin
		• Therefore, we need to use an analog to digital converter to obtain the user's pulse rate values
		• The pulse rate is obtained in units of bpm (beats per minute)
3	Accelerometer sensor	• Adxl335 accelerometer sensor is used
		• It is used to obtain the values of the coordinates of the individual
		• Here we use two accelerometer sensors
		• One is to detect the fall of the individual and the other is to detect the individual's jerking movements
		• These sensors play a crucial role in the prediction of different types of seizures
4	Vibration sensor	• We use an SW-420 vibration sensor
		• It plays a crucial role in confirming a seizure as it detects the individual's jerking movements to alert the contacts/emergency systems at the seizure session
5	Sound-detecting sensor	• We use a KY-037 sound-detecting sensor which enables us to detect the sounds of the individual
		• If the user's sound surpasses the threshold limit or declines below a low threshold value, the device immediately alerts the user
		• The device also alerts the contacts of the user
		• Deep neural networks are used to predict unusual sounds
6	GPS module	• We use a GPS module for monitoring the location coordinates of the individual at all times
		• The location coordinates in emergencies play a crucial role in saving the epileptic person from death
7	Buzzer	• We use a 5V buzzer that operates around the 2 kHz audible range
		• It plays a crucial role in alerting neighboring people during the seizure session

Table 2.5 Description of various sensors and modules.—cont'd

S. no	Type of sensor	Description
8	GSM module	• GSM stands for global system for mobile communication
		• We use a SIM900A GSM module to ensure a constant connection to the cloud
		• This helps in sending alert messages and alert emails to the contacts of the individual during emergencies
9	Raspberry Pi	• It is a tiny single-board computer
		• It is a small credit card-sized computer that can be connected to a monitor to perform several operations
		• The Pi can do everything that a standard laptop or desktop does
		• It consists of an inbuilt Wi-Fi module
		• It is the most commonly used platform for the development of applications after Arduino

ungovernable electrical disturbances in the brain. Thus, we use this neural network model to predict sudden seizures in individuals [30]. The flow chart of the neural network construction is shown in Fig. 2.5. The inputs to the neural network are parameters such as temperature, pulse rate, vibration levels of the body, frequencies of sounds, accelerometer readings, that is, the user's orientation. Data preprocessing techniques, such as standard scaler and minmax scaler, are applied to maintain all the parameters in the same range of standardized values. Then, the preprocessed data are fed to the artificial neural network and trained. The trained model is used to predict the probability of the occurrence of a seizure. This model also analyzes the user's vital parameters, detects the anomalies present, and sends the signal to the Pi module to take the necessary actions.

c. Deep natural language processing

Natural language processing helps in decreasing the gap between a device and humans [31]. The system also comprises a voice automation system that takes voice input from the user and produces the user's voice output. This increases the interactions between the user and the device. In this section, we discuss the role of deep NLP in the proposed system. The proposed device is an automated voice model that interacts with the user, engages, and keeps continuously updated with their condition. This automation develops an interactive environment between the user and the device. The use of the DNLP model provides a more efficient chatbot model for the device. The voice input is taken from the user and is converted into text using the speech-to-text conversion technique. The input text is then passed into the DNLP model to predict the given input's appropriate output. The output signal of the DNLP model is again sent back to the Pi module. Based on the model's signal, the Pi module produces the voice answer to the user's query [32].

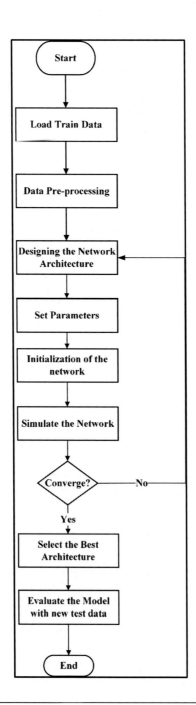

FIGURE 2.5

Complete flowchart of a neural network.

This model also performs various operations such as surfing through the Internet, playing songs from platforms such as YouTube, etc. The primary purpose of voice automation is to keep the user always active. The model also alerts the user to health conditions frequently to make monitoring easier. The device with voice automation makes the alerting more efficient. Fig. 2.6 clearly illustrates the flowchart of working of the voice automation in the device.

d. Mobile application

The discussions made in Section 3 depict the current emergence of remote health monitoring systems in the market. We also explain the advantages of this system, such as the emergence of telemedicine, efficient management of patients, etc. In this section, we discuss the role of mobile application and the cloud for the remote monitoring of epileptic patients. The device continuously monitors the user's vital parameters and sends the data to the cloud database through the Internet. The data from the cloud database can also be accessed by a web application and a mobile application.

The mobile application can monitor the individual remotely through the Internet. The user's vital parameters, such as temperature, pulse rate, etc., can be monitored using the mobile application. The mobile application also possesses an alert notification system which helps in a significant way during emergencies. Whenever the user has any anomalies in the vital parameters, the mobile application automatically alerts the person monitoring through a notification [33]. The workflow of the mobile application for seizure detection is shown in Fig. 2.7.

9. Proposed approach

In the previous section, we acquired complete knowledge of the different technologies involved in the proposed system. In this section, we discuss the proposed approach for predicting the occurrence of epileptic seizures and remote monitoring of the individual.

The development of the system is based on three main principles, which we call the 3P principle:

1. Prevent: The device helps epileptic individuals to prevent the occurrence of seizures by updating and alerting the individuals continuously about their health condition. The powerful voice automation of the device helps in keeping the individual interactive.
2. Predict: Prediction is the key feature of the device. The device uses the ANN to predict the occurrence of epileptic seizures. The device predicts the seizure before its occurrence, which helps epileptic individuals safeguard themselves from dangers caused by seizures. During the sudden occurrence of a seizure, the device immediately starts ringing a buzzer, and requests help through its powerful voice automation feature. It also sends alert messages to the individual's contacts and emergency services.
3. Protect: The device protects epileptic individuals throughout their lives through its robust monitoring and predicting seizures. In addition, the mobile application developed helps monitor individuals, helps track their health status, and tracks their location, thus helping to protecting individuals during any emergencies.

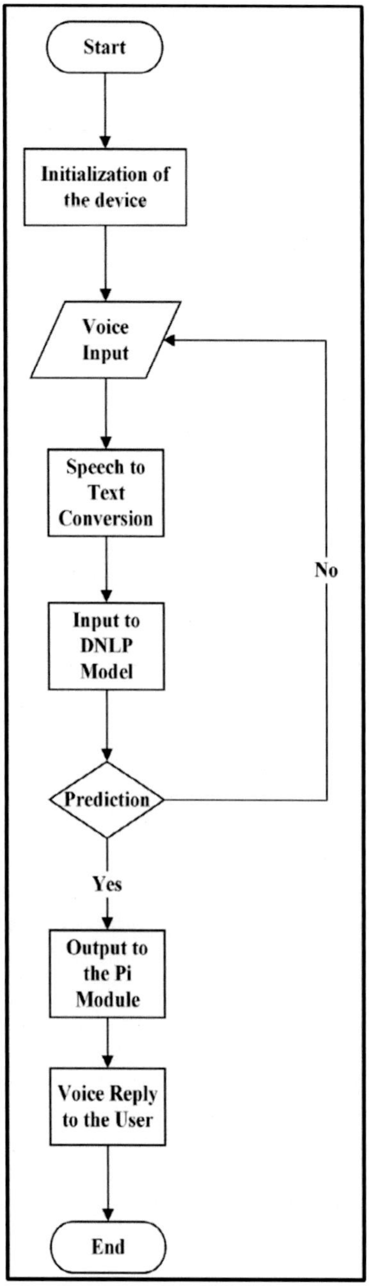

FIGURE 2.6

Workflow of the voice automation.

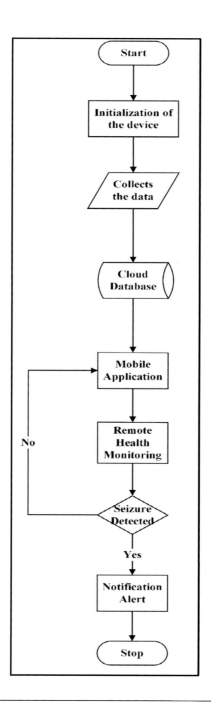

FIGURE 2.7

Workflow of the monitoring system.

9.1 Working of the system

The proposed system is a smart device that takes care of the epileptic individual. It is developed based on cognitive technology. The working of the system is described below.

1. Using the technology of the IoT, several corporal parameters are collected from the individual continuously.
2. The collected data are processed by the device and sent to the cloud through the Internet.
3. Simultaneously, the data are also fed to a deep neural network to detect any abnormalities present in the individual's health status.
4. Here, the neural network analyzes the individual's vital data collected through a variety of sensors.
5. If there is a discrepancy in the individual's vitals, the neural network immediately transmits a warning signal to the Pi module.
6. The Pi module prompts the user to confirm the state of health.
7. If the user confirms the health status positively, the device warns the user with the unusual vital parameter and asks the user to remain safe to prevent further harm.
8. If the individual is unresponsive or confirms a negative health status, the device immediately alerts the person's contacts and emergency services with the individual's location. The device also starts ringing a buzzer and asks for help through the speaker to alert people close by.
9. The system also provides an alert notification in the mobile application in the event of an emergency.
10. In this way, the device is designed to protect constantly the epileptic individual.

9.2 Device for different types of seizures

We can predict the occurrence of epileptic seizures, as explained above. To be more precise, we can also identify the type of seizure. As discussed in Section 2, two major types of seizures are described: generalized-onset seizures and focal-onset seizures. Therefore, we designed this device to be capable of predicting the occurrence of generalized-onset seizures. The generalized-onset seizures include tonic, myoclonic, atonic, clonic seizures, etc. This identification of different types of seizures helps significantly with the patient's medication. A demonstration of the various sensors to predict the various seizures is given in Table 2.6.

9.3 Device for health monitoring

Remote monitoring of the patient has many advantages. The safety and survival rate of the patient increases, and the cost of medication decreases. The system is designed to predict epileptic seizures with the remote health monitoring of patients using a mobile application.

We can incorporate various sensors to evaluate different vital parameters such as blood pressure, respiration rate, body temperature, pulse rate, etc. These vital parameters are collected from the device and transmitted through the Internet to the cloud database. The mobile application can access the data from the cloud. Health professionals or contacts can use the mobile application to monitor the patient's vital parameters remotely, thus increasing the survival rate of the patient from sudden unusual life-threatening situations.

S. no	Type of seizure	Characteristics	Demonstration
Table 2.6 Sensors for various seizures.			
1	Atonic seizure	1. Also called drop seizures 2. This causes a lack of muscle control and may lead to the person collapsing to the ground	A. We can consider the temperature variation and the fall of the individual to predict atonic seizures B. The temperature sensor and accelerometer sensors can be used
2	Myoclonic seizure	1. Appears as sudden small jerks in the arms and legs 2. Most common in children	A. We can consider the shaking of the hands and legs of the individual B. Vibrating sensors can be used to detect jerks in the individual
3	Tonic-clonic seizure	1. Also known as grand mal seizures 2. It is the most dangerous seizure 3. Can cause sudden loss of consciousness, body shaking, and stiffening of the body	A. We can consider the sudden fall of an individual for the loss of consciousness, vibration sensors for body shaking B. The fall of the patient can be demonstrated using accelerometer sensors and pulse rate sensors
4	Tonic seizure	1. Causes stiffening of muscles 2. It affects the back, arms, and legs drastically, which leads to the person falling	A. We can consider the pulse rate sensors to demonstrate this seizure B. Also, falling of the individual can be demonstrated by the accelerometer sensors

Specifications of the mobile application include:

1. It is helpful for the remote monitoring of the patient.
2. It possesses an alert system that produces an alert notification for any anomaly detected in the patient's health.
3. It stores all the data and them it based on the risk factor of the event.
    a. For example, the medical and other epileptic individual's data are stored in regular records in normal times.

    b. Meanwhile the medical data during the epileptic seizure are stored in the seizure records. In these seizure records, there is provision for data classification based on the type of seizure that occurred, such as focal seizure, clonic seizure, etc.

    c. The data are well organized and available to monitor the patient more efficiently.

4. The mobile application also allows us to track the location of the patient.

5. This location tracking of the patient helps significantly during emergencies.

6. The mobile application stores the medical data of the user collected at different intervals. These data help in the medication of the patient.

7. The mobile application allows health professionals and the patient's contacts to communicate remotely, increasing the patient's and carer's confidence in leading an everyday happy life.

10. Simulations and discussions

In the previous section, we discussed methodology of the proposed approach for predicting the occurrence of epileptic seizures and the remote monitoring of patients using a mobile application. In this section, we discuss the simulations and the results obtained by the system.

    The deep neural network is tested with a different number of hidden layers, and the percentage accuracy of the neural network concerning the number of hidden layers is shown in Fig. 2.8.

    The working of the device is classified into three different zones:

1. Preseizure: In this zone, the device continuously collects the medical data from the individual and stores them in the cloud database, monitoring the individuals. It issues alerts in the case of any sudden variation in the vital parameters.

2. During the seizure: In this zone, the device immediately alerts the contacts of the patient and emergency services with a phone call, text message, or email and sends an alert notification in the mobile application and starts ringing a buzzer. The probability of the occurrence of seizure in a specific test period is shown in Fig. 2.9.

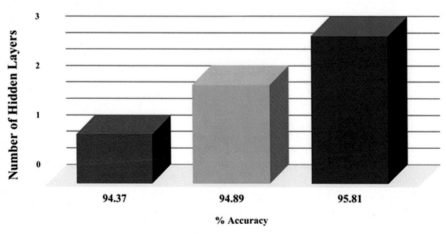

FIGURE 2.8

Comparison of accuracies with respect to hidden layers.

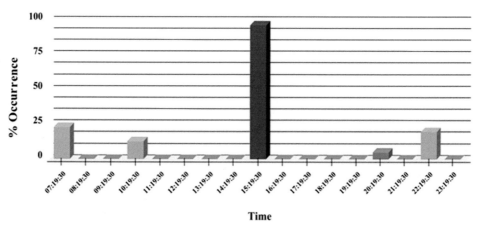

FIGURE 2.9

Probability of the occurrence of a seizure.

3. Post-seizure: In this zone, the device classifies and organizes the data collected. This helps in the future medication of epileptic individuals.

The device is tested on the person with epilepsy. The results obtained are plotted in Figs. 2.10–2.15, where the pulse rate readings are plotted in Fig. 2.10, temperature readings in Fig. 2.11, vibration levels in Fig. 2.12, and accelerometer readings in Fig. 2.13.

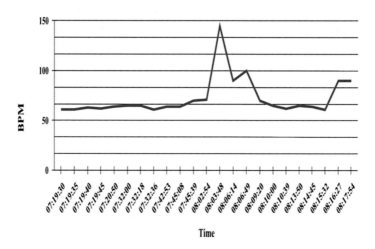

FIGURE 2.10

Pulse rate readings.

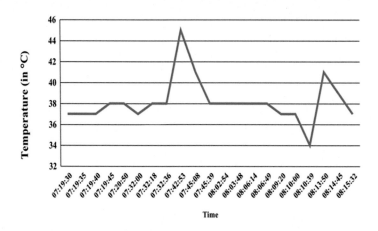

FIGURE 2.11

Temperature readings.

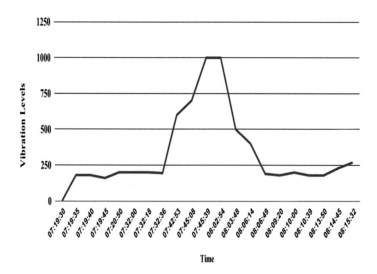

FIGURE 2.12

Vibration levels.

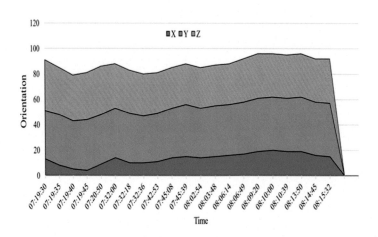

FIGURE 2.13

Accelerometer readings.

FIGURE 2.14

Registration page.

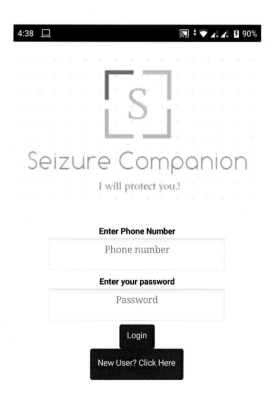

FIGURE 2.15

Login page.

Results of mobile application:

1. A mobile application named "Seizure Companion" was developed to monitor epileptic individuals remotely.
2. The users are registered in the registration portal and sign in to the application through the login portal, as shown in Figs. 2.14 and Fig. 2.15.
3. This application checks the health records: regular health records and seizure records are shown in Fig. 2.16.
4. Health professionals and contacts of the users can monitor the vital parameters such as temperature, pulse rate, vibration levels, sound levels, and location (shown in Fig. 2.17).
5. We also have an option to track the location of the individual, as shown in Fig. 2.17.
6. The application also provides an option to visualize the live readings of the individual's corporal parameters, as shown in Figs. 2.18 and 2.19.
7. This application also alerts the user in the case of any emergencies through an alert notification.

FIGURE 2.16

Welcome page.

FIGURE 2.17

Monitoring page.

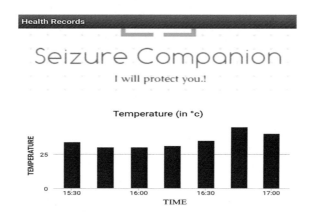

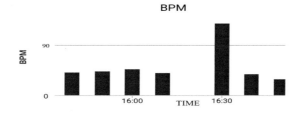

FIGURE 2.18

Live visualization of temperature of the user.

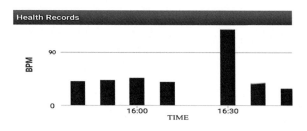

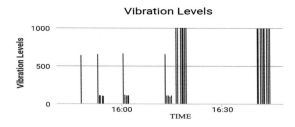

FIGURE 2.19

Live visualization of BPM and vibration levels of the user.

11. Conclusions

Machines mimicking human behavior is not something new. It has been tried and implemented over many years. The latest addition is cognitive technology. This chapter has focused on the development of a system to protect individuals from sudden deaths from epileptic seizures. In addition, the chapter also focused on developing a remote monitoring system that helps parents and healthcare professionals monitor patients remotely. The entire architecture of this device is based on CIoT technology, which means adding a layer of intelligence to the existing IoT technology. The three pillars of CIoT technology—deep learning, natural language processing (NLP), and IoT technology—helped to develop a robust, intelligent device. The proposed device is a powerful voice-controlled device that can protect epileptic people from sudden deaths, interacts with them, and always keeps them engaged. In addition, it predicts the onset of epileptic attacks very effectively. This device is a multifunctional device that also allows individuals to be monitored efficiently. The system is tested on different possible scenarios, and it has given very satisfactory results. Hence, it is proposed to demonstrate that cognitive technology is changing the world with a wide range of intelligent applications.

References

[1] L. In, K. Lee, The Internet of things (IoT): applications, investments, and challenges for enterprises, Bus. Horiz. 58 (4) (2015) 431–440.

[2] T. Wu, F. Wu, J. Redouté, M.R. Yuce, An autonomous wireless body area network implementation towards IoT connected healthcare applications, in: IEEE Access, vol. 5, 2017, pp. 11413–11422, https://doi.org/10.1109/ACCESS.2017.2716344.

[3] P. Pijush Kanti Dutta, S. Pal, P. Choudhury, Beyond Automation: The Cognitive IoT. Artificial Intelligence Brings Sense to the Internet of Things, Cognitive Computing for Big Data Systems over IoT, Springer, Cham, 2018, pp. 1–37.

[4] S. Oniani, G. Marques, S. Barnovi, I.M. Pires, A.K. Bhoi, Artificial intelligence for Internet of Things and enhanced medical systems, in: Bio-inspired Neurocomputing, Springer, Singapore, 2020, pp. 43–59.

[5] World Health Organisation, WHO, Epilepsy, 2019 (online). Available from: https://www.who.int/newsroom/factsheets/detail/epilepsy.

[6] E.B. Bromfield, J.E. Cavazos, J.I. Sirven (Eds.), An Introduction to Epilepsy (Internet), American Epilepsy Society, West Hartford (CT), 2006 (Chapter 2), Clinical Epilepsy. Available from: https://www.ncbi.nlm.nih.gov/books/NBK2511/.

[7] R.S. Fisher, et al., Epileptic seizures and epilepsy: definitions proposed by the International League Against Epilepsy (ILAE) and the International Bureau for Epilepsy (IBE), Epilepsia 46 (4) (2005) 470–472.

[8] About Epilepsy: The Basics, 12/2013 (online). Available from: https://www.epilepsy.com/learn/about-epilepsy-basics.

[9] R. Williamson, et al., Generalized-onset seizures with secondary focal evolution, Epilepsia 50 (7) (2009) 1827–1832.

[10] S.I. Johannessen, E. Ben-Menachem, Management of focal-onset seizures, Drugs 66 (13) (2006) 1701–1725.

[11] J. Sweller, Cognitive technology: some procedures for facilitating learning and problem solving in mathematics and science, J. Educ. Psychol. 81 (4) (1989) 457.

[12] B. Srivastava, J. Marecki, G. Tesauro (Eds.), 2nd Workshop on Cognitive Computing and Applications for Augmented Human Intelligence, in Conjunction with International Joint Conference on Artificial Intelligence (IJCAI), Buenos Aires, Argentina, 2015.

[13] B. Avitall, et al., Remote Health Monitoring System, U.S. Patent No. 6,171,237, 2001.

[14] G. Marques, N. Miranda, A. Kumar Bhoi, B. Garcia-Zapirain, S. Hamrioui, I. de la Torre Díez, Internet of Things and enhanced living environments: measuring and mapping air quality using cyber-physical systems and mobile computing technologies, Sensors 20 (3) (2020) 720.

[15] How IoT Works – 4 Main Components of IoT System (online). Available from: https://data-flair.training/blogs/how-iot-works/.

[16] S. Russell, N. Peter, Artificial Intelligence: A Modern Approach, 2002.

[17] A. Sheth, Internet of things to smart IoT through semantic, cognitive, and perceptual computing, IEEE Intell. Syst. 31 (2) (2016) 108–112.

[18] D. Johnston, et al., Active properties of neuronal dendrites, Annu. Rev. Neurosci. 19 (1) (1996) 165–186.

[19] S. Han, et al., Learning both weights and connections for efficient neural network, Adv. Neural Inf. Process. Syst. (2015).

[20] C. Szegedy, et al., Intriguing Properties of Neural Networks, arXiv, 2013. Preprint arXiv:1312.6199.

[21] F. Pauget, S. Lacaze, T. Valding, A global approach in seismic interpretation based on cost function minimization, in: SEG Technical Program Expanded Abstracts 2009, Society of Exploration Geophysicists, 2009, pp. 2592–2596.

[22] S. Schmidtlein, et al., A brute-force approach to vegetation classification, J. Veg. Sci. 21 (6) (2010) 1162–1171.

[23] Y.S. Abu-Mostafa, Learning from hints in neural networks, J. Complex 6 (2) (1990) 192–198.

[24] A. Khanna, et al., A study of today's ai through chatbots and rediscovery of machine intelligence, Int. J. u- e- Serv. Sci. Technol. 8 (7) (2015) 277–284.

[25] M. Briand, N. Martin, D. Virette, Parametric representation of multichannel audio based on principal component analysis, in: Audio Engineering Society Convention 120, Audio Engineering Society, 2006.

[26] R. Zhao, K. Mao, Fuzzy bag-of-words model for document representation, IEEE Transactions on Fuzzy Systems 26 (2) (2017) 794–804.

[27] S. Moriya, C. Shibata, Transfer learning method for very deep CNN for text classification and methods for its evaluation, in: 2018 IEEE 42nd Annual Computer Software and Applications Conference (COMPSAC), vol. 2, IEEE, 2018.

[28] A. Sriram, et al., Cold Fusion: training seq2seq Models Together With Language Models, arXiv, 2017. Preprint arXiv:1708.06426.

[29] C.W. Zhao, J. Jegatheesan, S. Chee Loon, Exploring iot application using raspberry pi, Int. J. Comput. Appl. 2 (1) (2015) 27–34.

[30] A.K. Bhoi, P.K. Mallick, C.M. Liu, V.E. Balas, Bio-inspired Neurocomputing, Springer, 2021.

[31] S. Bird, E. Klein, E. Loper, Natural Language Processing with Python: Analyzing Text with the Natural Language Toolkit, O'Reilly Media, Inc., 2009.

[32] D. Kummer, Voice-Recognition Home Automation System for Speaker-Dependent Commands. U.S. Patent Application No. 14/566,977.

[33] C. Raj, C. Jain, W. Arif, HEMAN: health monitoring and nous: an IoT based e-health care system for remote telemedicine, in: 2017 International Conference on Wireless Communications, Signal Processing and Networking (WiSPNET). IEEE, 2017.

Cognitive Internet of Things (IoT) and computational intelligence for mental well-being

Surendrabikram Thapa[1], Awishkar Ghimire[1], Surabhi Adhikari[1], Akash Kumar Bhoi[2,3] and
Paolo Barsocchi[3]

[1]*Department of Computer Science and Engineering, Delhi Technological University, Rohini, Delhi, India;* [2]*Department of Computer Science and Engineering, Sikkim Manipal Institute of Technology, Sikkim Manipal University, Majitar, Sikkim, India;* [3]*Institute of Information Science and Technologies, National Research Council, Pisa, Italy*

1. Introduction

In a world full of opportunities and competition, mental well-being has always been a topic that has been overlooked. The influence that a healthy mind can have on daily activities is often underestimated. Mental well-being is about the ability to bring constant positivity to the thoughts and feelings our mind processes. Mental well-being is also about how well we tackle our day-to-day problems, handle stresses, and move forward in life. With good mental well-being, people can realize their value, importance, and responsibilities. The interpersonal skills and the connections people can make depend upon how their mental health. Only a healthy mind can make people reach their fullest potential, through which they can make their contribution to family, community, nation, and humanity as a whole. Thus, mental well-being is a topic that should be treated with much importance and scrutiny.

Today, people's minds are regularly occupied with thoughts of competition, incompleteness, and many negative thoughts, in addition to mental illnesses. With technology pervading all areas of life, social interactions have become much less regular and the typical daily schedule has become hectic. Therefore, the problems of depression, anxiety, personality disorders, etc. have become very common. Mental disorder has been seen comparatively more in older age population, but the fact that the younger population is also susceptible to mental disorders should not be neglected. According to a World Health Organization report in 2015, suicide is the second most common cause of death in the population age group of 15–29 years globally [1]. The most common cause of suicide is depression. Depression is one of the largest causes of global illness, with an estimated 300 million or almost 5% of the world's population affected by it [1]. Depression is a very common yet serious medical condition that affects how a person feels, thinks, acts, and perceives things around themself. Apart from depression, there are other serious illnesses that can bring deadly consequences. Fortunately, however, many of these conditions can be treated effectively by pharmacotherapy or psychotherapy [2].

Cognitive and Soft Computing Techniques for the Analysis of Healthcare Data. **https://doi.org/10.1016/B978-0-323-85751-2.00004-9**

Computers and sensors have been around for a long time. Since the inception of the age of electronics, researchers have attempted to discover ways through which computers and sensors can be used for the benefit of humankind. From industrial applications to important healthcare applications, computers and sensors have their applications in a wide range of areas. The rapid growth in the field of electronics, especially the advancements in sensors, happened after the tremendous improvements in radar technologies, leading to wireless systems in the 1970s [3]. Over the last 40 years or so, with the increasing advancements in these infrastructures, wireless communication systems have been evolving rapidly [4].

More recently, with the advent of modern tools and technologies, there has been a paradigm shift in how patients with mental illnesses are treated. The incorporation of artificial intelligence (AI) and the Internet of Things (IoT) in human lives has enabled researchers to come up with innovative ways of tackling mental illnesses. Traditional health care relies on simple questionnaires and physical examinations to assess the mental well-being of patients. This is usually ineffective at times when there are many factors such as patient's background, education, unreliable autobiographical memory, and more to understand [5]. Thus, there was a much-needed transition on ways to cure mental illnesses. Lately, there has been increased usage of AI, the IoT, and intelligent systems for assessing mental well-being and curing mental illnesses. The Internet of Things, commonly known as the IoT, is an interconnected network of sensors that continuously collect various data. The data collected through the sensors are integrated to build more informative data. An analysis is then done on the available data to infer valuable information which can later be used for various purposes. For example, a heartbeat sensor can calculate the heartbeat of a person. The sensor continuously collects the heartbeat data and, if there is an abnormal heartbeat rate, the sensors are programmed to display the information on this abnormality. This information provided by the sensors can be used by the person to make informed medical decisions such as visiting a doctor or calling emergency helplines in the case of significant abnormality. Further, the same sensor can be made to automatically call an emergency helpline in the case of abrupt and fatal abnormal heartbeat rates. With that being said, cognitive computing can be defined as expert systems which have reasoning abilities and that can infer insights from data from humans [6]. Cognitive computing is a subset of artificial intelligence that also can assist humans in taking decisions.

Scientists have always been interested in how the human brain works and have been working on finding ways to mimic the human brain. With unprecedented developments in the field of natural language processing, computer vision, etc. there has been a spike in the development of deep learning as a field [7]. Previously, there were many barriers to deep learning. The main barrier was the processing power required for deep learning, as the algorithms required heavy mathematical operations. With increasing research in the field of parallel computation and computer architecture, deep learning has been developed multiple-fold in just the past few decades. The processing infrastructure has become so portable that it can even be fit onto small chips. This has given rise to an increasingly high variety of sensors and IoT devices. These devices have the power of cognition or, in other words, the power to decipher information from the data provided. The insights that sensors can derive from the given information have become increasingly accurate, adding a great deal of value to big data analytics.

Cognitive IoT, thus, is an extended version of IoT where IoT devices are given the power of cognition, giving them learning and reasoning abilities through which they can derive insightful information. Cognitive IoT blends the physical world we live in with the world of the Internet, data, and machine intelligence [8]. In the world we live in, billions of bytes of data are processed every second and this is estimated to increase multiple-fold in the near future. This ubiquitous data can be leveraged for social good and general well-being [9]. Currently, data are used in each and every sector and there is not a sector where big data has not been used. AI and big data are thus described as the fourth industrial revolution because of their ability to change everything [10]. As the development in big data continues, some impacts are being brought along which can influence our lives directly in many ways.

In this chapter, we primarily provide a detailed overview of how cognitive IoT and sensors, along with the power of computational intelligence, can be used to tackle problems of mental illnesses. The chapter discusses in detail how IoT and computational intelligence can be used in healthcare applications specifically for mental well-being. Computer vision (CV) and natural language processing (NLP), being the most prominent fields used in tackling mental disorders, are emphasized in the chapter while exploring the applications of CV and NLP for mental well-being. With more concrete examples of use cases in neurodegenerative diseases like Alzheimer disease (AD), Parkinson disease (PD), etc. and other mental illnesses like depression, schizophrenia, dementia, etc., the chapter also explores the possibilities for where computational intelligence can be used in conjunction with expert insight from medical practitioners. The chapter also focuses on the advantages and disadvantages of automated systems over trivial clinical practices and presents ways through which intelligent mental diagnostic systems can be made more robust.

2. Cognitive IoT and computational intelligence in health care

Computational systems are currently being used extensively in the diagnosis of various diseases as well as in the search for cures for various diseases that plague mankind. Computational intelligence has also been successfully used to tackle the current COVID-19 pandemic [11]. Artificial intelligence and machine learning have been successfully used to diagnose diseases including swine flu, the common cold, influenza, hepatitis, Alzheimer and Parkinson diseases, and even various types of cancer. In addition to the diagnoses of diseases, the various dimensions of health monitoring such as heartbeat calculation, calorie burn calculations, etc. are done by cognitive IoT. These devices have the ability to give intelligent outputs based on the basic inputs taken from IoT devices, which are mostly wearables [12].

Amrane et al. [13] carried out a study using machine learning models for the diagnosis of breast cancer. The data set they used was taken from the Wisconsin Breast Cancer Database. Nine characteristics were used in the study. The study compared the accuracy of different machine learning models namely, k-nearest neighbors and naive Bayes classifier. The highest accuracy was given by the naive Bayes classifier, with an accuracy of 97.51%. Esteva et al. [14] proposed a deep convolutional neural network that diagnoses skin cancer with a dermatologist's level of accuracy. The system they developed is as good as a real-life medical practitioner in diagnosing skin cancer from images of lesions. The data set they used consisted of 129,450 images. The highest accuracy of the CNN model in three-way classification was $72.1 \pm 0.9\%$. The highest accuracy obtained using a real dermatologist in the same experiment was 66.0%. This study shows that computation images are much better than actual dermatologists in diagnosing skin cancer using images.

Machine learning and computational intelligence can also be used to diagnose diseases like swine flu using patient data. Bhatt et al. [15] successfully used machine learning techniques like support vector machines, linear discriminant analysis, and neural networks for the diagnosis of swine flu. In their study, neural networks gave the highest accuracy. Banerjee et al. [16] used machine learning techniques like random forest classifier to diagnose COVID-19 in patients using a full blood count.

These are just a few examples in which computational intelligence has been used to diagnose different diseases. In the subsequent sections, we explore in detail different types of technologies that have been used to diagnose mental disorders.

3. Computer vision for early diagnosis of mental disorders using MRI

Computer vision is widely used currently to solve various real-world problems. Computer vision also finds applications in the medical industry, particularly in diagnosis by making use of medical imagery such as magnetic resonance imaging (MRI), computed tomography (CT), and X-ray. Computer vision as it is understood today mainly consists of image processing and deep learning techniques for extracting relevant data out of images or a video feed which is a sequence of images. Today, convolutional neural networks (CNNs) can be considered as the backbone of computer vision as they have been shown to be highly accurate among a range of different computational problems.

MRI is a technique that is used to generate images of the human physiological system. It makes use of strong magnetic fields, magnetic field gradients, and radio waves to generate imagery of different human body parts. MRI is considered to be safe and it finds myriad uses in today's healthcare industry. Different computer vision techniques have been applied to MRI images for the automatic diagnosis of numerous diseases. MRI images can be taken of different parts of the body, from the brain to the liver and gastrointestinal systems. In this section we discuss applications of artificial intelligence and computer vision for the diagnosis of mental disorders, such as Alzheimer disease, using MRI images [17].

MRI has been extensively used for the diagnosis of Alzheimer disease as it is a brain disease and the physical effect of Alzheimer's is clearly seen in the brain tissues. Farooq et al. [18] proposed a system that diagnoses a patient with Alzheimer disease using MRI images, as shown in Fig. 3.1. Along with the diagnosis of Alzheimer's, it also does the diagnosis of mild cognitive impairment and late

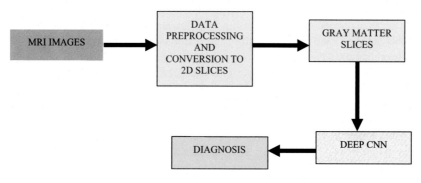

FIGURE 3.1

A high-level overview of the flow of steps in the diagnosis of AD.

mild cognitive impairment. Patients with these symptoms are more likely to develop Alzheimer's in the near future and hence their system can be considered as an early diagnosis of Alzheimer disease. Their system is a multiclass classifier and the classes are Alzheimer's, mild cognitive impairment, late mild cognitive impairment, and healthy individuals. Their system incorporates deep convolutional neural networks. The system's architecture pipeline mainly consists of two parts. The first part converts MRI volume to 2D slices, namely the data preprocessing step. The second part classifies the image into a four-class label, namely the classification part. Since MRI scans are provided in 3D form it is necessary to convert them into 2D slices so that the CNN can work on them. In the data pre-processing part of the system, gray matter segmentation and skull stripping are carried out through spatial normalization, bias corrections, and modulation using the SPM-8 tool. Using the python nibabel package, gray matter volume is converted into JPEG slices. Using these slices different convolutional neural network models are trained. They used standard CNN models such as GoogLeNet, ResNet-18, and ResNet-152. In their experiment, GoogLeNet performed best, with an accuracy of 98.88%. The data set they used to perform their experiment was the data set obtained from ADNI. The data set consisted of a total of 355 patients and hence of the 355 MRI volumes, 137 were healthy persons, 73 patients with Alzheimer's, 61 patients with late mild cognitive impairment, and 84 patients with mild cognitive impairment. Their paper has one of the highest recorded accuracies for Alzheimer's detection in this particular data set.

MRI of the brain is also used for the diagnosis of Parkinson disease as it is also a disease in which the physical pointers or effects are found in the brain. There have been studies that show that Parkinson's can be diagnosed using MRI with the help of computer vision techniques. Here we discuss one such relevant paper. Esmaeilzadeh et al. [19] used 3D convolutional neural networks for the accurate diagnosis of Parkinson disease. In their study, they used images from the PPMI database, which is a standard data set for diagnosis of Parkinson's. Each image is a 3D image and consists of about four million pixels. In their system, first data preprocessing is performed and further data augmentation is done so as to increase the cardinality of the data set. After that, training and testing are done using a 3D CNN model. In the data preprocessing step a standard skull stripping algorithm is used so as to remove noncerebral tissues in the image. The algorithm is called the brain extraction technique (BET). After this process, the image consists of around 800,000 pixels. In the data augmentation step, a new augmented image is formed by switching the left and right hemispheres of the brain. A 3D CNN model is used for the classification of the data set. In this model, a leaky relu activation function is used. Exponential learning rate decay is used for the optimizer. The accuracy of their model on the data set was 100%, which is staggeringly high and shows that their model is very effective. Using their model, they also created a heat map of the brain so as to determine which parts of the brain have more weightage in the diagnosis of Parkinson disease. The parts of the brain that they found to be more important in the diagnosis had been confirmed by medical doctors in earlier research. They also found that a particular part of the brain that medical practitioners had neglected in the diagnosis of Parkinson's was also very important. With this research, we can see that computation systems are not just effective at automated diagnosis but can also be used to derive important facts and knowledge about the human physiological system.

MRI also finds its use cases in the automated diagnosis of schizophrenia. This is possibly because schizophrenia directly affects the various parts of the physical brain. Hu et al. [20] proposed a 3D CNN system that is able to diagnose schizophrenia using MRI images with relatively high accuracy. In their study they compare the accuracy of CNN models with handcrafted featured engineered machine learning models and show that CNNs are the better option in this particular problem of schizophrenia diagnosis using MRI. They used two independent data sets so as to determine the cross-data set testing accuracy of the model. They tested various different CNN models among which a hybrid of inception and ResNet model gave the best accuracy. The testing accuracy was 79.27%. The accuracy, when tested on a different data set than that with which it was trained, came out at 70.98%. In the current literature, the accuracy of their paper is one of the highest ever recorded, and yet it could be considered quite low as it is lower than 80% and hence much research is yet to be done in the field of schizophrenia diagnosis using artificial intelligence and soft computing techniques.

Computer vision and CNN models have also been used in the diagnosis of attention deficit hyperactivity disorder (ADHD) using MRI. Zou et al. [21] proposed a 3D CNN model that diagnoses ADHD using structural MRI (3D) and functional MRI (4D). They performed their experiment on the ADHD-200 data set and achieved a state-of-the-art accuracy of 69.15%. In this research they carried out feature extraction first instead of directly plugging the data into the CNN model. This enabled their model to give higher accuracy.

CNN models have also been used to automatically diagnose depression and epilepsy in patients using MRI. Pominova et al. [17] compared the effectiveness of different CNN models as well as models with CNN and RNN (recurrent neural networks), in diagnosing epilepsy and depression using structural MRI and functional MRI. They achieved an ROC-AUC score of 0.73 when diagnosing depression against a control group. They also created a heat map of the brain using their trained models to show which parts of the brain had greater importance in the diagnosis of epilepsy and depression.

Brain tumors also cause mental disorders in patients, ranging from forgetfulness to loss of motor coordination. Much research has been carried out on the detection of brain tumors using computational resources. Shahzadi et al. [22] proposed a CNN + LSTM hybrid network that can be used for brain tumor classification using MRI. In their system VGC-16, a standard convolutional neural network was used for feature extraction, and then LSTM was used for the classification of brain tumors. The accuracy of the system was found to be 84%.

4. Feature selection techniques and optimization techniques used

Different machine learning techniques have been used for the diagnosis of diseases in computational health care. Apart from computer vision and deep learning, simple machine learning algorithms in conjunction with intelligent feature engineering, feature selection, and feature extraction methods have been successfully used for the diagnosis of many mental disorders from statistical data as well as medical imagery data. In this section, some of the more recent and state-of-the-art machine learning and feature selection techniques used for the diagnosis of mental disorders are discussed.

Forouzannezhad et al. [23] used support vector machines with radial basis function for the diagnosis of Alzheimer disease. The schema of the pipeline is shown in Fig. 3.2. In their study, the input data consisted of three parts, the PET (positron emission transmission) images, MRI (magnetic resonance imagery), and standard neuropsychological test scores. In the study, a total of 896 participants from the Alzheimer's Disease Neuroimaging Initiative (ADNI) was considered. This is a standard data set for Alzheimer disease diagnosis. They used standard software for feature extraction of MRI and PET. In the feature selection process, first ANOVA (analysis of variance) with a P value of 0.01 was used and further random forest based on "Gini" importance was applied. After that,

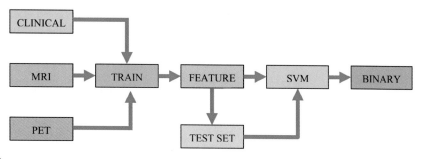

FIGURE 3.2

Schematic pipeline of the system for diagnosis of AD with SVM.

classification was done using SVM with radial basis function. Their study classified patients into four classes, namely control normal (CN), early mild cognitive impairment (EMCI), late mild cognitive impairment (LMCI), and Alzheimer's (AD). The classification is done binarily, that is, CN versus EMCI, CN versus LMCI, and CN versus AD is performed. Their proposed approach gave an accuracy of 81.1% in classifying CN versus EMCI, an accuracy of 91.9% in classifying CN versus LMCI, and an accuracy of 96.2% in classifying CN versus AD. This accuracy is expected because the physical effects of AD are much more pronounced in the brain compared to the physical effects of EMCI.

Various machine learning algorithms have also been successfully used to diagnose Parkinson disease. Ali et al. [24] proposed a machine learning model that uses the voice of patients to diagnose Parkinson's among them. The data set they used consists of 40 patients and from each patient 20 voice recording samples were taken.

Their proposed feature selection algorithm ranks the various features using a statistical model known as the chi-square test and then further searches the optimal subset of the features that are ranked and then selects the samples iteratively. The classifier they used was neural networks and it was shown that their system gave an accuracy of 97.5%, which is extremely high. Avuclu et al. [25] carried out a comparative evaluation of various machine learning algorithms and compared them on their accuracy in the diagnosis of Parkinson's based on voice-based features. The data set they used consisted of 31 people of whom 23 had Parkinson's. A total of 195 samples were collected from each subject. They compared four different machine learning methods, namely k-nearest neighbor, random forest, naive Bayes, and support vector machine.

An electroencephalogram (EEG) is a procedure that detects electrical activity in the brain using miniature electrodes attached to the scalp. EEG signals have been extensively used for analyzing the brain. They have also been used for the diagnosis of various mental disorders. We discuss one such use case of EEG in the diagnosis of depression. Hosseinifard et al. [26] used machine learning and nonlearning features extracted from EEG signals to classify depressive patients from normal subjects. The data set they used consisted of 45 normal subjects and 45 depressed patients. They experimented with different feature extraction algorithms such as Higuchi, detrended fluctuation analysis, correlation dimension, and Lyapunov exponent to extract features from the EEG signals. For optimal feature selection, they used genetic algorithms with an initial population of 50, crossover rate of 80%, and a mutation rate of 4%. The machine learning algorithms that were used in their experiments were k-nearest neighbors, linear discriminant analysis, and linear regression. The highest classification accuracy of 83.3% was achieved when the feature extraction technique used was correlation dimension and the machine learning model used was the linear regression model. Using all the nonlinear features extracted by all of the different feature extraction methods the accuracy of the system reached 90% when the linear regression model was used.

5. Natural language processing-based diagnostic system

NLP-based diagnostic systems can be phenomenal in making screening tests accessible. For example, the speech transcripts of patients with Alzheimer disease can be analyzed to get an overview of how speech deterioration occurs as the disease progresses.

The ability of a human to listen, speak, and communicate with others has undoubtedly been the greatest blessing to humankind. The ability to communicate with each other has unraveled endless opportunities for the civilization and advancement of humanity. Over the course of time, early humans discovered scripts, alphabets, and letters which again proved to be exceptionally important human discoveries as they helped in the management of records, historical events, and effective communication among a larger group of people [27]. These scripts, alphabets, linguistics, and other aspects of language have evolved highly to date. There is a great deal of text data generated every fraction of a second in social networks, search engines, microblogging platforms, etc. With the power of natural language processing (NLP), text data can be processed to gain valuable insights from it. The inception of NLP started in the 1950s as an intersection of artificial intelligence and linguistics [28]. Currently, it has applications in hundreds of fields such as customer service, business analytics, intelligent healthcare systems, etc.

The text we generate has its own features. Deep learning models now can classify between speech or text produced by a healthy individual and that from an individual with mental illness. Thus, it can be used for designing diagnostic systems for screening mental illnesses. For example, a patient with Alzheimer disease (AD) can be diagnosed with MRI, positron emission tomography (PET), CT, and other conventional scanning methods [9]. These techniques however need to be supervised by medical practitioners at each and every stage. On the other hand, the cognitive impairments in AD patients can also be evidenced by aphasia or the inability to understand and produce speech in daily activities [29]. Such anomalies in speech can be leveraged for building diagnostic systems for the early diagnosis of AD. NLP and deep learning can thus be used to build models that are able to automatically diagnose a disease. This application is, however, not just limited to AD and can be used in the diagnosis of any illnesses which can be characterized by cognitive impairments reflected in speech. Apart from the ease in applications, the NLP-based models can be much more powerful than conventional screening tests like the Mini-Mental State Examination (MMSE) [30], the Rowland Universal Dementia Assessment Scale (RUDAS) [31], etc. because the information in spontaneous speech can gain greater insights than questionnaires given for assessment. The assessments done using questionnaires are also influenced by backgrounds such as education, culture experienced, and a many other factors. Thus, the assessment techniques are not always accurate and hence patients who are diagnosed with mental illnesses using one assessment tool may be diagnosed as CN with another assessment tool [32]. Similarly, ethics over the collection of personal information in neuropsychological assessment is also a problem to be addressed [33]. In this context, NLP can be used to detect anomalies in the speech narratives of patients.

Different researchers in the past have used different modalities and algorithms to diagnose patients with different mental illnesses such as AD, Parkinson disease (PD), etc. Fraser et al. [34] used the speech narratives of healthy individuals and patients diagnosed with AD to build a diagnostic system based on a logistic regression algorithm. For their study, they used the corpus named DementiaBank. DementiaBank is a widely used corpus that has the speech narratives of patients with AD along with those of healthy control normal individuals [35]. The DementiaBank has both speech (audio) and text transcripts corresponding to that audio. The algorithm used on English speech transcripts gave an accuracy of 81.93%. The model used hand-picked features with machine learning algorithms. Hand-picked features are often highly dependent upon the person preparing the data and can lead to high variability. Thus, lately, there has been a shift toward using deep learning-based models for the diagnosis of Alzheimer disease. Karlekar et al. [36], with a motive to overcome the issues due to hand-picked features, used different deep learning models to build the diagnostic system using speech narratives from DementiaBank. Out of the different deep learning models used, the CNN-LSTM model performed the best, with an accuracy of 91.1%. The authors furthermore carried out analysis of what AD-related features of language the deep learning models are learning.

Apart from the speech narratives in the English language, work has been done in many other regional languages also. Vincze et al. [37] used the speech narratives of patients in the Hungarian language. A total of 84 patients, with 48 patients having mild cognitive impairment (MCI) and 36 having AD participated in the experiment. Rich feature sets that contained various linguistic features based on language morphology, sentiment, spontaneity in speech, and demography of participants were used for feeding the model. Such hand-picked features when used with SVM gave an accuracy of 75% at the best case when only more significant features were chosen. In addition, Thapa et al. [38] also presented an architecture for diagnosing patients with AD using Nepali speech transcripts. The baselines were established using various machine learning classifiers and, later, deep learning models were also used. Among the various deep learning architectures used, Kim's CNN architecture [39] performed the best with an accuracy of 0.96. Their study also used data from the DementiaBank which was translated into the Nepali language by native language speakers for the purposes of the experiment. Furthermore, a great deal of work has been done in other languages including Turkish [40], Portuguese [41], etc. However, the works done in regional languages are very limited. The nonavailability of prerequisites for natural language processing like word embeddings, language models, etc. creates a barrier when regional languages are dealt with [42].

In addition to Alzheimer disease, efforts have been made to build models for the diagnosis of Parkinson disease (PD) also. PD is a disease similar to AD which can be diagnosed using speech or text-based features. Toro et al. [43] proposed an SVM model for the diagnosis of PD from healthy control (HC) subjects. For their study, they used the speech narratives of 50 PD and 50 HC subjects. The speech was manually transcribed and later, NLP was used for building the models. The model which was built for the Spanish language had an accuracy of 72%. Similarly, Thapa et al. [44] used a twin SVM-based algorithm for diagnosis of PD using speech features. Using a feature selection algorithm, a total of 13 features were selected for a total of 23. With the feature selection-based twin SVM, an accuracy of 93.9% was achieved.

The research has been mainly concentrated on these two diseases, namely PD and AD, because of their worldwide prevalence and the growing number of patients. Research continues to find applications of language modality in building diagnostic systems for mental illnesses other than AD and PD. Some of the works carried out in the domain of diagnosis of mental illnesses can be found in Table 3.1.

Table 3.1 Diagnosis of mental illnesses with text and speech modality.

Authors	Year	Data set	Language	Use-case	Modality	Algorithms	ACC	Pre	Recall	F-score
Vincze et al. [37]	2016	48 MCI 36 CN (private)	Hungarian	Mild cognitive impairment	Text	SVM	75	75.8	75	75.1
Karlekar et al. [36]	2018	Dementia Bank	English	Alzheimer disease	Text	CNN-LSTM	91.1	–	–	–
Aluísio et al. [41]	2016	20 CN 20 MCI 20 AD (NILC dataset)	Portuguese	CN versus MCI versus AD	Text	Naive Bayes	–	–	–	0.82
				CN versus MCI		J48 algorithm	–	–	–	0.90
Thapa et al. [38]	2020	Dementia Bank	Nepali	CN versus AD	Text	Kim's CNN	0.96	0.97	0.96	0.96
Toro et al. [43]	2019	PC-GITA 50 PD, 50 HC	Spanish	Parkinson disease	Text	SVM	0.72	–	0.92	–
Thapa et al. [44]	2020	Little et al. [45]	English	Parkinson disease	Speech	Twin SVM	0.932	0.93	0.93	0.93
Khodabakhsh et al. [40]	2014	20 AD 20 CN (private)	Turkish	CN versus AD	Speech	SVM	0.9	–	–	–
Fraser et al. [34]	2016	Dementia Bank	English	Alzheimer disease	Text	Logistic regression	81.93	–	–	–
Fritsch et al. [46]	2016	Dementia Bank	English	Alzheimer disease	Text	LSTM	85.6	–	–	–
Chen et al. [47]	2019	Dementia Bank	English	Alzheimer disease	Text	Att-CNN + Att-BiGRU	97.42	–	–	–

In addition to the diagnosis of mental illnesses from speech narratives, the clinical texts can also be used to extract the symptoms of mental illnesses [73]. Furthermore, discourse analysis should be done to analyze how linguistic features of the speech are correlated with conversational outcomes [62].

6. Harnessing the power of NLP for the analysis of social media content for depression detection

With the availability of the Internet and mobile phones to a very large number of people around the world, a lot of activities are taking place in the Internet sphere every second. Social networking sites like Facebook, LinkedIn, etc., and microblogging sites like Twitter have given people the freedom to express their opinions, beliefs, personal experiences, feelings, etc. People tend to express many feelings to friends and family in their network through which inferences can be made about their mental state [27].

Depression has become a very common disease. Therefore, this has to be dealt with by measures that are readily available and accessible. Thus, computer-based diagnostic measures could prove to be very effective because of their easy availability and accessibility. The diagnostic systems based on computational intelligence rely on readily available data. Most of the past works use text data from readily available sources like Reddit, Twitter, Facebook, etc.

Tadesse et al. [58] used the posts of Reddit users to build an analytical model for depression detection from Reddit posts. With 1293 posts pertaining to the depressed category and 548 posts relating to the nondepressed category, an accuracy of 91% was achieved with multilayer perceptron. Similarly, Aldarwish et al. [60] took posts from multiple social networking sites to build their data sets. The data were taken from various social networking sites like LiveJournal, Twitter, Facebook, etc. to build the model. The naïve Bayes classifier gave a perfect precision of 100 but performed badly in terms of other performance measures like accuracy and recall. The accuracy and recall for the model were reported to be 63 and 58 on a scale of 100, respectively. Many works has been done in the English language, but few in other languages. However, researchers also are building diagnostic systems for other languages.

Katchapakirin et al. [55] built a system using the Facebook posts of Thai users. Facebook, being the most used social network in Thailand, is the platform where most of the users express their feelings freely. With 1105 posts taken from Facebook, a deep neural network was used to classify the users as depressed or nondepressed. With the activity of users in Facebook such as the length of posts, the time the user posts, etc. the model was able to classify with an accuracy of 85%.

In addition to tweets, spontaneous speeches can also be used to build the model for the detection of depression. Huang et al. [56] used the audio recordings taken from smartphones to detect depression. The characteristic vocal features like pauses and differences in pronunciations were leveraged by the LDA bigram model to diagnose the subjects with an accuracy of 78.70%. The smartphone-based techniques can be useful and easily available. Further, spontaneous speech can be rich in features and hence can help in accurate diagnosis.

7. Computational intelligence and cognitive IoT in suicide prevention

Suicide has been one of the most serious issues in modern society. The competition in society, with high expectations of oneself, and limited social interaction are among the factors that contribute to suicide. Every year, nearly a million people around the globe die from suicide [63]. This number is staggeringly high and suicide accounts for more deaths than war, homicide, or prevalent diseases like malaria. The figures might be even higher, as thousands of cases go unreported. Suicide not only takes the lives of our beloved, it also causes severe distress to those close to the victim. There are many examples of relatives and families left in financial and emotional burden after a suicide. Thus, suicide is a problem that not only kills individuals but also leaves the relatives in deep distress. Hence, there is a need to identify the risks of suicide as early as possible [64]. This can help psychiatrists, social activists, and concerned stakeholders to step in and carry out preventive measures.

The identification of suicidal behavior is a great challenge to psychiatrists and computational intelligence scientists. The diagnosis is difficult because there is not a single symptom that can be screened for. There are many social and relationship factors that need to be analyzed in greater detail. Despite complications posed by various factors, there have been efforts to uncover the risks and identify suicidal ideation. There are also some high-risk groups such as patients with terminal illnesses and no psychiatric counseling, people with significant financial burdens, and so on [65]. Factors like these can be reflected through electromedical health records, demographic information, etc. Such useful information is leveraged by machine learning algorithms to uncover the probability of suicide and take proactive measures accordingly. Also, lately, social media contents have been used for analysis by machine learning algorithms. With the wide availability of mobile phones and intelligent sensors, they are also being incorporated to assess the risks of suicide and prevent them. While assessing the risks, it is more likely that the patients will convey their information to smartphone-based data collection modalities. These data can be collected through online forms, voice recordings, call logs, etc. which can be leveraged for further analysis [66]. Cognitive IoT can also be used in such case. Such cognitive IoT devices can assess the risks in real time and allow the emergency helplines to communicate with the victims. In this way, cognitive IoT devices, especially wearables ones, can play a vital role.

Sawhney et al. [48] built a model for the prediction of suicidal ideation using various machine learning and evolutionary algorithms. The data were collected from Twitter for suicide and nonsuicide labels using Twitter API. The tweets that showed a tendency for self-harm or suicide were labeled as suicidal tweets, whereas the tweets that did not show any such tendencies were labeled as nonsuicidal tweets. Various machine learning and deep learning models were then used to evaluate the performance. Of the various deep learning and machine learning models some of which were used in conjunction with evolutionary algorithms, the random forest algorithm with binary firefly algorithm performed the best. The model Random Forest + Binary Firefly Algorithm showed the best performance in terms of accuracy, precision, and recall. The model had an accuracy of 88.82% with a precision and recall of 87.12 and 84.73 respectively on a scale of 100.

Depressed patients can have varying degrees of suicide susceptibility. Cheng et al. [51] used posts from Weibo, a popular social media site in China, to curate the data sets and build the models for the assessment of suicide risks. The authors carried out a detailed study to assess suicide risks along with the probabilistic suicidal possibility and levels of anxiety, depression, and stress. For the respondents who earlier had suicidal communications, a recall of 70 (on a scale of 100) was obtained for classifying respondents with severe anxiety. Similarly, those with severe depression and high suicide risks were classified with a sensitivity of 65% each.

Similarly, Fodeh et al. [52] built a k-nearest neighbor (KNN)-based algorithm to identify patients who were at risk and patients who were at high risk. The data set of 280 tweets of class "high risk" and

1614 tweets of class "at risk" were taken for the study. Using the down-sampling technique, the data were down-sampled to form a balanced data set of 280 tweets of class "high risk" and 285 tweets of class "at risk." The KNN-based classifier was able to classify the two classes with a precision of 0.853 and sensitivity of 0.933. Classification of the tweets in such a hierarchy would help rescuers to prioritize cases according to the degree of severity. Lin et al. [53] also proposed models for the prediction of suicidal ideation in military personnel. This work used six machine learning models by taking six important psychological stress domains as the features. Two classification problems were defined, one with any suicidal ideation and another with serious suicidal ideation. For any suicidal ideation, the performance measures for normal and suicidal subjects were 100% for accuracy, precision, and f-score with a multilayer perceptron (MLP) model. Similarly, for serious suicidal ideation, an accuracy of 99.9% was achieved with the MLP model (Table 3.2).

Despite the easy classification, there are many problems associated with machine learning models. The main problem arises from the data availability. Twitter, which is the main source of data in most of the earlier works, is sometimes unreliable. Sawhney et al. [48] point out the complications in analysis using tweets by doing a detailed error analysis. The authors found a high fluctuation in the meaning that words in tweets want to convey. Most of the time, the algorithms misclassify the tweets as tweets with suicidal ideation when they had characteristics words like "kill me," "I am done," etc. Some tweets containing such words might be suicidal tweets, but this is not always the case. Sometimes, people express humor or sarcasm with such words. Machine learning models fail to identify such occasions.

Apart from suicide prevention, machine learning can be used to analyze the data from past suicides and come up with proactive measures to prevent suicides. Various organizations have been using past data for modeling and analyzing the effects of various plans and policies for suicide prevention. Also, various chatbots and conversational bots have been developed recently to aid in suicide prevention [67]. Suicide prevention using computational intelligence is undoubtedly one of the most useful applications of machine learning and is promising because of the early detection and high accuracy exhibited by various algorithms. Though the measures have good outcomes, various ethical issues should also be addressed. Ethical issues while collection and processing data should be taken into consideration while building models based on computational intelligence [68]. Many other aspects go hand-in-hand with suicide prevention and, because of this, computational scientists along with other stakeholders must show a coordinated effort [69].

8. Wearables and IoT devices for mental well-being

One of the key challenges of mild mental well-being disorders, such as mild-level depression, is that people may not recognize it until it is too late. It has been reported that depression is particularly difficult to diagnose in a traditional way. Doctors usually diagnose depression using the traditional method of questions and answers. Since the autobiographical memory of people is not 100% accurate and also the answers from patients can be highly mood dependent, it is highly likely that depression can go undiagnosed even with the help of professional medical practitioners. There has been a rise in mental health monitoring apps for smartphones in the market today. There are many apps that act as a diary for the user to input details about their mental health. Recently, chatbots have been created using NLP that are able to chat with the user and determine their emotional state. State-of-the-art chatbots

Table 3.2 Use cases of natural language processing in depression diagnosis and suicide prevention.

Authors	Year	Language	Data set	Use-cases	Algorithm	Acc	Pre	Rec	F-score	AUC
Sawhney et al. [48]	2019	English	Tweets	Suicidal ideation detection	Random forest + binary firefly algorithm	88.82	87.12	84.73	85.91	–
Walsh et al. [49]	2017	English	Health records	Predicting risk of suicide attempts	Random forest	–	0.79	0.95	–	0.84
Braithwaite et al. [50]	2016	English	Tweets	Prediction of suicide	Decision trees	91.9	–	–	–	–
Cheng et al. [51]	2017	Chinese	Weibo posts	Suicide risk and emotional distress	SVM	–	–	0.70 (severe anxiety)	–	0.75
Fodeh et al. [52]	2019	English	Tweets	Detection of suicide risk	KNN	–	0.853	0.933	–	0.885
Lin et al. [53]	2020	English	Psychopathological observations	Detection of suicidal ideation	Multilayer perceptron	100	100	100	100	100
Zheng et al. [54]	2020	English	Electronic health records (EHR)	Suicide attempt	Deep neural network	–	–	–	–	0.792
Katchapakirin et al. [55]	2018	Thai	Facebook posts	Depression detection	Deep neural network	85	80	100	88.9	–
Huang et al. [56]	2019	English	Smartphone audio recording	Depression detection	LDA-bigram	78.70%	–	–	0.549	–
Orabi et al. [57]	2018	English	Tweets	Depression detection	CNN-based model	87.96	87.44	87.03	86.97	0.95
Tadesse et al. [58]	2019	English	Reddit posts	Depression detection	Multilayer perceptron	91	–	–	0.93	–
Choudhury et al. [59]	2013	English	Tweets and questionnaires	Depression detection	SVM	72.34	0.74	0.629	–	–
Aldarwish et al. [60]	2017	English	Multiple social networking sites	Depression detection	Naive Bayes	63	100	58	–	–
Deshpande et al. [61]	2017	English	Tweets	Depression detection	Naive Bayes	83	0.836	0.83	0.833	–

also attempt to uplift the user's mood using linguistic tricks. Wysa and Woebot are two such applications that are available which users have reported as being mood uplifting. The market for such applications has also been on the rise. An application called calm has been valued at a billion dollars, even though no research backs up its claim to improve mental health. Similarly, there are other applications such as Calm Harm which is designed to prevent self-harm and also prevent suicide [5].

Gjoreski et al. [70] created a system that is able to carry out real-time detection of stress in individuals. Stress is relatively harmless, but prolonged and continuous stress can cause irreversible damage to the human system; thus, it is very important to detect and manage stress. Their system consists of a wrist device that captures physiological data, primarily a photoplethysmogram (PPG). Using the data, the person is classified as having stress or not in that particular moment in time using machine learning. The machine-learning algorithm was trained in the laboratory by obtaining data from subjects by placing them in stressful situations.

Being in good physical health is a prerequisite for mental well-being because a person who is sick or has a disease is not able to be in complete mental ease. Thus, it is important to monitor the physical health of people. Nowadays, IoT systems have been developed that constantly monitor subjects in a nonintrusive manner and report any abnormalities in the physical system using different computational techniques. Saha et al. [71] proposed a system that can carry out real-time tracking of a person's pulse rate, echocardiogram rate of heart, pressure levels, temperature, as well as blood glucose levels using suitable sensors. These sensors send data to the smartphone that the person is carrying and then the phone further sends the data to the cloud for further analysis. Casaccia et al. [72] proposed a system that determines the well-being of elderly patients through domotic sensors and machine learning algorithms. The domotic sensor consists of three parts. The first part is the light status detector that detects whether the light is on or off. The second is a thermostat which monitors and controls their temperature, and the third is passive infrared sensors which monitor the presence of users. For the first 2 months a survey was taken at regular intervals and then using that survey and data the machine learning algorithm was trained. The accuracy and effectiveness of the system at determining and regulating the well-being of senior citizens was found to be acceptable.

9. Future scope of computational intelligence in mental well-being

It is well known that artificial intelligence and computational systems are practically driving today's world and they find applications in many different areas. One such area is the healthcare sector. Many computational technologies have already been developed for the accurate diagnosis of many diseases and disorders using various features from images, voices, blood samples, and so on. There could be many advances in the field of technological healthcare systems in the future. Some perspectives of the authors as to what could happen in the future are discussed below.

One of the major advances would probably be in the field of mental disorders diagnosis. There are systems that can automatically diagnose certain mental disorders such as Alzheimer disease, Parkinson disease, etc. with 100% accuracy using various data like MRI, PET, and medical records. The entire process of diagnosis could be done without the involvement of any humans, with the entire process being carried out by computational systems. Artificial intelligence systems that could potentially determine whether a person is likely to develop a mental disorder as much as 50 years into the future could be developed. These systems could scan the genetic makeup of a child and determine whether the child is likely to develop certain mental disorders in the future. There could be computational systems that could also determine what kind of environment is more likely to cause mental disorders in individuals and suggest the kind of environment for optimal mental well-being for a certain individual based on his/her personal history and physiological makeup.

There could even be certain computational technologies which could prevent and treat mental disease that would show up years in the future in certain individuals. Perhaps machines that could change the genetic makeup of individuals so as to cure diseases such as cancer would be made in the future. These machines could very well remove the genes that cause mental disorders. It could also potentially add genes that could potentially prevent any sort of mental disorder from happening to the DNA of an individual. However, we probably will not see these sorts of technologies in the near future, but as human civilization progresses these kinds of systems could possibly be made.

10. Conclusion

This chapter has discussed how computational intelligence and intelligent sensors can be used for mental well-being. Mental well-being, being one of the most important aspects of life, should be given greater emphasis and focus should be laid on making diagnostic systems as cheap and accessible as possible. Thus, more research needs to be done to aid people in living a happy life. Computational intelligence has developed immensely and, in the future, doctors might even be replaced by artificial intelligent machines. The clinical diagnosis could be done using intelligent expert chatbots that could correctly determine what disease a person has and automatically suggest tests and diagnosis methods that would confirm it. Surgeries would probably take place automatically. In fact, robots that are capable of performing neurosurgery have already been developed, however, they still need some level of human intervention. Perhaps in the near future these robots could successfully operate without any human intervention. The future of computational technologies is only limited by human imagination and creativity. Anything that we can think of could be done using computational technologies and artificial intelligence. The future is bright if we use these systems ethically and for the benefit of humanity.

References

[1] Suicide in the World: Global Health Estimates, World Health Organization, 2019.
[2] P. Cuijpers, et al., The efficacy of psychotherapy and pharmacotherapy in treating depressive and anxiety disorders: a meta-analysis of direct comparisons, World Psychiatr. 12 (2) (2013) 137–148.
[3] C. Gu, Short-range noncontact sensors for healthcare and other emerging applications: a review, Sensors 16 (8) (2016) 1169.
[4] S.K. Khan, et al., Performance evaluation of next-generation wireless (5G) UAV relay, Wirel. Pers. Commun. 113 (2) (2020) 945–960.
[5] K. Woodward, et al., Beyond mobile apps: a survey of technologies for mental well-being, IEEE Trans. Affect. Comput. (2020).
[6] S. Gupta, et al., Big data with cognitive computing: a review for the future, Int. J. Inf. Manag. 42 (2018) 78–89.
[7] M. Chen, F. Herrera, K. Hwang, Cognitive computing: architecture, technologies and intelligent applications, IEEE Access 6 (2018) 19774–19783.

[8] J. Ploennigs, A. Ba, M. Barry, Materializing the promises of cognitive IoT: how cognitive buildings are shaping the way, IEEE Internet Things J. 5 (4) (2017) 2367–2374.

[9] S. Thapa, et al., Data-driven approach based on feature selection technique for early diagnosis of Alzheimer's disease, in: 2020 International Joint Conference on Neural Networks (IJCNN), IEEE, 2020.

[10] A. Ghimire, et al., Accelerating business growth with big data and artificial intelligence, in: 2020 Fourth International Conference on I-SMAC (IoT in Social, Mobile, Analytics and Cloud) (I-SMAC), IEEE, 2020.

[11] A. Ghimire, et al., AI and IoT solutions for tackling COVID-19 pandemic, in: 2020 4th International Conference on Electronics, Communication and Aerospace Technology (ICECA), IEEE, 2020.

[12] S. Adhikari, et al., A comparative study of machine learning and NLP techniques for uses of stop words by patients in diagnosis of Alzheimer's disease, in: 2021 International Joint Conference on Neural Networks (IJCNN), IEEE, 2021.

[13] M. Amrane, et al., Breast cancer classification using machine learning, in: 2018 Electric Electronics, Computer Science, Biomedical Engineerings' Meeting (EBBT), IEEE, 2018.

[14] A. Esteva, et al., Dermatologist-level classification of skin cancer with deep neural networks, Nature 542 (7639) (2017) 115–118.

[15] D. Bhatt, et al., Swine flu predication using machine learning, in: Information and Communication Technology for Intelligent Systems, Springer, 2019, pp. 611–617.

[16] A. Banerjee, et al., Use of machine learning and artificial intelligence to predict SARS-CoV-2 infection from full blood counts in a population, Int. Immunopharm. 86 (2020) 106705.

[17] M. Pominova, et al., Voxelwise 3d convolutional and recurrent neural networks for epilepsy and depression diagnostics from structural and functional MRI data, in: 2018 IEEE International Conference on Data Mining Workshops (ICDMW), IEEE, 2018.

[18] A. Farooq, et al., A deep CNN based multi-class classification of Alzheimer's disease using MRI, in: 2017 IEEE International Conference on Imaging Systems and Techniques (IST), IEEE, 2017.

[19] S. Esmaeilzadeh, Y. Yang, E. Adeli, End-to-End Parkinson Disease Diagnosis Using Brain MR-Images by 3D-CNN, arXiv, 2018. Preprint arXiv:1806.05233.

[20] M. Hu, et al., Brain MRI-based 3D convolutional neural networks for classification of schizophrenia and controls, in: 2020 42nd Annual International Conference of the IEEE Engineering in Medicine & Biology Society (EMBC), IEEE, 2020.

[21] L. Zou, et al., 3D CNN based automatic diagnosis of attention deficit hyperactivity disorder using functional and structural MRI, IEEE Access 5 (2017) 23626–23636.

[22] I. Shahzadi, et al., CNN-LSTM: Cascaded framework for brain tumour classification, in: 2018 IEEE-EMBS Conference on Biomedical Engineering and Sciences (IECBES), IEEE, 2018.

[23] P. Forouzannezhad, et al., Early diagnosis of mild cognitive impairment using random forest feature selection, in: 2018 IEEE Biomedical Circuits and Systems Conference (BioCAS), IEEE, 2018.

[24] L. Ali, et al., Early diagnosis of Parkinson's disease from multiple voice recordings by simultaneous sample and feature selection, Expert Syst. Appl. 137 (2019) 22–28.

[25] E. Avuçlu, A. Elen, Evaluation of train and test performance of machine learning algorithms and Parkinson diagnosis with statistical measurements, Med. Biol. Eng. Comput. 58 (11) (2020) 2775–2788.

[26] B. Hosseinifard, M.H. Moradi, R. Rostami, Classifying depression patients and normal subjects using machine learning techniques and nonlinear features from EEG signal, Comput. Methods Progr. Biomed. 109 (3) (2013) 339–345.

[27] R.A. Calvo, et al., Natural language processing in mental health applications using non-clinical texts, Nat. Lang. Eng. 23 (5) (2017) 649–685.

[28] P.M. Nadkarni, L. Ohno-Machado, W.W. Chapman, Natural language processing: an introduction, J. Am. Med. Inf. Assoc. 18 (5) (2011) 544–551.

[29] K. Faber-Langendoen, et al., Aphasia in senile dementia of the Alzheimer type, Ann. Neurol. 23 (4) (1988) 365−370.

[30] J.R. Cockrell, M.F. Folstein, Mini-mental state examination, in: Principles and Practice of Geriatric Psychiatry, 2002, pp. 140−141.

[31] J.E. Storey, et al., The Rowland universal dementia assessment scale (RUDAS): a multicultural cognitive assessment scale, Int. Psychogeriatr. 16 (1) (2004) 13.

[32] R.J. Ellis, et al., Diagnostic validity of the dementia questionnaire for Alzheimer disease, Arch. Neurol. 55 (3) (1998) 360−365.

[33] P.J. Whitehouse, Ethical issues in early diagnosis and prevention of Alzheimer disease, Dialogues Clin. Neurosci. 21 (1) (2019) 101.

[34] K.C. Fraser, J.A. Meltzer, F. Rudzicz, Linguistic features identify Alzheimer's disease in narrative speech, J. Alzheim. Dis. 49 (2) (2016) 407−422.

[35] J.T. Becker, et al., The natural history of Alzheimer's disease: description of study cohort and accuracy of diagnosis, Arch. Neurol. 51 (6) (1994) 585−594.

[36] S. Karlekar, T. Niu, M. Bansal, Detecting Linguistic Characteristics of Alzheimer's Dementia by Interpreting Neural Models, arXiv, 2018. Preprint arXiv:1804.06440.

[37] V. Vincze, et al., Detecting Mild Cognitive Impairment by Exploiting Linguistic Information From Transcripts, Association for Computational Linguistics, 2016.

[38] S. Thapa, et al., Detecting Alzheimer's disease by exploiting linguistic information from Nepali transcript, in: International Conference on Neural Information Processing, Springer, 2020.

[39] Y. Kim, Convolutional Neural Networks for Sentence Classification, 2014.

[40] A. Khodabakhsh, S. Kuşxuoğlu, C. Demiroğlu, Natural language features for detection of Alzheimer's disease in conversational speech, in: IEEE-EMBS International Conference on Biomedical and Health Informatics (BHI), IEEE, 2014.

[41] S. Aluísio, A. Cunha, C. Scarton, Evaluating progression of Alzheimer's disease by regression and classification methods in a narrative language test in Portuguese, in: International Conference on Computational Processing of the Portuguese Language, Springer, 2016.

[42] S. Thapa, S. Adhikari, S. Mishra, Review of text summarization in Indian regional languages, in: 2020 International Conference on Computing Informatics & Networks, ICCIN), 2020.

[43] P.A. Pérez-Toro, et al., Natural language analysis to detect Parkinson's disease, in: International Conference on Text, Speech, and Dialogue, Springer, 2019.

[44] S. Thapa, et al., Feature selection based twin-support vector machine for the diagnosis of Parkinson's disease, in: 2020 IEEE 8th R10 Humanitarian Technology Conference (R10-HTC), 2020.

[45] M. Little, et al., Suitability of dysphonia measurements for telemonitoring of Parkinson's disease, Nat. Preced. (2008) 1.

[46] J. Fritsch, S. Wankerl, E. Nöth, Automatic diagnosis of Alzheimer's disease using neural network language models, in: ICASSP 2019-2019 IEEE International Conference on Acoustics, Speech and Signal Processing (ICASSP), IEEE, 2019.

[47] J. Chen, J. Zhu, J. Ye, An attention-based hybrid network for automatic detection of Alzheimer's disease from narrative speech, in: INTERSPEECH, 2019.

[48] R. Sawhney, et al., Exploring the impact of evolutionary computing based feature selection in suicidal ideation detection, in: 2019 IEEE International Conference on Fuzzy Systems (FUZZ-IEEE), IEEE, 2019.

[49] C.G. Walsh, J.D. Ribeiro, J.C. Franklin, Predicting risk of suicide attempts over time through machine learning, Clin. Psychol. Sci. 5 (3) (2017) 457−469.

[50] S.R. Braithwaite, et al., Validating machine learning algorithms for Twitter data against established measures of suicidality, JMIR Ment. Health 3 (2) (2016) e21.

[51] Q. Cheng, et al., Assessing suicide risk and emotional distress in Chinese social media: a text mining and machine learning study, J. Med. Internet Res. 19 (7) (2017) e243.

[52] S. Fodeh, et al., Using machine learning algorithms to detect suicide risk factors on twitter, in: 2019 International Conference on Data Mining Workshops (ICDMW), IEEE, 2019.

[53] G.-M. Lin, et al., Machine learning based suicide ideation prediction for military personnel, IEEE J. Biomed. Health Inform. 24 (7) (2020) 1907−1916.

[54] L. Zheng, et al., Development of an early-warning system for high-risk patients for suicide attempt using deep learning and electronic health records, Transl. Psychiatr. 10 (1) (2020) 1−10.

[55] K. Katchapakirin, et al., Facebook social media for depression detection in the Thai community, in: 2018 15th International Joint Conference on Computer Science and Software Engineering (JCSSE), IEEE, 2018.

[56] Z. Huang, J. Epps, D. Joachim, Speech landmark bigrams for depression detection from naturalistic smartphone speech, in: ICASSP 2019-2019 IEEE International Conference on Acoustics, Speech and Signal Processing (ICASSP), IEEE, 2019.

[57] A.H. Orabi, et al., Deep learning for depression detection of twitter users, in: Proceedings of the Fifth Workshop on Computational Linguistics and Clinical Psychology: From Keyboard to Clinic, 2018.

[58] M.M. Tadesse, et al., Detection of depression-related posts in reddit social media forum, IEEE Access 7 (2019) 44883−44893.

[59] M. De Choudhury, et al., Predicting depression via social media, in: Proceedings of the International AAAI Conference on Web and Social Media, 2013.

[60] M.M. Aldarwish, H.F. Ahmad, Predicting depression levels using social media posts, in: 2017 IEEE 13th International Symposium on Autonomous Decentralized System (ISADS), IEEE, 2017.

[61] M. Deshpande, V. Rao, Depression detection using emotion artificial intelligence, in: 2017 International Conference on Intelligent Sustainable Systems (ICISS), IEEE, 2017.

[62] T. Althoff, K. Clark, J. Leskovec, Large-scale analysis of counseling conversations: an application of natural language processing to mental health, Trans. Assoc. Comput. Linguist. 4 (2016) 463−476.

[63] W.H. Organization, Depression and Other Common Mental Disorders: Global Health Estimates, 2017. Available from: https://www.who.int/mental_health/management/depression/prevalence_global_health_estimates/en/.

[64] C.A. King, et al., Suicide risk screening in healthcare settings: identifying males and females at risk, J. Clin. Psychol. Med. Sett. 24 (1) (2017) 8−20.

[65] J. Torous, R. Walker, Leveraging digital health and machine learning toward reducing suicide—from panacea to practical tool, JAMA Psychiatr. 76 (10) (2019) 999−1000.

[66] J. Torous, et al., Smartphones, sensors, and machine learning to advance real-time prediction and interventions for suicide prevention: a review of current progress and next steps, Curr. Psychiatr. Rep. 20 (7) (2018) 1−6.

[67] A.N. Vaidyam, et al., Chatbots and conversational agents in mental health: a review of the psychiatric landscape, Can. J. Psychiatr. 64 (7) (2019) 456−464.

[68] G.M. Slavich, S. Taylor, R.W. Picard, Stress measurement using speech: recent advancements, validation issues, and ethical and privacy considerations, Stress 22 (4) (2019) 408−413.

[69] M. Rezaeian, A brief report on the components of national strategies for suicide prevention suggested by the World Health Organization, World Fam. Med. J. 99 (5480) (2017), 1−1.

[70] M. Gjoreski, et al., Monitoring stress with a wrist device using context, J. Biomed. Inf. 73 (2017) 159−170.

[71] H.N. Saha, et al., Health monitoring using Internet of Things (IoT), in: 2017 8th Annual Industrial Automation and Electromechanical Engineering Conference (IEMECON), IEEE, 2017.

[72] S. Casaccia, et al., Measurement of users' well-being through domotic sensors and machine learning algorithms, IEEE Sensor. J. 20 (14) (2020) 8029−8038.

[73] R.G. Jackson, et al., Natural language processing to extract symptoms of severe mental illness from clinical text: the Clinical Record Interactive Search Comprehensive Data Extraction (CRIS-CODE) project, BMJ Open 7 (1) (2017) e012012.

Artificial neural network-based approaches for computer-aided disease diagnosis and treatment

João Alexandre Lôbo Marques[1], Francisco Nauber Bernardo Gois[2], João Paulo do Vale Madeiro[3], Tengyue Li[4] and Simon James Fong[4]

[1]*University of Saint Joseph (USJ), Macau, Macau SAR, China;* [2]*Escola de Saúde Pública (ESP), Fortaleza, Brazil;* [3]*Federal University of Ceará (UFC), Fortaleza, Ceará, Brazil;* [4]*University of Macau (UM), Macau, Macau SAR, China*

1. Introduction

Dr. Goodwin is a cardiosurgeon who works with a very specific type of cardiac surgery, using a sophisticated computerized system to calculate in real time several metrics to support his decisions during the procedure. A probe is inserted into one of the heart chambers with an ultra-high-definition camera and several sensors, to record visually the chamber conditions and collect data from each heart beat and the overall activity of the heart. The sensors send the signals and image to a central computer which runs a powerful software to analyze and interpret the data. In addition the system has a special module that generates a 3D model of the electrical activity of the heart and indicates any unexpected changes, based on advanced artificial intelligence algorithms. In addition, the software also has a decision support subsystem which indicates the precise location of the heart where Dr. Goodwin should perform the intervention. With all this support, in the end, it is always a decision for whether Dr. Goodwin will follow the suggestions provided by the AI computerized system or perform the surgery in a different way.

Since he became one of the most prominent specialists in this area, Dr. Goodwin and other highly specialized members of his cardiovascular team also work in cooperation with the manufacturers of heart surgery support equipment, suggesting improvements, providing corrections, validating new techniques, and researching new approaches and metrics to enhance the diagnostic and intervention capabilities. It appears that advanced medical procedures, which were exclusively hardware-dependent before, relying on probes, sensors, and visualization screens, are also moving to rely increasingly on the software aiding diagnostics capabilities. Actually, several decisions and interventions are possible today because of these technological advances.

However, with so much valuable information provided by the equipment and software, will Dr. Goodwin or any other specialist from the cardiology team be able to disagree with the software? Is it really necessary to disagree with the computerized support sometimes?

In another example, think about Dr. Helen, an obstetrician who manages a unit that manages 35 labors per day in a public hospital (which aims to receive only patients from low-income families) located in a poor province of a developing country. The challenges are many: problematic infrastructure, lack of medical specialists and qualified support staff, overloaded capacity, no financial resources, patients' demographic and socioeconomic characteristics, among many others. A few years ago, Dr. Helen decided to analyze the performance and effectiveness of the maternal and fetal monitoring ambulatory processes, based on cardiotocography (CTG) examination, which monitors the fetal heart rate and the maternal uterine contractions, in parallel with maternal vital signs, such as heart rate, temperature, blood pressure, and oximetry. After analyzing historical data compiled by the ambulatory and clinical units in a handwritten report, it was possible to illustrate that the number of false positives or false negatives detected was above an acceptable rate, and it was highly likely that several other cases had not even been reported. Nevertheless, Dr. Helen is certain that this is not caused by individual or staff incompetence, but mainly because of the process and a consequence of the large number of issues faced by the hospital, as described above.

After applying three times to different funding opportunities, Dr. Helen and some of her colleagues received a request approval from a national funding agency which only releases these calls every 4 years. They acquired a fully computerized maternal–fetal monitoring solution, integrating 25 beds to a centralized computer which runs an intelligent computer-aided diagnostic and treatment system, based on artificial neural network classifiers. It had the potential to change the reality of the maternal–fetal ambulatory unit. Training sessions were performed on the system operation to perform and check data collection, generate the automatic diagnostic support, and insert the new system into the clinical workflow. A group of obstetricians promptly adopted the solution and started using the new monitoring system. Nevertheless, other professionals constantly disconnected the cables and turned the transmission units off in order to "have more freedom on moving the equipment" or because "the diagnostic provided by the system wasn't reliable," despite all the tests, validation, and training indicating that there were no reports of less mobility created by the cables or that the system was presenting problems on its operation. The effective benefits of the computerized solution were at risk and a new official hospital policy and procedures document was to be published to enforce the system adoption. Will a new policy affect the way the team sees the system? Are the obvious benefits of this kind of solution not so obvious for the clinical daily operations?

Both cases presented here are fictitious, but are based on real examples observed by the authors during their working experience in hospitals and ambulatory premises. They both bring relevant aspects that must be considered when using digital solutions to support diagnostic and treatment: technology dependence versus independence; technology acceptance versus avoidance; technology-intensive medical procedures; team capacity building and commitment with the new solutions; among several others.

This chapter presents a discussion on the challenges and trends of using computer-aided diagnostic and treatment supporting tools, focused on solutions based on different types and approaches of artificial neural networks (ANN).

1.1 Structure of this chapter

In Section 2, the general concepts related to the area of CAD and treatment systems and artificial neural networks (ANN) are presented. Trends and challenges are also discussed. After that, a general analysis about the benefits and applications of ANN to the cardiology area is presented, considering three areas: echocardiography (images), electrocardiography (time-series), and image analysis of angiograms during cardiovascular surgical intervention. Finally, in Section 4 a case study is presented based on the application of deep learning convolutional network together with a recent technique called transfer learning to detect brain tumors using an MRI images data set.

2. Artificial neural networks applied to computer-aided diagnosis and treatment

The development of computerized solutions to support disease diagnosis and treatment is a vast area of study, including not only health professionals but also engineers and computer science specialists, as the application of techniques for time series, clinical analysis, or image interpretation are becoming more and more complex. With the increasing computer processing power and the semiubiquitous interconnection between Internet of Things (IoT) devices and cloud infrastructure, several challenges still need to be overcome.

This section presents an overview about the state of the art in computer-aided diagnosis and treatment systems with the focus on artificial neural network solutions, which are a specific area of artificial intelligence systems.

2.1 Computer-aided diagnosis and treatment systems (CADTS)

Computerized systems to support disease diagnosis and treatment methods are already a common tool in clinical practice and a widely studied area in the scientific literature. With the technology advancements in the last 3 decades, several subspecializations have been developed, such as signal processing (when considering biological time-series analysis), image analysis (for radiology and medical imaging), classification (based on clinical parameters, laboratory analysis, etc.), clusterization (to create unforeseen groups of patients or symptoms), prediction and forecasting (to support decision-making related to a patient's procedures or the clinical flow in general), among others.

The first essential division is to comprehend the clear difference between diagnosis and treatment. These two areas are very different and the techniques applied to each of them can also follow different paths. In diagnosis, usually only the patient data are considered, such as an ECG signal, a CT scan, and vital signs. The computerized solution must analyze these data and provide a visual tool (a report, a segmented image, a dashboard, etc.) to the medical specialist in order to assist with the diagnosis. In treatment, other external databases must be brought to the table, including chemical reactions and possible effects of a treatment, historical data of medicines, prediction tools to forecast possible outcomes, and alternative solutions.

Other concepts that sometimes generate a mixed definition with CADTS are CDSS (clinical decision support systems and TDSS (therapeutic decision support systems, or CADe (computer-aided detection systems))). It is also common to find in the literature the acronym CADx, representing different possibilities of computer-aided diagnosis systems. In fact, all of these solutions have their definitions interconnected. They aim to provide a better support to medical decisions about diseases and the corresponding treatment. In the end, their common goal is to use computerized tools to help the patient.

In Fig. 4.1, a general flow of a CADTS is presented. In the input layer, the patient data are considered. The first item is the time-series, which is based on biological signal-monitoring examinations, such as the heart electrical activity [electrocardiography (ECG)] or the brain electrical

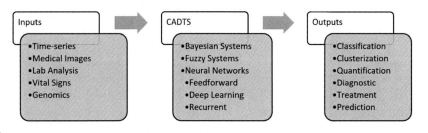

FIGURE 4.1

General representation of a CADT system with some examples of inputs, execution, and outputs.

activity [electroencephalography (EEG)]. The second item represents the wide set of medical images techniques, which can be originated from radiology equipment (X-ray, CT scan, mammography), ultrasound technologies (echocardiography, Doppler, etc.), optical sensors (fNIRS), magnetic field [magnetic resonance (MRI), magnetoencephalography (MEG)], or nuclear/radioactive isotopes (PET scans). Other inputs are also commonly considered, such as multiple results from laboratory analysis. In addition, as a recent trend that will soon increase in popularity and applications, the patient genomics should also be considered.

In the processing layer, called CADTS, several technologies are widely used such as Bayesian classifiers, fuzzy inference systems, and artificial neural networks, with three popular architectures: feed-forward, recurrent, and convolutional or deep learning. These architectures are presented and discussed in the following subsections.

Finally, the possibilities of outputs are also several, such as a classification, which can be a disease diagnosis itself or a previous step to support the medical decision. To clearly understand that, let us consider one example of a classification based on a quantification technique. One important task when analyzing a lung CT scans of patients with SARS-Cov2 pneumonia is to determine the percentage of the lung's affected areas. This is a time-consuming task for a radiologist to carry out by visual inspection. The computerized tool can use convolutional neural networks (CNNs) to calculate this area and generate indexes that will support the specialist and speed up the process. Other possible computerized outputs are clusterization, with the aim to organize input data in groups following supervised or unsupervised techniques. Finally, the task of prediction is also extremely relevant, using computational tools to predict future developments of a disease.

2.1.1 Challenges in CADTS

The recent advances in the development of CADTS are significant and are consistently changing the diagnosis and treatment capabilities. Nevertheless, some challenges still face CAD development that seriously inhibit its progress [1], from its design to the adherence to the medical application [2].

Three groups of challenges are discussed here to provide a brief overview to the reader and highlight trending aspects that must be considered during the development of any new application in the area.

- Big data and computational processing requirements: the current processing power required for large data sets such as CT scans and MRI is extremely high and will require GPU (graphical processing unit) farms working 24 h at full capacity to train, validate, and test one possible tuning solution. If the network is tuned, it will need to run again. This creates a burden for research teams with low-performance processing capabilities and also for hospital facilities with a lack of technical and human resources. Low-cost cloud computing technologies are available to minimize the impact of this, but the challenge tends to persist since new data require enormous volumes and new algorithms will require greater computational power.

- Increased data complexity: this item is directly related to the previous one, but highlighting the trends of medical data that are challenging the existing network infrastructure such as ultra-high-definition images and videos, molecular-based data with individual genomics processing tools for decision-making, and the integration between hundreds or thousands of IoT wearable biosensors integrated from home-care and clinical premises (ambulatory, interventions, ICU, etc.). The new 5G networks will represent a new frontier to deal with this kind of pervasive and ubiquitous data collection.

- Higher requirements of generalization and precision: with the increasing popularity of computer-aided diagnosis and treatment systems and their integration into the clinical flow, the dependency and requirements of a high-precision diagnostic system will significantly increase together with generalization capabilities. For example, in one PACS (picture archiving and communication system), which is the system responsible for managing medical imaging in a clinical facility, it will not be acceptable to have only high-performance algorithms to deal with lung X-rays or brain tumors. It will be necessary to cover as much analysis as possible with similar performance.

2.2 Artificial neural networks in medical diagnosis

According to Kröse and Smagt [3], ANNs can be most adequately characterized as computational models with particular properties such as the ability to adapt or learn, to generalize, to cluster or organize data, and the operation of which is based on parallel processing. Despite many of the capabilities also being able to be performed by other Bayesian or inference techniques, the ANNs provide the ability to present a superior classification performance in different applications. The aim of this section is to provide an overview of the most common models applied in the field of disease diagnosis and treatment, and not to provide exhaustive discussion on different models.

Typically, an ANN is represented by a number of artificial neurons (which are small processing units, with or without memory) interconnected between each other following different possible architectures, which define the information flow from one or more inputs to one or several outputs, in a feed-forward, feed-backward, or both directions. For each neuron, usually a numerical and dynamic weight is defined and will be responsible for increasing (activating) or decreasing (deactivating) the influence of that neuron as a processing unit of the entire network.

The neural network must be trained and tuned to perform a high-quality task. This means that training and validation phases are necessary to evaluate the network performance. Usually, available data are divided into three sub-data sets: training, validation, and test. The training data will be used to adjust network parameters and weights. The validation data will be used to test the training parameters and provide further adjustments. Finally, the test data set will be used to evaluate the network classification performance. Further adjustments after the testing phase may generate bias. If the results are not satisfactory, a new architecture and new data may be necessary to develop a reliable classifier.

During the last 40 years, several architectures of ANNs with different data-processing approaches have been proposed with different training approaches, and this continues, with the most recent focus on developing new more efficient unsupervised deep learning models, explainable artificial intelligence (XAI), or general adversative networks (GAN). To comprehend the general aspects of ANNs, it is necessary to understand which parameters must be generally considered for an efficient architecture design and performance achievement [4]:

- Model selection: the application and related data usually determine the ANN model to be considered. Medical imaging applications will not be able to use an architecture suitable to work with time series, and vice versa. A poor model selection will drastically impact on the learning and classification capacity of the desired solution;
- Learning algorithms: the convergence of a learning algorithm is dependent on several factors that are internal and external to the algorithm itself. Considered internally, the definition of several hyperparameters such as learning rate, number of epochs, convergence indexes, etc. will be essential for the learning performance. In addition, the risk of having data-dependent biased convergence should be carefully checked.
- Neural network robustness: after working on the previous two items (model and learning algorithm), the robustness of the proposed network should be considered. The network performance should be evaluated with new, larger, and noisy (spurious) data sets and still be able to provide coherent results.

2.3 ANN: types and applications

In Fig. 4.2, three different types of ANN are presented with a corresponding list of applications suitable for each specific type.

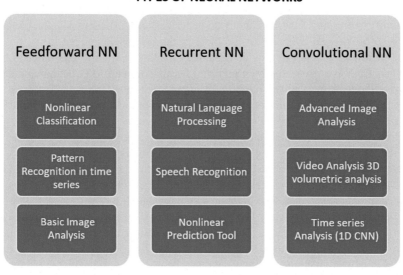

FIGURE 4.2

Types of artificial neural networks and their most suitable applications.

2.3.1 Feed-forward neural networks

A feed-forward neural network is structured in interconnected layers, each of them formed by neurons, as can be seen in Fig. 4.3. Note that there are no interconnections within the same layer.

The input layer receives the input data to be classified and transfers them to one or more hidden layers, where the classification tasks are performed, and transferred to the output layer, which represents the classes under analysis. For example, if we have eight different classes, eight output neurons will be used and only one positive output to one specific neuron will represent a classification match.

In order to better understand the network learning convergence, let us consider the backpropagation algorithm as an example. First, it is a supervised technique, that is, for each input X we have the corresponding desired output D that will be used as the reference of the classification. After submitting the input to the network, the output layer will generate a result Y that will be compared to the desired result D. The network error $E = Y - D$ is then verified. If the classification is not correct, the weights of each neuron are updated based on a parameter called learning rate, and the next input is tested. If the classification is correct, no changes are performed and the next input is tested. The analysis of all inputs is repeated several times (epochs) and the network should converge to a minimum error following a gradient-descent trend.

The application of feed-forward neural networks with backpropagation has been successfully adopted since the 1990s, achieving high performance when applied in areas such as nonlinear classifier, pattern recognition, and basic image analysis.

2.3.2 Recurrent neural networks

Recurrent networks also have neurons, weights, information flow, and error verification (Fig. 4.4). The main difference is that this type of network is applicable when the data sequence is essential for the processing, for example, in speech processing or natural language recognition [6].

A specific type of recurrent NN is LSTM (long-short-term memory) which is used as a high-performance nonlinear predictor. These networks were used during the COVID-19 pandemic to predict infectious trends and support clinical decision-making [8].

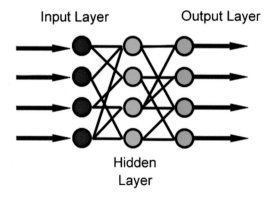

FIGURE 4.3

General model of a feed-forward neural network with input, hidden, and output layers [5].

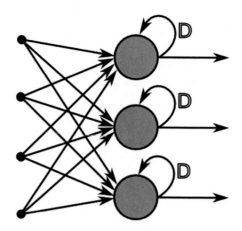

FIGURE 4.4

General model of a recurrent neural network [7].

2.3.3 Deep learning convolutional neural networks

The third type of ANN considered here was also the most popular application at the time of writing. One of the greatest advantages of deep learning networks relies on the fact that it is an unsupervised neural network, that is, previous labels are not necessary to improve the network convergence [9]. Additionally, they are powerful to work with two-dimensional (images) and three-dimensional (video) data, as can be seen in Fig. 4.5.

Because of that, the adoption of convolutional neural networks (CNNs) to deal with medical imaging has increased exponentially over the past 5 years and new architectures and algorithms are being continuously proposed. The technique has tended to become a standard in medical imaging and video processing. A comprehensive review about CNN applications in radiology can be found in Ref. [11].

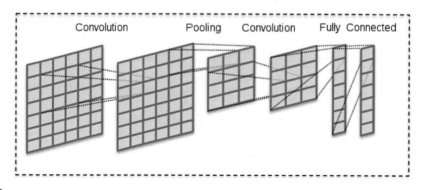

FIGURE 4.5

General model of a deep learning architecture with a convolutional and a pooling structure [10].

2.4 Future trends in ANN for disease diagnosis and treatment

Several areas show promising trends based on ANN architectures to support disease diagnosis and treatment. In this section, we discuss the trend of real personalized health care, which is, actually, a result of several advances and challenges that have been overcome during the last decade.

On one side, personalized health care deals with the integration of the whole range of patient data, including consultations, examinations, medical imaging, laboratory analyses, therapeutic interventions, chronic diseases, medications, personal observations and comments, healthcare mobile apps, and even social media facts to corroborate the patient history. Those data must be available regardless of the clinic or hospital the patient is attending. In addition, the adoption of wearable sensors in home-care will also boost the generation of multiple sources of data. In the other direction, rapid advances in DNA genotyping powered by automation technologies will change the whole computer-aided diagnosis industry. High-accuracy genome sequencing developed during the last few years, with increasing computational capacity and cheaper equipment and software, is favoring the development of new applications based on individual genomics data with the aim to detect patterns and correlations that are not visually available.

Effective and real personalized health care and medicine will be one of the key aspects of the next frontier in AI and diagnostic support.

The following sections will bring an overview about how the application of different types of ANN in cardiology are helping the development of computer-aided diagnosis and treatment in the area, followed by a case study of using deep learning and a recent technique called transfer learning to detect and classify brain tumors in MRI images.

3. Application of ANN in the diagnosis and treatment of cardiovascular diseases

Cardiology has been always positioned at the forefront of computer-aided diagnosis and treatment area, since the beginning of heartbeat electrical monitoring, a long time before the use of advanced image techniques to visualize the heart chambers working and pumping blood in real time.

Today, it is rare if not impossible to find one examination or intervention in cardiology which does not have a computerized solution to collect and analyze data for diagnosis and treatment support, from the simplest heart rate detection based on PPG (photoplethysmogram) with software module for precise heart rate detection and the analysis of HRV (heart rate variability); going through arrhythmia detection and classification based on the electrocardiogram (ECG) electrical signal; and the visual inspection of the dynamic performance of heart cavities and valves based on ultrasound images (echocardiography).

Specifically in the area of artificial intelligence in medicine, the use of ANN is a trend in signals and images and is the focus of this section. The Mayo Clinic recently published a review with a technical approach and considering different possibilities of using AI to support cardiology that can be found in Ref. [12].

However, any medical support system is still an algorithmic-based solution and suffers from the same challenges as any statistical approach to dealing with data. Some of these challenges were discussed earlier in this chapter, and we would like to emphasize the lack of generalizability of the techniques, something that is almost automatic for the human specialist with professional experience, and the risk of generating unforeseen bias when training, validating, and testing the computerized system.

3.1 Applications in cardiology

In Fig. 4.6 are three different areas of cardiology that already have experienced mature developments using AI tools.

Each area is discussed in more details below.

3.1.1 Echocardiography

Echocardiography is one of the most popular and cost-effective examinations to evaluate the physical structure and the functional behavior of the heart. The most challenging aspect of this kind of examination is that it is extremely dependent on the operator ability to position the ultrasound probe so as to visualize the heart chambers and valves and also to evaluate the blood flow in a detailed specific analysis called echo Doppler.

In Fig. 4.7, an example of an image of the heart during an echocardiography is presented.

Artificial intelligence tools based on machine learning or deep convolutional neural networks have been considered for probe positioning (to support specialists training or on-site operation difficulties), and also for image augmentation, segmentation, and classification. Several diseases can be classified such as valve disease, regional wall motion abnormalities, and cardiomyopathies [12,14].

The analysis of complex cardiac structures in echocardiography is a challenge that can also benefit from the use of AI tools, especially when time is a significant constraint to generate examination reports in clinical settings with overloaded capacity [15]. With a large amount of information

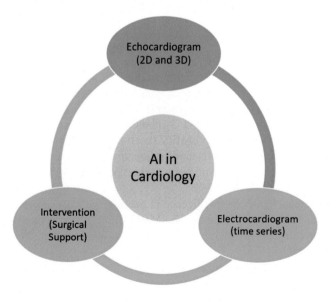

FIGURE 4.6

Three areas in cardiology that benefit from artificial neural networks.

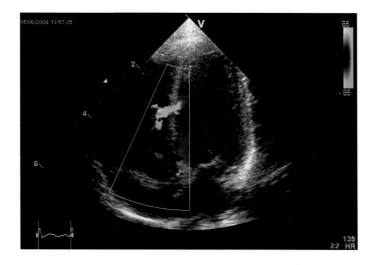

FIGURE 4.7

Example of an image detected during an echocardiography. AI is used to segment structures of the heart and also determine blood flow and volume [13].

generated in each echocardiography, it is not rare to have lots of useful data underutilized. In this aspect, AI-based systems for diagnostic support are able not only to use the whole range of information of one examination but also to compare and analyze various examinations in parallel.

3.1.2 Electrocardiography

The ECG (electrocardiogram) is a well-known and widely adopted noninvasive and low-cost technique to monitor the heart based on the detection of its electrical activity. It is classified as a gold standard diagnosis tool, since the data collected during the examination provide sufficient information to perform accurate diagnosis for particular heart conditions, such as arrythmia, myocardial infarction, conduction disturbance, among others.

A set of electrodes located on the patient's chest detects the whole cycle of a heartbeat, which consists of a sequence of well-defined electric signals as a result of the polarization and depolarization of the heard chambers, resulting in subsequent constriction and relaxation to pump the blood through the chambers and to the rest of the body. A representation of the PQRST complex or cycle (which is equivalent to one heart beat) is presented in Fig. 4.8.

The key tasks considered on the computerized analysis of the PQRST complex captures during one heartbeat in an electrocardiogram are represented in Fig. 4.9.

The application of different types of neural networks in ECG analysis has been widely published recently and a recent edition of the American Heart Association (AHA)'s *Circulation* [17] presented a compilation of relevant publications, such as an AI system for the detection and classification of left ventricular systolic dysfunction of patients with previous diagnosis of dyspnea [18]. In another publication, an enormous database of 53,549 patients was submitted to a deep convolutional neural network proposed by Hannun et al., to classify 12 classes of cardiac rhythm, capturing data with only a

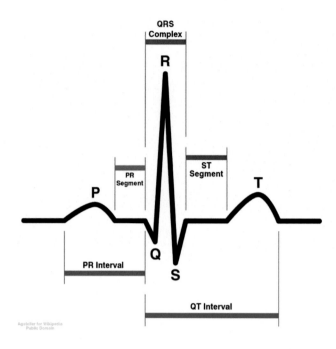

FIGURE 4.8

Representation of a complete PQRST cycle. Several applications of AI are possible such as QRS segmentation, T-wave detection and segmentation, and detection and classification of significant morphology changes (arrhythmia) [16].

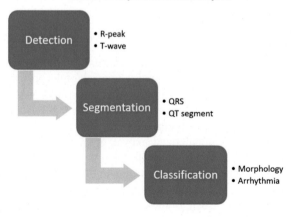

FIGURE 4.9

Common tasks performed by computerized AI systems on the analysis of electrocardiogram signals.

single-lead ambulatory ECG monitoring device. Considering the f1-score (check the following section for the f1-score equation) as a reference, the computerized system achieved 0.837, while the human performance was 0.780 achieved by a team of cardiologists [19].

3.1.3 Interventional cardiology: angiograms

Several cardiology interventions are also embracing the possibilities of using AI and ANN to support decision-making during medical procedures, for example, in angiograms, the identification and evaluation of coronary structural conditions [20]. In Fig. 4.10, an image of a coronary angiogram showing the left area of the heart is presented. Artificial intelligence systems based on deep convolutional architectures are used to identify lesions or even more predict fractional flow reserve, which substantially increases the risk of infarction of cardiovascular strokes [22].

After analyzing such different areas of application, such as ECG signals, cardiac imaging (echocardiography, MRI, CT scan, SPECT), and surgical interventions (angiogram), it is a natural consequence to conclude that cardiology can be considered a reference area to adopt computer-aided diagnosis and treatment systems since the existing solutions are mature and several possibilities are available.

The next section moves to a different part of the human body: the brain. A real case study is presented, developing a deep learning convolutional neural network to detect brain tumors using a public MRI brain images data set.

4. Case study: ANN and medical imaging—brain tumor detection

In this section, the adoption of ANN to support disease diagnosis and treatment is presented as a case study application.

The brain is a very complex organ, which is usually monitored based on its electrical activity and/or blood flow (and subsequent oxygen concentration). Brain tumors are the most lethal type of cancer,

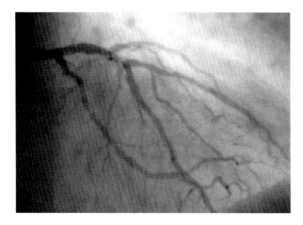

FIGURE 4.10

A coronary angiogram showing the left coronary circulation. AI tools can help during the intervention procedure to detect and locate problems [21].

with a short life expectancy at the advanced stages. Misdiagnosis of brain tumors results in ineffective medical interventions and decreases patients' chances of survival. Accurate diagnosis of brain tumors is critical for developing an effective treatment plan that will cure the disease and prolong the lives of patients. A brain tumor develops when cells divide uncontrollably, resulting in the formation of an abnormal group of cells surrounding or within the brain. This group of cells has the potential to impair the normal functioning of the brain and to destroy healthy cells [23,24].

Automated defect detection in medical imaging has emerged as a significant area of research in a variety of medical diagnostic applications. Automated tumor detection is critical because it provides information about abnormal tissues that are required for treatment planning. Human inspection is the conventional method for detecting defects in magnetic resonance brain images. This method is inefficient when dealing with large amounts of data. As a result, methods for automated tumor detection are being developed to save radiologists time. Due to the complexity and variability of tumors, brain tumor detection is a difficult task [25].

The task of tumor detection based on computerized systems using deep convolutional networks has been the subject of study of many research groups worldwide. In comparison to traditional feed-forward neural networks, deep convolutional architectures extract significant and robust features from the input space without supervision. This case study will consider the use of VGG16 convolutional neural network architectures to detect brain tumors using transfer learning techniques, such as fine-tuning and freezing, using an MRI data set of brain tumor images.

4.1 Proposed methodology

Recent works have established that deep convolutional networks do not require manually extracted features and prior domain knowledge, that is, the learning process is unsupervised. These networks incorporate the feature extraction phase into the self-learning process. It is not necessary to preprocess the data set (except in very specific cases), and the network converges to determine significant image features, even considering the semantic gap between the MRI images generated and the medical specialist interpretation. The efficacy of such a feature extraction framework is more important in terms of producing feature representations that accurately depict both low- and high-level information. To demonstrate the feasibility of the proposed content-based image retriever (CBIR) system, CNNs generate highly discriminative features automatically via a hierarchical learning approach. The first layers extract low-level features such as edges, shape, and texture, while the later layers deal with content-specific features, to combine the previous features and create abstract representations that integrate local and global information [26].

4.1.1 Convolutional neural networks

Convolutional neural networks (CNNs) are a subclass of feed-forward neural networks that are widely used for image-based classification, object detection, and recognition. The fundamental principle is convolution, which results in stacked filtered characteristic maps [27].

A CNN is a deep learning structure that measures the convolution between weights and a picture input. In contrast to conventional machine learning methods, it extracts attributes from the input data. Using a predefined cost function, the optimal values for the convolution coefficients are discovered during the learning process, from which the characteristics are automatically determined. Convolution is a technique that takes a small matrix of numbers (referred to as a kernel or filter), applies it to subparts of the image under analysis and generates a filtered image. The values of subsequent attribute maps are calculated using the following formula [28]:

$$G[m, n] = (f * h)[m, n] = \sum_{i}\sum_{k} h[j, k] f[m - j, n - k]$$

After the convolutional layer performs the dot product between all the defined kernels/filters and the entire subset of regions of the input image, the pooling layer performs a downsampling operation. In the convolutional neural system, the size of pooling layer output can be measured using the following formula [27]:

$$\frac{W - F + 2P}{S} - 1$$

4.1.2 Transfer learning

Transfer learning is a technique that utilizes a trained model's knowledge to learn another set of data. Transfer learning aims to improve learning in the target domain by leveraging knowledge from the source domain and learning task. Different transfer learning settings are defined based on the type of task and the nature of the data available in the source and target domains [29].

In the field of machine learning, transfer learning outperformed state-of-the-art methods. Improved performance in computer vision, in particular, prompted the use of deep learning in computer-based diagnosis and prediction. Transfer learning has gained considerable importance since it can work with little or no information in the training phase. That is, data that are well established are adjusted by move learning from one domain to another. Transfer learning is well suited to scenarios where a version performs poorly due to obsolete data or scant [30,31]. This form of transfer learning used in DL is known as an inductive transfer. This is where the reach of feasible models, that is, model bias, is narrowed in a practical way using a model match on a different but related task. Since AlexNet won the ImageNet competition, CNNs are utilized for a broad selection of DL applications. From 2012 to now, researchers have been attempting to apply CNN to several different tasks [32].

4.1.3 VGG16

VGG16 is a 16-layer network developed by the Visual Geometry Group (VGG) at Oxford. It competed in the ILSVRC-2014 ImageNet competition. One of the primary reasons VGG16 won the competition is that it was one of the first architectures to explore network depth by extending to 16−19 layers and employing extremely small (3 × 3) convolution filters. The VGG16 system is fashioned from 3 × 3 convolutional layers, 13 convolutional layers, and three fully connected layers, and can be attached to the pooling layer after every phase. The max-pooling layer follows some convolutional layers. The stride is set to 1 pixel. The five max-pooling layers use a determined stride of 2 pixels and a 2 × 2-pixel filter. A padding of 1 pixel is done for the 3 × 3 convolutional layers—all the layers of the network use ReLU as the activation function [33].

4.1.4 Proposed deep learning architecture

For the current application, the proposed method consists of using a VGG16 transfer learning network, modifying the last three layers to adapt it to the target domain. The fully connected (FC) layer in the original VGG16 was removed and a new FC layer with an output size of three was inserted. Finally, a fine tuning of the modified network was performed by training it with the MRI data set.

4.1.5 Data set

The data set was available on https://www.kaggle.com/sartajbhuvaji/brain-tumor-classification-mri. The data set is a collection of 3762 images with 1683 files with brain tumors and 2079 images with no brain tumor (Fig. 4.11). The images of the data set have different shapes and lengths. The images were cropped to a uniform size and shape (Fig. 4.12). A total of 3009 images were used for training and 602 images for testing.

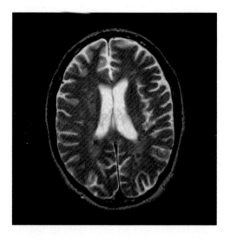

(a) Example of image with no Brain Tumor

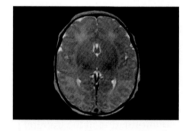

(b) Example of image with no Brain Tumor

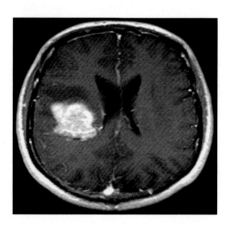

(c) Example of image with Brain Tumor

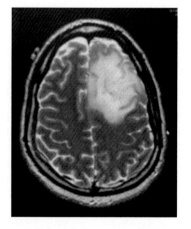

(d) Example of image with Brain Tumor

FIGURE 4.11

Image samples for the data set.

Original Image

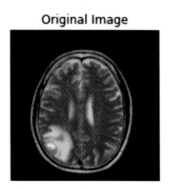

Cropped Image

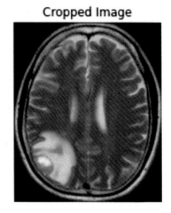

FIGURE 4.12

Example of a cropped image from the data set.

4.2 Model analysis

Accuracy, precision, and recall are the metrics considered to evaluate the model performance.

4.2.1 Confusion matrix

Let I(x,y): $\mathbb{R}^2 \to \mathbb{R}$ be a medical image and S(I(x,y)):$\mathbb{R}^2 \to \Omega, \Omega = 0, 1$ a binary decision of picture I(x,y). The assumed gold standard is represented by the function H and the result as M. Following that, each fold can be classified as:

- TP: $H(x, y) = 1 \char"02C6 M(x, y) = 1,$
- FP: $H(x, y) = 0 \char"02C6 M(x, y) = 1,$
- TN: $H(x, y) = 0 \char"02C6 M(x, y) = 0,$
- FN: $H(x, y) = 1 \char"02C6 M(x, y) = 0,$

  where TP is true positive, FP is false positive, TN is true negative, and FN is false negative.

4.2.2 Precision

The precision (P) is given by

$$P = \frac{TP}{TF + TP}$$

4.2.3 Recall

The recall is given by:

$$R = \frac{TP}{TP + FN}$$

where R is the recall. The optimal result is 1, and the worst value for the recall is 0.

4.2.4 Accuracy

Accuracy is a metric for deciding the model's performance in categorizing positive and negative classes. Assessing all detailed data with all data calculates the rating. It is given by:

$$\text{Accuracy} = \frac{TP + TN}{TP + TN + FP + FN}$$

4.3 Experiments and results

We use a 180-epoch training with a reduce learning rate on the plateau component. The number of images in each class was equalized. For Adam, a learning rate of 0.01 was chosen as the initial rate. By selecting a large value, the loss function can be prevented from converging and thus causing over-shoots. Additionally, a slow rate of learning prolongs the training period. The minibatch size was set to 38. The choice involves balancing training speed and computational requirements.

In the fully connected layer, we use two 1024-neuron layers, a 0.5-neuron dropout, and a batch normalization layer. Batch normalization (BN) is a technique for normalizing activation in deep neural network intermediate layers. Due to its proclivity for increasing accuracy and accelerating training, BN has become a popular technique in deep learning. Dropout is based on stochastically "dropping out" neurons during training to avoid feature detectors coadapting.

The confusion matrix for the results is shown in Table 4.1. We can see the model's specificity (prediction of no brain tumor). There are 16 incorrect predictions out of 316 where the patient has no brain tumor image.

Table 4.2 summarizes the experiment's findings. According to the findings, the model has a high degree of specificity (precision of 0.93 and recall of 0.94 for images with no brain tumor) and can be used as a screening tool for images that do not contain a brain tumor. The f1-score for images with brain tumor was 0.93.

Table 4.1 Confusion matrix.

	Predicted no brain tumor	Predicted brain tumor
No brain tumor	316	16
Brain tumor	23	247

Table 4.2 Obtained precision, recall, and f1-scored from the experiment.

	Precision	Recall	f1-score	Support
0	0.93	0.95	0.94	332
1	0.94	0.91	0.93	270
Accuracy			0.94	602
Macro average	0.94	0.93	0.93	602
Weighted average	0.94	0.94	0.94	602

The results achieved are promising considering the f1-score as a reference. The proposed CNN using transfer learning may be considered to be used as a computer-aided diagnosis tool. Future works will consider other techniques and compare them with the one presented here.

5. Final considerations

Multiple medical areas are using computer-aided diagnosis and treatment systems based on different types of artificial neural networks to accomplish several tasks such as classification, clusterization, pattern identification, among others.

Despite the large number of scientific publications and commercial products based on AI developments to support diagnosis and treatment, several challenges persist in the area. The risk of unforeseen bias during the model training and validation phases is a relevant problem that must be carefully addressed. This may be generated during the system modeling/tuning or the lack of variety in the available data sets. Furthermore, the adoption of the automatic diagnostic support system in the clinical flow is always challenging, since it is common to detect significant resistance from medical specialists to follow or even consider as valid the system interpretations.

This chapter presented the main concepts and a discussion about the challenges and trends in the areas of computer-aided support systems and also the application of different types of ANNs, such as feed-forward, recurrent, and convolutional architectures. A specific section with a comprehensive overview of the application of ANN to the area of cardiology was presented. In addition, a case study of a deep convolutional neural network architecture together with a recent approach of transfer learning applied to the detection of brain tumors on MRI images was presented.

References

[1] J. Yanase, E. Triantaphyllou, The seven key challenges for the future of computer-aided diagnosis in medicine, Int. J. Med. Inform. (2019), https://doi.org/10.1016/j.ijmedinf.2019.06.017. https://pubmed.ncbi.nlm.nih.gov/31445285/.

[2] O. Faust, U.R. Acharya, T. Tamura, Formal design methods for reliable computer-aided diagnosis: a review, IEEE Rev. Biomed. Eng. (2012), https://doi.org/10.1109/RBME.2012.2184750.

[3] B. Kröse, P. van der Smagt, An Introduction to Neural Networks, 1993.

[4] D. Lin, A.V. Vasilakos, Y. Tang, Y. Yao, Neural networks for computer-aided diagnosis in medicine: a review, Neurocomputing 216 (2016) 700−708.

[5] File:Feed forward neural net.gif - Wikipedia. https://en.wikipedia.org/wiki/File:Feed_forward_neural_net.gif.

[6] Boca Raton London New York Washington L. Medsker, D.L. Jain, Recurrent neural networks, in: Design and Applications, Technical Report, 2001.

[7] File:RecurrentLayerNeuralNetwork.png - Wikimedia Commons. https://commons.wikimedia.org/wiki/File:RecurrentLayerNeuralNetwork.png.

[8] J.A.L. Marques, F.N.B. Gois, J. Xavier-Neto, S.J. Fong, Prediction for decision support during the COVID-19 pandemic, in: SpringerBriefs in Applied Sciences and Technology, Springer Science and Business Media Deutschland GmbH, 2021, pp. 1−13, https://doi.org/10.1007/978-3-030-61913-8_1.

[9] C.C. Aggarwal, Neural Networks and Deep Learning, Springer International Publishing, 2018, https://doi.org/10.1007/978-3-319-94463-0.

[10] File:ConvolutionAndPooling.svg - Wikimedia Commons. https://commons.wikimedia.org/wiki/File: ConvolutionAndPooling.svg.

[11] R. Yamashita, M. Nishio, R.K.G. Do, K. Togashi, Convolutional neural networks: an overview and application in radiology, Insights Imag. (2018), https://doi.org/10.1007/s13244-018-0639-9. https://link.springer.com/articles/10.1007/s13244-018-0639-9.

[12] F. Lopez-Jimenez, Z. Attia, A.M. Arruda-Olson, R. Carter, P. Chareonthaitawee, H. Jouni, S. Kapa, A. Lerman, C. Luong, J.R. Medina-Inojosa, P.A. Noseworthy, P.A. Pellikka, M.M. Redfield, V.L. Roger, G.S. Sandhu, C. Senecal, P.A. Friedman, Artificial intelligence in cardiology: present and future, Mayo Clin. Proc. (2020), https://doi.org/10.1016/j.mayocp.2020.01.038.

[13] File:Ventricular Septal Defect.jpg -Wikimedia Commons. https://commons.wikimedia.org/wiki/File: Ventricular_Septal_Defect.jpg.

[14] M. Alsharqi, W.J. Woodward, J.A. Mumith, D.C. Markham, R. Upton, P. Leeson, Artificial intelligence and echocardiography, Echo Res. Pract. 5 (2018) R115−R125.

[15] P.P. Sengupta, Y.M. Huang, A. Bansal, A. Ashrafi, M. Fisher, K. Shameer, W. Gall, J.T. Dudley, Cognitive machine-learning algorithm for cardiac imaging; A pilot study for differentiating constrictive pericarditis from restrictive cardiomyopathy, circulation, Cardiovasc. Imaging 9 (2016).

[16] File:SinusRhythmLabels.png - Wikipedia. https://en.wikipedia.org/wiki/File:SinusRhythmLabels.png.

[17] K.T. Haq, S.J. Howell, L.G. Tereshchenko, Applying artificial intelligence to ECG analysis: promise of a better future, Circ. Arrhythm. Electrophysiol. (2020), https://doi.org/10.1161/CIRCEP.120.009111. https://www.ahajournals.org/doi/abs/10.1161/CIRCEP.120.009111.

[18] D. Adedinsewo, R.E. Carter, Z. Attia, P. Johnson, A.H. Kashou, J.L. Dugan, M. Albus, J.M. Sheele, F. Bellolio, P.A. Friedman, F. Lopez-Jimenez, P.A. Noseworthy, Artificial intelligence-enabled ECG algorithm to identify patients with left ventricular systolic dysfunction presenting to the emergency department with dyspnea, Circ. Arrhythm. Electrophysiol. 13 (2020).

[19] A.Y. Hannun, P. Rajpurkar, M. Haghpanahi, G.H. Tison, C. Bourn, M.P. Turakhia, A.Y. Ng, Cardiologist-level arrhythmia detection and classification in ambulatory electrocardiograms using a deep neural network, Nat. Med. 25 (2019) 65−69.

[20] A. De Marvao, T.J. Dawes, J.P. Howard, D.P. O'Regan, Artificial intelligence and the cardiologist: What you need to know for 2020, BMJ (2020), https://doi.org/10.1136/heartjnl-2019-316033. http://heart.bmj.com/.

[21] R.C. Hendel, D.S. Berman, M.F. Di Carli, P.A. Heidenreich, R.E. Henkin, P.A. Pellikka, G.M. Pohost, K.A. Williams, Appropriate use criteria for cardiac radionuclide imaging. A report of the american college of cardiology foundation, J. Am. Coll. Cardiol. (2009), https://doi.org/10.1016/j.jacc.2009.02.013.

[22] H. Cho, J.G. Lee, S.J. Kang, W.J. Kim, S.Y. Choi, J. Ko, H.S. Min, G.H. Choi, D.Y. Kang, P.H. Lee, J.M. Ahn, D.W. Park, S.W. Lee, Y.H. Kim, C.W. Lee, S.W. Park, S.J. Park, Angiography-based machine learning for predicting fractional flow reserve in intermediate coronary artery lesions, J. Am. Heart Assoc. 8 (2019).

[23] H. Mohsen, E.S.A. El-dahshan, E.S.M. El-horbaty, A.B.M. Salem, Classification using deep learning neural networks for brain tumors, Fut. Comput. Inform. J. 3 (2018) 68−71.

[24] A. Rehman, S. Naz, M. Imran, F. Akram, M. Imran, A deep learning-based framework for automatic brain tumors classification using transfer learning, Circuits Syst. Signal Process. (2019).

[25] K. Sharma, A. Kaur, S. Gujral, Brain tumor detection based on machine learning algorithms, Int. J. Comput. Appl. (2014) 15−20.

[26] Z.A.R. Nawab, K. Swati, Q. Zhao, M. Kabir, Z. Ali, S. Ahmed, J. Lu, F. Ali, Content-based brain tumor retrieval for MR images using transfer learning, IEEE Access 7 (2019) 17809−17822.

[27] S. Mehta, C. Paunwala, B. Vaidya, CNN based traffic sign classification using adam optimizer, in: 2019 International Conference on Intelligent Computing and Control Systems, ICCS 2019, 2019, pp. 1293−1298.

[28] M. Yemini, Y. Zigel, D. Lederman, Detecting masses in mammograms using convolutional neural networks and transfer learning, in: 2018 IEEE International Conference on the Science of Electrical Engineering in Israel, ICSEE 2018, 2019, pp. 1−4.

[29] S. Deepak, P.M. Ameer, Brain tumor classification using deep CNN features via transfer learning, Comput. Biol. Med. 111 (2019) 103345.

[30] X. Liu, Z. Liu, G. Wang, Z. Cai, H. Zhang, Ensemble transfer learning algorithm, IEEE Access 6 (2017) 2389−2396.

[31] H. Zuo, J. Lu, G. Zhang, F. Liu, Fuzzy transfer learning using an infinite Gaussian mixture model and active learning, IEEE Trans. Fuzzy Syst. 27 (2019) 291−303.

[32] A.M. Pour, H. Seyedarabi, S.H.A. Jahromi, A. Javadzadeh, Automatic detection and monitoring of diabetic retinopathy using efficient convolutional neural networks and contrast limited adaptive histogram equalization, IEEE Access (2020) 1.

[33] Z. Qu, J. Mei, L. Liu, D.Y. Zhou, Crack detection of concrete pavement with cross-entropy loss function and improved VGG16 network model, IEEE Access 8 (2020) 54564−54573.

AI and deep learning for processing the huge amount of patient-centric data that assist in clinical decisions

João Alexandre Lôbo Marques[1], Francisco Nauber Bernardo Gois[2], Jarbas Aryel Nunes da Silveira[3], Tengyue Li[4] and Simon James Fong[4]

[1]*University of Saint Joseph (USJ), Macau, Macau SAR, China;* [2]*Escola de Saúde Pública (ESP), Fortaleza, Brazil;* [3]*Federal University of Ceará (UFC), Fortaleza, Brazil;* [4]*University of Macau (UM), Macau, Macau SAR, China*

1. Introduction

The exponential increase in the amount of data focused on clinical analysis, together with the large number of computational systems to support medical diagnostics, is revolutionizing hospital and ambulatory premises with new tools, processes, roles, and risks to be considered within their operational and decision-making processes. Multiple stakeholders are involved in this challenging endeavor, such as medical specialists, who are, in the end, responsible for the diagnostics, nurses and technicians, who are responsible for the operations, biomedical engineers and computer science specialists, who should provide support to the other parties, and, in a broader sense, also administrative and juridical teams.

Information systems are already playing a substantial role in clinical environments with a strong operational dependence on electronic medical records (EMR) systems, medical images management systems, clinical analysis laboratories (where equipment and software are completely interdependent), diagnostic equipment, among several other examples. This is a result of a digital transformation process, in which the patient data became digital, the processes became computer-dependent, and the teams needed to adjust their operational skills to interact with information systems in both ways, that is, provide input data/information/diagnostic/prescription or receive outputs such as diagnostic support. Within this reality, advanced computational systems are being developed to increase aided-diagnostic capabilities, where artificial intelligence (AI) is playing a significant role in this new trend.

In a very general and introductory definition of AI, we can consider it as a set of integrated hardware and software systems with the aim of implementing intelligence-based tasks performed by humans, such as classification, clusterization, and generalization. This can be achieved from the simplest differentiation between two colors or tones in a digital image, to very complex inference systems to detect specific structures in a computerized tomography (CT) scan brain image, or to predict patient prognosis considering limited vital signs and clinical analysis results. It is important to highlight that within the medical community, several physicians and clinicians are skeptical about the feasibility of obtaining help from AI computerized systems. Nevertheless, as the processing become more transparent and focused on the medical support, this resistance has tended to reduce, for example, when AI decisions are embedded into a PACS (picture archiving and communications system) and brings direct support to the radiologist on the process of identifying structures and providing diagnostics.

Considering the specific area of clinical decisions, several different computerized systems are available in the market, focusing on specific areas, from stand-alone applications for private practice facilities to comprehensive solutions integrated to electronic health record (EHR) systems. These are known as clinical decision support systems (CDSSs) and a successful implementation comprehends the development of biomedical knowledge, person-specific data, and a set of inference rules or processing network generating classification from data and present high-value information to support medical decisions [1].

The resulting workflow of a CDSS implementation must not be focused on the technology, but on improving the physician or staff processes. The information provided by the system must be collected, stored, processed, and presented to interested parties in order to allow reliable and efficient decisions. Since there are several types of applications for CDSS, specific developments are being considered, from the design, reporting capabilities, technical precision and even interface adjustments, stand-alone systems or fully integrated to EHRs. In addition, the large amount of information submitted to physicians who are in responsible for the clinical decisions, demands increasing use of computerized systems to support, organize, and compile data.

It is relevant to include in this complex scenario some dimensions highlighted as follows. First, the necessity of modeling systems to handle patient-centered data from multiple sources, which means that the technical resources should be planned to not create any mental or physical distress to the patient. Second, the increasing number of clinical tests and analysis to be considered, such as genomics and proteomics, which creates a burden on specialist training and analysis capacity. Finally, the increasing number of patients to be diagnosed constrained by limited time to determine an output diagnostic, which demand clinician-friendly workflows integrated to the CDSS.

This chapter presents a discussion on the challenges and trends of using artificial intelligence and deep learning-based systems to deal with the large amounts of patient-centered data (with big data formal requirements or not) and effectively support clinical decisions.

1.1 Structure of this chapter

In Section 2, an introductory literature review is presented with selected relevant publications on each topic previously introduced. After that, two case studies are discussed from real applications. The first presents a clinical decision support solution for a maternal and fetal ambulatory monitoring system using multiple sensors, real-time diagnostic support based on inference rules, a signal processing feature extraction module, and an AI/deep learning classifier. The second case study is based on the development of a real application developed during the COVID-19 pandemic to the Government of the State of Ceara, in Brazil, to predict the spread of the disease based on two AI subsystems. Finally, the following section discusses the most recent challenges and trends of big data and artificial intelligence related to medical applications and how the next steps will affect the patient and the clinical flow.

2. Challenges and trends

The development of computerized solutions to assist clinical decisions has been widely studied and the scientific literature already has a vast number of publications, including technique propositions, validations, and development of new applications. Nevertheless, the adoption of artificial intelligence in addition to the traditional workflow and, more specifically, deep learning systems focused on patient-centered data to assist clinical decisions are a trend and also will need to overcome significant challenges.

This section also aims to introduce some relevant publications about the topic to allow the reader to get an overview about the evolution presented in the area and also the new recent developments.

Before moving to the literature review about the topic, it is necessary to present a list of essential concepts to clarify to the reader the selected scope of our analysis in this chapter.

2.1 Clinical decision support systems (CDSSs)

Clinical decision support systems are designed to provide clinicians, staff, patients, and/or other individuals with several levels of knowledge and person-specific information. This retrieval process varies from one system to another, intelligently filtering or presenting information at appropriate times, to enhance patient health care. It is important to comprehend that a CDS system may include different modules and pieces of software to support the process of making a decision in the clinical environment. This might include not only reporting but also alarming, remote interactions and distributed computing solutions.

Two common concepts that sometimes generate a mixed definition with CDSS are the computer-aided diagnostic (CAD) and therapeutic decision support (TDS) systems. Obviously there is an interconnection between them, since they rely on the computerized analysis of patient data to provide support to the medical or clinical operational flow. Nevertheless, the scopes are different. A CAD system focuses on specific diagnostic support actions, for example, an AI designed to analyze an MRI set of brain images for tumor detection, segmentation, and classification, or a computerized system to analyze maternal and fetal monitoring systems and provide more accurate diagnostic possibilities, given the higher level of false negatives or false positives. When considering a TDS, the scope focused on the optimization and individualized treatment of a patient, including diet, drug treatment, or radiotherapy [2]. The concept of CDSS brings a broader scope, which includes CAD, TDS, and other concepts. It considers the overall clinical flow of the patient, including medication prescription and patient outcome, which may result in even more general analysis such as clinical flow redesign or operational costs reduction.

2.2 Artificial intelligence × knowledge base systems

There are two main strategies adopted by CDSS to implement automatic decision support. One is based on a knowledge base architecture and the second on artificial intelligence models. In a general representation, both strategies have an impressive similarity, as can be seen in Fig. 5.1, despite their implementation following completely different computational algorithms and strategies.

For a better comprehension of the solutions discussed in this chapter, it is important to highlight the components from Fig. 5.2. First, the system user interfaces are evolving to provide intelligent

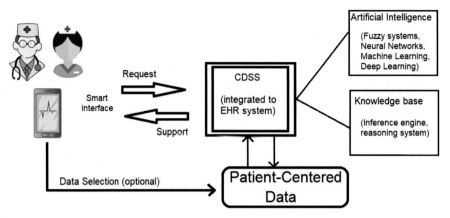

FIGURE 5.1

Block diagram of a general CDSS with AI and knowledge base supporting technologies.

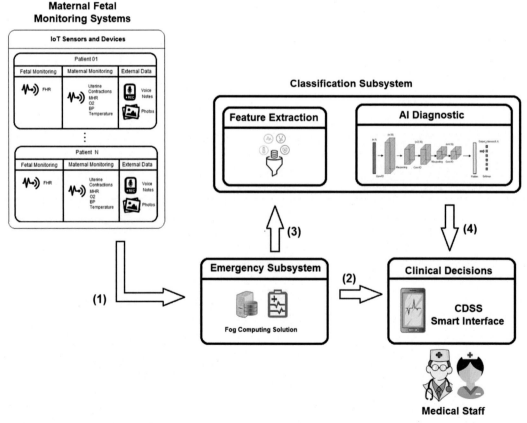

FIGURE 5.2

Proposed solution for the clinical maternal and fetal monitoring and decision support system.

interactions with the user and create a role-based personal experience, essentially integrated to the usual workflow and avoiding technicalities and additional steps which will create user resistance to adoption. Second, the smart interface communicates with the CDSS itself, that is desirably integrated into the EHR system. This simple communication step is rapidly evolving to complex distributed cloud-based multivendor integrated systems and demands a higher level of technical support, usually provided by third-party/outsourcing companies.

In addition, the patient-centered data block represents the challenge of integrating patient data from different sources, such as clinical, laboratory analysis, point of care, consultation, image examinations (PACS), and diagnostics. There is a connection between the user interface and the data module, which will allow the user to eventually select/remove specific patient data to add to the analysis. This probably is a more technical step, but can be achieved by implementing a level of abstraction to the medical staff user to avoid too technical descriptions. For example, the physicians can select if they want to move a previous medical imaging diagnosis to the current analysis or add historical data from similar patients to compare baselines or reference models to the patient under analysis.

Finally, as previously presented, the decision support subsystem from the CDSS will be implemented mainly based on two architectures. The first relies on artificial intelligence systems, which can be based on several different approaches such as fuzzy logic systems, machine learning algorithms, artificial neural networks (ANNs), and deep learning. The second architecture is focused on knowledge base systems, with different strategies to develop the inference engines and the reasoning subsystem.

2.3 The adoption of CDSSs

A CDSS is intended to improve healthcare delivery by enhancing medical decisions with targeted clinical knowledge, patient information, and other health information.

The adoption of CDSSs has seen a strong trend in clinical environments and the benefits are discussed widely in the literature, following three main different dimensions: improvements in the care process, clinical outcomes, and economic outcomes [1]. A systematic review from 2005 can be found focused on the improvements to practitioner performance [3]. Since then, several computational tools and capabilities have been achieved in clinical and ambulatory premises. A valuable overview of 25 years of CDSS was provided in Ref. [4] focusing on the medical literature with an iterative review and discussion among the authors, generating a division into six axes to be considered: data (handling and analysis), knowledge management, inference systems, proposed architecture and technology, processes of implementation and integration, and the users, who should receive special attention in any CDSS adoption. More recently, the adoption of artificial intelligence tools will boost and accelerate the process to achieve continuous improvements in several areas [5].

As an example, several researches and proposals of clinical decision models have been conducted on drug or medication management. For example, the application of a CDS can reduce adverse events from drug−drug interactions (DDI) [6,7], analyzing different sources of problems such as medication dosing [8], identification of duplicate therapies, any type of allergy, and the possible effects of drug−drug interactions (DDIs), connected to a dynamic knowledge base generating alerts at several levels.

As already mentioned, benefits in operations are also obtained when adopting CDSS. Felcher et al. presented the cost and operational improvements detecting unnecessary laboratory testing of vitamin D levels with the CDS integrated to the electronic health record (EHR) of a patient [9]. A broader view of cost savings associated with hospital-based pharmacy interventions can be found in Ref. [10].

From the diagnostic perspective, the adoption of CDSS is widely recommended to support the prevention of cardiovascular diseases (CVDs) [11] since there are a significant number of publications presenting positive results and clinical flow improvements. One interesting case reported that a reduction of cardiovascular risk in patients with type II diabetes could be obtained by integrating the computerized system and a patient feedback process created in the nursery area [12]. In the context of primary care practice in New Zealand, the adoption of an integrated electronic decision support could quadruple the efficacy of a CVD risk assessment process after only one cycle of routine patient visits [13].

Finally, from the public health side, the use of CDSS is already widely considered and should be analyzed with close attention. For example, in Ref. [14] the decision support messaging system was controlled, which resulted in a significant increase in laboratory testing, which generated an improvement in public health outcomes associated with outbreaks of foodborne illness.

2.4 The challenge of the increasing amounts of data available for clinical decision-making

When analyzing the evolution and applications of CDS systems as previously described, the increasing amount of patient-centered data is one of the most significant aspects that might be considered for the effectiveness and efficacy of a CDSS implementation. Considering the clinical flow, data from different sources are normally necessary to increase the computerized system capacity of analysis. For example, one supporting system that considers only patient demographics data and vital signs is much more limited in its analysis than another that also adds laboratory analysis results, medical images automatic processing and classification, historical data of medicine prescriptions and possible effects, and even integration with other systems from other clinical institutions. All these data sources together will create big data applications for clinical decision-making.

With that in mind, the first essential classification to be considered is that the fact of having a clinical solution generating large amounts of data does not necessarily mean that it fits into the definition of a big data application. For a system to be classified as big data, usually five requirements should be evaluated and classified, which are known as the five Vs (5Vs): variety, veracity, volume, velocity, and value [15].

The first V comes from variety and is a basic requirement of big data applications, which means that several data sources should be considered during the analysis. For example, images, clinical laboratory results, biological signals monitoring, among others can be briefly described examples. The second V, veracity, is related to the reliability of data collection, processing, storage, and manipulation. In information security, the integrity goal represents part of what is necessary to be achieved by the veracity dimension and all of these processes need to be monitored, controlled, and audited to keep the data valid and reliable. Third is the volume, which is the most significant criterion used to classify a big data application and also is the closest concept related to the general perception. With applications moving to cloud-based infrastructures, the volume of data generated has become even more critical. Velocity, the fourth V, is not related directly to the speed of communication, but the speed of data generation. Today, with the increasing numbers of sensors, health IoT systems, real-time monitors, and low-cost examination equipment, the speed of generated data is exponentially increasing. Finally, value is considered the requirement for the application to generate data that are valuable for the clinical decision-making process. Applications creating huge amounts of data with no value to the final analysis may be considered useless and not applicable in real life.

an interesting discussion of the impact of the 5Vs on the innovation competency of a corporate environment is provided in ref. [16]. The results presented that data velocity, variety, and veracity may enhance effective insights generation, while volume would not necessarily impact on it. In addition, the efficacy of descriptive and predictive data analysis was higher than when considering prescriptive tools. This means that, not necessarily advanced AI-based prescription tools will generate a positive impact on businesses and, consequently, the healthcare applications.

A valid discussion that should be considered is also about the data complexity that may impact on the processing requirements, even if it is not really a huge amount of data. In Ref. [15], a simple comparison allows this discussion. If you compare 500 TB of log data from a web site, with historical transaction occurrences, with a CDS system with a total of 1 TB per patient, containing encoded clinical data, images, data from multiple sensors, among others, which one of these two data collections should be considered big data? Not only the amount of data (volume) should be considered; the complexity of data (which can be expressed in terms of variety and value) are the key for future developments of applications.

Nevertheless, new applications that will be present in clinical analysis as a trend will generate significant amounts of data. For example, new genomics-based technologies produce very large amounts of raw data about the complex biochemical processes that regulate a living organism, which can exceed 1 TB. These analyses are difficult to interpret, but when it is possible to link genomics results to a closer connection to the patient pathological signs, observed at tissue, organ, and organism scales, many benefits are created and this will be possible with big data and AI-based CDSS.

2.4.1 Big data requirements and developing countries

Since the authors have extensive experience working with clinical setups in developing countries, such medical equipment installation and operation, adoption of automatic diagnostic support tools, and the process of decision-making based on CDSS, it became necessary to highlight some relevant parts of the challenges required by the increasing amount of data (or big data) applications as a mandatory part of the operational workflow for CDSS.

Medical institutions in developing countries are, as a matter of fact, complex and amazing structures, saving numerous lives and playing an essential social role in alleviating socioeconomic and psychological pressures in their communities. Nevertheless, the successful implementation of programs and adoption of innovations are very talent dependent. This means that, often, a group of heroic team members of the medical staff work day and night to implement changes and improvements, despite the lack of infrastructure or clear operational processes and procedures. Sometimes, they succeed, sometimes, they continue struggling without improvements to their working conditions. From this scenario, the 5Vs can be divided into two subgroups for a better understanding. First, the authors propose considering value and veracity as process-based requirements. The other group is based on infrastructure, which are volume, velocity, and variety.

For the first group, the organizational management maturity level is the key to success. Mature organizations are usually able to work on the elaboration, implementation, and auditing of policies and procedures. For example, the development of a corporate information security policy (ISP) to define roles and responsibilities and processes related to the mitigation of risks related to veracity, such as patient data handling, user authentication methods, and physical access control to the IT server room or the critical equipment room (radiology or cardiology, for example). On another dimension, staff training and involvement programs are also very important to comprehend the value of the data and to execute the veracity-related processes. Finally, change management capacity will also make it possible to implement the necessary changes to achieve determined goals and objectives.

For the infrastructure group (the second group with volume, velocity, and variety), the challenge is more resource based and less people dependent and is quite dependent on investment capacity. It is necessary to deal with a variety of data of different equipment and systems, generating an enormous volume of data, which require high-speed transmission not only in local premises but also interconnecting different units and usually providing telemedicine capabilities. This scenario is challenging to developing countries, because the investment in infrastructure is not a stand-alone action. If one hospital installs a set of innovative equipment, using a fibcroptics high-speed network, and a new AI-based DSS system in a brand-new server and there is no team to support their operation, the risk of operational disruption is extremely high.

Actually, the physical resources are the easiest part. It is common to find well-equipped health institutions in those countries with expensive equipment in constant underuse or stopped due to operational or maintenance issues. The authors already worked in a significant number of hospitals in Africa, for example, with a comprehensive set of radiology equipment such as mammography, CT scan, MRI, and even digital X-ray machines which are not available for operation simply because there are no technicians able to provide the relevant support to the medical teams. Also, the cost to maintain a team of specialists is sometimes much higher than the equipment acquisition and installation.

To conclude, the solution to implement big data and intelligent CDSS must consider not only the infrastructure challenges, but also the overall environment that results from this adoption.

2.5 Artificial intelligence and deep learning for CDSS

The concept of AI has been presented in the previous Section and there is a vast scientific literature on the adoption of these techniques as a tool to improve CDSS capabilities. It is important to understand from the beginning that the application of AI tools is designed focused on different levels of the clinical flow. For example, there is a significant percentage of systems developed to solve specific issues of the clinical process, such as CT scan image classification, laboratory analysis, diagnostic output, etc. On the other hand, some AI systems are more focused on the output of other clinical subsystems to support the higher level decision-making process.

An interesting approach was performed where CDS systems based on machine and deep learning solutions were analyzed based on the following criteria: selection, acceptance testing, commissioning, implementation, and quality assurance on the operation phase [17].

2.6 Engineers and medical researchers

The clinical setup is by nature a multidisciplinary environment, normally including physicians, nurses, assistants, technical staff, among others. Since the complexity of several activities is increasing, the presence of new types of professionals is frequently demanding, such as clinical engineers and biomedical engineers. For example, this clearly happened when medical imaging equipment started to play an essential role in the diagnostic field. Cardiac or brain CT scans or MRIs are examinations that will tend to be increasingly common in daily operation, but there are such a large number of requirements not only clinical but also technical, that equipment specialists are usually necessary to be available (if not present) to support the successful execution of the procedure.

In addition to the operations challenge, the design and adoption of CDSS are also controversial, when considering different types of professionals, such as engineers and medical researchers. Among the physicians it is not rare to find those who will never consider a computer-aided diagnostic output. In contrast, we also find a number of physicians who completely trust the computerized outputs. From the engineers' side, it is also easy to find some who believe that the whole set of clinical decisions should be based on intelligent computerized systems, and another group who believe that engineering systems should always be an operation and never be mixed with the role of providing a final diagnostic support.

Despite both areas (engineering and medicine) sharing similar premises and assumptions on problem solving, focusing always on finding a solution, even if requires further studies to be completely clear how and why it worked, nevertheless, it is common to find disagreement on problem identification and solving strategies, tactics, and actions.

According to Ref. [15] the fundamental difference is that engineers' mindset is prepared to identify phenomena related to the problem under study, since their training is based on the laws of physics or chemistry. If any of the laws are not applicable, then empirical approaches are considered to find a solution. This solution certainly creates a sense of fragility and will be always considered as non-reliable, until a formal solution is determined.

Medical researchers, on the other hand, base their decisions on reliable and recognized knowledge bases, which sometimes are exclusively qualitative (especially for rare diseases or difficult diagnoses) and the clinical approach positions the individual above the group quantitative analysis. Therefore, the search for a general law to solve the problem is considered simplistic.

In fact, the two philosophies of problem-solving modeling are applicable to particular cases. Computer-based systems for diagnostic and clinical decisions must be considered as an essential tool to approximate these approaches and increase the credibility and reliability of their use in clinical practice.

2.7 Developments and trends in big data and AI for CDSS

Trends in big data and artificial intelligence systems for clinical decision support systems are quite exciting and a great opportunity currently [18]. The challenges are the motivation to perform active research in the area and to propose effective and more efficient solutions. If this book was written no more than 10 years ago, several other challenges would have been listed, some that have been already overcome. For example, a global wide area network (WAN) with extremely high transmission rates and low latency was classified as impossible because of technology limitations of the existing satellite and digital transmissions. Today, the implementation of 5G networks worldwide is a reality and discussed not only by technicians but also by the ultimate consumers.

From the big data perspective, it is amazing to follow how the technology is evolving and creating new applications and solutions every day. For example, data-intensive diagnosis based on molecular levels. These data are coming from the individual genomics, that is, the DNA (deoxyribonucleic acid) or epigenomics, which is related to modifications of the DNA from any external sources such as stress, the environment, or even clinical interventions.

In another dimension, medical imaging can be considered to be the future of diagnostics. And it is going to demand a lot of volume and velocity. Over the decades, medical diagnostics was based on assumptions and approximations from external observations, such as visual inspection using the eyes, eventual patient abdominal inflammation, or the electrical activity of the heart, known as the electrocardiogram (ECG) examination. With new low-cost and high-resolution medical imaging equipment, the cardiologist will follow the muscle contractions, the blood flow, and electrical activity of the heart simultaneously and, with the help of intelligent computer-aided diagnostic systems, will be able to provide a precise and reliable diagnosis. Today, this is already possible, but the complexity and high cost of a cardiac MRI still prohibits its use for a large part of the population.

For the development of high-precision artificial intelligence deep learning diagnostic tools, the existence of training data is a requirement that is difficult to overcome. At present, huge integrated databases containing the historical data of the patient and integrated with other patients with similar diagnoses or conditions are under development and are allowing the development of precise computerized diagnostic tools.

A patient's health records will certainly be distributed and interconnected to other data sources such as education, social programs, financial status, previous medication, and other environmental factors. The data are personal but will be modeled in a global database. In the future, data analytic systems will be able to collect, compare, analyze, and predict local and global trends in chronic diseases such as diabetes or hypertension, but also will be better prepared for new eventual pandemics, such as the SARS-COV2 which is devastating lives and economies around the world as this chapter is being written.

3. Case study 1: multiple Internet of Things (IoT) monitoring systems and deep learning classification systems to support ambulatory maternal–fetal clinical decisions

The first case study presented in this chapter is related to the adoption of a multiparametric maternal and fetal monitoring system for ambulatory care units. This analysis is based on the results published by the authors in Refs. [19–21]. Before discussing the deep learning classifier, it is necessary to understand that the literature already extensively considered the problem of poor interobserver and intraobserver diagnostics reliability during maternal and fetal monitoring, resulting in higher rates of false positives or false negatives when based only on visual inspection of the cardiotocographic (CTG) traces [22].

The proposed system is based on the collection of the fetal heart rate (FHR) and maternal uterine contractions (UC) from CTG examinations in parallel with maternal vital signs, creating a network of Internet of Things (IoT) sensors and devices, and also allows the collection of unstructured data originated from the ambulatory staff observations such as voice notes and photos. This overall approach, including subjective analysis, was considered because, historically, a significant number of decisions were based on false-positive and false-negative interpretations of the CTG traces during maternal–fetal ambulatory monitoring. The whole solution is designed as a real-time classification tool based on the analysis of different data sources through a deep learning classifier to provide the computerized diagnostic support.

The adoption of IoT sensors to create integrated CDS solutions for the clinical healthcare industry is gaining attention with a large variety of solutions, although a challenging environment of obstacles to surpass remains a reality. IoT monitoring devices integrated usually to one or more sensors are a feasible solution for patient monitoring, not only to transform the process into being automatic, but also to meet the lack of medical specialists, especially in ambulatory premises.

Healthcare automatic decision systems are capable of handling large amounts of clinical data, and creating positive impacts in cost reduction and clinical efficiency. Nevertheless, as previously discussed, this trend demands more storage space for electronic health records that are accessible electronically [23]. In ambulatory premises integrating different types of IoT sensors, the amount of data tends to exponentially increase, requiring an adequate infrastructure to store and retrieve these data, following compliance regulations and clinical requirements. Aspects such as data security and privacy, data storage/retrieval techniques, communication systems and infrastructure, and data analysis techniques, that might rely on artificial intelligence classification systems to support medical decision-making are being continuously implemented and proposed.

From the network infrastructure perspective, the adoption of cloud-based solutions is significantly increasing [24], considering also fog computing solutions on the design, since it may provide an intermediate level of data storage and processing between hundreds or thousands of IoT sensors and devices [25,26]. This is extremely relevant for the case of developing countries, as discussed in the previous sections and especially for the case study under analysis here. The application of fault tolerance concepts may help increase the system reliability and availability constraints, such as Internet connection speed or availability [27].

Because of personal and critical data, information security is also of great concern when considering clinical data applications. The scientific literature already extensively addresses the topic and some important topics for the present analysis can be divided into three strategies. The first is to implement levels of protection to the network itself, considering physical and logical requirements [28]. The second is to consider the sensor side (maternal and fetal sensors in our case) in fault tolerance planning [29]. Finally, the third strategy would be to consider intelligent systems designed for trust-boundary protection in specific environments, a concept that comes from adversarial industrial IoT [30].

Ambulatory simultaneous maternal and fetal monitoring is used throughout the world, from high-luxury developing clinics to the most remote places with an extreme lack of infrastructure. Despite the simplicity of the methods and examinations, misinterpretation of these examinations is usually common, given the clinical setup and the long-term nature of the ambulatory monitoring. Previous work from the authors has already implemented signal processing techniques based on Hilbert transform and adaptive threshold technique for feature extraction from cardiotocography examinations [20]. Identification and extraction of relevant nonlinear metrics to support medical diagnostic capabilities were also proposed in Ref. [21]. AI systems are a suitable tool to deal with such a large number of metrics and parameters.

The proposed solution in this case study is based on a network of IoT sensors and devices to collect maternal and fetal signals, implementing a first-level emergency subsystem and a feature extraction layer to calculate linear and nonlinear features form the fetal heart rate and maternal uterine contractions and vital signs, submitting these metrics to classify the fetal and maternal health status. A flowchart representing the four phases of the proposed solution is presented in Fig. 5.3.

3.1 Preliminary CDSS

An AI fuzzy system was developed based on 26 inference rules and 24 deterministic rules to support a first-level diagnostic subsystem, which was called the emergency subsystem. The goal was to detect aberrances or significant changes automatically. The results were based on false-positive and false-negative rates and the overall accuracy is presented in Table 5.1.

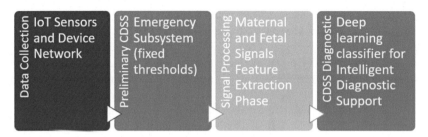

FIGURE 5.3

Flowchart of the maternal and fetal monitoring system.

Table 5.1 Performance of the preliminary CDS system based on the false-positive rate, false-negative rate, and accuracy.

Output	False-positive rate (%)	False-negative rate (%)	Accuracy (%)
Maternal emergency	8.70	9.09	91.74
Fetal emergency	7.32	13.56	90.09
Maternal and fetal emergency	16.67	6.82	92.59

3.2 Deep learning classifier

During the system modeling, the medical specialists working on the system design defined the adoption of six classes (PC1 to PC6) for the diagnostic prediction, considering all the possibilities of classifying the maternal and fetal status. The information about the six classes is presented in Table 5.2.

The classification task for the clinical decision support is based on a deep learning classifier system, which is a solution based on a large number of hyperparameters and their definition/tuning is an essential task to improve the overall classification performance. For the proposed deep learning classifier, the final modeling was achieved after executing a total of four implementations. First, four

Table 5.2 Definition of the six possible diagnostic classifications, according to the medical specialists.

Diagnostic classification	
PC1	Normal—fetus and mother
PC2	Suspicious—fetus
PC3	Distress—fetus
PC4	Suspicious—mother
PC5	Harmful—mother
PC6	Harmful—fetus and mother

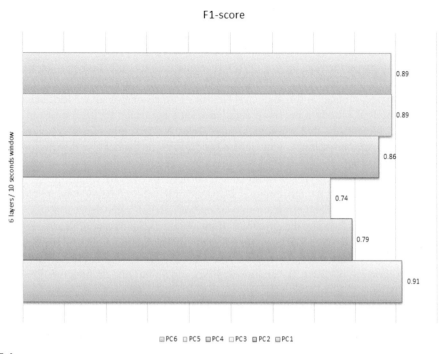

FIGURE 5.4

Final performance test of the deep learning classier system for clinical decision support.

and six convolutional layers were tested, considering a time series of 5 and 10 s as inputs. The detailed results can be found in Ref. [19]. After executing the tests, the best results were obtained by a network architecture with six convolutional layers and a time-series window size of 10 s.

In Fig. 5.4, a bar plot with the corresponding F1-score for each classification possibility is presented. Considering the fetal health status, we have F1-score (PC2) = 0.79 (suspicious cases) and F1-score (PC3) = 0.74 (fetal distress condition). Considering the maternal health status the results were higher than the fetal ones, with suspicious status F1-score (PC4) = 0.86 and for maternal status classified as harmful F1-score (PC5) = 0.89. The best F1-score was for the case where the mother and fetus were classified as healthy, PC1 = 0.91, while for the worst clinical case of the mother and the fetus under risk condition, the classification performance was F1-score (PC6) = 0.89.

3.3 Conclusion

In this section, a case study about the development of a big data and AI classification system for maternal and fetal ambulatory monitoring was presented. The best results were obtained by a network architecture with six convolutional layers and a time-series window size of 10 s, achieving an F1-score (PC6) = 0.89 for the case of both maternal and fetal as harmful. The system was designed to support maternal–fetal ambulatory premises in developing countries, where the demand is extremely high and the number of medical specialists is very low.

4. Case study 2: artificial intelligence epidemiology prediction system during the COVID-19 pandemic to assist in clinical decisions

The second case study is focused on a COVID-19 epidemiology infection predictor, considering several different artificial intelligence techniques and comparing their accuracy and computational performance to support clinical and managerial decisions on resources allocation and cost optimization. This case study is based on the more detailed results published by the authors in Ref. [31].

The problem of forecasting epidemiological time series is challenging for decision-making since the goal is to predict patterns or trends with severe time constraints and a low margin for errors [32]. The technique proposed here to cope with this problem is based on the application of recurrent neural networks (RNNs), which are a type of artificial neural network (ANN) where the structure of the network node is arranged to follow the temporal sequence of the classification data, making it suitable to use with speech recognition and clinical time-series, for example. Recurrent long-term short-term memory (LSTM) networks focus on the dynamics of the time series and its nonlinearities to effectively predict data. Nevertheless, RNN models contain a large number of parameters, and the optimization of the training phase and network tuning becomes a relevant task. The evolution during the last few years has allowed the validation of different versions of RNNs, including the architecture known as long-term short-term memory (LSTM) [32,33].

This case study considers the application of LSTM RNN to predict infection spread in Brazil during the COVID-19 pandemic. A second approach is based on the use of a new tool called H2O auto machine learning (H2O AutoML), which executes several different machine learning techniques and selects the best results achieved by each of them. This may possibly reduce modeling and testing phases and allows the selection of the best predictor, according to the considered time series.

4.1 Long-term short-term memory networks (LSTM)

Recurrent long-term short-term memory (LSTM) is based on the concept of cell states, which are considered as long- or short-term memories of the network, mitigating problems of recurrent networks such as vanishing gradient and exploding gradient, as can be found in Ref. [34]. Each LSTM block performs at different times and forwards its output to the subsequent block until the last LSTM piece produces a sequential output [32]. Considering the state H and the input X, and the output is a value between [0,1]. The decision on C_{t-1} means completely forgotten, 1 means completely remembered or kept on memory, which can be represented as [33]:

$$F_t = \sigma\left(w_f[H,x] + b_f\right)$$

$$G_t = \sigma\left(w_g[H,x] + b_g\right) \tag{5.1}$$

$$P_t = \sigma\left(w_p[H,x] + b_p\right)$$

where:

F_t = function used in the input layer;
G_t = forget function;
P_t = function used in the output layer;
X = input data;

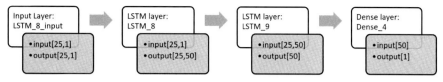

FIGURE 5.5

LSTM model used for the experiments.

H = data resulting from previous step;
W_f = weights matrix/vector;
b_f = neuronal bias function.

In Fig. 5.5 is the result of the prediction using the LSTM recurrent neural network. Each LSTM model was trained considering the following hyperparameters: 200 epochs, learning rate of 0.2, and patience factor equal to 2.

For the proposed experiment, a 10-fold cross-validation is performed, and R2 score, mean square error (MSE), and mean absolute error (MAE) are considered as the performance evaluation criteria. The results are presented based on the first wave of infections in Brazil, between March and September of 2020.

4.2 Auto machine learning approach (AutoML)

The platform H2O is an open-source and distributed machine learning online system designed to be able to analyze large data sets and integrate with several programming languages such as Java or Python, through its API. The tool provides a learning algorithm which is called H2O AutoML, which overlooks the process of finding candidate models. The result is a rated list of best models for the data set under analysis [35].

4.3 Results and discussion

The prediction results using LSTM and AutoML are presented in two parts and presented in the following subsections.

4.3.1 LSTM predictions for Brazil

In this section are presented four intervals of the COVID-19 infections in Brazil, considered as testing samples and the corresponding prediction time-series for each of them. The evaluation criteria are R^2, MSE (mean squared error), and MAE (mean accumulated error). A detailed description of each criterion and their application can be found in Ref. [31]. The following figures and the evaluation criteria are used to discuss the prediction performance of the LSTM model.

The model obtained an average R^2 score metric of 0.93 and an average MAE of $40,604.4$. For the MSE, since it is a quadratic measure, the average does not make really make sense to consider, because the penalties for larger individual errors are emphasized.

Considering the proposed model, the visual inspection of each curve can show that the convergence of the prediction takes a significant number of samples and this error in the beginning is reflected in all of the evaluation criteria. In addition, the error metrics such as MAE are also considered in the analysis.

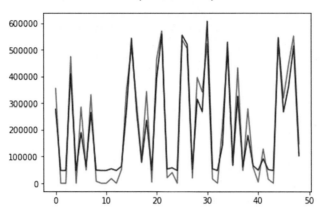

FIGURE 5.6

Sample 1 results: R2 score, 0.9312; MSE score, 2,943,184,750.2875; MAE score, 46,825.2641. Blue: original time series. Red: prediction time series.

The best R^2 score performance was 0.9939, achieved for sample 3, presented on Fig. 5.6, while the worse result is 0.9232 for sample 2, as seen in Fig. 5.7.

According to the results, the lowest MAE score was 10,437.99 for sample 3, while the highest MAE result was 50,401.91 for sample 4, as presented in Fig. 5.8. In this analysis, sample 2 presented the lowest R^2 score and also the highest MAE.

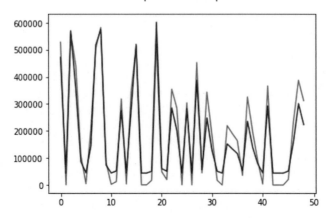

FIGURE 5.7

Sample 2 results: R2 score, 0.9232; MSE score, 2,791,157,146.2131; MAE score, 46,851.8443. Blue: original time series. Red: prediction time series.

4.3.2 H2O AutoML results for Brazil

A first round of execution for predicting the COVID-19 infections in Brazil is presented in Fig. 5.9.

The evaluation criteria for this example are R2 score, 0.9967; MSE score, 147,906,045.9071; and MAE score, 8341.1037. For this specific example, the performance of the predictor is superior to other techniques considered during the data analysis, such as autoregressive models (ARIMA) or nonlinear approaches based on Kalman filters [31] (Fig. 5.10).

After submitting the Brazilian COVID-19 time series to the AutoML framework, tens of machine learning techniques were executed and their results are presented in Table 5.3. The model column brings a description of the technique and the root mean squared error (RMSE) is considered as the performance criterion. As can be seen, for this case, the "stacked ensemble" approach presented the best performance. Actually, it is a model averaging ensemble that combines the predictions from multiple trained models. The other three best models are based on the XGBoost approach, also known as gradient boosted trees approach, which is based on decision trees.

4.4 Conclusion

This section considered two artificial intelligence approaches to provide efficient prediction of infections for clinical decision support during the COVID-19 pandemic in Brazil. First, LSTM recurrent neural networks were considered with the model obtaining $R^2 = 0.93$ and $MAE = 40,604.4$, in average. For time-series sample 3 the best result was achieved with $R^2 = 0.9939$. Second, an open-source framework called H2O AutoML considered with the "stacked ensemble" approach presented the best performance followed by XGBoost. Brazil has been one of the most challenging environments during the pandemic where efficient predictions may be the difference in saving lives.

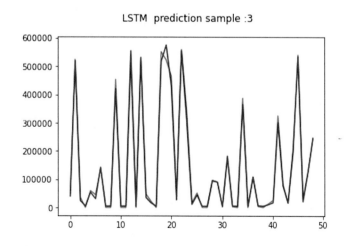

FIGURE 5.8

Sample 3 results: R2 score, 0.9939; MSE score, 232,427,798.3638; MAE score, 10,437.9951. Blue: original time series. Red: prediction time series.

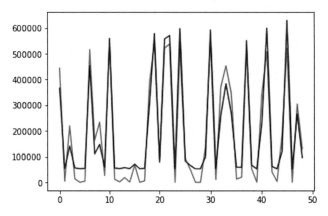

FIGURE 5.9

Sample 4 results: R2 score: 0.9291, MSE score, 3,192,973,911.3634; MAE score, 50,401.8199. Blue: original time series. Red: prediction time series.

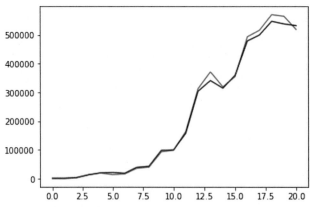

FIGURE 5.10

Prediction results of the H2O AutoML model for samples of COVID-19 active cases time series from Brazil. Blue: original time series. Red: prediction time series.

Table 5.3 Performance of different machine learning techniques for predicting the COVID-19 infections in Brazil.

Model	RMSE	MSE	MAE
StackedEnsemble_AutoML_033,205	12,161.7	1.47906e+08	8341.1
XGBoost_grid__1_AutoML_033,205_model_2	12,681.9	1.60829e+08	8472.79
XGBoost_grid__1_AutoML_033,205_model_1	13,718.4	1.88194e+08	8794.79
XGBoost_grid__1_AutoML_033,205_model_3	14,790.9	2.1877e+08	9455.89
GBM_grid__1_AutoML_033,205_model_1	14,899.1	2.21982e+08	10,059.9
DRF_1_AutoML_033,205	15,491.9	2.39999e+08	10,249.1

5. Final considerations

The adoption of clinical decision support systems will continue to increase and play essential roles in clinical practice with the use of large amounts of patient-centered data and artificial intelligence modules to support several steps of the process.

In several different environments, a large number of systems are already collecting patients' data and integrating them with automatic diagnostic or clinical decision support systems (CDSSs). This abundance of data (or big data if some or all 5V requirements are achieved) will create possibilities of technical developments and applied research that never existed previously. No more than a decade ago, local governments and international institutions, such as the World Health Organization (WHO), would have access only to static reports based on a limited time span, since data availability and computer processing were limited [18]. Recently, during the COVID-19 pandemic, an unprecedented effort of data sharing and integration allowed the creation of real-time dashboards and prediction tools to support the clinical and logistics decision-making process [31].

This chapter has presented the main concepts and a discussion about the challenges and trends in the area. Two case studies were presented. The first was based on a multiple monitoring system for maternal and fetal ambulatory care, modeled on a foggy and cloud architecture and using an AI deep learning subsystem to provide diagnostic support for medical staff. The second case considered an AI-based predictor developed to support the decision-making process of the Government of the State of Ceara in Brazil during the COVID-19 pandemic.

To conclude, the question that remains is: who will benefit from this increasing number of big data intelligent systems? A number of ethical issues are raised in this regard, considering the short- and long-term applications. Will the technology help humanity to overcome existing problems or will it increase even more the difference between rich and poor countries? In this direction, several initiatives are creating incentives to fund the development of low-cost technologies and providing solutions to everyone, and this is the key decision that researchers, specialists, government, and private organizations should embrace.

References

[1] N.M. Edu, J.E. Tcheng, S. Bakken, D.W. Bates, H. Bonner, I. Tejal, K. Gandhi, M. Josephs, K. Kawamoto, E.A. Lomotan, E. Mackay, B. Middleton, J.M. Teich, Scott, W. Marianne, H. Lopez, The Learning Health System Series Optimizing Strategies for Clinical Decision Support Summary of a Meeting Series, 2017. URL, https://lccn.loc.gov/2017055006.

[2] S. Golemati, S. Mougiakakou, J. Stoitsis, I. Valavanis, K.S. Nikita, Clinical decision support systems: basic principles and applications in diagnosis and therapy, Clin. Knowl. Manage. Opport. Chall. (2005) 251–270.

[3] A.X. Garg, N.K. Adhikari, H. McDonald, M.P. Rosas-Arellano, P.J. Devereaux, J. Beyene, J. Sam, R.B. Haynes, Effects of computerized clinical decision support systems on practitioner performance and patient outcomes: a systematic review, J. Am. Med. Assoc. 293 (2005) 1223–1238.

[4] B. Middleton, D.F. Sittig, A. Wright, Clinical decision support: a 25 year retrospective and a 25 year vision, Yearb. Med. Inf. Suppl 1 (2016) S103–S116.

[5] R.T. Sutton, D. Pincock, D.C. Baumgart, D.C. Sadowski, R.N. Fedorak, K.I. Kroeker, An overview of clinical decision support systems: benefits, risks, and strategies for success, Npj Digit. Med. 3 (2020) 1–10.

[6] P.L. Smithburger, M.S. Buckley, S. Bejian, K. Burenheide, S.L. Kane-Gill, A critical evaluation of clinical decision support for the detection of drugdrug interactions, Expet Opin. Drug Saf. 10 (2011) 871–882.

[7] A. Sonnichsen, U.S. Trampisch, A. Rieckert, G. Piccolori, A. VÖgele, M. Flamm, T. Johansson, A. Esmail, D. Reeves, C. LÖffler, J.H. Öck, R. Klaassen-Mielke, H.J. Trampisch, I. Kunnamo, Polypharmacy in chronic diseases—reduction of inappropriate medication and adverse drug events in older populations by electronic decision support (prima-eds): study protocol for a randomized controlled trial, Trials 17 (2016) 57.

[8] D. Fritz, A. Ceschi, I. Curkovic, M. Huber, M. Egbring, G.A. Kullak-Ublick, S. Russmann, Comparative evaluation of three clinical decision support systems: prospective screening for medication errors in 100 medical inpatients, Eur. J. Clin. Pharmacol. 68 (2012) 1209–1219.

[9] A.H. Felcher, R. Gold, D.M. Mosen, A.B. Stoneburner, Decrease in unnecessary vitamin d testing using clinical decision support tools: making it harder to do the wrong thing, J. Am. Med. Inf. Assoc. 24 (2017) 776–780.

[10] S. Calloway, H. Akilo, K. Bierman, Impact of a clinical decision support system on pharmacy clinical interventions, documentation efforts, and costs, Hosp. Pharm. 48 (2013) 744–752.

[11] D.P. Hopkins, Clinical Decision Support Systems Recommended to Prevent Cardiovascular Disease, 2015, https://doi.org/10.1016/j.amepre.2015.03.041.

[12] F.G. Cleveringa, K.J. Gorter, M.D. Van Donk, G.E. Rutten, Combined task delegation, computerized decision support, and feedback improve cardiovascular risk for type 2 diabetic patients, Diabetes Care 31 (2008) 2273–2275.

[13] S. Wells, S. Furness, N. Rafter, E. Horn, R. Whittaker, A. Stewart, K. Moodabe, P. Roseman, V. Selak, D. Bramley, R. Jackson, Integrated electronic decision support increases cardiovascular disease risk assessment four fold in routine primary care practice, Eur. J. Prev. Cardiol. 15 (2008) 173–178.

[14] W.Y. Wu, G. Hripcsak, J. Lurio, M. Pichardo, R. Berg, M.D. Buck, F.P. Morrison, K. Kitson, N. Calman, F. Mostashari, Impact of integrating public health clinical decision support alerts into electronic health records on testing for gastrointestinal illness, J. Publ. Health Manag. Pract. 18 (2012) 224–227.

[15] M. Viceconti, P. Hunter, R. Hose, Big data, big knowledge: big data for personalized healthcare, IEEE J. Biomed. Health Inf. 19 (2015) 1209–1215.

[16] M. Ghasemaghaei, G. Calic, Does big data enhance firm innovation competency? The mediating role of data-driven insights, J. Bus. Res. 104 (2019) 69–84.

[17] G. Mahadevaiah, P. RV, I. Bermejo, D. Jaffray, A. Dekker, L. Wee, Artificial intelligence—based clinical decision support in modern medical physics: selection, acceptance, commissioning, and quality assurance, Med. Phys. 47 (2020) e228–e235.

[18] E.B. Sloane, R.J. Silva, Artificial intelligence in medical devices and clinical decision support systems, in: Clinical Engineering Handbook, second ed., Elsevier, 2019, pp. 556–568.

[19] J.A.L. Marques, P.C. Cortez, J.P. Madeiro, V.H.C. de Albuquerque, S.J. Fong, F.S. Schlindwein, Nonlinear characterization and complexity analysis of cardiotocographic examinations using entropy measures, J. Supercomput. 76 (2020a) 1305–1320.

[20] J.A.L. Marques, T. Han, W. Wu, J.P.d.V. Madeiro, A.V. Neto, R. Gravina, G. Fortino, V.H.C. de Albuquerque, IoT-based smart health system for ambulatory maternal and fetal monitoring, IEEE Internet of Things J. (2020) 1, https://doi.org/10.1109/JIOT.2020.3037759.

[21] J.A.L. Marques, P.C. Cortez, J.P.D.V. Madeiro, S.J. Fong, F.S. Schlindwein, V.H.C. Albuquerque, Automatic Cardiotocography diagnostic system based on Hilbert transform and adaptive threshold technique, IEEE Access 7 (2019) 73085–73094.

[22] G.A. Macones, Intrapartum Fetal Heart Rate Monitoring: Nomenclature, Interpretation, and General Management Principles, 2009, https://doi.org/10.1097/AOG.0b013e3181aef106. URL, https://pubmed.ncbi.nlm.nih.gov/19546798/.

[23] Y. Zhang, L. Sun, H. Song, X. Cao, Ubiquitous WSN for healthcare: recent advances and future prospects, IEEE Internet of Things J. 1 (2014) 311–318.

[24] L.A. Tawalbeh, R. Mehmood, E. Benkhlifa, H. Song, Mobile cloud computing model and big data analysis for healthcare applications, IEEE Access 4 (2016) 6171−6180.

[25] H. Li, K. Ota, M. Dong, Learning IoT in edge: deep learning for the Internet of Things with edge computing, IEEE Netw. 32 (2018) 96−101.

[26] W. Rafique, L. Qi, I. Yaqoob, M. Imran, R.U. Rasool, W. Dou, Complementing IoT services through software defined networking and edge computing: a comprehensive survey, IEEE Commun. Surv. Tutor. 22 (2020) 1761−1804.

[27] K. Wang, Y. Shao, L. Xie, J. Wu, S. Guo, Adaptive and fault-tolerant data processing in healthcare IoT based on fog computing, IEEE Trans. Netw. Sci. Eng. 7 (2020) 263−273.

[28] R.R. Guimarães, L.A. Passos, R.H. Filho, V.H.C. De Albuquerque, J.J. Rodrigues, M.M. Komarov, J.P. Papa, Intelligent network security monitoring based on optimum-path forest clustering, IEEE Netw. 33 (2019) 126−131.

[29] O.S. Albahri, A.S. Albahri, A.A. Zaidan, B.B. Zaidan, M.A. Alsalem, A.H. Mohsin, K.I. Mohammed, A.H. Alamoodi, S. Nidhal, O. Enaizan, M.A. Chyad, K.H. Abdulkareem, E.M. Almahdi, G.A. Al Shafeey, M.J. Baqer, A.N. Jasim, N.S. Jalood, A.H. Shareef, Fault-tolerant mHealth framework in the context of IoT-based real-time wearable health data sensors, IEEE Access 7 (2019) 50052−50080.

[30] M.M. Hassan, M.R. Hassan, S. Huda, V.H.C. de Albuquerque, A robust deep learning enabled trust-boundary protection for adversarial industrial IoT environment, IEEE Internet of Things J. (2020) 9611−9621, https://doi.org/10.1109/JIOT.2020.3019225.

[31] J.A.L. Marques, F.N.B. Gois, J. Xavier-Neto, S.J. Fong, Prediction for decision support during the COVID-19 pandemic, in: SpringerBriefs in Applied Sciences and Technology, Springer Science and Business Media Deutschland GmbH, 2021, pp. 1−13, https://doi.org/10.1007/978-3-030-61913-8_1.

[32] V.K.R. Chimmula, L. Zhang, Time series forecasting of COVID-19 transmission in Canada using LSTM networks, Chaos, Solit. Fractals 135 (2020).

[33] M. Zubair Asghar, A. Khan, F. Subhan, M. Imran, F. Masud Kundi, A. Khan, S. Shamshirband, A. Mosavi, P. Csiba, A.R. Varkonyi Koczy, Performance Evaluation of Supervised Machine Learning Techniques for Efficient Detection of Emotions from Online Content Design Optimization of Electric Machines View Project Business Modeling View Project Performance Evaluation of Supervised Machine Learning Techniques for Efficient Detection of Emotions from Online Content, 2020.

[34] P. Arora, H. Kumar, B.K. Panigrahi, Prediction and analysis of COVID-19 positive cases using deep learning models: a descriptive case study of India, Chaos, Solit. Fractals 139 (2020).

[35] E. Ledell, S. Poirier, H2O AutoML: Scalable Automatic Machine Learning, 2020.

Universal intraensemble method using nonlinear AI techniques for regression modeling of small medical data sets

Ivan Izonin[1] and Roman Tkachenko[2]

[1]*Department of Artificial Intelligence, Lviv Polytechnic National University, Lviv, Ukraine;* [2]*Department of Publishing Information Technologies, Lviv Polytechnic National University, Lviv, Ukraine*

1. Introduction and problem statement

The development of computer power, artificial intelligence tools, as well as the growth of the number of sensors and devices based on the Internet of Things (IoT) have set new trends [1,2] in the development of various industries, medicine, economics, etc. The ability to collect a huge amount of data based on the Internet of Things devices, to use advanced neural network tools for its processing, and powerful hardware to provide necessary computing resources allow it to effectively solve the big data tasks. Today many frameworks provide the specialist with everything necessary for accurate and relatively fast processing of large volumes of data. This situation is typical for modern medicine. A variety of patient information collection devices based on the IoT provide the physician with a huge amount of information necessary for diagnosis and/or treatment [3]. The use of artificial intelligence tools helps to make the right, accurate, and timely decision during the diagnosis and observation of the patient or his treatment [4,5]. This greatly simplifies the work of specialists in the field of medicine and this area is set to develop rapidly in the future [6].

However, there are cases when data for diagnosis, prevention, or treatment are scarce [7–9]. This applies to personalized treatment, diagnosis, and choice of treatment for rare diseases, etc. [10]. Existing machine learning methods or artificial neural network tools do not provide satisfactory results of intellectual analysis in this case [11]. This is due to a number of potential problems when processing short data sets by computational intelligence tools:

— overfitting problems, which are very typical when processing short data sets;
— huge impact of noise components, missing values, and outliers;
— sharp variables fluctuations inside the short data set;
— very low ability to generalization when processing of short data sets;
— very small dimension of the validation sample for the optimal parameters selection procedures;
— small dimension of the test sample for a certain generalization of assessments of the effectiveness of a particular method;

— problems of finding the optimal complexity model in the case of using data augmentation methods;
— measurement errors during processing of short data sets;
— problems of objectivity of data in case of their small quantity;
— and so on.

Despite this number of serious problems, solving the task of efficient processing of short data sets remains a very important task today. This is explained by a number of factors, considered in detail, described, and analyzed in Ref. [7]. However, the main one is the ability to obtain no less accurate results of intellectual analysis using a much smaller amount of data, material, technological, and time resources (in comparison with using big data technologies). In addition, in some cases, small data may even provide information that does not provide big data [12].

The aim of this chapter is to develop an effective method of processing short data sets that would be a universal basis for the use of various computational intelligence tools. On the one hand, it should be fairly simple, but on the other hand, it should take into account nonlinearities and complex relationships between the variables of a short data set that meets the requirements of tasks from different fields of medicine [13].

Therefore, the main contributions of this chapter can be summarized as follows:

1. A universal intraensemble method is designed for processing short sets of medical data, which is based on the use of nonlinear computational intelligence tools;
2. Various algorithmic implementations of the designed universal intraensemble method with the use of both a machine learning algorithm and artificial neural networks are presented; procedures for their training and application within the designed method are described;
3. An experimental investigation of the efficiency of work of all proposed algorithms based on two short medical data sets is carried out; the increasing prediction accuracy based on the designed universal intraensemble method by comparison with parental regressors is shown.

The reminder of this chapter is organized as follows: in Section 2 we analyze the related concepts, in Section 3 we describe the proposed universal intraensemble method and its three different algorithmic realizations. Practical implementation of the proposed algorithms, and the procedures of its optimal parameters selection are described in Section 4. Comparison with existing methods and conclusions are described in Sections 5 and 6, respectively.

2. Related concepts

The prediction accuracy of solving the regression tasks in the case of processing short data sets is an important task in various fields of medicine. Today, there are many challenges in this area, which are characterized by insufficient data for various reasons. This work is dedicated to the effective solution of such problems.

There is a small number of works and research in the peer-reviewed literature devoted to the problem of "a small data approach." If we use the following query in the Scopus database: TITLE-ABS-KEY-AUTH ("small data approach") we get only 16 publications. The number of publications is growing every year, which indicates a significant interest in these tasks, but the problem of developing effective tools to solve such tasks is becoming more widespread. It covers a variety of fields, from archeology to medicine. If we discuss unreviewed literature and expert articles, they briefly but rather objectively describe the problems and tasks of "a small data approach." However, they do not offer any technical solutions.

In our opinion, the best peer-reviewed study in the direction of small data approach today is in Ref. [7]. The authors have collected many facts and arguments, but very clearly provide detailed information about the importance and value of a small data approach for today. In addition, they show how this approach can help improve a number of healthcare studies. The authors outline possible ways to develop a small data approach and even provide hypotheses about complementing the big data approach with the results obtained using the small data approach. Despite the theoretical nature of this work, its significance is difficult to estimate.

If we talk about the techniques of a small data approach, then one of the newest books on data analytics based on small data sets is Ref. [14], which was published in 2021. The authors of that book prepared a manual for students, which outlines the basic techniques of data analysis and simple machine learning models, which, moreover, are mainly used to process medium data sets. Some are based on the assumption of a lack of nonlinearity and relationships between the elements of the data set, which in most cases is incorrect. Other models are known and are often used to analyze data in medicine and other fields. Nevertheless, this work will help the student to take their first steps in the direction of their own research when processing short data sets. A similar idea is carried out in Ref. [15]. The authors of that work investigate the existing tools for their application in the processing of short data sets, but in education. The authors argue that most of the tasks in this area are accompanied by very brief historical data and the development of a small data approach is very important here.

In Ref. [16] the problems and prospects of the application of big and small data models are analyzed. The authors of the article emphasize the development and implementation of small data models and their use in the healthcare system. In particular, the authors developed a small data model to predict the length of a patient's hospital stay. The developed model demonstrates acceptable accuracy, and can be integrated into the big data model. In Ref. [17] the author also focuses on a small data approach, which considers a person or household as a sample unit for further analysis. The author collected and analyzed various existing data analysis frameworks for their effective use for implementation of the small data approach.

In Ref. [11], a new approach to the application of artificial neural networks to solve the task of processing short data sets is proposed. The developed method demonstrates high prediction accuracy, but requires many resources for its work. In addition, it is based on the use of only artificial neural networks and therefore is not universal. In Ref. [18], the authors also consider the artificial neural networks to solve the stated task. However, in this case, they used GAN as a numerical data augmentation tool for efficient processing of short data sets. The advantages of this approach are independence from the type of variables or distribution laws within the data set. However, the developed method is only a tool for data augmentation. However, for solving classification or regression tasks based on an extended data set, it is necessary to use additional tools. In Ref. [19], the authors developed an ensemble within a single neural network. This approach significantly reduced the computing resources required to train and use multiple neural networks, as part of an ensemble model. Moreover, it provided greater efficiency compared to a single neural network model.

The last three studies have given us the impetus to develop our universal intraensemble method for effective processing of short data sets. It combines the advantages of all three methods, by using some of their elements; provides the ability to expand data and use the principles of ensemble learning within a single computational intelligence tool; and is a universal basis for the development of algorithmic implementations based on a variety of nonlinear computational intelligence tools.

3. Universal intraensemble method for handling small medical data

This section describes the developed universal intraensemble method. In addition, three algorithmic implementations of the training and application procedures for different nonlinear computational intelligence tools are described.

3.1 Design of the universal intraensemble method

As a basic idea of the universal intraensemble method for processing of short data sets, a combination of two existing approaches is put forward: numerical data augmentation and basic principles of the ensemble learning. The proposed approach is implemented based on using only one nonlinear computational intelligence tool (artificial neural network or machine learning algorithm). Algorithmic implementation of the method involves a quadratic increase in the volume of the available training sample by simple combinations inside the initial data set. The purpose of learning a nonlinear computational intelligence tool on a new data set is to increase the generalization properties. In addition, the use of elements of the theory of ensemble learning, namely the principle of averaging the results and partial mutual compensation of random errors of different signs during the application of the developed method will improve the accuracy of the output signal.

The developed method, depending on the selected nonlinear kernel and the features of the selected computational intelligence tool, operates in the modes of iterative or noniterative training and application. For a nonlinear core of a GRNN network, the training mode is virtually absent.

The training mode, in turn, can be divided into two main procedures: data preprocessing and the actual training procedure. The main purpose of the data preprocessing stage is to increase the dimensionality of the initial data set according to the author's algorithm. As described in the first section, this strategy demonstrates a significant increase in the prediction accuracy of computational intelligence tools when processing short (in the case of solving a regression or classification task) or even unbalanced data sets (in the case of solving a classification task). The main effect of the application of the strategy of increasing the data set according to the proposed algorithm in this chapter is achieved by a quadratic increase in the number of sampling vectors for training the selected nonlinear computational intelligence tools, to improve the generalization properties based on it. The training phase takes place according to the classical procedures of the chosen computational intelligence tool, however, on a new, enlarged data set.

In the application mode, the algorithmic implementation of the proposed method also involves the implementation of two stages: the preliminary processing of the input observation and the actual prediction procedure. In the preprocessing step, the current vector with an unknown output signal is combined with each vector of the initial training sample. Next, partial predictions are made for each of the twice-extended vectors, by the pretrained regressor, which are averaged as a result. This ensures the principles of ensemble learning, namely the averaging of the result. The main difference here is that only one computational intelligence tool is used (which is why the intraensemble method is used).

The final result of the universal method is formed by taking into account the known outputs of the initial training data set and the averaged result obtained at the above step, in accordance with the algorithmic implementation of the method. It should be noted that the use of the linear core of the selected computational intelligence tool in this case does not provide effective results.

Let us consider the basic mathematical expressions of the universal intraensemble method. Let the training data set be presented in the form of a normalized set of vectors in the form:

$$\overline{x_i} \rightarrow y_i, \tag{6.1}$$

for which the initial value y_i is known. The dimension of the set of vectors is $dim\{\overline{x_i}\} \rightarrow N$.

Step 1. We create a new, extended set of data by combining all possible pairs of vectors in the form:

$$\overline{x_m x_i} \rightarrow z_{m,i} \tag{6.2}$$

where the dimension of the set of vectors (2) is $dim\{\overline{x_m x_i}\} \rightarrow N^2$, and output $z_{m,i}$, $m = 1, N$ for each of Eq. (6.2) are forming in the following way:

$$z_{m,i} = y_m - y_{,i}, \tag{6.3}$$

where $m = \overline{1, N}$, $i = \overline{1, N}$. It should be noted that Eqs. (6.2) and (6.3) implement the principle of data augmentation based on the author's approach.

Step 2. We adjust the necessary parameters of the selected nonlinear kernel of the chosen computational intelligence tool and perform the procedure of its training, if any.

Step 3. Based on the u-th input vector $\overline{x_u}$, for which it is necessary to predict the initial value, we form a set of temporary vectors by combining it with each available vector from the initial set of training data:

$$\overline{x_u x_i} \rightarrow z_{u,i}^{pred} \tag{6.4}$$

where the dimension of the set of vectors is $dim\{\overline{x_u x_i}\} = N$, and $z_{u,i}^{pred}$ is an unknown intermediate value to be predicted'

Step 4. We obtain the predicted values of $z_{u,i}^{pred}$ by applying each vector in Eq. (6.4) to a pretrained nonlinear computational intelligence tool'

Step 5. We form the desired value of the output signal y_u^{pred} for u-th input vector $\overline{x_u}$, according to the equation:

$$y_u^{pred} \cong \frac{\sum_1^N z_{u,i}^{pred} + c}{N} \tag{6.5}$$

where c is the average value of the sum of known output signals for all vectors from Eq. (6.1) (constant):

$$c = \frac{\sum_1^N y_i}{N} \tag{6.6}$$

It should be noted that in Eq. (6.5), due to $\frac{\sum_1^N z_{u,i}^{pred}}{N}$, the principle of averaging that is characteristic of ensemble methods is implemented.

Since the effectiveness of the developed method for the processing of short medical data sets is provided by the use of nonlinear computational intelligence tools, let us consider the developed algorithms for its operation.

3.2 Algorithm 1: support vector regression using nonlinear kernels

The first algorithmic implementation of the universal intraensemble method is based on the use of the machine learning method. The authors chose support vector regression (SVR) with two nonlinear kernels (polynomial and *rbf*), as this method is often used to process medical data sets [20,21]. The universal intraensemble method based on SVR (nonlinear kernel) works in two modes: training and application.

Algorithmic implementation of the training procedure of the developed method involves the following steps [22]:

1. to create an extended data set according to Eqs. (6.2) and (6.3);
2. to choose a nonlinear kernel of the method (*rbf* or polynomial);
3. to set the optimal parameters of the method (degree of the polynomial, if the polynomial kernel is selected, the number of iterations, etc.);
4. to perform the training procedure.

In the application mode for the u-th input vector $\overline{x_u}$, it is necessary to predict the value of the output signal. To do this, according to the algorithmic implementation of the method is necessary:

1. to form a set of temporary vectors according to Eq. (6.4) based on the input vector, with an unknown output signal;
2. to predict the intermediate values of the output signals for all generated additional vectors;
3. to form the result of the method using Eq. (6.5).

3.3 Algorithm 2: general regression neural network

The second algorithmic implementation of the universal intraensemble method is based on the use of the general regression neural network (GRNN). The GRNN topology is shown in Fig. 6.1. Details of the procedures for its operation are given in Ref. [23].

This choice is due to a number of advantages of this nonlinear computational intelligence tool among the existing ones [24]. In particular, it is necessary to highlight the highest generalization properties among the existing types of artificial neural networks, the lack of training procedures and high speed in the case of processing short data sets [23]. Algorithmic implementation of the universal intraensemble method based on the use of GRNN involves the following steps [23,25]:

1. to form an extended set of available input data in Eq. (6.1) according to Eqs. (6.2) and (6.3);
2. to form a set of temporary vectors according to Eq. (6.4) on the basis of input one $\overline{x_u}$, with unknown output signal;
3. to calculate the Euclidean distances $d_{u,i}$, between each temporary vector $\overline{x_u}$, and all other vectors obtained in the first step of the procedure;
4. to calculate Gaussian functions g_i from $d_{u,i}$ with the choice of the optimal value σ (smooth factor). It should be noted that the correct selection of the parameter σ will affect the efficiency of the developed method;
5. to predict the values of the output signals $z_{u,i}^{pred}$ for all temporary vectors formed in step 2 according to the formula for calculation of the output signal of the GRNN method (Fig. 6.2).
6. to form the result of the method using Eq. (6.5).

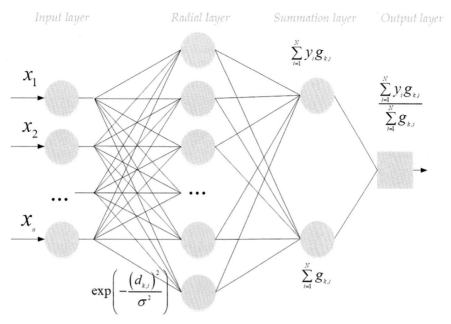

FIGURE 6.1

GRNN architecture.

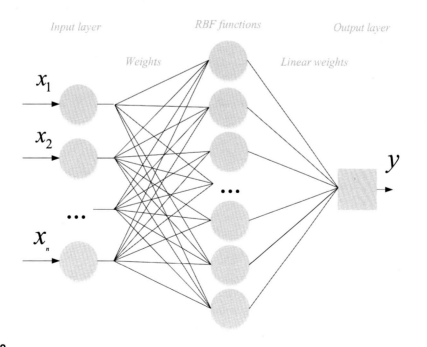

FIGURE 6.2

RBF architecture.

3.4 Algorithm 3: RBF neural network

The third algorithmic implementation of the universal intraensemble method is based on the use of an iterative RBF neural network. The RBF topology is shown in Fig. 6.1. Details of the procedures for its training and application are given in Ref. [26].

This choice is argued for by the high prediction accuracy of neural networks of this type when solving various real tasks [27]. A universal intraensemble method based on an RBF neural network operates in two modes: training and application.

Algorithmic implementation of the training procedure of the developed method involves the following steps [28]:

1. to create an extended data set according to Eqs. (6.2) and (6.3);
2. to carry out clustering by the *k-nn* method with the selected value of the number of clusters;
3. to select the optimal parameters of the method, including the number of epochs, σ value, etc.;
4. to carry out training of the RBF neural network where the number of neurons in the hidden layer (number of *rbf* centers) is equal to the number of clusters determined in the previous step.

It should be noted that the correct selection of the number of clusters, the number of iterations, and the selection of the parameter σ would significantly affect the efficiency of the developed method. The selection of optimal parameters can be performed using a validation sample using the selected loss function [29].

In the application mode for the u-th input vector $\overline{x_u}$, it is necessary to predict the value of the output signal. To do this, according to the algorithmic implementation of the method it is necessary:

1. to form a set of temporary vectors according to Eq. (6.4) based on the input vector $\overline{x_u}$, with an unknown output;
2. to carry out clustering by the *k-nn* method with the value of the number of clusters, specified in step 2 of the training procedure;
3. to predict the temporary values of the output signals $z_{u,i}^{\text{pred}}$ for all generated additional vectors according to the RBF ANN;
4. to form the result of the method using Eq. (6.5).

---

4. Practical implementation

This section presents the results of experimental modeling of the developed method using two short medical data sets. A number of procedures have been performed to select the optimal operating parameters of the three algorithms based on the use of two data sets. The accuracy and speed of three algorithmic implementations of the universal intraensemble method are experimentally established.

4.1 Data sets for experimental modeling

The processes of diagnosis, control, and treatment of various disorders and pathologies are accompanied by data on patients [9]. Sometimes there is a lot of such information, but in some cases, there is a shortage of available historical data for a particular disease. In this chapter, we worked with such tasks. The authors used two short medical data sets to model the operation of three algorithmic implementations of the developed method. After cleaning, deleting observations with omissions, etc., the dimension of the first data set was 35 observations, and the dimension of the second set was 77 observations. The original data sets are available at Refs. [9,11,30], respectively.

The purpose of the first task based on the first data set was to predict the compressive strength of trabecular bone (CS in MPa) in patients with osteoarthritis. This intellectual analysis was based on five independent variables. The urgency of this task is to determine the optimal load on the bone to avoid injury or disability. Such cases are very common for the elderly.

The second data set contains of a set of six independent attributes that were used to predict the level of the calcium concentration in urine. In general, a urine test is a basic test in diagnosing, determining the effectiveness of treatment, or simply monitoring a patient. However, this specific task is important in the diagnosis and control of treatment of urolithiasis (the presence of stones in the urinary tract), as well as nephrocalcinosis (i.e., saturation of the renal pyramids with calcium salts).

The basic characteristics of both data sets are given in Tables 6.1 and 6.2, respectively.

Table 6.1 The basic characteristics of the first data set.

Variable	Minimum value	Maximum value	Mean value
Patient's age	41.7	87.0	64.8
Patient's gender	0	1	–
Structure model index (SMI)	0.04	2.1	0.65
Tissue porosity (BV/TV)	9.68	43.5	26.22
Trabecular thickness factor (tb.th)	154.0	419.0	259.69
CS (in MPa)	1.93	28.8	16.4

Table 6.2 The basic characteristics of the second data set.

Variable	Minimum value	Maximum value	Mean value
The osmolarity of the urine	187	1236	613.61
The conductivity of the urine	5.1	38	20.901
The urea concentration in millimoles per liter	10	620	264.141
The pH reading of the urine	4.76	7.94	6.042
The specific gravity of the urine	1.005	1.04	1.018
Indicator of the presence of calcium oxalate crystals	0	1	0.436
The calcium concentration in millimoles per liter	0.17	14.34	4.161

4.2 Performance indicators

The errors of each algorithmic implementation of the designed method were determined based on two indicators:

$$\text{RMSE} = \sqrt{\frac{\sum_{u=1}^{T}\left(y_u^{\text{pred}} - y_u\right)}{T}}$$ (6.7)

$$\text{MAE} = \frac{1}{T}\sum_{u=1}^{T}\left|y_u^{\text{pred}} - y_u\right|$$ (6.8)

where y_u is the actual value; y_u^{pred} is the predicted value; and T is the dimension of the test sample.

In addition, the training time (where necessary) of the selected nonlinear computational intelligence tools, which is the basis for the specific implementation of the designed method, was taken into account. In particular, the duration of the training procedure was determined for the first and third algorithmic implementations of the method. For the second algorithm, the training time was not determined, because GRNN does not actually require such a procedure.

4.3 Optimal parameters selection

This chapter presents three different algorithmic implementations of the universal intraensemble method. Their main difference is the use of a specific nonlinear computational intelligence tool as the basis of the different algorithms. This greatly affects the modes of operation of the method, the time of its operation, as well as the accuracy of the method.

An experimental modeling was based on two short sets of medical data. They were divided into training and test samples in the ratio of 80% to 20%. It should be noted that the data were normalized using the StandartScaller () function of Python.

Let us consider the features of the selection of optimal parameters for each algorithmic implementation of the universal intraensemble method in more detail.

4.4 Algorithm 1: support vector regression using nonlinear kernels

The first algorithm of the universal intraensemble method is based on the SVR with a nonlinear kernels. The authors developed their own software based on the use of a ready-made implementation of SVR from the Python library [31]. We used two kernels:

- polynomial [Algorithm 1(polynomial)];
- and *rbf*-kernel [Algorithm 1(*rbf*)].

Among the optimal parameters of the method the following should be selected: the number of iterations of the training procedure for both implementations of the algorithm (with different kernels), as well as the degree of the polynomial for Algorithm 1 (polynomial). Other parameters of the method do not significantly affect the accuracy and speed of its work.

Let us select the optimal parameters of Algorithm 1 (polynomial) and Algorithm 1 (*rbf*) for both sets of medical data. Basic parameters of the method are: kernel coefficient *gamma* = "*scale*", independent term in kernel function *coef0 = 0.0*. The input data set is prenormalized using a function *StandartScaller* () from the Python library.

Figs. 6.3 and 6.4 show the change in regression metrics values for different numbers of iterations [500, 5000] for both implementations of the method under otherwise equal conditions for the second short set of medical data. It should be noted that the degree of the polynomial for Algorithm 1 (polynomial) in this experiment is set by default (equal to 3).

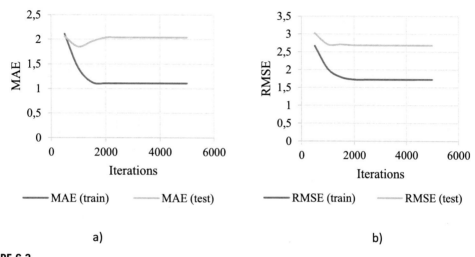

a)   b)

FIGURE 6.3

Regression metrics for different numbers of the iterations for Algorithm 1 (*rbf*): (A) MAE; (B) RMSE.

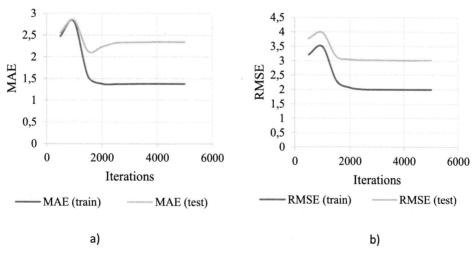

a)   b)

FIGURE 6.4

Regression metrics for different numbers of the iterations for Algorithm 1 (polynomial): (A) MAE; (B) RMSE.

Table 6.3 summarizes the results of experimental selection of the optimal value of the degree of the polynomial for Algorithm 1 (polynomial) under otherwise equal conditions.

In the case of processing the first set of medical data, the change in the number of iterations of the method did not significantly affect the value of regression metrics in Eqs. (6.7) and (6.8). In particular, the average value of RMSE and MAE in the test mode when changing the number of iterations from 500 to 500 was 4.11 and 3.56 for Algorithm 1 (polynomial); and 5.9 and 4.54 for Algorithm 1 (*rbf*), respectively. However, changing the polynomial degree from 2 to 6 for Algorithm 1 (polynomial) showed significant changes to the prediction accuracy of the method. Such dynamics for both modes of operation of this algorithmic implementation of the method are summarized in Table 6.4.

4.5 Algorithm 2: general regression neural network

The second algorithm of the universal intraensemble method is based on the general regression neural network. This nonlinear neural network provides efficient processing of short data sets. The authors have developed their own software in Python. A feature of this neural network is the actual absence of a training procedure. In addition, a neural network of this type requires the setting of only one parameter—the smooth factor (σ) [23].

We conducted experimental research on the selection of the optimal value of σ to ensure the highest accuracy of the universal intraensemble method. The experiment consisted of a complete search of values σ in the interval $\sigma \in [0.001, 10]$ with a step 0.001. The results of this experiment for both data sets are presented in Figs. 6.5 and 6.6, respectively.

Table 6.3 Performance indicators for different polynomial degree [Algorithm 1 (polynomial)] when handling the second data set.

Mode	Performance indicator title	Polynomial degree = 2	Polynomial degree = 3	Polynomial degree = 4	Polynomial degree = 5	Polynomial degree = 6
Training mode	Training time	0,314,159	0,446,804	0,451,751	065,824	0,831,776
	RMSE	2,734,631	199,635	2,052,394	1,934,205	2,009,342
	MAE	2,163,466	1,378,102	14,196	1,286,136	1,377,202
Test mode	RMSE	3,204,296	3,018,386	2,985,867	3,072,635	3,130,561
	MAE	255,376	2,346,974	2,484,168	2,437,382	2,589,195

Table 6.4 Performance indicators for different polynomial degree [Algorithm 1(polynomial)] when handling the first data set.

Mode	Performance indicator title	Polynomial degree = 2	Polynomial degree = 3	Polynomial degree = 4	Polynomial degree = 5	Polynomial degree = 6
Training mode	Training time	0,016,963	0,019,946	0,017,952	0,018,949	00,255
	RMSE	5,921,146	4,701,108	5,155,709	4,759,955	5,116,417
	MAE	4,682,827	3,938,528	3,989,654	3,858,347	3,973,738
Test mode	RMSE	6,240,367	5,896,869	5,841,411	5,929,349	5,866,395
	MAE	5,191,123	4,540,275	4,674,377	4,557,808	4,496,008

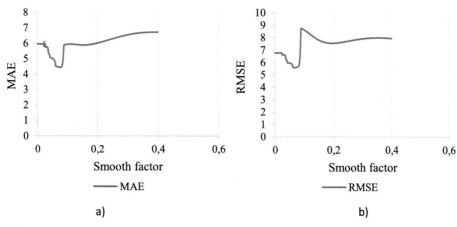

a)   b)

FIGURE 6.5

Regression metrics for different values of σ (σ∈ [0.001, 0.4]) for the first data set: (A) MAE; (B) RMSE.

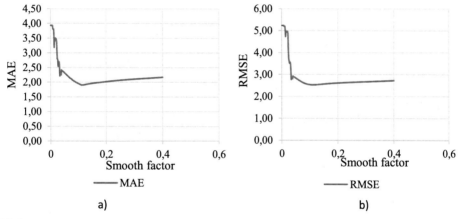

a)   b)

FIGURE 6.6

Regression metrics for different values of σ (σ∈ [0.001, 0.4]) for the second data set: (A) MAE; (B) RMSE.

It should be noted that Figs. 6.5. and 6.6 show the results for σ∈ [0.001, 0.4], because a further increase of this parameter did not reduce the values of regression matrix in Eqs. (6.7) and (6.8).

4.6 Algorithm 3: RBF neural network

The third algorithm of the universal intraensemble method is based on RBF neural networks. This type of neural network using *rbf* functions as activation functions and provides the ability to approximate the function with high accuracy. For the practical implementation of the algorithm, the authors have developed their own software in Python. Among the main parameters that are necessary for the effective operation of algorithmic implementation of the universal intraensemble method the following should be noted:

- the number of the centers of clusters;
- the number of iterations of the RBF neural network.

We conducted experimental studies on the selection of optimal values of these parameters that provide the highest accuracy of the method. In the case of this algorithmic implementation of the universal intraensemble, 10% of the observations of the training sample were randomly selected for the validation sample. It was the basis of optimal parameters selection for the proposed method using the MSE loss function.

The first experiment was performed to determine the optimal number of iterations for the effective operation of the method. The results of the loss function for both data samples when changing the number of iterations are presented in Fig. 6.7.

From the two graphs (Fig. 6.7) it can be seen that retraining is not observed. This is taking into account the quadratic increase of the training sample size and the processing of twice the number of input attributes. However, increasing the number of iterations during the operation of the method may cause overfitting, which will negatively affect the operation of the method as a whole.

The next experiment involved selecting the optimal number of clusters for the *k-nn* algorithm during data clustering. The experiment was performed at a smooth factor equal to 0.8 and 300 epochs, other things being equal. Because the choice of cluster centers is random during each method run, we used the process of running the method 100 times and determining the minimum, maximum, and average values based on the obtained data. Figs. 6.8 and 6.9 shows graphs of MAE and RMSE dependence when changing the number of cluster on the interval [15,100] for both data sets, respectively.

The next experiment involved determining the optimal value σ to ensure the highest accuracy of the RBF-based universal intraensemble method. To do this, a search of the values σ in the interval $\sigma \in [0.1, 1]$ has been performed. The results of this experiment for both data sets are presented in Figs. 6.10 and 6.11, respectively.

As can be seen from both figures, the best indicators of the prediction accuracy of this algorithm are obtained at values of σ that are in the range $\sigma \in [0.7, 0.9]$.

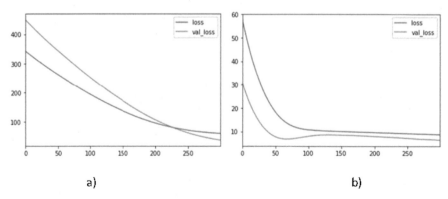

a)   b)

FIGURE 6.7

Dependency of MSE loss function (*oy*-axis) values on the number of iterations [1300]: (A) first data set; (B) second data set.

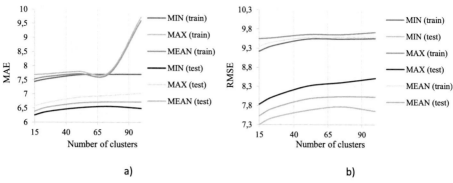

FIGURE 6.8

Dependency graphs showing how averaged (100 runs) minimum, maximum, and mean value of regression metrics depend on the number of *k-nn* algorithm clusters (averaged value for 100 runs) for the second small data set: (A) MAE; (B) RMSE.

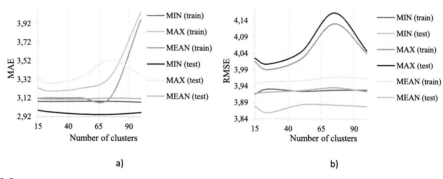

FIGURE 6.9

Dependency graphs showing how averaged (100 runs) minimum, maximum, and mean value of regression metrics depend on the number of *k-nn* algorithm clusters (averaged value for 100 runs) for the second small data set: (A) MAE; (B) RMSE.

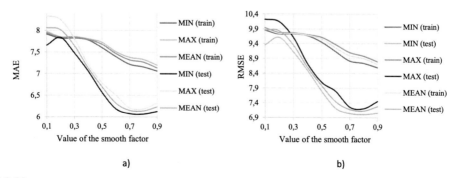

FIGURE 6.10

Dependency of averaged (10 runs) regression metrics (oy-axis) on the value $\sigma \in [0.1, 1]$ for the first data set: (A) MAE; (B) RMSE.

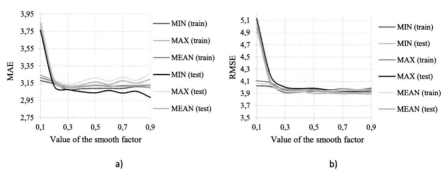

FIGURE 6.11

Dependency of averaged (10 runs) regression metrics (oy-axis) on the value $\sigma \in [0.1, 1]$ for the second data set: (A) MAE; (B) RMSE.

As a result of experimental research, the optimal operating parameters of all three algorithmic implementations of the universal intraensemble method were established, which provide the most effective results. It should be noted that further, during the comparison, the minimum values of errors of the last algorithmic implementation of the designed method in the application mode would be taken into account. This is due to the possibility of fixing the *rbf* centers, which will provide an unambiguous solution during the practical application of the designed method.

4.7 Results

Using the selected optimal parameters of each of the three algorithmic implementations of the universal intraensemble method, the prediction accuracy and the time of training (where appropriate) were obtained. These results are summarized in Tables 6.5 and 6.6 for the first and second medical data sets, respectively.

Table 6.5 Optimal parameters and performance indicators of the three algorithmic realizations of the universal intraensemble method for the first data set.

Algorithm	Basic parameters	Optimal additional parameters	MAE	RMSE	Training time (s)
Algorithm 1 (polynomial)	10 inputs, 1 output; gamma: "auto"; coef0: 0.0; Epsilon: 0.001; 80% training data set; 20% test data set	Polynomial degree: 6; 1500 epoch	Train mode: 3.974 | Test mode: 4.496	5.116 | 5.866	0.0255 | a
Algorithm 1 (*rbf*)	10 inputs, 1 output; gamma: "auto"; coef0: 0.0; Epsilon: 0.001; 80% training data set; 20% test data set	1500 epoch	Train mode: 2.671 | Test mode: 3.559	3.462 | 4.118	0.0179 | a

Table 6.5 Optimal parameters and performance indicators of the three algorithmic realizations of the universal intraensemble method for the first data set.—cont'd

Algorithm	Basic parameters	Optimal additional parameters	MAE	RMSE	Training time (s)
Algorithm 2	10 neurons in the input layer, 1 output; 80% preparation data set; 20% test data set	Smooth factor is 0.076;	Application mode: 5.614	4.439	a
Algorithm 3	10 neurons in the input layer, 1 output; *k-nn* clustering algorithm with 100 epoch; MSE loss function; 70% training data set, 10% validation data set; 20% test data set	300 epoch; smooth factor is 0.8; 25 clusters	Train mode: 7.157 Test mode: 6.064	8.739 7.005	13.906 a

Not applicable.

Table 6.6 Optimal parameters and performance indicators of the three algorithmic realizations of the universal intraensemble method for the second data set.

Algorithm	Basic parameters	Optimal additional parameters	MAE	RMSE	Training time (s)
Algorithm 1 (polynomial)	12 inputs, 1 output; gamma: "auto"; coef0: 0.0; Epsilon: 0.001; 80% training data set; 20% test data set	Polynomial degree: 3; 4000 epoch	Train mode: 1.377 Test mode: 2.341	1.996 3.016	0.601 a
Algorithm 1 (*rbf*)	12 inputs, 1 output; gamma: "auto"; coef0: 0.0; Epsilon: 0.001; 80% training data set; 20% test data set	5000 epoch	Train mode: 1.108 Test mode: 2.037	1.726 2.684	0.516 a
Algorithm 2	12 neurons in the input layer, 1 output; 80% preparation data set; 20% test data set	Smooth factor is 0.111;	Application mode: 2.512	1.865	a
Algorithm 3	12 neurons in the input layer, 1 output; *k-nn* clustering algorithm with 100 epoch; MSE loss function; 70% training data set, 10% validation data set; 20% test data set	300 epoch; smooth factor is 0.4; 25 clusters	Train mode: 3.085 Test mode: 3.049	3.936 3.943	23,31 a

Not applicable.

The values of the performance indicators for the three developed algorithms from Tables 6.5 and 6.6 were taken into account when comparing the efficiency of their work based on regression metrics and training time with parental methods.

5. Comparison and discussion

This section presents the results of comparing the work of the developed algorithmic implementations of the universal intraensemble method. The comparison of accuracy based on Eqs. (6.7) and (6.8) and speed of work of three algorithms of the designed method is carried out. In addition, a comparison of their effectiveness with nonlinear computational intelligence tools, which are the basis of the corresponding algorithmic implementations of the designed method, is carried out.

5.1 A comparative study of three different algorithms

Figs. 6.12 and 6.13 shows a comparison of the regression metrics in training and test modes for three developed algorithms using two different short medical data sets.

As can be seen from Figs. 6.12 and 6.13, the highest values of the prediction accuracy on both data sets are shown by Algorithm 1 with *rbf* kernel. In only one of the four cases, Algorithm 2 demonstrates less RMSE when processing a short data set. If we analyze the work of Algorithm 3,

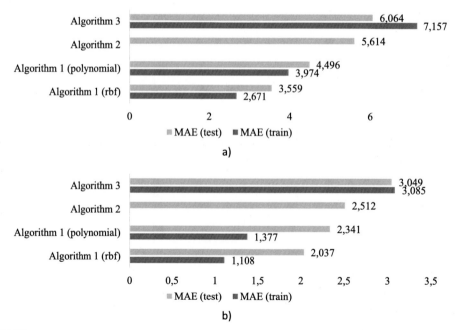

FIGURE 6.12

Comparison of the MAE values in the training and test modes for three developed algorithms: (A) for the first data set; (B) for the second data set.

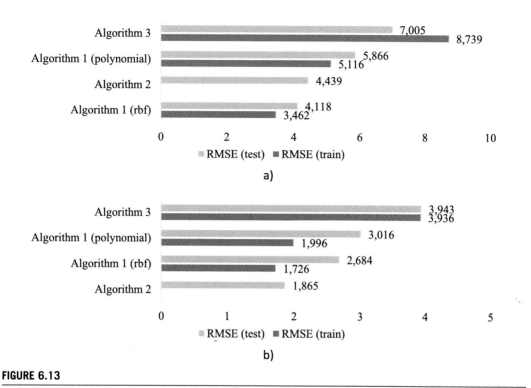

FIGURE 6.13

Comparison of the RMSE values in the training and test modes for the three algorithms developed: (A) for the first data set; (B) for the second data set.

then Figs. 6.12 and 6.13 clearly show a significant overcomplication of the model due to the increase in both the number of input attributes and the size of the training sample. Here there is an overfitting of the method, as evidenced by regression metrics in both modes of operation. In particular, for both data sets, the error of application of the algorithm is much smaller than the error of its training.

In addition, this method requires much more time to implement the training procedure compared to the other two algorithms. This is clearly seen in Fig. 6.14 for both data sets.

It should be noted that Fig. 6.14 does not show results for Algorithm 2, as it does not require a training procedure.

In view of all the above, Algorithm 1 (*rbf*) is recommended for practical application for solving prediction tasks based on the processing of short sets of medical data.

5.2 Comparison with parental regressors

Let us consider the results of comparing all three algorithmic implementations of the developed method with nonlinear computational intelligence tools, which are the basis of the corresponding algorithms of the universal intraensemble method. For this purpose, there is a comparison with SVR with nonlinear kernels (*rbf* and polynomial), GRNN, and classical RBF neural network.

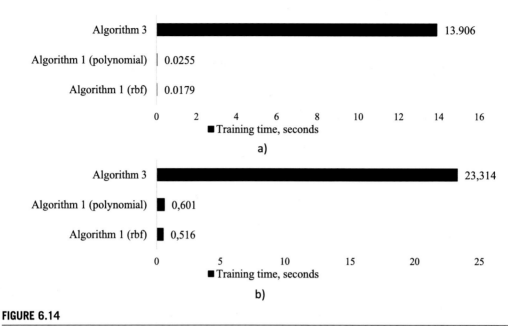

FIGURE 6.14

Training time (in seconds) for algorithms developed: (A) for the first data set; (B) for the second data set.

The main parameters of the parent methods are the same as in the algorithmic implementations of the method, developed on their basis (Tables 6.5 and 6.6). The only exceptions here were the other number of inputs (the initial number of inputs was taken for the parental methods) and the other dimension of the data sample (for the parental methods the initial size of the corresponding data set was used).

The results of such a study for both data sets are summarized in Tables 6.7 and 6.8. In addition, for the visual assessment of the results obtained in Appendix A, the obtained regression metrics and training time are summarized in the form of histograms for all studied methods.

Based on the results summarized in Tables 6.6 and 6.7, the following can be stated:

1. The developed universal intraensemble method based on the both nonlinear AI tools: machine learning methods and artificial neural networks, demonstrates high efficiency of solving regression tasks during processing of short data sets from different branches of medicine.
2. All three developed algorithmic implementations of the universal intraensemble method showed an accuracy increase based on both: MAE and RMSE in comparison with the parent regressors, which are the basis of each specific algorithmic implementation of the developed method.
3. All developed algorithms are characterized by a significant increase in the working time (training or preparation) due to the peculiarities of the developed universal intraensemble method. However, given the need to process short data sets, this shortcoming is not critical.
4. During the implementation of Algorithm 3, using both data sets, overcomplication of the model is observed, due to the procedure of quadratic increase of the dimension of the initial training data set and doubling the number of input features of each vector of the data set. This leads to

Table 6.7 Optimal parameters and performance indicators for all methods investigated based on the first data set.

Algorithm	MAE	RMSE	Training time (s)
Algorithm 1 (polynomial)	Train mode:		
	3.974	5.116	0.026
	Test mode:		
	4.496	5.866	a
Algorithm 1 (*rbf*)	Train mode:		
	2.671	3.462	0.018
	Test mode:		
	3.559	4.118	a
Algorithm 2	Application mode:		
	5.614	4.439	a
Algorithm 3	Train mode:		
	7.157	8.739	13.906
	Test mode:		
	6.064	7.005	a
Classical RBF neural network	Train mode:		
	7.762	9.039	9.669
	Test mode:		
	6.425	7.552	a
Classical GRNN	Application mode:		
	5.658	4.642	a
Classical SVR with *rbf* kernel	Train mode:		
	5.756	7.046	0.002
	Test mode:		
	6.056	7.352	a
Classical SVR with polynomial kernel	Train mode:		
	5.992	7.422	0.001
	Test mode:		
	6.256	7.511	a

[a]*Not applicable.*

overfitting of the model and eliminates its practical use in this form for solving real medical tasks. Avoiding such a situation requires the development of a support universal intraensemble method, in particular in the direction of improving the procedures for forming a training data set. This possibility exists and is described in the conclusion section.

5. Algorithm 1 (*rbf*) demonstrates the highest accuracy at the shortest training time. This allows its practical application in solving various tasks in the field of medicine, provided that it is necessary to process short data sets.

Table 6.8 Optimal parameters and performance indicators for all methods investigated based on the second data set.

Algorithm	MAE	RMSE	Training time (s)
Algorithm 1 (polynomial)	Train mode:		
	1.377	1.996	0.601
	Test mode:		
	2.341	3.016	a
Algorithm 1 (*rbf*)	Train mode:		
	1.108	1.726	0.516
	Test mode:		
	2.037	2.684	a
Algorithm 2	Application mode:		
	2.512	1.865	a
Algorithm 3	Train mode:		
	3.085	3.936	23,31
	Test mode:		
	3.049	3.943	a
Classical RBF neural network	Train mode:		
	3.063	3.863	9.669
	Test mode:		
	3.171	3.985	a
Classical GRNN	Application mode:		
	2.525	1.899	a
Classical SVR with *rbf* kernel	Train mode:		
	1.529	2.31	0.002
	Test mode:		
	2.162	2.949	a
Classical SVR with polynomial kernel	Train mode:		
	1.565	2.315	0.001
	Test mode:		
	2.437	3.228	a

*a*Not applicable.

In addition to the above, it should be noted that the developed universal intraensemble method in addition to solving regression tasks can be adapted to solve classification tasks in medicine and in many other areas [32,33] where there is a problem of a lack of historical data for effective intellectual analysis.

6. Conclusion and future work

This chapter proposes a new approach to the processing of short data sets. It is based on a combination of two existing approaches: numerical data augmentation and basic principles of ensemble learning. Its implementation is performed based on only one nonlinear computational intelligence tool. The effectiveness of this approach is determined by increasing the generalization properties of the method and, as a consequence, by increasing the accuracy of the output signal formation. This is ensured by increasing the dimensionality of the training sample and averaging the predicted results. The final issue is essentially an element of the theory of ensemble learning.

As a result, the authors have developed a new universal intraensemble method for processing short sets of medical data. Three of its algorithmic implementations using both machine learning methods and artificial neural networks are presented. The procedures of training (preparation) and application of each of the proposed algorithms are described.

Experimental modeling was performed using two short data sets from different fields of medicine. Procedures for operational parameters selection of each of the developed algorithms are given, and their optimal values are selected experimentally. The efficiency of all proposed algorithms is compared based on the regression metrics and training time. It is experimentally established that Algorithm 1 (*rbf*) provides the highest accuracy of work with the shortest duration of the training procedure. In addition, a comparison of the efficiency of the developed algorithms with the parent regressors has been conducted. It is experimentally established that the developed algorithms show an accuracy increase in comparison with nonlinear computational intelligence methods, which are the basis of each specific algorithmic implementation of the universal intraensemble method. In some cases, the error reduction is not very large. This is explained by the use of only one method of generating the output signals (Eq. 6.3) during the data set expansion procedure (step 2). That is why further work will be carried out in the following directions:

1. an approbation of the method's effectiveness using medical data sets of different volumes (small and medium) with the use of other nonlinear computational intelligence tools as the basis of new algorithmic implementations of the universal intraensemble method;
2. the design of an additive universal intraensemble method, which will take into account various options for generating output signals (Eq. 6.3) during the implementation of the procedure for expanding the data set (step 2) and as a consequence, changing Eq. (6.5) for formation of the output signal of the new method. This approach will provide partial mutual compensation of errors of different signs in the new equality, which will increase the accuracy of the method as whole;
3. the design of the support universal intraensemble method by reducing the dimensionality of the artificial data set based on Eq. (6.2) in the case of more than 100 initial observations in the medical data set. This approach is possible by choosing a certain multiplication of supportive observations (rather than the formation of all possible pairs, as provided by the developed method) and the formation of a new data set based on Eq. (6.2) only with their use;
4. the design of the weighted universal intraensemble method by replacing the summation procedure for $\sum_{u=1}^{N} z_{u,i}^{pred}$ from Eq. (6.5) with weighted summation with displacement based on the use of SGTM neural-like structure [17]. This approach, in the case of a large number of initial observations of initial short data set (over 100), will increase the accuracy of the method with a slight increase in the duration of the training procedure.

Appendix A

See Figs. A.1 to A.3.

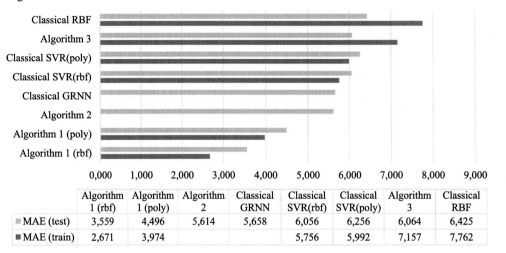

	Algorithm 1 (rbf)	Algorithm 1 (poly)	Algorithm 2	Classical GRNN	Classical SVR(rbf)	Classical SVR(poly)	Algorithm 3	Classical RBF
▪ MAE (test)	3,559	4,496	5,614	5,658	6,056	6,256	6,064	6,425
▪ MAE (train)	2,671	3,974			5,756	5,992	7,157	7,762

a)

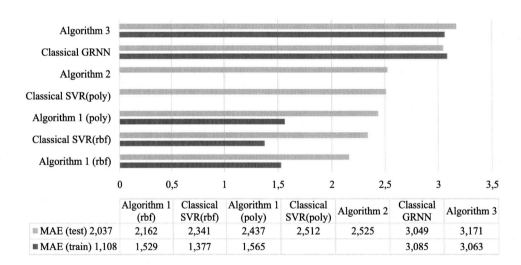

	Algorithm 1 (rbf)	Classical SVR(rbf)	Algorithm 1 (poly)	Classical SVR(poly)	Algorithm 2	Classical GRNN	Algorithm 3
▪ MAE (test)	2,037	2,162	2,341	2,437	2,512	2,525	3,049	3,171
▪ MAE (train)	1,108	1,529	1,377	1,565			3,085	3,063

b)

FIG. A.1

MAE values in training and test modes for all methods investigated: (A) for the first data set; (B) for the second data set.

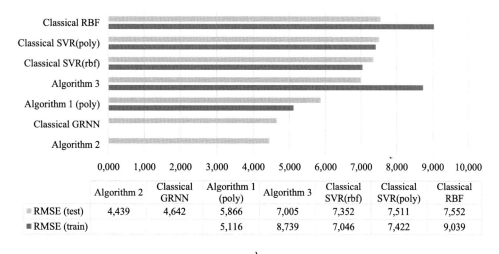

	Algorithm 2	Classical GRNN	Algorithm 1 (poly)	Algorithm 3	Classical SVR(rbf)	Classical SVR(poly)	Classical RBF
▨ RMSE (test)	4,439	4,642	5,866	7,005	7,352	7,511	7,552
▪ RMSE (train)			5,116	8,739	7,046	7,422	9,039

a)

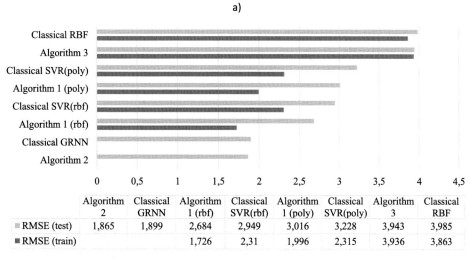

	Algorithm 2	Classical GRNN	Algorithm 1 (rbf)	Classical SVR(rbf)	Algorithm 1 (poly)	Classical SVR(poly)	Algorithm 3	Classical RBF
▨ RMSE (test)	1,865	1,899	2,684	2,949	3,016	3,228	3,943	3,985
▪ RMSE (train)			1,726	2,31	1,996	2,315	3,936	3,863

b)

FIG. A.2

RMSE values in training and test modes for all methods investigated: (A) for the first data set; (B) for the second data set.

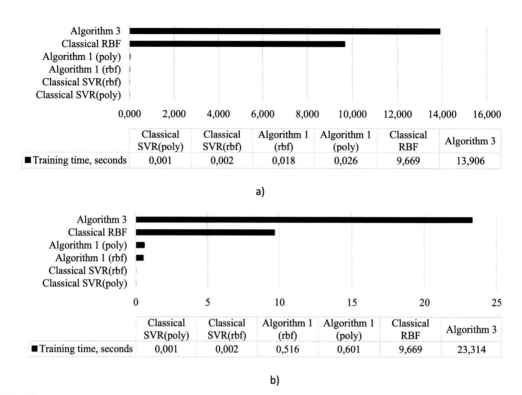

	Classical SVR(poly)	Classical SVR(rbf)	Algorithm 1 (rbf)	Algorithm 1 (poly)	Classical RBF	Algorithm 3
■ Training time, seconds	0,001	0,002	0,018	0,026	9,669	13,906

a)

	Classical SVR(poly)	Classical SVR(rbf)	Algorithm 1 (rbf)	Algorithm 1 (poly)	Classical RBF	Algorithm 3
■ Training time, seconds	0,001	0,002	0,516	0,601	9,669	23,314

b)

FIG. A.3

Training time (in seconds) for all methods investigated: (A) for the first data set; (B) for the second data set.

References

[1] R. Kitchin, T.P. Lauriault, Small data in the era of big data, GeoJournal 80 (2015) 463−475, https://doi.org/10.1007/s10708-014-9601-7.

[2] S. Fedushko, T. Ustyianovych, M. Gregus, Real-time high-load infrastructure transaction status output prediction using operational intelligence and big data technologies, Electronics 9 (2020) 668, https://doi.org/10.3390/electronics9040668.

[3] S. Fedushko, N. Shakhovska, Verifying the medical specialty from user profile of online community for health-related advices, in: Proceedings of the 1st International Workshop on Informatics & Data-Driven Medicine (IDDM 2018) Lviv, Ukraine, November 28−30, 2018, vol. 2255, n.d., pp. 301−310.

[4] N. Boyko, L. Mochurad, U. Parpan, O. Basystiuk, Usage of machine-based translation methods for analyzing open data in legal cases, in: Proceedings of the International Workshop on Cyber Hygiene (CybHyg-2019) Co-Located with 1st International Conference on Cyber Hygiene and Conflict Management in Global Information Networks (CyberConf 2019) Kyiv, Ukraine, November 30, 2019, vol. 2654, n.d., pp. 328−338.

[5] N. Boyko, L. Mochurad, I. Andrusiak, Y. Drevnytskyi, Organizational and legal aspects of managing the process of recognition of objects in the image, in: Proceedings of the International Workshop on Cyber Hygiene (CybHyg-2019) Co-Located with 1st International Conference on Cyber Hygiene and Conflict Management in Global Information Networks (CyberConf 2019) Kyiv, Ukraine, November 30, 2019, vol. 2654, 2019, pp. 571−592.

[6] S. Mishra, H.K. Tripathy, P.K. Mallick, A.K. Bhoi, P. Barsocchi, EAGA-MLP—an enhanced and adaptive hybrid classification model for diabetes diagnosis, Sensors 20 (2020) 4036, https://doi.org/10.3390/s20144036.

[7] E.B. Hekler, P. Klasnja, G. Chevance, N.M. Golaszewski, D. Lewis, I. Sim, Why we need a small data paradigm, BMC Med. 17 (2019) 133, https://doi.org/10.1186/s12916-019-1366-x.

[8] A.E. Deeb, What to Do with "Small" Data?, Rants on Machine Learning, 2015. https://medium.com/rants-on-machine-learning/what-to-do-with-small-data-d253254d1a89. (Accessed 6 April 2019).

[9] M.A. Lateh, A.K. Muda, Z.I.M. Yusof, N.A. Muda, M.S. Azmi, Handling a small dataset problem in prediction model by employ artificial data generation approach: a review, J. Phys. Conf. Ser. 892 (2017) 012016, https://doi.org/10.1088/1742-6596/892/1/012016.

[10] N. Melnykova, V. Melnykov, E. Vasilevskis, The personalized approach to the processing and analysis of patients' medical data, in: Proceedings of the 1st International Workshop on Informatics & Data-Driven Medicine (IDDM 2018) Lviv, Ukraine, November 28–30, 2018, vol. 2255, n.d., pp. 103–112.

[11] T. Shaikhina, N.A. Khovanova, Handling limited datasets with neural networks in medical applications: a small-data approach, Artif. Intell. Med. 75 (2017) 51–63, https://doi.org/10.1016/j.artmed.2016.12.003.

[12] M. Ali, P.I. Sholihah, K. Ahmed, Sri, P. Prabandari, Small Data and Big Data: Combination Make Better Decision, 2016. https://paper/Small-Data-and-Big-Data-%3A-Combination-make-better-Ali-Sholihah/b15e7f500734146c32f3e621b5cccd9a95df4d5d (Accessed 16 January, 2021).

[13] O. Ryabukha, I. Dronyuk, Applying Regression Analysis to Study the Interdependence of Thyroid, Adrenal Glands, Liver, and Body Weight in Hypothyroidism and Hyperthyroidism, vol. 2488, CEUR-WS.org, 2019, pp. 155–164.

[14] Data Analytics: A Small Data Approach, Routledge & CRC Press, n.d. https://www.routledge.com/Data-Analytics-A-Small-Data-Approach/Huang-Deng/p/book/9780367609504. (Accessed 17 January 2021).

[15] T.E. Lombardi, A.M. Holland-Minkley, Educators as clinicians: small data for education research, in: S.B. Fee, A.M. Holland-Minkley, T.E. Lombardi (Eds.), New Directions for Computing Education: Embedding Computing Across Disciplines, Springer International Publishing, Cham, 2017, pp. 277–293, https://doi.org/10.1007/978-3-319-54226-3_16.

[16] R.P. Mann, F. Mushtaq, A.D. White, G. Mata-Cervantes, T. Pike, D. Coker, S. Murdoch, T. Hiles, C. Smith, D. Berridge, S. Hinchliffe, G. Hall, S. Smye, R.M. Wilkie, J.P.A. Lodge, M. Mon-Williams, The problem with big data: operating on smaller datasets to bridge the implementation gap, Front. Public Health 4 (2016), https://doi.org/10.3389/fpubh.2016.00248.

[17] M. Thinyane, Investigating an architectural framework for small data platforms, in: Data for Societal Challenges-17th European Conference on Digital Government (ECDG 2017), n.d., pp. 220–227.

[18] L. Xu, M. Skoularidou, A. Cuesta-Infante, K. Veeramachaneni, Modeling Tabular Data Using Conditional GAN, 2019. https://arxiv.org/abs/1907.00503v2. (Accessed 26 December 2020).

[19] Y. Gao, Z. Cai, L. Yu, Intra-Ensemble in Neural Networks, 2019. https://arxiv.org/abs/1904.04466v2. (Accessed 2 January 2021).

[20] G. Battineni, N. Chintalapudi, F. Amenta, Machine learning in medicine: performance calculation of dementia prediction by support vector machines (SVM), Inform. Med. Unlocked 16 (2019) 100200, https://doi.org/10.1016/j.imu.2019.100200.

[21] Y. Bodyanskiy, A. Deineko, F. Brodetskyi, D. Kosmin, Adaptive Least-Squares Support Vector Machine and its Online Learning vol. 2762, CEUR-WS, 2020, pp. 58–72.

[22] I. Izonin, R. Tkachenko, M. Gregus, K. Zub, N. Lotoshunska, Input doubling method based on SVR with RBF kernel in clinical practice: focus on small data, Proc.Comput. Sci. 184 (2021) 606–613.

[23] I. Izonin, R. Tkachenko, V. Verhun, K. Zub, An approach towards missing data management using improved GRNN-SGTM ensemble method, Int. J. Eng. Sci. Technol. 24 (3) (2021) 749–759, https://doi.org/10.1016/j.jestch.2020.10.005.

[24] Y.V. Bodyanskiy, A.O. Deineko, Y.V. Kutsenko, On-line kernel clustering based on the general regression neural network and T. Kohonen's self-organizing map, Automat. Contr. Comput. Sci. 51 (2017) 55−62, https://doi.org/10.3103/S0146411617010023.

[25] I. Izonin, R. Tkachenko, M. Gregus ml, K. Zub, P. Tkachenko, A GRNN-based approach towards prediction from small datasets in medical application, Proc.Comput. Sci. 184 (2021) 242−249.

[26] C.S.K. Dash, A.K. Behera, S. Dehuri, S.B. Cho, Radial basis function neural networks: a topical state-of-the-art survey, Open Comput. Sci. 6 (2016) 33−63, https://doi.org/10.1515/comp-2016-0005.

[27] S. Subbotin, Radial-basis function neural network synthesis on the basis of decision tree, Opt. Mem. Neural Network. 29 (2020) 7−18, https://doi.org/10.3103/S1060992X20010051.

[28] I. Izonin, R. Tkachenko, S. Fedushko, D. Koziy, K. Zub, O. Vovk, RBF-based input doubling method for small medical data processing, in: Hu Z. (Ed.), Advances in Artificial Systems for Logistics Engineering. ICAILE2021: The First International Conference on Artificial Intelligence and Logistics Engineering 82, Springer, Cham, 2021, pp. 23−31 (in press).

[29] M. Pramanik, R. Pradhan, P. Nandy, A.K. Bhoi, P. Barsocchi, Machine learning methods with decision forests for Parkinson's detection, Appl. Sci. 11 (2021) 581, https://doi.org/10.3390/app11020581.

[30] R: Urine Analysis Data, n.d. https://vincentarelbundock.github.io/Rdatasets/doc/boot/urine.html. (Accessed 12 December 2020).

[31] sklearn.svm.SVR — scikit-learn 0.24.0 Documentation, n.d. https://scikit-learn.org/stable/modules/generated/sklearn.svm.SVR.html. (Accessed 8 January 2021).

[32] N. Chukhrai, O. Grytsai, Diagnosing the efficiency of cost management of innovative processes at machine-building enterprises, Actual Probl. Econ. 146 (2013) 75−80.

[33] N. Chukhrai, Z. Koval, Essence and classification of assessment methods for marketing strategies' efficiency of cost-oriented enterprises, Actual Probl. Econ. 145 (2013) 118−129.

Comparisons among different stochastic selections of activation layers for convolutional neural networks for health care

Loris Nanni[1], Alessandra Lumini[2], Stefano Ghidoni[1] and Gianluca Maguolo[1]

[1]*DEI, University of Padua, Padua, Italy;* [2]*DISI, Università di Bologna, Cesena, Italy*

1. Introduction

Deep learning has received increased attention in recent years because it was able to set new levels of performance in a variety of fields such as image processing and natural language processing [1]. Like other neural networks, deep networks make use of nonlinear activation functions (e.g., tanh, ReLU) that have a strong influence on the performance that can be achieved as they provide the network the ability to approximate an arbitrarily complex function.

Given the effect on the network performance, in this chapter, we compare a large number of activation functions used in convolutional neural networks (CNNs) for image classification tasks on multiple and diverse data sets. Our backbone network is ResNet50 [3], and we modify it by changing its original activation functions with others proposed in the literature. This process returns a large number of different networks that we use to create ensembles of CNNs.

At first, we introduce the activation functions that we shall substitute in the original network. At that point, we introduce our approach to randomly substitute all the activations in the original network. We substitute them with new ones chosen among those that we introduced earlier. The key idea is that the selection of the activations is independent in every layer. Hence, this procedure always yields a different network, thereby providing a large number of partially independent classifiers. The classifiers can be fused together to create an ensemble of CNNs. Ensembles of classifiers have been proven to be more effective than stand-alone CNNs due to the instability of their training [4]; hence, our methods boost the performance of single CNNs.

We evaluate our approach on several medical data sets following our protocol that includes a fine-tuning of each model considered on each data set. Medical images are a good test for CNNs because they show a variety of low- and mid-level patterns of different dimensions [5]. CNNs have already been demonstrated to be effective in analyzing images in a variety of applications like carcinoma and melanoma detection [6], classification of subcellular and stem cell images [7], thyroid nodules classification [8], and breast cancer detection [9].

Cognitive and Soft Computing Techniques for the Analysis of Healthcare Data. https://doi.org/10.1016/B978-0-323-85751-2.00003-7

Our experiments show that the proposed ensembles work well in all the tested problems gaining state-of-the-art classification performance [10].

The code developed for this work will be available at https://github.com/LorisNanni.

2. Literature review

Deep learning started a new era in several fields, including pattern recognition, object detection, and many others in computer vision [11]. Convolutional neural networks (CNNs) are widely used for processing images, thanks to their convolutional layers that process an image considering the local neighborhood. The layered approach [12] has proven to be very effective in analyzing the low- and mid-level patterns in image processing. Researchers gradually increased the number of layers, as this was able to improve the representation learned by the models and to increase the performance in several domains. However, this came at the expense of requiring very large data sets and an increased risk of overfitting, which further pushed toward a large use of data augmentation, regularization techniques, and more effective activation functions.

The role of activation functions is sometimes underestimated, but it is central to gain high performance, as it introduces a strong nonlinear component. This is a topic that has been attracting the attention of several researchers [13,14]. One of the main advances was the introduction of the rectified linear unit (ReLU) [15], a piecewise linear function that substituted the sigmoid function because it is extremely fast to compute and offers very good performance. Building on this success, a family of activation functions based on ReLU was developed: (1) leaky ReLU [16], that shows a small slope (α) for negative inputs; (2) ELU (exponential linear unit) [14], showing an exponential decrease to a limit point α in the negative domain; (3) SELU (scaled exponential linear unit) [17], a scaled version of ELU by a constant λ; and (4) RLReLU (randomized leaky ReLU) [18], based on a nonlinear random coefficient.

The functions (1)−(4) mentioned above are static, because they depend on a set of parameters that are chosen and kept constant throughout the whole training process. A more advanced activation function design is capable of adjusting the parameter set at training time, thus adapting the activation function to the training data, making the function dynamic. Dynamic functions usually train a different set of parameters for each layer or, in some cases, for each neuron. This, however, increases the number of learnable parameters, which can increase overfitting. Activation functions belonging to this second group are: (5) PReLU (parametric ReLU) [19], a parametric version of ReLU similar to Leaky ReLU for which the parameter α is not static but, rather, learned; (6) APLU (adaptive piecewise linear unit) [13], that is a piecewise function determined by a set of parameters that are learned separately for each neuron at training time; (7) trained activation function [20], whose shape is learned by means of a linear regression model—two variants are proposed in Ref. [21]: linear sigmoidal activation and adaptive linear sigmoidal activation. According to Ref. [22], two of the best performing functions are (8) swish, a sigmoid function based on a trainable parameter, and (9) Mexican ReLU (MeLU) [23], a piecewise linear activation function obtained by summing PReLU and a number of Mexican hat functions.

In this work, we consider mixtures of static and dynamic activation functions, with the aim of combining the advantages of both, thereby mitigating their weak points.

3. Activation functions

In this chapter we consider several different activations. We now briefly introduce them. Many of these activations depend on a hyperparameter called *maxInput*, which is used to normalize the activation depending on whether the input is in [0,1] or [0,255].

The first activation is ReLU [15], which is defined as:

$$y_i = f(x_i) = \begin{cases} 0, & x_i < 0 \\ x_i, & x_i \geq 0 \end{cases} \tag{7.1}$$

and its derivative is given by:

$$\frac{dy_i}{dx_i} = f'(x_i) = \begin{cases} 0, & x_i < 0 \\ 1, & x_i \geq 0 \end{cases} \tag{7.2}$$

Many variants of ReLU have been proposed in the literature. The first that we consider is leaky ReLU [16], which is defined as:

$$y_i = f(x_i) = \begin{cases} ax_i, & x_i < 0 \\ x_i, & x_i \geq 0 \end{cases} \tag{7.3}$$

where the a is a small and positive number (0.01 in this work). The main strength of leaky ReLU is that its derivative is always positive:

$$\frac{dy_i}{dx_i} = f'(x_i) = \begin{cases} a, & x_i < 0 \\ 1, & x_i \geq 0 \end{cases} \tag{7.4}$$

The second variant of ReLU that we consider is exponential linear unit (ELU) [14], which is defined as:

$$y_i = f(x_i) = \begin{cases} a(\exp x_i - 1), & x_i < 0 \\ x_i, & x_i \geq 0 \end{cases} \tag{7.5}$$

where a is a positive number (1 in this study). ELU has also a positive gradient and is also continuous:

$$\frac{dy_i}{dx_i} = f'(x_i) = \begin{cases} a \exp(x_i), & x_i < 0 \\ 1, & x_i \geq 0 \end{cases} \tag{7.6}$$

Parametric ReLU (PReLU) [24] is a learnable variant of leaky ReLU. It is defined by:

$$y_i = f(x_i) = \begin{cases} a_c x_i, & x_i < 0 \\ x_i, & x_i \geq 0 \end{cases} \tag{7.7}$$

where a_c are different real numbers, one for each input channel. PReLU is similar to leaky ReLU, the only difference being that the a_c parameters are learnable. The gradients of PReLU are:

$$\frac{dy_i}{dx_i} = f'(x_i) = \begin{cases} a_c, & x_i < 0 \\ 1, & x_i \geq 0 \end{cases} \quad \text{and} \quad \frac{dy_i}{da_c} = \begin{cases} x_i, & x_i < 0 \\ 0, & x_i \geq 0 \end{cases} \tag{7.8}$$

S-shaped ReLU (SReLU) [25] is the fourth variant or ReLU that we include in this study. It is defined as a piecewise linear function:

$$y_i = f(x_i) = \begin{cases} t^l + a^l(x_i - t^l), & x_i < t^l \\ x_i, & t^l \le x_i \le t^r \\ t^r + a^r(x_i - t^r), & x_i > t^r \end{cases} \tag{7.9}$$

SReLU depends on four sets of learnable parameters: t^l, t^r, a^l, and a^r. In this chapter, they are initialized to $a^l = 0$, $t^l = 0$, $a^r = 1$, $t^r = $ maxInput. Hence, its initialization makes it equal to ReLU in the first training step. The gradients are given by:

$$\frac{dy_i}{dx_i} = f'(x_i) = \begin{cases} a^l, & x_i < t^l \\ 1, & t^l \le x_i \le t^r \\ a^r, & x_i > t^r \end{cases} \tag{7.10}$$

$$\frac{dy_i}{da^l} = \begin{cases} x_i - t^l, & x_i < t^l \\ 0, & x_i \ge t^l \end{cases}, \text{ and} \tag{7.11}$$

$$\frac{dy_i}{dt^l} = \begin{cases} 1 - a^l, & x_i < t^l \\ 0, & x_i \ge t^l \end{cases} \tag{7.12}$$

Adaptive piecewise linear unit (APLU) [13] is a piecewise linear function whose slopes and points of nondifferentiability are learnable. It is defined as:

$$y_i = \text{ReLU}(x_i) + \sum_{c=1}^{n} a_c \max(0, -x_i + b_c) \tag{7.13}$$

where n is a hyperparameter defining the number of hinges; a_c and b_c are real numbers, one for each input channel. Its gradients are:

$$\frac{df(x, a)}{da_c} = \begin{cases} -x + b_c, & x < b_c \\ 0, & x \ge b_c \end{cases} \text{ and } \frac{df(x, a)}{db_c} = \begin{cases} -a_c, & x < b_c \\ 0, & x \ge b_c \end{cases} \tag{7.14}$$

We initialized the parameters a_c to zero, and the points of nondifferentiability are randomly selected. We also added an L^2-penalty of 0.001 to the norm of the parameters a_c, as suggested by its creators.

Mexican ReLU (MeLU) [23] is a variant of ReLU derived from the Mexican hat functions. These functions are defined as:

$$\phi^{a, \lambda}(x) = \max(\lambda \cdot \text{maxInput} - |x - a \cdot \text{maxInput}|, 0) \tag{7.15}$$

where a and λ are real numbers. The output of MeLU is defined as:

$$y_i = \text{MeLU}(x_i) = \text{PReLU}^{c_0}(x_i) + \sum_{j=1}^{k-1} c_j \, \phi^{\alpha_j, \lambda_j}(x_i) \tag{7.16}$$

MeLU is the weighted sum of PReLU and $k - 1$ Mexican hat functions. The weights in PReLU and of those that multiply the Mexican functions are the learnable parameters. α_j and λ_j are fixed parameters chosen recursively. We refer to the original paper for a more detailed explanation of how they are chosen. MeLU is continuous and piecewise differentiable. Besides, MeLU generalizes ReLU in the sense that when all the c_i parameters are set to zero, the two functions coincide. This is a useful property because MeLU can be substituted in any ReLU network allowing an efficient transfer learning, if it is properly initialized.

The gradient of MeLU is simply the weighted sum of the gradients of PReLU and those of the Mexican hat functions.

In this work, we used two values of k. In our experiments, we call MeLU the implementation where $k = 4$, and wMeLU is the implementation where $k = 8$, where wMeLU stands for wider MeLU.

Gaussian ReLU, also called GaLU [26], is an activation function based on the so-called Gaussian-like functions:

$$
\begin{aligned}
\phi_g^{a,\,\lambda}(x) = {} & \max(\lambda \cdot \text{maxInput} - |x - a \cdot \text{maxInput}|, 0) \\
& + \min(|x - a \cdot \text{maxInput} - 2\lambda \cdot \text{maxInput}| - \lambda \cdot \text{maxInput}, 0) \\
& + \min(|x - a \cdot \textit{maxInput} - 2\lambda \cdot \textit{maxInput}| - \lambda \cdot \textit{maxInput}, 0)
\end{aligned}
\tag{7.19}
$$

where a and λ are real numbers. GaLU is defined as:

$$
y_i = \text{GaLU}(x_i) = \text{PReLU}^{c_0}(x_i) + \sum_{j=1}^{k-1} c_j \, \phi_g^{a_j,\,\lambda_j}(x_i)
\tag{7.20}
$$

which is the homologous of MeLU for Gaussian-type functions. In the experiments we call GaLU the implementation with $k = 4$ and sGaLU (for smaller GaLU) the one with $k = 2$.

Parametric deformable exponential linear unit (PDELU) was introduced in [40] and is defined as:

$$
y_i = f(x_i) =
\begin{cases}
x_i, & x_i > 0 \\
a_i \cdot \left([1 + (1 - t)x_i]_+^{\frac{1}{1-t}} - 1 \right), & x_i \leq 0
\end{cases}
$$

It has zero mean and, according to its creators, this speeds up the training process.

Swish is an activation function introduced in Ref. [22]. Its creators used reinforcement learning to assemble different basis functions using sum, multiplication, and composition. The output of this learning was a smooth and nonmonotonic function defined as:

$$
y = f(x) = x \cdot \text{sigmoid}(\beta x) = \frac{x}{1 + e^{-\beta x}}
$$

where β is a parameter that can optionally be learnable. In our tests, we initialize it to 1.

Mish is an activation function introduced in Ref. [27]. It is defined as

$$
y = f(x) = x \cdot \tanh(\text{softplus}(\alpha x)) = x \cdot \tanh(\ln(1 + e^{\alpha x}))
$$

where α is a learnable parameter.

Soft root sign (SRS) is an activation introduced in Ref. [28]. It is defined as:

$$y = f(x) = \frac{x}{\dfrac{x}{\alpha} + e^{-\frac{x}{\beta}}}$$

where α and β are learnable and nonnegative parameters. SRS is neither monotone nor positive. If the distribution of the input is a standard normal, its shape allows it to have zero mean, which again should enable faster training.

Soft learnable is a new activation function proposed in Ref. [28], which is defined as:

$$y = f(x) = \begin{cases} x, & x > 0 \\ \alpha \cdot \ln\left(\dfrac{1 + e^{\beta x}}{2}\right), & x \leq 0 \end{cases}$$

where α, β are positive parameters. We used two different versions of this activation, depending on whether the parameter β is fixed (SoftLearnable) or learnable (SoftLearnable2).

In order to avoid any overfitting to the data, we used the same parameter setting that the original authors of each activation suggest in their papers.

4. Materials and methods

In this section, we detail the data sets used for performing experimental evaluation, the backbone architectures, and the stochastic methods proposed to design new CNN models and the ensembles.

Experimental evaluation is carried out for medical image classification, performing experiments on several well-known medical data sets which are summarized in Table 7.1. For each data set the following information is included: data set name and reference, a short abbreviation, the number of samples and classes, the size of the images and the testing protocol, which is fivefold cross-validation (5CV) in almost all cases except when expressly specified by the authors of the data set (tenfold cross-validation (10CV) for CO and a threefold division for the LAR [33]). Even if data sets include images of different size and aspect ratios, all the images have been resized to the fixed squared size of 224 × 224 required from the input size of the most known CNN model.

Performance evaluation and comparison among all the proposed models and ensembles is performed according to image classification accuracy, that is, the rate of correct classifications; moreover, the superiority of a method over another is validated according to the Wilcoxon signed rank test [39].

The methods for pattern classification are ensembles composed of CNN models stochastically designed from a starting architecture by replacing the activation layers. In this section, we describe how we derive ensembles of new CNNs starting from a base architecture—this is selected among the best-performing general-purpose networks for image classification, like AlexNet [29], GoogleNet [30], VGGNet [31], ResNet [3], and DenseNet [32].

Starting from the above-cited base architectures, several stochastic ensembles are created by the fusion of N stochastic models obtained using the pseudo-code reported in Fig. 7.1. GenStochasticModel takes as input a CNN base model (IM), and a set of activation functions (AS). It returns a new model obtained by randomly replacing all the activation layers of the input model IM with activation

Table 7.1 Summary of the medical image data sets used for image classification: short same (ShortN), name, number of classes (#C), number of samples (#S), image size, testing protocol, reference.

ShortN	Name	#C	#S	Image size	Protocol	Ref
CH	Chinese hamster ovary cells	5	327	512×382	5CV	[34]
HE	2D HELA	10	862	512×382	5CV	[34]
LO	Locate endogenous	10	502	768×512	5CV	[35]
TR	Locate transfected	11	553	768×512	5CV	[35]
RN	Fly cell	10	200	1024×1024	5CV	[36]
TB	Terminal bulb aging	7	970	768×512	5CV	[36]
LY	Lymphoma	3	375	1388×1040	5CV	[36]
MA	Muscle aging	4	237	1600×1200	5CV	[36]
LG	Liver gender	2	265	1388×1040	5CV	[36]
LA	Liver aging	4	529	1388×1040	5CV	[36]
CO	Human colorectal cancer	8	5000	150×150	10CV	[37]
BGR	Breast grading carcinoma	3	300	1280×960	5CV	[38]
LAR	Laryngeal dataset	4	1320	1280×960	Tr-Te	[33]

```
Function GenStochasticModel
Input:
  Base model: IM
  Set of activation functions AS
Output:
  Output model: OM
Algorithm:
  Let L be the set of layers of IM
  For each activation l∈ L
        Randomly draw an activation function l' from AS
        Replace l with l'
End
```

FIGURE 7.1

Pseudo code of the algorithm for the creation of a stand-alone stochastic model.

layers randomly drawn from AS. For the ensemble creation, first all the N stochastic models are fine-tuned on the training set, then they are fused together in an ensemble using the sum rule, that is, by summing the outputs of their last softmax layer. The final decision is obtained by applying an argmax function.

In this work, we have selected as the "backbone" network ResNet50 [3], which is composed of 50 layers and is one of the most widely used architectures for image classification. The reported experiments could also be replicated for different architectures. The original ResNet50 architecture, which contains ReLu layers to be substituted by different activation functions, is coupled with three different sets of activation functions to be used as input in the GenStochasticModel procedure. The first set, denoted as OldAS, includes the nine activation functions proposed in Ref. [26]: MeLU(k = 8), leakyReLU, ELU, MeLU(k = 4), PReLU, SReLU, APLU, GaLU, and sGaLU. The second set, denoted as FullAS, includes the whole set of activation functions described in Section 3, i.e., the same nine functions of OldAS and a further set of seven activation functions: ReLU, SoftLearnable, PDeLU, learnableMish, SRS, SwishLearnable, and Swish. Finally, in order to evaluate the effectiveness of the new proposed activation functions, a third set is built, named BaseAS, excluding from FullAS all the activation functions proposed by the authors of this chapter; this last set is a baseline for our work and includes the following 11 functions: leakyReLU, ELU, PReLU, SReLU, APLU, ReLU, PDeLU, learnableMish, SRS, SwishLearnable, and Swish.

The fine tuning of the stochastic CNN models to each image classification problem has been performed according to the following training option: batch size 30, max epoch 30, learning rate 0.0001 (for all the networks, no freezing); data augmentation includes image reflections on the two axes and random rescaling using a factor uniformly sampled in the range [1,2].

5. Results

In this section, we compare the classification performance of the stochastic ensembles proposed in the previous section with several stand-alone CNNs and ensembles of classifiers. The first experiment is aimed at comparing the different activation functions presented in Section 3 and the stochastic method for the design of a new model. In Table 7.2, we compare all the variants of the ResNet50 architecture obtained by deterministically substituting each activation layer by one of the activation functions described in Section 3 (the same function for all the networks): such CNNs are denoted with the name of the activation function. Some activation functions depend on the training parameter *maxInput*, which has been set to 1e or 255 (as reported in parentheses). Moreover the last rows in Table 7.2 report the performance of some stochastic models obtained by the calling the GenStochasticModel method with ResNet50 and the three different activation sets detailed in Section 4: the resulting models (they are stand-alone methods) are denoted as SOldAs, SFullAS, and SBaseAS, respectively.

In the second experiment, reported in Table 7.3, we compare the performance of several ensembles obtained by the fusion of the previous approaches:

- *FusOldAS10/FusOldAS10(255)* are the fusion by the sum rule of the above models whose activation function belongs to the set OldAS; as denoted by their name, such ensembles are made of 10 classifiers.
- *FusFullAS16(255)* is the fusion by the sum rule of the 16 above models whose activation function belongs to the set FullAS.
- *Sto<setName><K>(maxInput)* denotes the ensembles of stochastic models, that is, *StoOldAS10* and *StoOldAS10(255)*; they are ensembles obtained by the fusion of K=10 SOldAS stochastic models; we test ensembles composed of 5, 10, and 15 stochastic models in order to study the dependence of the performance on the number models.

Table 7.2 Performance of the several ResNet50 variants in the medical image data sets (accuracy): the last two columns report the average accuracy (Avg) and the rank (evaluated on Avg).

Method	Data set													Avg	Rank
	CH	HE	LO	TR	RN	TB	LY	MA	LG	LA	CO	BG	LAR		
ReLU	93.5	89.9	95.6	90.0	55.0	58.5	77.9	90.0	93.0	85.1	94.9	88.7	87.1	84.55	6
leakyReLU	89.2	87.1	92.8	84.2	34.0	57.1	70.9	79.2	93.7	82.5	95.7	90.3	87.3	80.30	22
ELU	90.2	86.7	94.0	85.8	48.0	60.8	65.3	85.0	96.0	90.1	95.1	89.3	89.9	82.80	20
SReLU	91.4	85.6	92.6	83.3	30.0	55.9	69.3	75.0	88.0	82.1	95.7	89.0	89.5	79.02	24
APLU	92.3	87.1	93.2	80.9	25.0	54.1	67.2	76.7	93.0	82.7	95.5	90.3	88.9	78.99	25
GaLU	92.9	88.4	92.2	90.4	41.5	57.8	73.6	89.2	92.7	88.8	94.9	90.3	90.0	83.28	17
sGaLU	92.3	87.9	93.2	91.1	52.0	60.0	72.5	90.0	95.3	87.4	95.4	87.7	88.8	84.13	8
PReLU	92.0	85.4	91.4	81.6	33.5	57.1	68.8	76.3	88.3	82.1	95.7	88.7	89.6	79.26	23
MeLU	91.1	85.4	92.8	84.9	27.5	55.4	68.5	77.1	90.0	79.4	95.3	89.3	87.2	78.76	27
wMeLU	92.9	86.4	91.8	82.9	25.5	56.3	67.5	76.3	91.0	82.5	94.8	89.7	88.8	78.95	26
softLearnable2	93.9	87.3	93.6	92.5	46.0	60.3	69.0	89.5	94.6	86.1	95.0	89.6	87.0	83.41	15
softLearnable	94.1	87.4	93.4	90.3	47.0	59.1	67.7	88.3	95.0	85.5	95.5	89.3	88.2	83.13	19
pdeluLayer	94.1	87.2	92.0	91.6	51.5	56.7	70.9	89.5	96.3	86.6	95.0	89.6	88.1	83.77	12
learnableMishLayer	95.0	87.5	93.2	91.8	45.0	58.4	69.0	86.6	95.3	86.6	95.4	90.0	88.4	83.24	18
SRSLayer	93.2	88.8	93.4	91.0	51.5	60.1	69.8	88.7	95.0	86.4	95.7	88.3	89.4	83.94	10
swishLearnable	93.5	87.9	94.4	91.6	48.0	59.2	69.3	88.7	95.3	83.2	96.1	90.0	89.3	83.57	14
swishLayer	94.1	88.0	94.2	90.7	48.5	59.9	70.1	89.1	92.6	86.1	95.6	87.6	87.6	83.39	16
SReLU(255)	92.3	89.4	93.0	90.7	56.5	59.7	73.3	91.7	98.3	89.0	95.5	89.7	87.9	85.15	4
APLU(255)	95.1	89.2	93.6	90.7	47.5	56.9	75.2	89.2	97.3	87.1	95.7	89.7	89.5	84.35	7
GaLU(255)	92.9	87.2	92.0	91.3	47.5	60.1	74.1	87.9	96.0	86.9	95.6	89.3	87.7	83.73	13
sGaLU(255)	93.5	87.8	95.6	89.8	55.0	63.1	76.0	90.4	95.0	85.3	95.1	89.7	89.8	85.09	5
MeLU(255)	92.9	90.2	95.0	91.8	57.0	59.8	78.4	87.5	97.3	85.1	95.7	89.3	88.3	85.26	2
wMeLU(255)	94.5	89.3	94.2	92.2	54.0	61.9	75.7	89.2	97.0	88.6	95.6	87.7	88.7	85.27	1
SOIdAS	90.2	90.0	94.2	91.6	54.5	62.0	77.3	90.8	95.7	90.5	95.1	89.0	87.1	85.23	3
SOIdAS(255)	93.2	88.5	94.4	91.6	51.5	59.1	73.9	88.3	94.0	89.1	95.1	86.7	88.0	84.11	9
SFullAS(255)	94.1	87.2	93.0	87.3	54.5	60.1	72.3	89.2	94.7	83.6	94.6	89.0	89.9	83.80	11
SBaseAS	92.6	88.0	92.4	93.1	55.5	56.8	71.7	80.4	86.7	87.2	94.6	87.0	88.5	82.65	21

Table 7.3 Performance of the proposed ensembles in the medical image data sets (accuracy); the last two columns report the average accuracy (Avg) and the rank (evaluated on Avg).

Method	Dataset													Avg	Rank
	CH	HE	LO	TR	RN	TB	LY	MA	LG	LA	CO	BG	LAR		
FusOldAS10	93.5	90.7	97.2	92.7	56.0	63.9	77.6	90.8	96.3	91.4	96.4	90.0	90.0	86.67	20
FusOldAS10(255)	95.1	91.3	96.2	94.2	63.0	64.9	78.7	92.5	97.7	87.6	96.5	89.7	89.8	87.46	13
FusFullAS16(255)	97.2	91.3	97.4	95.5	60.0	64.5	76.0	94.2	98.3	89.1	96.8	90.0	90.3	87.74	12
StoOldAS10	95.4	91.3	95.8	95.1	63.0	64.2	78.9	93.8	98.7	91.1	96.5	90.3	90.2	88.02	10
StoOldAS(255)	96.6	90.8	97.0	96.0	55.5	65.1	78.1	92.1	98.3	90.1	96.3	88.7	90.0	87.27	14
StoOldAS10(255)	96.9	91.2	96.8	96.2	58.5	66.6	79.7	92.5	98.3	91.6	96.6	89.7	91.1	88.13	9
StoOldAS15(255)	97.8	91.5	96.6	95.8	60.0	65.8	80.0	92.9	99.0	91.2	96.6	90.7	91.0	88.37	8
StoFullAS5(255)	98.1	92.3	96.6	95.5	64.0	64.6	83.2	93.8	99.0	92.6	96.6	91.3	92.1	89.20	6
StoFullAS10(255)	98.8	92.9	97.6	95.8	66.5	65.7	84.3	93.7	99.3	94.1	96.8	90.3	92.3	89.85	4
StoFullAS15(255)	98.8	93.4	97.8	96.4	65.5	66.9	85.6	92.9	99.7	94.3	96.6	91.3	92.3	90.11	2
StoBaseAS5(255)	99.4	91.0	97.6	95.6	61.5	64.1	80.0	88.3	94.7	91.8	96.5	90.3	90.4	87.78	11
StoBaseAS10(255)	99.4	93.5	97.8	95.6	65.5	65.8	81.3	89.6	96.3	94.9	96.7	91.0	90.8	89.09	7
StoBaseAS15(255)	99.4	93.9	98.0	96.0	64.5	66.4	83.2	90.0	96.0	93.9	96.7	92.0	91.3	89.33	5
StoBaseAS8(255) + StoFullAS7(255)	99.4	93.8	98.0	96.0	67.5	66.3	83.5	92.1	98.0	95.1	96.7	91.7	91.7	89.98	3
StoBaseAS15(255) + StoFullAS15(255)	99.4	93.8	98.0	96.5	67.5	67.0	85.9	91.2	98.7	94.9	96.9	92.0	92.3	90.31	1
FusOldAS3(255)	93.9	91.5	94.8	93.1	58.5	63.5	77.6	91.3	98.3	88.0	96.3	89.0	89.4	86.55	21
StoOldAS3(255)	96.3	90.9	95.6	95.1	54.0	62.9	78.7	92.5	98.7	90.9	96.2	90.0	90.5	87.10	16
FusRelu5	95.0	90.5	96.2	94.7	56.0	63.7	77.1	94.1	95.6	89.1	96.4	89.0	89.5	86.68	19
FusRelu10	94.5	91.6	95.8	94.5	56.5	64.5	76.0	93.3	97.7	89.1	96.6	89.6	90.2	86.91	17
FusRelu15	95.4	91.1	96.2	95.1	58.5	64.8	76.0	92.9	97.3	89.3	96.3	90.0	90.4	87.17	15
FusRelu30	95.4	91.5	96.2	94.7	59.0	63.9	75.7	92.5	97.3	88.2	96.4	89.0	90.1	86.91	18

- *FusReLu<K>* denotes the ensembles of K standard ResNet50 models (with ReLu activation functions): it is used to demonstrate the usefulness of stochastic selection of the activation functions, which increases the diversity in the creation of ensembles.
- *FusOldAS3* and *StoOLDAS3* are the fusion of three models taken, respectively, from the best fixed activation models and three stochastic models.
- *A + B* means sum rule between A and B.

We now summarize the most relevant results reported in Tables 7.2 and 7.3:

- Ensemble methods outperform stand-alone networks. Hence, changing the activation functions is an effective way to create ensembles of networks.
- Among stand-alone networks, ReLU is not the best one. The activations that reach the highest performance are the two MeLUs with *maxInput* equal to 255. This results is achieved even though the ResNet architecture was originally designed for ReLU.
- The performance of the networks that use different activations in the same architecture is not consistently better than the other stand-alone networks, but they show their power when combined to create an ensemble. When used together, they reach the best overall results.
- Considering the ensembles *FusReLu<K>*, which is an ensemble of K standard ResNet50, a baseline for ensemble approaches; it performs well due to instability of tuning in small datasets, but it is outperformed by almost all the stochastic approaches (*Sto<setName><K>(maxInput)*).
- The four *FusReLu<K>* ensembles have similar performance (*P*-value >.1), but any of them outperforms stand-alone ReLU (*P*-value .005)
- Considering the number of models in each ensemble, we can see that increasing K from 5 to 10 to 15 to 30 increases ensemble performance; regardless, there is no statistical evidence of a difference from 15 to 30.
- The nonstochastic ensemble *FusFullAS16*(255) outperforms with a *P*-value .05 the ensemble of ReseNet50 and *FusReLu15*; instead, *FusOldAS10(255)* obtains performance statistically similar to *FusReLu10* and *FusReLu15*. The stochastic ensemble *StoOldAS15(255)* outperforms with a *P*-value of .1 *FusFullAS16(255)*.
- Designing the model by means of stochastic activation functions gives valuable results, especially in the creation of ensembles. Indeed, these approaches are the first-ranked methods tested in these experiments.
- The comparison between the two "light" ensembles, *FusOldAS3* and *StoOLDAS3*, which are made of fixed and stochastic models, respectively, suggests again that using stochastic activation functions improves the performance in ensembles.
- According to the Wilcoxon signed rank test *StoFullAS15(255)* outperforms *StoOldAS15*(255) FusRanOLD15 with a *P*-value of .0001 and *StoBaseAS15(255)* with a *P*-value of .1. There is no statistical difference between *StoFullAS15*(255) versus *StoBaseAS8(255)+StoFullAS7(255)* and *StoFullAS15*(255) versus *StoFullAS15*(255) + *StoBaseIAS15*(255).

In our experiments, we used a GTX1080 GPU. ResNet50 can classify more than 40 images; hence, a 20-network ensemble can classify two images per second using a single GTX1080. We report a graphical summary of some representative networks in Fig. 7.2.

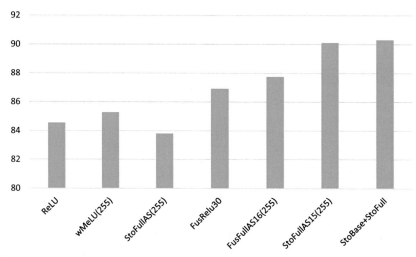

FIGURE 7.2

Average accuracies of the stand-alone networks and of the best ensembles.

6. Conclusions

In this chapter, we have presented three different methods for modifying an existing CNN architecture to obtain new high-performance and diverse networks. The core idea of our methods is replacing the activation functions in the original network with others, which can be different in every layer. This process allowed us to create new networks well suited to be included in an ensemble. We showed that our methods outperform standard ResNet50, all our stand-alone methods, and all our ensemble baselines on a variety of biomedical data sets. In this chapter, we only used ResNet50 as the backbone architecture, but we plan to test lighter networks suitable for mobile devices in the future. Studying ensembles of CNNs requires sizable computational power and long, memory-expensive experiments.

All the code will be available at https://github.com/LorisNanni in order to encourage the replication of our work.

Acknowledgments

We gratefully acknowledge the support of NVIDIA Corporation for the "NVIDIA Hardware Donation Grant" of a Titan X used in this research.

Part of this work was supported by MIUR (Italian Ministry for Education) under the initiative Departments of Excellence (Law 232/2016).

References

[1] I. Goodfellow, Y. Bengio, A. Courville, Deep Learning, MIT Press, 2016.

[2] Y. Cho, L.K. Saul, Large-margin classification in infinite neural networks, Neural Comput. (2010).

[3] K. He, X. Zhang, S. Ren, J. Sun, Deep residual learning for image recognition, in: Proceedings of the 2016 IEEE Conference on Computer Vision and Pattern Recognition, CVPR, 2016, pp. 770–778.

[4] L.K. Hansen, P. Salamon, Neural network ensembles, IEEE Trans. Pattern Anal. Mach. Intell. (1990), https://doi.org/10.1109/34.58871.

[5] P. Ghosh, S. Antani, L.R. Long, G.R. Thoma, Review of medical image retrieval systems and future directions, in: Proceedings of the IEEE Symposium on Computer-Based Medical Systems, 2011.

[6] A. Esteva, B. Kuprel, R.A. Novoa, J. Ko, S.M. Swetter, H.M. Blau, S. Thrun, Dermatologist-level classification of skin cancer with deep neural networks, Nature 542 (2017) 115–118, https://doi.org/10.1038/nature21056.

[7] M. Paci, L. Nanni, A. Lahti, K. Aalto-Setala, J. Hyttinen, S. Severi, Non-binary coding for texture descriptors in sub-cellular and stem cell image classification, Curr. Bioinform. (2013), https://doi.org/10.2174/1574893611308020009.

[8] J. Chi, E. Walia, P. Babyn, J. Wang, G. Groot, M. Eramian, Thyroid nodule classification in ultrasound images by fine-tuning deep convolutional neural network, J. Digit. Imag. 30 (2017) 477–486.

[9] M. Byra, Discriminant analysis of neural style representations for breast lesion classification in ultrasound, Biocybern. Biomed. Eng. 38 (2018) 684–690.

[10] L. Nanni, S. Brahnam, S. Ghidoni, A. Lumini, Bioimage classification with handcrafted and learned features, IEEE/ACM Trans. Comput. Biol. Bioinform. (2018), https://doi.org/10.1109/TCBB.2018.2821127.

[11] M.Z. Alom, T.M. Taha, C. Yakopcic, S. Westberg, P. Sidike, M.S. Nasrin, M. Hasan, B.C. Van Essen, A.A.S. Awwal, V.K. Asari, A state-of-the-art survey on deep learning theory and architectures, Electronics 8 (2019) 292, https://doi.org/10.3390/electronics8030292.

[12] W. Liu, Z. Wang, X. Liu, N. Zeng, Y. Liu, F.E. Alsaadi, A survey of deep neural network architectures and their applications, Neurocomputing (2017), https://doi.org/10.1016/j.neucom.2016.12.038.

[13] F. Agostinelli, M. Hoffman, P. Sadowski, P. Baldi, Learning activation functions to improve deep neural networks, in: Proceedings of the 3rd International Conference on Learning Representations, ICLR 2015 — Workshop Track Proceedings, 2015.

[14] D.A. Clevert, T. Unterthiner, S. Hochreiter, Fast and accurate deep network learning by exponential linear units (ELUs), in: Proceedings of the 4th International Conference on Learning Representations, ICLR 2016 — Conference Track Proceedings, 2016.

[15] X. Glorot, A. Bordes, Y. Bengio, Deep sparse rectifier neural networks, in: Proceedings of the Journal of Machine Learning Research, 2011.

[16] A.L. Maas, A.Y. Hannun, A.Y. Ng, Rectifier nonlinearities improve neural network acoustic models, in: Proceedings of the in ICML Workshop on Deep Learning for Audio, Speech and Language Processing, 2013.

[17] G. Klambauer, T. Unterthiner, A. Mayr, S. Hochreiter, Self-normalizing neural networks, in: Proceedings of the NIPS, 2017.

[18] B. Xu, N. Wang, T. Chen, M. Li, Empirical Evaluation of Rectified Activations in Convolutional Network, 2015.

[19] K. He, X. Zhang, S. Ren, J. Sun, Delving deep into rectifiers: surpassing human-level performance on imagenet classification, Proc. IEEE Int. Conf. Comput. Vis. 2015 Inter (2015) 1026–1034, https://doi.org/10.1109/ICCV.2015.123.

[20] Ö.F. Ertuğrul, A novel type of activation function in artificial neural networks: trained activation function, Neural Network. 99 (2018) 148–157, https://doi.org/10.1016/J.NEUNET.2018.01.007.

[21] V.S. Bawa, V. Kumar, Linearized sigmoidal activation: a novel activation function with tractable non-linear characteristics to boost representation capability, Expert Syst. Appl. 120 (2019) 346–356, https://doi.org/10.1016/J.ESWA.2018.11.042.

[22] P. Ramachandran, Z. Barret, Q.V. Le, Searching for activation functions, in: Proceedings of the 6th International Conference on Learning Representations, ICLR 2018 — Workshop Track Proceedings, 2018.

[23] G. Maguolo, L. Nanni, S. Ghidoni, Ensemble of Convolutional Neural Networks Trained with Different Activation Functions, 2019.

[24] K. He, X. Zhang, S. Ren, J. Sun, Delving deep into rectifiers: surpassing human-level performance on imagenet classification, in: Proceedings of the IEEE International Conference on Computer Vision, 2015.

[25] X. Jin, C. Xu, J. Feng, Y. Wei, J. Xiong, S. Yan, Deep learning with S-shaped rectified linear activation units, in: Proceedings of the 30th AAAI Conference on Artificial Intelligence, AAAI 2016, 2016.

[26] L. Nanni, A. Lumini, S. Ghidoni, G. Maguolo, Stochastic selection of activation layers for convolutional neural networks, Sensors (2020), https://doi.org/10.3390/s20061626.

[27] D. Misra, Mish: A Self Regularized Non-monotonic Activation Function.

[28] Y. Zhou, D. Li, S. Huo, S.-Y. Kung, Soft-Root-Sign Activation Function, 2020.

[29] A. Krizhevsky, I. Sutskever, G.E. Hinton, ImageNet classification with deep convolutional neural networks, Adv. Neural Inf. Process. Syst. (2012) 1—9, https://doi.org/10.1016/j.protcy.2014.09.007.

[30] C. Szegedy, W. Liu, Y. Jia, P. Sermanet, S. Reed, D. Anguelov, D. Erhan, V. Vanhoucke, A. Rabinovich, Going deeper with convolutions, in: Proceedings of the Proceedings of the IEEE Computer Society Conference on Computer Vision and Pattern Recognition, 07—12 June, 2015, pp. 1—9.

[31] K. Simonyan, A. Zisserman, Very deep convolutional networks for large-scale image recognition, Int. Conf. Learn. Represent. (2015) 1—14, https://doi.org/10.1016/j.infsof.2008.09.005.

[32] G. Huang, Z. Liu, L. Van Der Maaten, K.Q. Weinberger, Densely connected convolutional networks, in: Proceedings of the Proceedings - 30th IEEE Conference on Computer Vision and Pattern Recognition, CVPR 2017, 2017.

[33] S. Moccia, E. De Momi, M. Guarnaschelli, M. Savazzi, A. Laborai, L. Guastini, G. Peretti, L.S. Mattos, Confident texture-based laryngeal tissue classification for early stage diagnosis support, J. Med. Imag. 4 (2017) 34502.

[34] M.V. Boland, R.F. Murphy, A neural network classifier capable of recognizing the patterns of all major subcellular structures in fluorescence microscope images of HeLa cells, Bioinformatics 17 (2001) 1213—1223, https://doi.org/10.1093/bioinformatics/17.12.1213.

[35] N.A. Hamilton, R.S. Pantelic, K. Hanson, R.D. Teasdale, Fast automated cell phenotype image classification, BMC Bioinform. 8 (2007) 110, https://doi.org/10.1186/1471-2105-8-110.

[36] L. Shamir, N. Orlov, D. Mark Eckley, T.J. Macura, I.G. Goldberg, IICBU 2008: a proposed benchmark suite for biological image analysis, Med. Biol. Eng. Comput. 46 (2008) 943—947, https://doi.org/10.1007/s11517-008-0380-5.

[37] J.N. Kather, C.-A. Weis, F. Bianconi, S.M. Melchers, L.R. Schad, T. Gaiser, A. Marx, F.G. Zöllner, Multiclass texture analysis in colorectal cancer histology, Sci. Rep. 6 (2016) 27988, https://doi.org/10.1038/srep27988.

[38] K. Dimitropoulos, P. Barmpoutis, C. Zioga, A. Kamas, K. Patsiaoura, N. Grammalidis, Grading of invasive breast carcinoma through Grassmannian VLAD encoding, PLoS One 12 (2017) 1—18, https://doi.org/10.1371/journal.pone.0185110.

[39] J. Demšar, Statistical comparisons of classifiers over multiple data sets, J. Mach. Learn. Res. 7 (2006) 1—30, https://doi.org/10.1016/j.jecp.2010.03.005.

[40] Q. Cheng, H.L. Li, Q. Wu, L. Ma, Parametric deformable exponential linear units for deep neural networks, Neural Netw. 125 (2020) 281—289, https://doi.org/10.1016/j.neunet.2020.02.012.

Natural computing and unsupervised learning methods in smart healthcare data-centric operations

Joseph Bamidele Awotunde[1], **Abidemi Emmanuel Adeniyi**[2], **Sunday Adeola Ajagbe**[3] and **Alfonso González-Briones**[4,5,6]

[1]*Department of Computer Science, University of Ilorin, Ilorin, Kwara, Nigeria;* [2]*Department of Computer Science, Landmark University, Omu-Aran, Kwara, Nigeria;* [3]*Department of Computer Engineering, Ladoke Akintola University of Technology, Ogbomoso, Oyo, Nigeria;* [4]*Research Group on Agent-Based, Social and Interdisciplinary Applications (GRASIA), Complutense University of Madrid, Madrid, Spain;* [5]*BISITE Research Group, University of Salamanca, Salamanca, Spain;* [6]*Air Institute, IoT Digital Innovation Hub, Salamanca, Spain*

1. Introduction

Natural computing (NC) is the area of knowledge that examines nature-inspired models and computational methods and, dually, it attempts to describe the environment around us in terms of data analysis [1]. It is a multidisciplinary research area, both at the level of digital infrastructure and at the stage of fundamental science, connecting natural sciences with computer science [2]. NC comes in different areas and subjects such as pure theoretical science, algorithms, and applications [3–5]. The significant principle of NC is that every type of computation takes place in nature, and that it is necessary to recognize, model, interpret, and use computing capacities for different goals and in diverse situations. A computational model as an illustration is influenced by artificial immune systems as a subsystem of a biological organism, with artificial life seeking to mimic nature in what it means to be alive. It is assumed that one of the most significant contributions of natural computation to healthcare sectors may be the creation of an acceptable language to define healthcare concepts and processes effectively and articulately, and to explain them. The ideas of information processing are quickly absorbed by the natural sciences, and the nature of computation evolves as it incorporates natural science principles with the unique privilege of engaging in some such metamorphoses.

NC is a concept implemented to include three types of methods: (1) innovative problem-solving techniques motived by nature; (2) the use of machines in producing natural phenomena; and (3) all those that mimic the use of synthetic resources (e.g., molecules). There are several fields of research that have been created to make up these three branches, including swarm intelligence, artificial immune systems, DNA computing, quantum computing, artificial neural networks, evolutionary algorithms, fractal geometry, artificial life, etc.

Cognitive and Soft Computing Techniques for the Analysis of Healthcare Data. https://doi.org/10.1016/B978-0-323-85751-2.00005-0

Unsupervised learning has helped to address the drawbacks of the concept of supervised feature space by dynamically defining patterns in data and constraints by learning a lightweight and universal description that makes things simpler for collecting valuable information automatically when creating classifiers or some other determinants. Given the quality of this text, interactive, and broadcasting feature learning [6], and the growing prevalence of deep learning [7] (i.e., training based on deep neural network hierarchies), these strategies have not been widely used with data from the healthcare sector.

When looking back at healthcare analytics generally, there is no denying that advanced analytics will play a key role in improving outcomes in healthcare environments. Hence, a stronger strategic drive in the healthcare industry is driving toward more data-centric operations. There is, however, a very significant difference within a few independent empirical observations and being "properly" data-centric for a medical center. The push through data-centricity needs to be faster, particularly if people understand what it means for a medical professional to be data-centric, and more so if you consider the amount and varieties of information generated in the healthcare setting. Therefore, the importance of data-centric operations in the healthcare industry can never be overemphasized, and the healthcare industry should be thinking of how to become data-centric operators in nature. The introduction of NC and unsupervised learning methods in healthcare data-centric operations has become important when considering the significance of these on big data analytics generally. Imitator and mimic of human being and animals have been one of the aims of the NC and unspervised learning, and this has really help in data-centric operations. These are part of computer science, with no operational computational algorithms when considering complicated problems.

Over time, NC has been used in different fields by acting as a patron for further approaches [8,9]. Methods of NC and unsupervised learning have produced increased focus within the research community. As outlined in many recent findings, their approaches offer valuable detection accuracy in comparison with other data classification techniques [8–10]. To achieve appropriate precaution programming, conspicuous correctness in forecasting is significantly relevant, but this may create diversity in the system methodologies. Hence, during a disease outbreak projection in a healthcare system, recognizing proficient devices is fundamental in order to enable accuracy. In policymaking, these techniques are very successful in solving systematic and real-life difficulties. The performance of various NC and unsupervised learning approaches for the categorization of diseases in healthcare systems is summarized.

The commonly used NC approaches in the healthcare industry are: computing inspired by nature like artificial neural networks (ANNs), evolutionary computation (EC), swarm intelligence (SI), artificial immune systems (AISs); algorithms like fuzzy C-means, K-medoids, hidden Markov model, Gaussian combination, neural network, and hierarchical, which are some of the most frequently engaged unsupervised learning methods. The inclusion of the objectives makes NC and unsupervised learning multifaceted in nature, and intellectual for acquiring ophthalmic observation and language understanding since individual intelligence is multifaceted. Hitherto, the implementations of their methods have shown positive results in numerous healthcare environments to discover new behaviors and identify potential for the future. The recent modern systems, such as ANN, SI, AIS, K-means, and neural network techniques, have shown positive outcomes in the extraction from a massive data set of nonlinear dynamic structures.

Therefore, this chapter shows that natural computation and unsupervised learning are applied to consolidated medical information at the preprocess patient level, with outcomes in interpretations that are adequately interpreted by the mechanism and that greatly enhance analytical scientific prototypes for a variety of clinical situations in a data-centric operations nature. The remainder of this chapter is structured as follows: Section 2 discusses NC in healthcare, and Section 3 presents applications of unsupervised learning in smart healthcare systems. Section 4 discusses the applicability of NC and supervised learning in healthcare data-centric intelligence operations in smart healthcare systems. Section 5 presents a case study and Section 6 outlines the results. Finally, Section 7 concludes the chapter.

2. Natural computing in the healthcare industry

NC is the digital equivalent of the method of capturing concepts from the environment to create computational structures or to perform computations using natural constituents (e.g., molecules) [11−13]. From a spectrum of viewpoints, both knowledge and computation are concepts and occurrences that are still being intensively investigated. The architecture of computation must be sufficient to be able to effectively model the universe as a computing network. There remains some confusion when it comes to generalization of the concept of computation [14]. The recurring one is about the relationship between the machine and the universe. It must be stressed that the universe is not in any real way identical to a PC, and when we speak about the computing universe with the richness of phenomena contained in nature being able to be represented, the notion of computation must be generalized. NC is subdivided into three main branches [11,15]:

(1) Nature-inspired technology: uses nature as a motivation for the creation of new methods for problem-solving. The core insight of this segment is to create computational data instruments (algorithms) for the modeling of various difficulties by taking inspiration from nature.

(2) Through computer science, and the modeling and optimization of nature: This is essentially a naturally derived process that aims to create trends, facets, behavior patterns, and organisms that accurately depict "existence" (not inherently). Its components can be used to simulate various physical processes, thereby extending our understanding of nature and computational model perspectives.

(3) Computing of synthetic resources: This coincides with the use of naturally derived computing components, thus representing a true unique computing paradigm that substitutes or complements current computers based on silicon.

The establishment of innovative techniques was inspired by NC in hardware, software, and wetware for solving problems [4,16]. These led to the synthesis of natural patterns, species, and habits inspired by nature, and can contribute to the exploration of constructing microprocessors using natural features for computation. NC is also a scientific area that attests the dominance of science fields [17−19]. With its three key fields of research, it shows that knowledge is necessary in different fields for a full experience of this paradigm. This knowledge is necessary for the simulation and analysis of natural practices and controls in the creation of new philosophies in computation. It therefore becomes important for all functions to share ideas and expertise for the workability of NC, examples include computer scientists, astronomers, pharmacologists, designers, psychologists, etc. [12,20].

A significant part NC's computational methods is focused on greatly simplified representations of the structures and procedures that are present in the underlying natural processes. The explanations are numerous for such simplifying assumptions and heuristics. First, to enable a model to be workable for a huge number of individuals, many simplifications are required. It may also be helpful to demonstrate

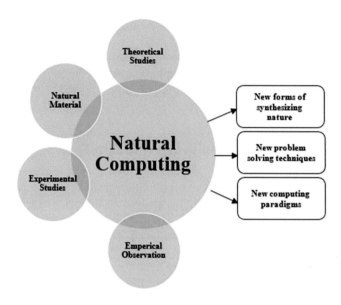

FIGURE 8.1

Methodologies used to develop NC with its branches.

the executive summary required to allow the replication of certain unique aspects of implementation and to observe certain emerging technologies. Whatever the level of exploration and interpretation is most suitable depends on the empirical issue, what kind of problem one needs to tackle, or the processes of nature to be reproduced. In order to achieve its objectives, NC typically incorporates theoretical and experimental natural science, physical science and chemistry, scientific findings from landscapes, and many other theories, findings, and mechanisms from various levels of research into nature, as outlined in Fig. 8.1.

2.1 Computing inspired by nature (CIN)

Nature-inspired computing (CIN) is a computational method that incorporates the computer science category with other scientific fields of knowledge, such as physical science, chemistry, natural science, engineering, and mathematics, to allow new computer tools including algorithms and hardware to be created [21]. CIN intelligence is a technique of optimization focused on living organisms' actions. A CIN model aims to accomplish a goal within a set of constraints to be met, and an objectives function known as the success index calculates the optimal solution [21]. In finding a global optimal solution, the algorithms use naturally endowed random hunting skills of animals [22], the nature-inspired algorithm will investigate and optimize the computational complexity. Primarily, CIN algorithms are classified into EAs by focusing on SI algorithms. EAs are focused natural systems on evolutionary behavior like the genetic algorithm (GA), while SI simulates the collaborative behavior inspired by a swarm naturally, such as ant colony (ACO) [23] wolf [24], ANT [25], dung beetle [26], PSO [27,28] and BAT [29], among many others. Table 8.1 displays the algorithms and application domains in the healthcare industry that are nature-inspired.

Table 8.1 Applications of natural computation algorithms in healthcare systems.

Natural computation algorithms	Application areas
GA	This algorithm is very useful in features selection in healthcare systems; the GA is very effective when it is combined with various algorithms. Also, it uses bandwidth, computing assets, and data dependencies. The GA algorithm has been extended to cloud-based data and computing facilities [30–33]
SA and WOA	This is a big data optimization technique based on simulated annealing using the whale optimization algorithm to design distinct characteristic selection. The SA algorithm helps to enhance the precision of the classification and chooses the most useful attributes for classification problems [34,35]
PSO	This can be used for data analytics, especially on a big data set to diagnose and predict various diseases. The PSO is very useful in image registration, remote sensing, and time series estimate [36,37]
SA based on feature selection	The SAFS is very useful in computer vision and big data analytics. The algorithm is used in reducing the size of a data set by selecting the relevant features that are suitable for data analytics; the procedure eliminates parameters and tightens sparse restrictions [38]
Artificial bee colony (ABC)	The ABC algorithm-based big data frameworks allow determination of the best cluster and optimize for various sizes of data sets. When applied in a map/reduce-based Hadoop ecosystem, the ABC algorithm helps to reduce the time complexity and enhances the precision of clustering. In the preparation of neural networks for pattern recognition, the ABC algorithm is very useful and important [39–41]
Firefly swarm optimization (FSO)	The FSO hybrid algorithm (FSOH) is focused on six multiobjectives in a data optimization strategy, and difficulties in minimizing implementation costs, but has a high complexity and running time [42,43]. It is used in the prediction of heart disease, image processing, brain tissue segmentation, clustering, and classification of hyperspectral images and protein complexes [44]
Gray wolf optimization algorithm (GWO)	This algorithm is very useful in features selection, group identification, diagnosis, and prediction of various diseases [45–48]
Cat swarm optimization (CSO)	In a text classification experiment for big data, the CSO-based method is best for big data classification for features selections, and for text classification experiments in data analytics [49,50]. The word frequency—inverse document frequency is used by the CSO algorithm to increase the accuracy of the selection of features [51–53]
Ant colony optimization (ACO)	This is used in order to pick optimal decision-making features for mobile big data, which helps to efficiently handle social network big data (tweets and posts) [54,55]. it is also used in predictive monitoring for nonlinear processes, identification of anomalies, treatment of omitted values in data sets, denoising of clinical images, and classification of hyperspectral images [56–58]
Improved ACO algorithm (IACO)	This is a big data analytical approach for clinical data management, such as patient, radiology, and operational data that can be used by doctors within the shortest time to retrieve necessary data [55,59]
Shuffled frog leaping (SFL)	The SFL is useful in high-dimensional biomedical data for features selection. Possible subsets are exploring to obtain the set of features that are relevant within a data set, and irrelevant features are removed; the SFL algorithm maximizes predictive precision [60,61]

Continued

Table 8.1 Applications of natural computation algorithms in healthcare systems.—cont'd

Natural computation algorithms	Application areas
Bacterial foraging optimization (BFO) algorithm	Insightful and efficacious content from medical websites and blogs should be graded. The "MAYO" was used to test the correctness of the medical data set to retrieve the necessary details [62]
Kestrel-based search algorithm (KSA)	This algorithm is use for features selection in bioinformatics high-dimensional data sets, and can also be relevant as a parameter-tuning model for optimization possibility [27]
Lion optimization algorithm (LOA)/lion cooperation characteristic	This is used for optimization for the extraction of liver from abdominal CT images and is very relevant in data clustering [58]
Whale optimization algorithm (WOA)	The WOA is used in the diagnosis and prediction of various illnesses, and employed sometimes in feature selection of high-dimensional analytics data, especially in big data analytics in IoT-based platforms [63,64]
Flock by leader	This is used in local proximity in an artificial virtual space, and is very relevant in data clustering [65]

2.2 Recent works using NC algorithms in solving various problems in healthcare systems

Researchers in data analytics need high-quality and appropriate data from the vast amount of data collected. The methodology of feature selection (FS) helps to minimize the complexity of features by removing distorted, unnecessary, or insignificant data from which inventiveness in prediction performance is achieved with the least information extraction. There is a turn to preserving the files relevant to each individual due to the inclusion of dimensionality of features and records in data repositories. More recently, data-mining techniques have been formally used to distinguish a precious and novel pattern from conventional data. Many simple methods of analysis are still required to solve problems. The classification system mostly provides a valid outcome for the classification of the data sets. Typically, complicated information with errors is used in high and large dimensional data sets, and the classification method plays an important role in such a situation.

First, to quantify a function subset, Zheng and Wang [66] calculated the joint maximum information entropy (JMIE). Next, to explore the optimum function subset, a binary particle swarm optimization (BPSO) algorithm is suggested. Finally, UCI companies are listed to verify the efficiency of the proposed system compared to the standard method of mutual knowledge (MI), CHI, as well as a binary variant of the selection of features of particle swarm optimization-support vector machines (BPSO-SVMs). Research reveals that FS-JMIE achieves a score equal to or better than MI, CHI, and BPSO-SVM. In addition, to the number of groups, FS-JMIE demonstrates marginally improved robustness. In addition, the technique demonstrates better time efficiency and greater accuracy than BPSO-SVM.

Oztekin et al. [67], together with the creation and design of several highly accurate classification algorithms, demonstrated the hybrid GA-based feature selection technique to identify the critical features in the feature-rich and broad UNOS lung transplant data set. Jain et al. [68] demonstrated a two-phase hybrid model linking correlation-based feature selection (CFS) with enhanced binary particle swarm optimization for cancer classification (iBPSO). The proposed iBPSO also tests the question of immediate rivalry with the conventional BPSO's local optimum. On 11 benchmark microarray data sets of various cancer forms, the suggested architecture was estimated. In comparison with seven several well-defined approaches, clinical trials have shown better results regarding the number of selected genes and the accuracy of classification in most cases. In particular, for these 11 data sets, seven with a minimum-sized prognostic gene subset (up to 1:5%) achieved up to 100% classification accuracy.

Nandhini et al. [40], using the artificial bee colony (ABC) algorithm and an optimization strategy to construct an efficient associative algorithm, attempted to produce necessary automobiles. An associative algorithm, designed to use the ABC invented vehicles, achieved high accuracy and interesting prognosis values. The ABC-based AC produced promising results when tests were carried out utilizing medical insurance databases from the UCI machine learning library. A novel feature selection method was proposed by Shilaskar and Ghatol [69] for the arrangement of high-dimensionality disease microarrays utilizing signal-to-noise ratio (SNR) filtering and particle swarm optimization (PSO). The data collection is first grouped using the k-means of clustering and genes are ranked by SNR score. In order to form a new function subset, high-scored genes are derived from each cluster. Second, PSO accepts a developed subset of features and produces an optimized subset of features. Support vector machine (SVM), k-nearest neighbor (k-NN), and probabilistic neural network (PNN) grouping approaches with a one-off cross-validation technique are used to test the function subsets. The findings show that the suggested technique using PSO provides better results than the other methods.

ABC was suggested as a way to minimize the data component of classifiers [70]. From the initial high-dimensional results, an optimal selection of measurements is chosen. The k-NN technique is then used for appropriateness assessment inside the ABC system. ABC and k-NN have been revised to produce an active dimensionality technique. The activity of three categories of bees, including bees operating, bees observing, and bees spying, is used by ABC, and the wrapping of ABC and k-NN classifier is referred to as proposed type. k-NN is used for capability measurement to measure the activity importance of ABC nutrients. After the development of the new applicant nutrients of the working bees and prospective bees, which are a subclass of identified factors, k-NN is conducted to determine the accuracy of the classifier of the new candidate feed ingredients. Correctness is used as a benchmark for the best subset of functionality to be selected. The novel treatment approaches concentrate on the assessment of observations and actions, which is very time-consuming. Studies with data on gene regulation and autism data sets have been conducted. The findings of the DNA expression investigation revealed that the ABC−k-NN approach can successfully minimize the data length while retaining highly accurate results.

The revised binary particle swarm optimization (RBPSO) collection function has helped refine the collection of features while concurrently optimizing the layout of the SVM kernel parameter. Vieira et al. [71] used this in septic patients to assess mortality. An updated form of the binary particle swarm optimization (BPSO) was introduced to minimize untimely merging of the BPSO procedure. Using speed and comparison between the best swarm strategies, MBPSO handles swarm heterogeneity. This technique utilizes SVM in the binding method, where kernel variables are configured at the exact same time. The cohort of prototypes to evaluate the threat of death in sepsis patients is a significant medical issue. An analysis was conducted to evaluate the outcome of patients with septic shock (survived or deceased). RBPSO has been verified and matched to other PSO-based techniques and genetic procedures with many benchmark data sets (GA). The test results demonstrated that, equal to other PSO-based procedures, the suggested technique would properly select the discriminating input features and also accomplish highly accurate results. RBPSO is similar in terms of precision to GA, but there are fewer attributes selected in subgroup methods.

Mafarja and Mirjalili [72] proposed a simulated annealing (SA) algorithm-based big data optimization method for architect diverse feature selection approaches using the whale optimization algorithm (WOA) to minimize manipulation by evaluating the most competent areas. The proposed approach aims to improve the consistency of the description and selects the most helpful applications for the categorization tasks. Further, Barbu et al. [38] suggested an SAFS hybrid algorithm that used big data learning and computer vision. The SAFS algorithm eliminates variables based on a criterion and constricts a sparsity limit, which progressively decreases the difficult size through repetitions, making it particularly ideal for studying big data. Big data research focusing on the FSO and SA-based hybrid (FSOSAH) method to stochastic dynamic facilities layout-based multiobjective data management has been recommended [73]. Saida, Nadjet, and Omar [74] suggested the use of cuckoo search optimization (CO) algorithms based on large data analytics methodology for clustering data. In addition, the validation of the CO algorithm by experimental results has been considered by various UCI deep learning repository databases, and data sets do better in terms of computational performance and integration consistency.

Dheeba et al. [75] proposed and optimized a wavelet neural network (PSOWNN) using a particle swarm to study another method of characterizing the region of breast differences in abnormal mammograms. The sole backbone to this technique is the collection of material and power measurements from mammograms and the organization of suspicious areas with the use of an example classifier. The potential approach is implemented using the actual clinical inventory of 216 mammograms collected through mammogram scanning and using the reader operational characteristics (ROC) curve for performance measurements. The findings show that the region of the suggested calculation under the ROC curve is 0.96853% with a sensitivity of 94.167% and precision of 92.105%.

Mohebian et al. [76], in an attempt to assess the clinical and pathological performance of 579 patients with malignant in breast tumors using duplication prediction, and the results gave a repeated prevalence of 19.30%. Ensemble learning is expressed in training and particle swarm optimization (PSO) has further enhanced its usability. The minimal responsiveness, reliability, accuracy, and precision of the method delivered were 77%, 93%, 95%, and 85%, respectively, for the whole cross-validation fold and the hold-out test fold, and thus it surpassed the other classification model evaluated.

3. Unsupervised learning techniques in healthcare systems

Unsupervised learning uses an algorithm where the input data (X) must only be inserted and no corresponding output variables must be placed. In order to help learners understand more about the data, the main purpose of unsupervised learning is to help model the underlying structure or even the distribution of the data. These are called unsupervised learning because there are no correct responses and there is no instructor, unlike in supervised learning described above. To help discover and present the fascinating structure that is present in the data, algorithms are left to their own devices. It is also possible to group unsupervised learning problems into clusters and create association problems in advance.

3.1 Clustering

Clustering indicates what you want to discover and helps in inherent groupings of the data, such as grouping customers based on their purchasing behavior.

3.2 Association

The learning problem is known as the association rule. This is where the exact rules that define the vast amounts of knowledge can be discovered, for example, people who purchase X also prefer to purchase Y.

Many data management technologies, namely data gathering, clinical applications, pattern detection, and social concepts, are of key significance for the classification of objects. Items which have already been categorized are classified in supervised labeled classes, while those that have not been labeled are divided into unsupervised classified groups. Benchmark k-means grouping strategies are very useful in the healthcare sector with variants such as fuzzy k-means. Graph theoretic approaches generate correlations using diagrams. Data objects are created by several probability distributions in combination with density-dependent techniques and can be obtained from various density function types (e.g., Gaussian multivariate or t-distribution) or from the same family but with varying metrics. STING (statistic knowledge grid approach) is a highly versatile algorithm which has the ability to break down data collection to various levels of detail.

The grid-based gathering strategies include the following. The evolutionary clustering methods begin with a distributed populace of contestant solutions that would be optimized with some fitness function. In documents that share a similar template, the document clustering algorithm helps to find classes. It was used without any user control to automatically find clusters in a set [77]. The main purpose of clustering is to find meaningful classes so that, compared to seeing it as a whole set, the study of all the documents within clusters is much simpler. Information retrieval, record organization, genetics, weather forecasting, medical imaging, etc., are some of the most popular clustering applications [78,79]. There are numerous methods for records to be grouped, however two common forms of methods of clustering are partitional and hierarchical clustering. By splitting a set of documents based on an objective function, a partitional clustering algorithm finds all the nonoverlapping clusters at once. These algorithms aim to minimize an objective function or optimize it. The majority of partition clustering algorithms are prototype-based, where a prototype is chosen for each cluster and the documents are grouped on the basis of the prototypes. These algorithms normally work many times before a convergence takes place or an optimal condition is reached. By splitting/mixing each group at each stage, hierarchical clustering produces a tree of clusters until the preferred cluster quantities are created.

This tree is also referred to as a dendrogram. To build a dendrogram, hierarchical clustering may use either the top-down method (divisive) or the bottom-up method (agglomerative). Agglomerative clustering starts with an initial document in each category and, at each point, periodically combines two clusters that are most identical in their sequence before a single cluster is produced from all records. Divisive grouping, on the other hand, begins as a single group for all reports and divides them before the singleton groups into clusters. These classification forms are more commonly used because the underlying representation of their hierarchical clusters matches their application areas. Hierarchical agglomerative clustering methods combine pairs of clusters at each stage based on one of the preceding connection parameters for calculating cluster proximity [80,81]. A single relation algorithm (SLA) tests the cumulative pairwise resemblance of each cluster to integrate the nearest neighbors [82]. This form of clustering is often described as the relationship, the least process, or the closest neighbor approach. In singular cluster formation, a single layer pairing, that is, those two components (one in each group) that are nearest to one another, provides a link between the two groups. In this cluster, the distance between two points is described by the nearest distance from any component of one group to any member of the other group, which also indicates the resemblance. The resemblance between a couple of groups is considered to be the greatest correlation between any component of a group and any participant of the other category if the data have similarities.

Exploratory data methods are commonly applicable to the high-dimensional models established by today's scientist, such as cluster analysis [83]. In areas like microbiology, atmospheric science, medicine, physics, and marketing, technical advances have dramatically altered the format and amount of data obtained. It is vital to ensure a decent methodology for estimating designs, and choosing variables of interest and structure models in high-dimensional environments as a means of capturing and preserving ever-greater volumes of data. For instance, in Ref. [84], where the number of genes increases the amount of specimens significantly, the focus was on gene expression data analysis. The paper proposed a new hierarchical classification approach called the hierarchical organized partition and collapsing hybrid (HOPACH) designed to overcome some of the limitations of presently available strategies for grouping gene expression results. As related concerns can possible arise in other high-dimensional data contexts, the HOPACH procedure could be used in several fields to analyze databases.

Clustering is a form of unsupervised learning in which homogeneous groups are divided into a collection of elements. Suppose that we are interested in the clustering of elements $p, X_j, \{1, \ldots, p\}$ and that each element X_j is a vector of dimensions n, vector$(x_{1j}, \ldots, x_{nj})^T$. Let $d(X_j, X_{j'})$ connote the differences among entities j and j' and let D be the disparity of the symmetric matrix $p \times p$. Euclidean distance, 1 minus correlation, 1 minus total correlation, and 1 minus cosine angle are typical options for differences. Clustering procedures map the distance from matrix D to p category tags (either implicitly or explicitly).

It is possible to separate the nonparametric clustering techniques into separating and categorized architectures. Segregating approaches such as self-organization charts (SOM) [85], medoid partitioning (PAM) [86], and k-means identify the quantity of groups specified by the worker and assign a cluster to each element. Hierarchical strategies include creating a category tree in which the base is a unique group comprising all the items, each of which comprises just one component in the leaves. When it is required to promote groups at a number of stages of information, such as the stage of the final tree, which is the systematic structure of the components, using hierarchical approaches. As far as the subject-matter scientist is concerned, such a set, wherein the surrounding components are equivalent, is much more valuable than a selection of broad, unordered classes.

The structural tree may be either divisive (i.e., constructed by iteratively updating of the components from the top down) or agglomerative (i.e., assembled from the bottom-most up by recursively merging the components). DIANA [87] is an illustration of ordered clustering procedure, while AGNES [87] and cluster [88] are examples of agglomerative hierarchical algorithms. With various forms of linkage, agglomerative approaches may be employed. The distance between two clusters in average linkage methods seems to be the average distance between the values in one category and the values in the other category. The difference between two clusters is the least difference between a position in the sixth group and a position in the second group with a single connection process (nearest neighbor methods).

Clustering is a method for splitting data sets into multiple subsets whose components share similar attributes. Among clustering algorithms, the two most common and classic methods are hierarchical and k-means clustering. Both have innate drawbacks, however. Hierarchical clustering is unable to reflect distinct clusters with identical patterns of speech. Also, the actual expression patterns become less important as clusters increase in size. The clustering of K-means involves a defined number of clusters in advance and randomly selects initial centroids; it is also sensitive to outliers. For microarray data, agglomerative (bottom-up) hierarchical clustering algorithms are important analysis tools. In order to reveal biologically interesting patterns, they are useful for organizing genes and samples from a series of microarray experiments. In particular, hierarchical approaches are useful because they allow researchers to analyze data groupings simultaneously into several small clusters (e.g., repeated samples from the same patient) and a few large clusters (e.g., different prognosis groups) [89,90]. Using a single hierarchical model means that groups are nested at various levels of information, making understanding simpler [91,92].

Bottom-up clustering, which connects artifacts successively, is effective at identifying small clusters, but can provide suboptimal performance for a few large clusters to be found. Top-down strategies, on the other hand, are effective at finding a few large clusters, but worse at identifying several tiny clusters. We aim to combine the strengths of both methods with knowledge obtained from an introductory bottom-up gathering, adjusting top-down procedures. A new central idea, that of a "mutual cluster," promotes this mix. As a group of objects collectively closer to each other than to any other object, a mutual cluster is described. Table 8.2 displays the algorithms and application domains that use unsupervised learning in the healthcare industry.

Table 8.2 Applications of unsupervised learning in healthcare systems.

Nature-inspired algorithms	Application areas
k-Means	The algorithm is very useful in large data sets to analyze disease data samples in healthcare systems, it is very effective when combined with some other algorithms. The k-means algorithm has been extended to cloud-based architecture with k-means MapReduce computing facilities [93]. The complexity of homecare clients who use recovery facilities to recognize previously unknown trends of diagnostic criteria has been investigated by k-means [94]. A useful way to segment a heterogeneous recovery client population into more homogeneous subgroups has been given by the K-means algorithm. This research offers improved recognition of the preferences and needs of patients and allows rehabilitation programs for home healthcare clients to be better customized accordingly. Uncovering natural classes within a diverse community, k-means clustering is used on given data [95,96]
K-medoids	The K-medoids algorithm can be useful in disease diagnosis, prediction, and forecasting [97–99]. The K-medoids algorithm also very helps in enhancing the precision of the classification and chooses the most useful attributes for classification. The major advantage of this weighing approach is the acquisition of linearly separable data sets by transforming the nonlinear data set and enhancing classification efficiency during the medical data set [97,98]

Continued

Table 8.2 Applications of unsupervised learning in healthcare systems.—cont'd

Nature-inspired algorithms	Application areas
Fuzzy C-means	This algorithm can be used to improve the classification of disease data during diagnosis and prediction. The algorithm will also improve attribute selection with it is used with other algorithms. Time series prediction, medical data classification, and selection of remote sensing images are some of the examples of using K-medoids. The algorithm will assemble a set of unmarked items into several classes in such a manner that a related category of information is available in each group. The fuzzy C-means can also be used on big data analytics to detect useful data among huge amounts of data from IoT-based devices [100−102]
Hierarchical	The algorithm can be used in big data analytics to reduce the size problem making it especially suitable for analytic learning in big data problems. The hierarchical algorithm can take advantage of both cloud and fog computing features and introduces a tailor-made management approach for IoT-based healthcare services [103]. The algorithm can be used for association rule mining for frequent feature extraction, to categorize the contraceptive method [104]
Gaussian mixture	The Gaussian mixture algorithm-based big data frameworks allow determination of the best cluster and optimizes for various sizes of data sets. The Gaussian mixture can be applied in a map/reduce-based Hadoop ecosystem to reduce the time complexity and enhances the precision of clustering [105]. The algorithm can be useful in hidden conditional random fields for the human activity recognition problem to eliminate the lack of enhancement in the learning method [106]. The algorithm is very useful in feature extractions of medical data [105]
Hidden Markov model	The hidden Markov model algorithm is very useful in the big data optimization approach. The algorithm can be used in medical image processing to provide more precise views in medical and healthcare management systems [107,108]. Medical image background and foreground segmentation can be performed using this algorithm [109,110]
Neural network	This algorithm can be useful in the diagnosis and prediction of various diseases, and group identification of signs and symptoms. The algorithm is very useful in features selection in healthcare systems, and is very useful when combined with various other algorithms. Also, the usage of bandwidth, computing assets, and data dependencies can be optimized using the algorithm. Applications of the neural network have the ability to inform decision-making at various levels of healthcare organizations. Despite belonging to a class of statistical processes, the structural elements used to characterize a neural network are conceptually similar to those used in neuroscience [111]

In many fields, like data mining, information processing, predictive analytics, artificial intelligence, and segmentation techniques, k-means is a common data partition tool. The machine learning and data mining groups consider this method to be an unsupervised learning technique as it looks for structures among input parameters without using the output layer to decide how the structure is generated. In other terms, clustering with k-means is a method to use data within a particular community to explore natural clusters. The algorithm starts by first attaching data points to random groups in order to determine structures. Based on the ranges across each data point and the team facilities, the community facilities are defined and the community memberships redeployed. This method is replicated until there are no improvements from the previous iteration of community members. All the parameters included in the k-means cluster analysis were dichotomized, with the exception of generation. This promotes clear interpretation as the overall mean of a dichotomous metric is specifically related to the number of clients with a rating of 1.

Clustering approaches such as fuzzy grouping are often unsupervised where not much attention is set to the training process [112]. Randomly chosen cluster centers are iteratively modified together with the degree of membership of each data set in the case of fuzzy clustering methods. Related to the degree of participation and the duration of the data point from the cluster centers, an objective function is determined. The iteration of these kinds of algorithms persists until they approximate the objective function. The quantity of repetitions, however, hinges on the space between the same data points for the cluster and its center for the cluster. The number of iterations can be reduced by a semisupervised method by supplying the fuzzy C-means (FCM) procedure with the original cluster centroid. Therefore, it is possible to decrease the package cost and implementation time automatically. In any classification scheme, the more irrelevant features exist, the greater the likelihood of inappropriate grouping of data. The inappropriate set of characteristics will force an incorrect cluster to include valid data. Elimination of unrelated features from a grouping model will enhance the system's accuracy and minimize the execution time of programs and costs. Therefore, in order to increase the precision of any classification scheme, appropriate-only collection of features should be used.

4. The data-centric operations in healthcare systems

How we offer treatment and medication is specifically mirrored in all health data. In nature, it is necessarily networked and continually modified. This will create tremendous clinical value by accepting the connectedness of this knowledge, both safely and effectively. The importance of this is in its direct relation to how advanced analytical policy and a supporting infrastructure ecosystem are developed by a healthcare provider. It is not easy to unlock the complexities and accept the connectivity of these data at the patient level, but focusing heavily on a ground-breaking data-centric method offers new techniques to do so.

For any industry that wishes to display or see the value of clients documents, the data must be part of day-to-day actions in the workplace. It suggests that staff and patients understand why they really need to give more details on their wellbeing with a larger perspective within the healthcare system, as more details can be collated. Encouragement to share this information will go a long way toward advocating this from managers and senior-level teams and contributing to the change and effect that data may be accessible from every medical professional. This incentive, however, can only take effect if the organization as a whole adopts a data-centric approach, follows stringent data governance, and introduces a mature and structured data policy. The use of natural computing and unsupervised learning on these data gives meaningful insight into those data for proper policy-making at the level of healthcare management and government in general.

In the face of the rising obstacles faced by the healthcare sector, stakeholders must stay current with or keep abreast of competitiveness. Through developing a smart healthcare system using natural computing and unsupervised learning solutions to allow better management and decisions on an everyday basis, data-centric operations will assist healthcare agencies, payers, and hospitals to improve their competitive advantage. Data-centric intelligence practices allow the healthcare industry to tap into its many databases and provide personnel, management, and healthcare stakeholders with easy-to-understand insight. Thousands of healthcare industries are now using data-centric intelligence practices to identify fresh income prospects, minimize expenses, reallocate capital, and enhance functioning proficiency.

Data-centric intelligence operations provide the information needed to maximize efficiency, minimize costs, and comply with industry regulations and requirements when properly applied to data within the healthcare industry. Furthermore, companies are offered the resources needed to make the best use of the large quantities of data accessible to them, helping them to work more effectively and enhance the comfort of patients. Healthcare providers will grow and use specific competencies, whether starting with one or many applications, to use data-centric intelligence applications: a convenient standardized web server with extranet and intranet functionality, access for thousands of users, control and monitoring of enormous volumes of data from various outlets, visual analysis tools and consistency reviews for the board, nonconstraint of the natural computing and unsupervised learning will play a prominent role in helping this to happen.

4.1 Applications of data-centric intelligence to healthcare systems

Premier, Inc. is a United States-owned medical alliance of 200 nonprofit hospitals and healthcare networks. It serves 1700 hospitals and more than 46,500 other healthcare institutions, and is committed to enhancing the quality of patient services, while efficiently lowering the cost of treatment. Micro-Strategy supports Premier's data applications that help track health reliability and patient welfare, market and customer approaches, utilization of clinical services, operational effectiveness, and competitiveness for more than 500 of its hospital customers. There are various ways in which medical professionals should use a data-centric information system to make good decisions in the healthcare sector through multiple challenges, as described next.

Security measures would need to be adopted by all medical institutions to protect their records, both organized and unorganized, as well as the confidentiality of patients. If there is genuine confidence in data collection, buy-in from clinicians, and surgical and clinical consumers is of utmost importance, and this goes back to tight security and privacy measures. In the meantime, hospitals must establish their own methods of accessing as much patient data as possible. Note that the word access, not necessarily collect, is used in this context. The use of modern analytical platforms is a paramount tool in this direction, but it needs data sophistication and data-centricity, that are not prevalent in many medical institutions, in order to do this safely, effectively, and successfully. The need is there, several completely data-centered data solutions being put together is difficult enough, never mind them being enforced.

There is a lot more important information than just what is gathered by hospitals. When you realize a patient has had three visits to his GP and four to the emergency department since his last admission to the clinic, think how great you can triage and evaluate a client? Potentially, in the emergency department of another hospital, hospitals would be able to perform surveys and analyze insights from medical information accessible around the country and historical medical information at any particular time with a more all-encompassing data-centricity. When all the critical data are finally available to medical professionals they would be able to see from a single computer display more quickly what a patient requires, in line with what has already been achieved in many other countries, making the system easier and more effective.

Data-centric intelligence helps healthcare providers to dig into quantitative cost and income analyses from reports and view basic working capital reports, which equates to planned versus real sales and variance results. Quantitative capabilities help caregivers to analyze emerging patterns in care services and detect outdated or underrated initiatives, perform net income analyses, gather predictions, and monitor payment requirements. Investigating technologies enable medical professionals to conform to regulatory reporting requirements and to guarantee transparency to business unit management, executives, and directors from financial analysts.

In order to assess the probability of growing consumption of services focused on knowledge, such as quick use of healthcare infrastructure, drug use, and statistics of patients, data-centric intelligence operations will examine the history and risk profiles of an individual. By using evidence-based performance data, monitoring quality differences, delivering client dashboards, and alerting and verifying drug reactions, clinicians maximize efficiency. Reliability, care quality, customer loyalty, utilization, and profitability measures are achieved by evaluating the quality of the services in compliance with insurance plan, employer data, and knowledge system (HEDIS) requirements developed by the National Accreditation Committee. Data-centric intelligence operation will help medical professionals and insurers to define the greatest potential risks and establish the most efficient payment systems by evaluating and monitoring complaints. Proper handling of health records also allows medical providers and payers to optimize cost, improve claim turnaround times, and foil false statements. Advanced computational tools provide statistical software that allows healthcare companies to assess risks throughout the platform, identify error-related or fraudulent claim anomalies, improve claim-payment flow predictability, and identify loss potential for particular geographical areas.

Organizations may monitor vast quantities of knowledge resulting from clinical operations and determine the most appropriate practices by providing analysis from several sources at once. This aids providers in recognizing patterns and irregularities, and in clinical care, examining risk. By working separately as individual silos, caregivers, hospitals, and medical institutions are finding that they do not offer the best maintenance. In every layer of the architecture, centralized management and bullet-proof protection ensure that medical facilities have industry-leading safety initiatives. Some clinicians may detect and administer more effectively and offer superior care with a sense of satisfaction, safety, and critical clinical details.

By increasing the exchange of knowledge with patients and providing self-service functions to patients, healthcare industries use data-centric intelligence to permit patients to take control of their treatment, leading to better results. Data-centric activity helps the most appropriate people have access to the appropriate details at the right moment, providing healthcare professionals with a single channel to exchange patient information for improved decision-making and connecting patients through hospitals, nursing homes, medical offices, and social support environments throughout the community. It supports the provision of safe treatment, and supports physicians in promoting the integrated delivery of treatment through healthcare settings through scientific diagnosis and treatment. Providers are able to monitor and predict patient diagnosis and use of healthcare services to maximize patient treatment, reduce long waiting lists, and provide more timely treatment.

Access to high-quality data and analysis is key to the strategic objectives of a leading healthcare provider, including the practice of specialized treatment and the implementation of research findings by maximizing the efficacy of scientific trials, decreasing the cycle times from testing to clinical care and thereby enhancing the lifespan efficiency and durability. The consistency and volumes of information are critical factors in the provision of this analysis. It is widely recognized, for instance, that oncology is the field of medicine in which knowledge is more quickly produced (It is reported that keeping up with the poetry can take up to 160 hours per week for a clinician.). This requires access to, supervision, and management of a vast volume of ever-changing information, much of it structureless. The identification, processing, and application of data rather than the more traditional approach of "data processing, flow and data integration," linkage with pace and agility of research data and clinical results requires a radically different type of revolutionary data integration. This, in essence, makes for a great standard of data-centricity to be accomplished while minimizing the cost and complexity with functional scaling. In the healthcare sector, the ramifications of data-centric operations are far-reaching and can become the foundation on which an organization takes action and makes important decisions. Undoubtedly, those businesses that exploit strong data-centered structures for superior insights, mobility, and outstanding data delivery technologies are more competitive in the market.

5. Case study for application of the particle swarm optimization model for the diagnosis of heart disease

The PSO algorithm is a population-based optimization technique that uses a population of particles to try to find the best solution to a problem. A swarm is a collection of particles, and each particle is an individual. PSO, like other search-based evolutionary procedures, is a methodology that examines a problem's search space in order to determine the parameters required to maximize a specific goal. Optimal control mechanisms are used to find the highest and minimum values of a function or process [113]. The PSO's simplicity of implementation and the fact that no gradient information is necessary are two of its most appealing aspects. In PSO, the problem's solution space is modeled as a search space. Every point in the search space represents a possible solution to the problem. Each particle has a role to participate in the discovery of the best position or best solution in the solution space. The velocity of each particle determines how fast it moves. The particle movement is estimated as follows for each iteration [114]:

$$X_i(t+1) \leftarrow X_i(t) + V_i(t) \tag{8.1}$$

$$V_i(t+1) \leftarrow WV_i(t) + c_1 r_1(pbest_i(t) - X_i(t)) + c_2 r_2(gbest_i(t)) - -X_i(t) \tag{8.2}$$

In Eqs. (8.1) and (8.2), $X_i(t)$ is the position of particle i at time t, $v_i(t)$ is the velocity of particle i at time t, $pbest_i(t)$ is the best position found by the particle itself so far, $gbest_i(t)$ is the best position found by the whole swarm so far, ω is an inertia weight scaling the previous time step velocity, c_1 and c_2 are two acceleration coefficients that scale the effect of the best personal position of the particle, $(pbest_i(t))$ and the best global position $(gbest_i(t))$ and r_1 and r_2 are random variables within the range of 0 and 1.

Hence, $i\varepsilon 1...s$

$$pbest_i(t+1) = \begin{cases} pbest_i(t) \text{ if } (pbest(t) \leq f(X_i(t+1))) \\ X_t(t+1)(t) \text{ if } (pbest(t)) \leq f(X_i(t+1)) \end{cases}$$

$$pbest_i(t) = \min\{f(y), f(gbest(t))\} \tag{8.3}$$

where, $y\varepsilon\{pbest_o(t), pbest_1(t), pbest_2(t), ...pbest_i(t)\}$ \tag{8.4}

At time t, Eqs. (8.3) and (8.4) describe how the personal and global best values are changed. The swarm is considered to have s particles, and the objective function f is utilized to compute the particles' fitness using a minimization problem.

Cardiac arrest is a severe condition that is common in Western countries. Cardiovascular disease (CVD) is defined by a number of disorders that affect the heart and blood vessels, such as atherosclerosis, which is caused by plaque deposition in the arteries. Plaque can build and form clots, resulting in a block plate. A smooth flow of blood in the artery can trigger a heart attack or stroke [115]. CVD has a variety of adverse effects, including mitral valve prolapse, pulmonary stenosis, dilated cardiomyopathy, congenital heart disease, arrhythmia, and coronary artery disease, among others. CVD is a major global disease as compared with other communicable illnesses because of the increase in age, urbanization, and globalization [116]. In 2005, 30% of global deaths, or 17 million people, were due to CVD illness, with 7.2 and 5.7 million deaths due to heart attacks and stroke, respectively; 80% of these deaths were reported in developing countries, and the WHO estimates that another 24 million deaths could occur if the trend is not reversed by 2033 [117].

The main determinant of CVD has decreased the average age of death between 1990 and 2015, and heart disease has caused the highest incidence of death in Africa, as well as sudden fatalities internationally [118]. Effective diagnosis of such fatal diseases would also go a long way toward lowering global death rates. Predicting who is liable to suffer from CVD has been a key research challenge around the world [119]. Various characteristics such as smoking habits, age, and drug usage have been used to predict CVD sufferers, but none have yet proven to be accurate prediction models [120]. The increase in the number of infectious and chronic illnesses is due to an increase in the global population [121]. The exponential growth in the volume, speed, and diversity of disease and health-related data has necessitated the development of smarter and more robust healthcare systems for effective data storage and control in order to meet the demands of large data sets [121]. Natural computing models on medical data are highly significant for achieving the accuracy, efficiency, management, and identification of significant areas for CVD prediction [122].

5.1 The heart disease data set characteristics

There are 303 instances of 14 attributes in this heart disease data set [53]. Table 8.3 gives a description of this data set.

5.2 Performance evaluation metrics

True negative (TN), true positive (TN), false negative (FN), and false positive (FP) are used for performance evaluation in this chapter, where:

TN = positively diagnosed diabetes by the model, the healthy people;
TP = positively diagnosed diabetic mellitus patients in the data set used;
FN = negatively diagnosed individuals diagnosed with diabetes mellitus healthy patients;
FP = false positively diabetic patients but not diagnosed by the model.

6. Results and discussion

The PSO models were used on the training data set, and the results of the preliminary performance evaluation using all 13 input parameters are presented in this section. The results of experiments show better performance when compared with some selected other algorithms, as shown in Table 8.4 and

Table 8.3 The details and features of the CVD data set.

S. no.	Features	Data values	Data type	Description
1	Age		Numeric	Age in years
2	Sex	0 = Male 1 = Female	Numeric	NIL
3	Cp	1: Typical angina 2: Atypical angina 3: Nonanginal pain 4: Asymptomatic	Numeric	Chest pain type
4	Treetops	NIL	Numeric	Resting blood pressure (in mmHg on admission to hospital)
5	Chol	NIL	Numeric	Serum cholesterol in mg/dL
6	Fbs	1 = true 0 = false	Numeric	Fasting blood sugar >120 mg/dL
7	Resting	0: Normal 1: Having ST-T wave abnormality 2: Showing probable or definite left ventricular hypertrophy by Estes' criteria	Numeric	Resting electrocardiographic results
8	Thalach		Numeric	Maximum heart rate achieved
9	Exang	1 = Yes 0 = No	Numeric	Exercise-induced angina
10	Oldpeak		Numeric	Oldpeak = ST depression induced by exercise relative to rest
11	Slope	1: Upsloping 2: Flat 3: Downsloping	Numeric	The slope of the peak exercise ST segment
12	Ca		Numeric	Number of major vessels (0–3) colored by fluoroscopy
13	Thal	0; 1; 2;	Numeric	Thal: 0 = normal; 1 = fixed defect; 2 = reversible defect
14	Target	0 = No heart disease 1 = Heart disease	Numeric	The predicted attribute

Table 8.4 Performance of PSO on regular classifiers with the heart disease data set.

Models	Accuracy	Sensitivity	Specificity	False positive	ROC-AUC
KNN	94.06	91.56	93.00	9.00	92.11
SVM	97.54	97.78	96.32	4.00	97.08
Decision tree	88.67	85.43	85.84	13.5	89.06
Naïve Bayes	95.78	94.32	95.20	2.42	95.00
Proposed model	98.40	97.94	96.98	3.75	98.00

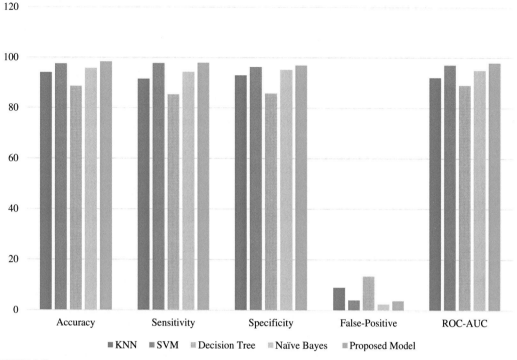

Performance Evaluation of various Models

FIGURE 8.2

A comparison of the proposed model performance with some of the state-of-the-art models.

Fig. 8.2. This means that the performance of the algorithm is good at recording accuracy, with recall and accuracy values of 98.4%, 97.9%, and 97.5%, respectively. This outcome is encouraging in heart diseases with previously implemented algorithms. A total of 98% of the test data are correctly identified by the model, and the sensitivity is balanced between the two target class groups. In terms of accuracy, PSO effectively registered 98.4%, demonstrating its ability to reliably provide accurate results. In addition, an ROC-AUC value of 98% reported by the model indicates that it has a good dissimilarity measure. This means it has a 98% chance of reliably determining between the existence and avoidance of heart disease from the patient data.

There are 13 instances in the heart disease data set used. The classification result in Fig. 8.1 shows that the PSO classifier has the highest score with an accuracy of 98.4%. Its sensitivity and false-positive rates are 97.94% and 3.75%, respectively. The worst of the classifiers is DT, with 88.67% accuracy and 13.50% false-positive error rate. Besides DT and KNN classifiers with higher false-positive error rates, other classifiers demonstrate a potent index in all the metrics. This indicates that the proposed model was good for the classification of heart disease and can still be use in other infectious diseases for better diagnosis and classification.

7. Conclusion

Natural computing is of interest in smart healthcare mainly because it can be used to model real-life problems using biological phenomena. The NC is relevant in other various fields of study such as cognitive science, economics, chemistry, physics, art, and even ethics. For instance, engineers can use NC to control complex behaviors that are difficult to generate and it offers methods to regulate traditional methods. Natural computing is important for individuals because it facilitates the development of novel technologies that can be used as entertainment, science tools, and to help people perform problematic or unpleasant tasks. The system in smart healthcare has taught us to think computationally about nature and think "naturally" about computation. The approaches from all NC yield exciting and novel capabilities for various fields, especially healthcare systems and bioinformatics. The combination of nature and computing has helped scientists and engineers to gain a very rich paradigm for exploration of the healthcare system. Therefore, NC has taught us that any model of a natural occurrence can be used as the basis for the creation of new computational problem-solving technologies; computers can simulate/emulate a large array of natural events; and computational materials can be used. However, the full potential of NC is far from being reached in healthcare systems, although the fruits of it exploration are extremely attractive for new technological solutions to and explanations of old and more recent problems. Unsupervised learning is mainly categorized into clusters and hierarchical algorithms. Clusters are created by iteratively splitting patterns (instances) into top-down or bottom-up agglomerative procedures in a hierarchical type using categorization methods, and with hierarchical grouping techniques that are contentious. Unlike hierarchical clustering, by optimizing some criterion or feature, partitional classification applies data to k clusters with no hierarchical arrangement. The most suitable technique is to identify the Euclidean distance between the positions of each cluster available and to apply the point to the minimum distance of the clusters. Therefore, this chapter presents the areas of application of NC, and unsupervised learning methods in a healthcare data-centric approach to increase trust, cost-effectiveness, and security of data in the healthcare sector. The chapter also discussed several outstanding opportunities created by NC and unsupervised learning in the healthcare industry and the research challenges to deployment in the healthcare system. In order to assess the probability of increased resource use based on information, such as rapid usage of healthcare facilities, substance use, and patient demographics, data-centric intelligence operations examine the history and risk profiles of individuals. Natural computing and unsupervised learning data-centric intelligence operation can help healthcare providers and payers identify the greatest risk areas and formulate the most effective rate structures by assessing and tracking claims. Proper management of claims data also helps healthcare organizations and payers to maximize cost, and reduce the response time, and thwart false claims. Advanced analytical capabilities include predictive analysis that helps healthcare industries to analyze risk across the network, identify error-related or fraudulent claim anomalies, improve claim-payment flow predictability, and identify the loss potential for particular geographical areas.

References

[1] L. Kari, G. Rozenberg, The many facets of natural computing, Commun. ACM 51 (10) (2008) 72–83.
[2] Z. Zuo, K. Zhao, The more multidisciplinary the better? —The prevalence and interdisciplinarity of research collaborations in multidisciplinary institutions, J. Inform. 12 (3) (2018) 736–756.
[3] N.H. Siddique, H. Adeli, Nature-Inspired Computing: Physics and Chemistry-Based Algorithms, CRC Press, 2017.

[4] J.M. Górriz, J. Ramírez, A. Ortíz, F.J. Martínez-Murcia, F. Segovia, J. Suckling, et al., Artificial intelligence within the interplay between natural and artificial computation: advances in data science, trends and applications, Neurocomputing 410 (2020) 237–270.

[5] S. Miguel-Tomé, The influence of computational traits on the natural selection of the nervous system, Nat. Comput. 17 (2) (2018) 403–425.

[6] Y. Bengio, A. Courville, P. Vincent, Representation learning: a review and new perspectives, IEEE Trans. Pattern Anal. Mach. Intell. 35 (8) (2013) 1798–1828.

[7] Y. LeCun, Y. Bengio, G. Hinton, Deep learning, Nature 521 (7553) (2015) 436–444.

[8] F.E. Ayo, R.O. Ogundokun, J.B. Awotunde, M.O. Adebiyi, A.E. Adeniyi, Severe acne skin disease: a fuzzy-based method for diagnosis, in: Lecture Notes in Computer Science (Including Subseries Lecture Notes in Artificial Intelligence and Lecture Notes in Bioinformatics), 2020, 12254 LNCS, 2020, pp. 320–334.

[9] J.B. Awotunde, O.E. Matiluko, O.W. Fatai, Medical diagnosis system using fuzzy logic, Afr. J. Comput. ICTs 7 (2) (2014) 99–106.

[10] T.O. Oladele, R.O. Ogundokun, J.B. Awotunde, M.O. Adebiyi, J.K. Adeniyi, Diagmal: a malaria coactive neuro-fuzzy expert system, in: Lecture Notes in Computer Science (Including Subseries Lecture Notes in Artificial Intelligence and Lecture Notes in Bioinformatics), 2020, 12254 LNCS, 2020, pp. 428–441.

[11] L.N. de Castro, Fundamentals of natural computing: an overview, Phys. Life Rev. 4 (1) (2007) 1–36.

[12] R. Pathak, S.S. Gupta, A study on natural computing: a review, in: ICDSMLA 2019, Springer, Singapore, 2020, pp. 1975–1983.

[13] Z. Konkoli, S. Nichele, M. Dale, S. Stepney, Reservoir computing with computational matter, in: Computational Matter, Springer, Cham, 2018, pp. 269–293.

[14] G. Dodig Crnkovic, Dynamics of information as natural computation, Information 2 (3) (2011) 460–477.

[15] A. Johanson, W. Hasselbring, Software engineering for computational science: past, present, future, Comput. Sci. Eng. (2018).

[16] M.T. Emmerich, A.H. Deutz, A tutorial on multiobjective optimization: fundamentals and evolutionary methods, Nat. Comput. 17 (3) (2018) 585–609.

[17] U. Rüde, K. Willcox, L.C. McInnes, H.D. Sterck, Research and education in computational science and engineering, SIAM Rev. 60 (3) (2018) 707–754.

[18] K.S. Bonham, M.I. Stefan, Women are underrepresented in computational biology: an analysis of the scholarly literature in biology, computer science and computational biology, PLoS Computational Biol. 13 (10) (2017) e1005134.

[19] B.K. Sovacool, J. Axsen, S. Sorrell, Promoting novelty, rigor, and style in energy social science: towards codes of practice for appropriate methods and research design, Energy Res. Soc. Sci. 45 (2018) 12–42.

[20] N. Abd-Alsabour, Nature as a source for inspiring new optimization algorithms, in: Proceedings of the 9th International Conference on Signal Processing Systems, 2017, pp. 51–56.

[21] N. Siddique, H. Adeli, Nature inspired computing: an overview and some future directions, Cogn. Comput. 7 (6) (2015) 706–714.

[22] I.E. Agbehadji, R.C. Millham, S.J. Fong, H. Yang, Bioinspired computational approach to missing value estimation, Math. Probl. Eng. 2018 (2018).

[23] G.A.E.N.A. Said, Nature inspired algorithms in cloud computing: a survey, Int. J. Intell. Inf. Syst. 5 (5) (2016) 60–64.

[24] R. Tang, S. Fong, X.S. Yang, S. Deb, Wolf search algorithm with ephemeral memory, in: Seventh International Conference on Digital Information Management (ICDIM 2012), IEEE, 2012, pp. 165–172.

[25] M. Dorigo, M. Birattari, T. Stutzle, Ant colony optimization, IEEE Comput. Intell. Mag. 1 (4) (2006) 28–39.

[26] I.E. Agbehadji, R. Millham, S. Thakur, H. Yang, H. Addo, Visualization of frequently changed patterns based on the behaviour of dung beetles, in: International Conference on Soft Computing in Data Science, Springer, Singapore, 2018, pp. 230–245.

[27] I.E. Agbehadji, R. Millham, S.J. Fong, H. Yang, Kestrel-based search algorithm (KSA) for parameter tuning unto long short term memory (LSTM) network for feature selection in classification of high-dimensional bioinformatics datasets, in: 2018 Federated Conference on Computer Science and Information Systems (FedCSIS), IEEE, 2018, pp. 15–20.

[28] S. Fong, R. Wong, A.V. Vasilakos, Accelerated PSO swarm search feature selection for data stream mining big data, IEEE Trans. Ser. Comput. 9 (1) (2015) 33–45.

[29] A.H. Gandomi, X.S. Yang, Chaotic bat algorithm, J. Comput. Sci. 5 (2) (2014) 224–232.

[30] Y. Shi, T. Boudouh, O. Grunder, A hybrid genetic algorithm for a home health care routing problem with time window and fuzzy demand, Expert Syst. Appl. 72 (2017) 160–176.

[31] E. Sulis, P. Terna, A. Di Leva, G. Boella, A. Boccuzzi, Agent-oriented decision support system for business processes management with genetic algorithm optimization: an application in healthcare, J. Med. Syst. 44 (9) (2020) 1–7.

[32] M. Tahir, A. Tubaishat, F. Al-Obeidat, B. Shah, Z. Halim, M. Waqas, A novel binary chaotic genetic algorithm for feature selection and its utility in affective computing and healthcare, Neural Comput. Appl. (2020) 1–22.

[33] R. Ahmed, T. Zayed, F. Nasiri, A hybrid genetic algorithm-based fuzzy Markovian model for the deterioration modeling of healthcare facilities, Algorithms 13 (9) (2020) 210.

[34] M. Abdel-Basset, L. Abdle-Fatah, A.K. Sangaiah, An improved Lévy based whale optimization algorithm for bandwidth-efficient virtual machine placement in cloud computing environment, Cluster Comput. 22 (4) (2019) 8319–8334.

[35] G.I. Rajathi, G.W. Jiji, Chronic liver disease classification using hybrid whale optimization with simulated annealing and ensemble classifier, Symmetry 11 (1) (2019) 33.

[36] A. Abdelaziz, M. Elhoseny, A.S. Salama, A.M. Riad, A.E. Hassanien, Intelligent algorithms for optimal selection of virtual machine in cloud environment, towards enhance healthcare services, in: International Conference on Advanced Intelligent Systems and Informatics, Springer, Cham, 2017, pp. 289–298.

[37] V. Dutt, P.S. Rathore, K. Chauhan, Support vector in healthcare using SVM/PSO in various domains: a review, Swarm Intell. Optim. Algorithm Appl. (2020) 291–307.

[38] A. Barbu, Y. She, L. Ding, G. Gramajo, Feature selection with annealing for computer vision and big data learning, IEEE Trans. Pattern Anal. Mach. Intell. 39 (2) (2016) 272–286.

[39] J. Yan, Y. Peng, D. Shen, X. Yan, Q. Deng, An artificial bee colony-based green routing mechanism in WBANs for sensor-based e-healthcare systems, Sensors 18 (10) (2018) 3268.

[40] M. Nandhini, S.N. Sivanandam, S. Renugadevi, Artificial bee colony-based associative classifier for healthcare data diagnosis, in: Handbook of Research on Disease Prediction Through Data Analytics and Machine Learning, IGI Global, 2020, pp. 237–253.

[41] B. Subanya, R.R. Rajalaxmi, Feature selection using artificial bee colony for cardiovascular disease classification, in: 2014 International Conference on Electronics and Communication Systems (ICECS), IEEE, 2014, pp. 1–6.

[42] I.E. Agbehadji, B.O. Awuzie, A.B. Ngowi, R.C. Millham, Review of big data analytics, artificial intelligence and nature-inspired computing models towards accurate detection of COVID-19 pandemic cases and contact tracing, Int. J. Environ. Res. Publ. Health 17 (15) (2020) 5330.

[43] P. Pattnaik, S. Mishra, B.S.P. Mishra, Optimization techniques for intelligent IoT applications, in: Fog, Edge, and Pervasive Computing in Intelligent IoT Driven Applications, 2020, pp. 311–331.

[44] N. Dey, H. Das, B. Naik, H.S. Behera (Eds.), Big Data Analytics for Intelligent Healthcare Management, Academic Press, 2019.

[45] P.S. Game, V. Vaze, M. Emmanuel, Optimized decision tree rules using divergence based grey wolf optimization for big data classification in health care, Evol. Intell. (2019) 1–17.

[46] P. Sharma, A. Gupta, A. Aggarwal, D. Gupta, A. Khanna, A.E. Hassanien, V.H.C. de Albuquerque, The health of things for classification of protein structure using improved grey wolf optimization, J. Supercomput. 76 (2) (2020) 1226–1241.

[47] S.B. Babu, A. Suneetha, G.C. Babu, Y.J.N. Kumar, G. Karuna, Medical disease prediction using grey wolf optimization and auto encoder based recurrent neural network, Period. Eng. Nat. Sci. 6 (1) (2018) 229−240.

[48] P. Sharma, S. Sundaram, M. Sharma, A. Sharma, D. Gupta, Diagnosis of Parkinson's disease using modified grey wolf optimization, Cognit. Syst. Res. 54 (2019) 100−115.

[49] A. Alameen, A. Gupta, Optimization driven deep learning approach for health monitoring and risk assessment in wireless body sensor networks, Int. J. Bus. Data Commun. Netw. 16 (1) (2020) 70−93.

[50] D. Moldovan, P. Stefan, C. Vuscan, V.R. Chifu, I. Anghel, T. Cioara, I. Salomie, Diet generator for elders using cat swarm optimization and wolf search, in: International Conference on Advancements of Medicine and Health Care through Technology; 12th-15th October 2016, Cluj-Napoca, Romania, Springer, Cham, 2017, pp. 238−243.

[51] L.M. Abualigah, A.T. Khader, E.S. Hanandeh, A new feature selection method to improve the document clustering using particle swarm optimization algorithm, J. Comput. Sci. 25 (2018) 456−466.

[52] L.M. Abualigah, A.T. Khader, Unsupervised text feature selection technique based on hybrid particle swarm optimization algorithm with genetic operators for the text clustering, J. Supercomput. 73 (11) (2017) 4773−4795.

[53] M. Tubishat, S. Ja'afar, M. Alswaitti, S. Mirjalili, N. Idris, M.A. Ismail, M.S. Omar, Dynamic Salp swarm algorithm for feature selection, Expert Syst. Appl. 164 (2020) 113873.

[54] S. Banerjee, Y. Badr, Evaluating decision analytics from mobile big data using rough set based ant colony, in: Mobile Big Data, Springer, Cham, 2018, pp. 217−231.

[55] S. Changxin, M. Ke, Research on big data mining method of bioinformatics, in: Proceedings of the 5th International Conference on Distance Education and Learning, 2020, pp. 166−169.

[56] R. Behmanesh, I. Rahimi, M. Zandieh, A.H. Gandomi, Advanced ant colony optimization in healthcare scheduling, Evol. Comput. Sched. (2020) 37−72.

[57] W. Xiang, J. Yin, G. Lim, An ant colony optimization approach for solving an operating room surgery scheduling problem, Comput. Ind. Eng. 85 (2015) 335−345.

[58] O. Zedadra, A. Guerrieri, N. Jouandeau, G. Spezzano, H. Seridi, G. Fortino, Swarm intelligence-based algorithms within IoT-based systems: a review, J. Parallel Distr. Comput. 122 (2018) 173−187.

[59] S.S. Gill, R. Buyya, Bio-inspired algorithms for big data analytics: a survey, taxonomy, and open challenges, in: Big Data Analytics for Intelligent Healthcare Management, Academic Press, 2019, pp. 1−17.

[60] X.M. Pan, Application of improved ant colony algorithm in intelligent medical system: from the perspective of big data, Chem. Eng. Trans. 51 (2016) 523−528.

[61] B. Hu, Y. Dai, Y. Su, P. Moore, X. Zhang, C. Mao, et al., Feature selection for optimized high-dimensional biomedical data using an improved shuffled frog leaping algorithm, IEEE ACM Trans. Comput. Biol. Bioinf. 15 (6) (2016) 1765−1773.

[62] E.A. Neeba, S. Koteeswaran, Bacterial foraging information swarm optimizer for detecting affective and informative content in medical blogs, Cluster Comput. 22 (5) (2019) 10743−10756.

[63] M. Abdel-basset, R. Mohamed, M. Elhoseny, R.K. Chakrabortty, M.A. Ryan, Hybrid COVID-19 detection model using an improved marine predators algorithm and a ranking-based diversity reduction strategy, IEEE Access 8 (2020) 79521−79540.

[64] G. Carrasco-Escobar, M.C. Castro, J.L. Barboza, J. Ruiz-Cabrejos, A. Llanos-Cuentas, J.M. Vinetz, D. Gamboa, Use of open mobile mapping tool to assess human mobility traceability in rural offline populations with contrasting malaria dynamics, PeerJ 7 (2019) e6298.

[65] M. Abdel-Basset, H. Hawash, M. Elhoseny, R.K. Chakrabortty, M. Ryan, DeepH-DTA: deep learning for predicting drug-target interactions: a case study of COVID-19 drug repurposing, IEEE Access 8 (2020) 170433−170451.

[66] K. Zheng, X. Wang, Feature selection method with joint maximal information entropy between features and class, Pattern Recogn. 77 (2018) 20−29.

[67] A. Oztekin, L. Al-Ebbini, Z. Sevkli, D. Delen, A decision analytic approach to predicting quality of life for lung transplant recipients: a hybrid genetic algorithms-based methodology, Eur. J. Oper. Res. 266 (2) (2018) 639–651.

[68] I. Jain, V.K. Jain, R. Jain, Correlation feature selection based improved-binary particle swarm optimization for gene selection and cancer classification, Appl. Soft Comput. 62 (2018) 203–215.

[69] S. Shilaskar, A. Ghatol, Feature selection for medical diagnosis: evaluation for cardiovascular diseases, Expert Syst. Appl. 40 (10) (2013) 4146–4153.

[70] T. Prasartvit, A. Banharnsakun, B. Kaewkamnerdpong, T. Achalakul, Reducing bioinformatics data dimension with ABC-kNN, Neurocomputing 116 (2013) 367–381.

[71] S.M. Vieira, L.F. Mendonça, G.J. Farinha, J.M. Sousa, Modified binary PSO for feature selection using SVM applied to mortality prediction of septic patients, Appl. Soft Comput. 13 (8) (2013) 3494–3504.

[72] M.M. Mafarja, S. Mirjalili, Hybrid whale optimization algorithm with simulated annealing for feature selection, Neurocomputing 260 (2017) 302–312.

[73] A. Tayal, S.P. Singh, Integrating big data analytic and hybrid firefly-chaotic simulated annealing approach for facility layout problem, Ann. Oper. Res. 270 (1–2) (2018) 489–514.

[74] I.B. Saida, K. Nadjet, B. Omar, A new algorithm for data clustering based on cuckoo search optimization, in: Genetic and Evolutionary Computing, Springer, Cham, 2014, pp. 55–64.

[75] J. Dheeba, N.A. Singh, S.T. Selvi, Computer-aided detection of breast cancer on mammograms: a swarm intelligence optimized wavelet neural network approach, J. Biomed. Inf. 49 (2014) 45–52.

[76] M.R. Mohebian, H.R. Marateb, M. Mansourian, M.A. Mañanas, F. Mokarian, A hybrid computer-aided-diagnosis system for prediction of breast cancer recurrence (HPBCR) using optimized ensemble learning, Comput. Struct. Biotechnol. J. 15 (2017) 75–85.

[77] E. Sherkat, S. Nourashrafeddin, E.E. Milios, R. Minghim, Interactive document clustering revisited: a visual analytics approach, in: 23rd International Conference on Intelligent User Interfaces, 2018, pp. 281–292.

[78] M. Ramadas, A. Abraham, Metaheuristics for Data Clustering and Image Segmentation, Springer, 2019.

[79] A. Saxena, M. Prasad, A. Gupta, N. Bharill, O.P. Patel, A. Tiwari, et al., A review of clustering techniques and developments, Neurocomputing 267 (2017) 664–681.

[80] A. Lurka, Spatio-temporal hierarchical cluster analysis of mining-induced seismicity in coal mines using Ward's minimum variance method, J. Appl. Geophys. (2020) 104249.

[81] F. Murtagh, P. Contreras, Algorithms for hierarchical clustering: an overview, II, Wiley Interdiscipl. Rev. Data Min. Knowl. Discov. 7 (6) (2017) e1219.

[82] L. Shooshtarian, D. Lan, A. Taherkordi, A clustering-based approach to efficient resource allocation in fog computing, in: International Symposium on Pervasive Systems, Algorithms and Networks, Springer, Cham, 2019, pp. 207–224.

[83] M. Pavithra, R.M.S. Parvathi, A survey on clustering high dimensional data techniques, Int. J. Appl. Eng. Res. 12 (11) (2017) 2893–2899.

[84] M.J. Van der Laan, K.S. Pollard, A new algorithm for hybrid hierarchical clustering with visualization and the bootstrap, J. Stat. Plann. Inference 117 (2) (2003) 275–303.

[85] J.A.F. Costa, M.L. de Andrade Netto, Clustering of complex shaped data sets via Kohonen maps and mathematical morphology, in: Data Mining and Knowledge Discovery: Theory, Tools, and Technology III, vol. 4384, International Society for Optics and Photonics, 2001, pp. 16–27.

[86] Z. Li, G. Wang, G. He, Milling tool wear state recognition based on partitioning around medoids (PAM) clustering, Int. J. Adv. Manuf. Technol. 88 (5–8) (2017) 1203–1213.

[87] L. Kaufman, P.J. Rousseeuw, Finding Groups in Data: An Introduction to Cluster Analysis, vol. 344, John Wiley & Sons, 2009.

[88] M.B. Eisen, P.T. Spellman, P.O. Brown, D. Botstein, Cluster analysis and display of genome-wide expression patterns, Proc. Natl. Acad. Sci. USA 95 (25) (1998) 14863−14868.

[89] H. Chipman, R. Tibshirani, Hybrid hierarchical clustering with applications to microarray data, Biostatistics 7 (2) (2006) 286−301.

[90] K. Hemming, M. Taljaard, A. Forbes, Analysis of cluster randomised stepped wedge trials with repeated cross-sectional samples, Trials 18 (1) (2017) 101.

[91] Q. Wu, C.R. Lane, L. Wang, M.K. Vanderhoof, J.R. Christensen, H. Liu, Efficient delineation of nested depression hierarchy in digital elevation models for hydrological analysis using level-set method, JAWRA J. Am. Water Resour. Assoc. 55 (2) (2019) 354−368.

[92] M.K. Forbes, R. Kotov, C.J. Ruggero, D. Watson, M. Zimmerman, R.F. Krueger, Delineating the joint hierarchical structure of clinical and personality disorders in an outpatient psychiatric sample, Compr. Psychiatr. 79 (2017) 19−30.

[93] P.M. Shakeel, S. Baskar, V.S. Dhulipala, M.M. Jaber, Cloud based framework for diagnosis of diabetes mellitus using K-means clustering, Health Inf. Sci. Syst. 6 (1) (2018) 16.

[94] J.J. Armstrong, M. Zhu, J.P. Hirdes, P. Stolee, K-means cluster analysis of rehabilitation service users in the home health care system of Ontario: examining the heterogeneity of a complex geriatric population, Arch. Phys. Med. Rehabil. 93 (12) (2012) 2198−2205.

[95] Z.K. Feng, W.J. Niu, R. Zhang, S. Wang, C.T. Cheng, Operation rule derivation of hydropower reservoir by k-means clustering method and extreme learning machine based on particle swarm optimization, J. Hydrol. 576 (2019) 229−238.

[96] L.D.L. Fuente-Tomas, B. Arranz, G. Safont, P. Sierra, M. Sanchez-Autet, A. Garcia-Blanco, M.P. Garcia-Portilla, Classification of patients with bipolar disorder using k-means clustering, PLoS One 14 (1) (2019) e0210314.

[97] A. Rai, S.H. Upadhyay, Bearing performance degradation assessment based on a combination of empirical mode decomposition and k-medoids clustering, Mech. Syst. Signal Process. 93 (2017) 16−29.

[98] E. Irwansyah, E.S. Pratama, M. Ohyver, Clustering of Cardiovascular Disease Patients Using Data Mining Techniques with Principal Component Analysis and K-Medoids, 2020.

[99] M. Peker, A decision support system to improve medical diagnosis using a combination of k-medoids clustering based attribute weighting and SVM, J. Med. Syst. 40 (5) (2016) 116.

[100] N.A.H. Haldar, F.A. Khan, A. Ali, H. Abbas, Arrhythmia classification using Mahalanobis distance based improved fuzzy C-means clustering for mobile health monitoring systems, Neurocomputing 220 (2017) 221−235.

[101] S. Winiarti, S. Kusumadewi, I. Muhimmah, H. Yuliansyah, Determining the nutrition of patient based on food packaging product using fuzzy C means algorithm, in: 2017 4th International Conference on Electrical Engineering, Computer Science and Informatics (EECSI), IEEE, 2017, pp. 1−6.

[102] N. Purandhar, S. Ayyasamy, N.M. Saravanakumar, Clustering healthcare big data using advanced and enhanced fuzzy C-means algorithm, Int. J. Commun. Syst. 34 (1) (2021) e4629.

[103] I. Azimi, A. Anzanpour, A.M. Rahmani, T. Pahikkala, M. Levorato, P. Liljeberg, N. Dutt, Hich: hierarchical fog-assisted computing architecture for healthcare IoT, ACM Trans. Embed. Comput. Syst. 16 (5s) (2017) 1−20.

[104] S. Kushwaha, S. Das, Hierarchical agglomerative clustering approach for automated attribute classification of the health care domain from user generated reviews on web 2.0, in: 2020 IEEE International Conference on Computing, Power and Communication Technologies (GUCON), IEEE, 2020, pp. 671−676.

[105] S. Kanrar, P.K. Mandal, E-health monitoring system enhancement with Gaussian mixture model, Multimed. Tool. Appl. 76 (8) (2017) 10801−10823.

[106] M.H. Siddiqi, M. Alruwaili, A. Ali, S. Alanazi, F. Zeshan, Human activity recognition using Gaussian mixture hidden conditional random fields, in: Computational Intelligence and Neuroscience, vol. 2019, 2019.

[107] G. Manogaran, V. Vijayakumar, R. Varatharajan, P.M. Kumar, R. Sundarasekar, C.H. Hsu, Machine learning based big data processing framework for cancer diagnosis using hidden Markov model and GM clustering, Wirel. Pers. Commun. 102 (3) (2018) 2099–2116.

[108] J. Son, P.F. Brennan, S. Zhou, Correlated gamma-based hidden Markov model for the smart asthma management based on rescue inhaler usage, Stat. Med. 36 (10) (2017) 1619–1637.

[109] S.N.N. Htun, T.T. Zin, P. Tin, Image processing technique and hidden Markov model for an elderly care monitoring system, J. Imag. 6 (6) (2020) 49.

[110] J. Oliveira, C. Sousa, M.T. Coimbra, Coupled hidden Markov model for automatic ECG and PCG segmentation, in: 2017 IEEE International Conference on Acoustics, Speech and Signal Processing (ICASSP), IEEE, 2017, pp. 1023–1027.

[111] P. Melin, J.C. Monica, D. Sanchez, O. Castillo, Multiple ensemble neural network models with fuzzy response aggregation for predicting COVID-19 time series: the case of Mexico, Healthcare vol. 8 (2) (2020) 181 (Multidisciplinary Digital Publishing Institute).

[112] S. Ghosh, S.K. Dubey, Comparative analysis of k-means and fuzzy C-means algorithms, Int. J. Adv. Comput. Sci. Appl. 4 (4) (2013).

[113] S. Mishra, Y. Chouhan, A review on PSO and association rule mining for item set generation, Int. J. Innov. Res. Comput. Commun. Eng. 5 (1) (2017) 480–484.

[114] A.A. Esmin, R.A. Coelho, S. Matwin, A review on particle swarm optimization algorithm and its variants to clustering high-dimensional data, Artif. Intell. Rev. 44 (1) (2015) 23–45.

[115] J.R. Smith, M.J. Joyner, T.B. Curry, B.A. Borlaug, M.L. Keller-Ross, E.H. Van Iterson, T.P. Olson, Locomotor muscle group III/IV afferents constrain stroke volume and contribute to exercise intolerance in human heart failure, J. Physiol. 598 (23) (2020) 5379–5390.

[116] R. De Rosa, T. Palmerini, M. De Servi, G. Belmonte, S. Crimi, S. Cornara, et al., High on-treatment platelet reactivity and outcome in elderly with non-ST-segment elevation acute coronary syndrome-Insight from the GEPRESS study, Int. J. Cardiol. 259 (2018) 20–25.

[117] A. Aggarwal, S. Srivastava, M. Velmurugan, Newer perspectives of coronary artery disease in young, World J. Cardiol. 8 (12) (2016) 728.

[118] G.A. Roth, C. Johnson, A. Abajobir, F. Abd-Allah, S.F. Abera, G. Abyu, et al., Global, regional, and national burden of cardiovascular diseases for 10 causes, 1990 to 2015, J. Am. Coll. Cardiol. 70 (1) (2017) 1–25.

[119] E. Björnson, J. Borén, A. Mardinoglu, Personalized cardiovascular disease prediction and treatment—a review of existing strategies and novel systems medicine tools, Front. Physiol. 7 (2016) 2.

[120] L.N. Yasnitsky, A.A. Dumler, A.N. Poleshchuk, C.V. Bogdanov, F.M. Cherepanov, Artificial neural networks for obtaining new medical knowledge: diagnostics and prediction of cardiovascular disease progression, Biol. Med. 7 (2) (2015).

[121] A. Alamri, Big data with integrated cloud computing for prediction of health conditions, in: 2019 International Conference on Platform Technology and Service (PlatCon), IEEE, 2019, pp. 1–6.

[122] A. Kalantari, A. Kamsin, S. Shamshirband, A. Gani, H. Alinejad-Rokny, A.T. Chronopoulos, Computational intelligence approaches for classification of medical data: state-of-the-art, future challenges, and research directions, Neurocomputing 276 (2018) 2–22.

Optimized adaptive tree seed Kalman filter for a diabetes recommendation system—bilevel performance improvement strategy for healthcare applications

P. Nagaraj[1], P. Deepalakshmi[1] and Muhammad Fazal Ijaz[2]

[1]*School of Computing, Department of Computer Science and Engineering, Kalasalingam Academy of Research and Education, Krishnankoil, India;* [2]*Department of Intelligent Mechatronics Engineering, Sejong University, Seoul, South Korea*

1. Introduction

Type 1 diabetes (T1D) is a life-threatening disease caused by inadequate insulin delivery and, as an extreme case, it leads to dysregulation of blood glucose. Maintaining blood glucose at 70–180 mg/dL helps in preventing hyperglycemia (>180 mg/dL) and hypoglycemia (<70 mg/dL), which can cause T1D. Many different insulin injections are available with long- and rapid-acting formulations that are employed to determine the automated insulin delivery (AID) [1]. Recently, the availability of AID has expanded progressively, however people largely unaware of it due to the price, inconvenience, and problems with the form factor. People with T1D balance their glucose level using an insulin pump that delivers fast-acting insulin by continuous subcutaneous insulin infusion (CSII) before meals. The multiple daily injection (MDI) mechanism follows the self-administer fast-acting insulin, and long-acting insulin has to be regularly consumed before food, twice daily.

MDI is the initial approach used by a huge number of people globally. It is considered to be a most challenging problem when the parameters that affect insulin dosing, such as the preprandial glucose level, grams of carbohydrate, insulin sensitivity, insulin-to-carbohydrate ratio, and insulin-on-board (IOB), are at high levels. It is highly complicated for an individual to carry out the MDI strategy, which differs from person to person, using a bolus calculator, with various insulin pens having been introduced. Recently developed methods of heuristic-related guidelines for patients have been used to determine the insulin production for patients with T1D. Moreover, some people lack the skills required to measure their insulin level. Ref. [2] illustrated that most patients miscalculate the prandial insulin level, resulting in hypoglycemia and hyperglycemia. Also, some patients suffer from extensive health problems with daily and occasional differences in insulin demands and they can wait around 12–24 weeks to receive insulin from their doctors.

Enhanced health-related mobile computing, as well as continuous glucose monitors (CGM), have paved the way for automatic decision support systems (DSSs) for T1D. DSS offers an effective solution for those affected with T1D by enabling better prediction using a mobile interface, or information directly from received from patients is used by mobile applications to provide the required suggestions. When smartphone-related DSSs were used in clinical work, the simulation outcome was efficient and it provides enhanced glycemic results, whereas others methods will not provide efficient results.

Artificial intelligence (AI) is derived from computational models which are applied to activate machines to compute intelligent problem solving and achieve sophisticated operations. Machine learning (ML) is a subclass of AI that enhances the performance of tasks with prior knowledge. AI applications offer DSS for users with T1D. Such approaches provide the general insulin dosage during physician visits. If the CGM sensors are combined with real-time glucose evaluations, AI-related DSS models offer personalized hypoglycemia detection. Then, AI-based models have exhibited the capability for limiting hypoglycemia within a short time.

Building an accurate recommendation system for various diseases is important. Suitable data, when provided to recommender systems, yield excellent outcomes. The result of the recommender system will also vary by changing its adaptability to the problem and the input used. In this work, we define an optimized AKF technique for diabetic recommendation systems. Despite the Kalman filter being known for its efficacy in forecasting time changes and event prediction, its dependency on static attributes makes it somewhat restricted to real-time dynamic problems. Generally, all healthcare problems are dynamic. It is a general fact that the insulin requirement of a diabetes patient is always a dynamic problem since its deciding factors are usually determined by several time-varying biological parameters.

2. Literature review

Mertz [3] described a creative method used for commercialization which integrates four significant portions which were (1) a company-developed model which embeds AI and ML, (2) a mobile application, (3) no finger-stick glucose-monitoring scheme named FreeStyle Libre, and (4) a Bluetooth-based insulin pump. Alian et al. [4] outlined a personalized recommendation system (RS) for resolving diabetes self-management using an ontological profile with normal clinical diabetes recommendations and the only disadvantage is that it doesnot have mobile application for meal recommendation as well as food analyzing abilities.

Zheng et al. [5] performed a study that aimed to create a simple diabetes self-management system. Patients with T2D were randomly assigned to control the group. No meal RS was employed in this study. The Chronic Care Model described in Ref. [6], embeds major elements of team-based care in chronic disease management. No activity tracking of diabetic patients and interactive visual interface was evolved. Yang et al. [7] introduced Yum-me, a personalized nutrient-related meal RS to meet the user's vitamin requirements, diet conditions, and healthy foods. Yum-me offered a novel web learning mechanism to illustrate food preferences for both item-wise and pair-wise modules. Also, the RS model ensures efficiency; however, it lacks a diabetes Q&A system where complete knowledge of diabetes is available.

Toledo et al. [8] illustrated a common method to present a regular meal plan RS in conjunction with real-time management of nutritional-aware and preference-aware information. Here, prefiltering was carried out using AHPSort as a multicriteria decision-analyzing device for food organization; however, it is not applicable for affected patients. Gu et al. [9] described SugarMate, a mobile application which was a blood glucose inference system which is a partial CGM detector. Also, observing food, medicines, and insulin consumption mitigates an individual's physical activity.

Mokdara et al. [10] provide a combination of a deep neural network (DNN) and a recommendation system for Thai food. The presented method gathers essential ingredients from a group of recipes; however, it lacks a Diabetes Q&A chatbot. Bianchini et al. [11] presented a food recommender system which is suitable to give users a personalized and normal menu, which considers user preferences as well as clinical prescriptions. Prescriptions that categorize an ideal user's nutrition from constraints implied by a specific user's phenotype does not provide adequate information about diabetes. Xie et al. [12] established a mobile-based diabetes question-answering (Q&A) and early-warning system called Dia-AID, which guides diabetes patients and the general population. The Dia-AID system is composed of three modalities which include knowledge-based Q&A, frequently asked question-based Q&A, and web-based Q&A. It lacks a medicine reminder notification on smartphones, meal suggestions, and food-analyzing capabilities.

Mishra et al. [13] proposed the Enhanced Adaptive-Genetic Algorithm-Multilayer Perceptron (EAGA-MLP) model for the characterization of and suggestions regarding diabetes. This model presentation was additionally attempted with several disease data sets. The accuracy acquired was 94.7%. In this manner, the proposed model can assist medical expert recommendations by analyzing the risk components of type 2 diabetes. It can be utilized to help medical services specialists to discover patients affected by diabetes.

Mishra et al. [14] proposed another crossover attribute evaluator strategy to upgrade the recommendations of diabetes disease. The authors adequately incorporated the upgraded K-means clustering with CFS filter techniques and BFS covering techniques. Moreover, this hybrid technique was assessed with an improved decision tree classifier. The improved decision tree classifier is consolidated with clustering and classification. It was substantiated on 14 distinctive constant infection data sets and its performance was maintained. An ideal, steady characterization and execution were noted, and the accuracy obtained was 96.7%.

Oniani et al. [15] reviewed AI for Internet of Things (IoT) and medical frameworks, which incorporated the use and practice of various medication philosophies. The study results show that k-nearest neighbor, naive Bayes, support vector machine, logistic regression, support vector regression, classification tree, regression tree, and random forest are the most utilized AI strategies [16]. These strategies are applied to dissect and quantify the patient's information to improve their medical recommendations. For a coronary disease diagnosis, the essential utilization of AI techniques is naive Bayes, support vector machine, and deep learning multilayer perceptron, RFRS, cluster investigation, and EDPDCS. In prescient techniques, the most utilized strategies are CNN and K-nearest neighbor [17].

Nagaraj et al. [18] discussed the recommendations in the field of electronic health services and its e-medical services. It focuses on exhaustive and restorative services based on new medical cases with complete pre- and posttreatment protection in terms of the healthcare recommendation system.

3. The proposed AKF-TSA-based insulin recommendation system

Fig. 9.1 shows the working principle involved in the presented AKF-TSA model to recommend basal insulin for diabetic patients. The figure shows the AKF-TSA model that includes two major processes,

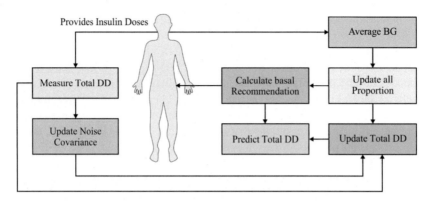

FIGURE 9.1

Block diagram of the AKF-TSA model.

namely AKF-based predict/recommend and the TSA-based tuning process. The working of the major process is discussed in the subsequent sections.

3.1 Kalman filtering technique

In general, KF is defined as a recursive estimator applied to incur attributes from indirect, imprecise, and irregular observations [19]. It is comprised of two steps, namely, the one-step-ahead state and the prediction of a state.

Consider a state x_z that is monitored by a system control series u_z and an equivalent noise w_z, the next state x_{z+1} can be expressed as

$$x_{z+1} = A \cdot x_z + B \cdot (u_z + w_z) \tag{9.1}$$

where A value implies the state transition method and B denotes a control-input technique.

Observations are depicted as,

$$\widehat{y}_z = H \cdot x_z + v_z \tag{9.2}$$

where y_z, H, and v_k are the observed state, observation of the method, and the observation noise, respectively.

Moreover, examination of the upcoming condition is illustrated as:

$$\widehat{x}_{z+1|z} = A \cdot \widehat{x}_{z|z} + B \cdot u_z \tag{9.3}$$

$$\widehat{x}_{z|z} = \widehat{x}_{z|z-1} + K_z \left(y_z - \widehat{x}_{z|z-1} \right) \tag{9.4}$$

in which $\widehat{x}_{z+1\,|z}$ denotes the monitored TDD for time $z + 1$, $\widehat{x}_{z|z}$ represents the evaluated TDD for time n conditioned measurements till z, and K_z signifies the Kalman gain.

The Kalman gain is expressed based on where R_z refers to the observation noise covariance at an n-th time as well as $P_{z|z-1}$ and $P_{z|z}$ being expressed using Eqs. (9.6) and (9.7) and refers to the covariance of the prediction error of $\widehat{x}_{z|z-1}$ and the corresponding update. Q_z exhibits good covariance of noise at the z-th time.

$$K_z = A \cdot P_{z|z-1} \cdot H^T \cdot \left(H \cdot P_{z|z-1} \cdot H^T + R_n \right) \tag{9.5}$$

$$P_{z|z-1} = A \cdot P_{z-1|z-1} \cdot A^T + Q_{z-1} \tag{9.6}$$

$$P_{z|z} = (I - K_z \cdot H) \cdot P_{z|z-1} \tag{9.7}$$

where w_z and v_z represent Gaussian white noise $w_z \sim N(0,\ Q)$ and $v_z \sim N(0,\ R)$, the Kalman filter reduces the mean square error (MSE) of the determined attributes.

The KF performs well when accurate knowledge of system information (A, B and H), and the statistical features [20,21] (Q and R) are provided. To accomplish an optimal function, the infrastructure of a system should be a priori. In the newly developed model, when the state variable x_z defines TDD, a control variable u_z signifies the regular bolus dose, and Eq. (9.3) forecasts the TDD for day $z + 1 \left(\hat{x}_{z+1|z} \right)$, as provided in the evaluation of TDD on day $z \left(\hat{x}_{z|z} \right)$ and count of bolus insulin used on a day n. As u_z implies the bolus insulin count on a day n and it can be learned, which is considered as $B = 1$. Followed by A develops the basal insulin in predicting TDD for the upcoming iteration.

Usually, physicians determine the basal insulin which it is determined by using TDD, that is, $A = \frac{1}{12}$. Therefore, it modifies the behavior of the method. In this work, a model has been presented for iterative A which depends upon the average BG level based on Eq. (9.8), in which A_k is an evaluated transition approach at the k-th iteration of a model, α refers to a learning rate, μ_G implies the average BG as the final maximization of A, and G_{sp} depicts a glucose set point.

$$A_{k+1} = A_k + \alpha \frac{\mu_G - G_{sp}}{G_{sp}} \tag{9.8}$$

It is clear that the average of CGM measures is described as $\mu_G = \frac{1}{M} \sum_{m=t-M}^{t} G_m$ in which G_m denotes the m-th BG values, M implies the count of BG instances applied, and t exhibits the time if A_{k+1} is determined as

$$\mu_{G_m} = \frac{m-1}{m} \mu_{G_{-1}} + \frac{1}{m} G_m \tag{9.9}$$

where m represents the count of BG instances, μ_{G_m} is the m-th update; and μ_G and G_m denote the m-th BG instances, which means a BG reading.

In addition, α implies a design variable that is similar in all cases, and G_{sp} is simply fixed to A. This is followed by H, which signifies the observation approach. The value of x_z defines the positive TDD and y_z implies the calculated TDD, which is considered to be $H = 1$.

3.2 The adaptive Kalman filtering (AKF) technique

In this study, the AKF technique is employed to seamlessly determine and adjust unseen or uncertain method variables and noise, whereas filtering the observed data to minimize the process errors makes the filtering outcome closer to the true value [22]. Here, the estimation of noise Q and R is a tedious process compared to designing a system. Therefore, AKF is applied to modify Q and R and has a strong influence on the Kalman filter. Once the Q/R value is found (see below), then the filtering output is largely based on the forecasted value. Similarly, once the Q/R value is found to be high, the filtering outcome is largely based on the measured value. The innovation-based adaptive evaluation filter is applied to modify the Q and R values for time. In every phase of the Kalman filter iterative computation, the Q and R values can be estimated and updated to give a precise outcome. The processes involved in the AKF technique are described below.

Prediction step:

$$L(z|z-1) = L(z-1|z-1) + W(z)$$
$$P(z|z-1) = P(z-1|z-1) + Q(z-1)$$

Update step:

$$K(z) = kP(z|z-1)\left[k^2P(z|z-1) + R(z-1)\right] - 1$$
$$L(z|z) = L(z|z-1) + K(z)[U(z) - kX(z|z-1)]$$
$$P(z|z) = [1 - K(z)k]P(z|z-1)$$
$$v(z) = U(z) - kL(z|z-1)$$
$$Cov(v(z)) = Cov(v(z-1)) + \frac{1}{N}\left(v(z)v(z)^Z - v(z-N)(z-N)^Z\right)$$
$$R(z) = Cov\ (v(z)) - k^2P\ (z|z-1)$$
$$Q(z) = K(z)^2 Cov(v(z))$$

where $v(z)$ is the innovation series which defines the variation among the measured and forecast values and $Cov(v(z))$ is the theoretical covariance of $v(z)$.

3.3 Tree seeding optimization algorithm

The adaptability performance of the AKF technique is further boosted with the use of a bioinspired optimization algorithm called TSA [23]. This is a population-based technique, commonly used to solve optimization problems. Naturally, the tree seeds are dispersed on the soil surface, and they grow over time to generate new trees. When the surface of the tree is assumed to be the research field, the positions of the tree and seed denote the probable solution for the optimization problem. Therefore, the significance of the position of the seed is increased due to the tree formation. Two individual equations represent the searching field. The initial concern is the generation of the seed for the optimal position of the tree population which enables the local search strength of the technique to be enhanced. Next, the distinct positions of the tree are utilized for the generation of new seeds [24].

$$S_{ij} = T_{i,j} + \alpha_{i,j}x(B_j - T_{r,j}) \tag{9.10}$$

$$S_{i,j} = T_{i,j} + \alpha_{i,j}x(T_{i,j} - T_{r,j}) \tag{9.11}$$

where S_{ij} denotes the j-th dimension of the i-th seed; T_{ij} implies the j-th dimension of the i-th tree; B_j means the j-th dimension; $T_{r,j}$ indicates the j-th dimension of the r-th tree as selected randomly; and α means the scaling factor among $[-1,1]$. Among the available seed values, two equations are chosen to determine the positions of novel seeds, and the selection is controlled using the ST control variable in the range of $[0, 1]$.

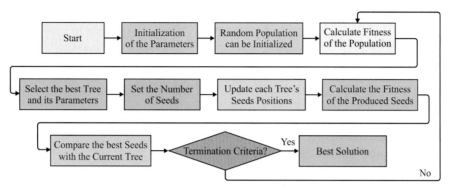

FIGURE 9.2

Flowchart of TSA.

At the initial stage of TSA, tree positions that are the probable solution for the optimization problem are defined using the equation below.

$$T_{i,j} = L_{j,\,min} + r_{i,j}\left(H_{j,\,max} - L_{j,\,min}\right) \tag{9.12}$$

where $L_{j,\,min}$ and $H_{j,\,max}$ are the lower and higher boundary limits of the search space, $r_{i,j}$ is a random number produced at every dimension and position in the interval of 0 and 1. The optimal solution chosen from the population of minimization is provided below.

$$B = \min\left\{f\left(\overrightarrow{T_i}\right)\right\} i = 1,\,2,\,...,N \tag{9.13}$$

where N indicates the tree count in the population. Once the new position of the seed is generated for the tree, the seed count (NS) is based on the population size. The seeds are generated arbitrarily in TSA [25,26]; where 10% and 25% of the population belong to the count of seeds generated with the minimum and maximum values. The generation of NS in TSA is attained using an arbitrary method, and the workflow of TSA is depicted in Fig. 9.2.

3.4 Recommendation process

The newly projected model is composed of KF theory to estimate the upcoming day's TDD according to the basal insulin dose. Hence, the KF is comprised of predicting the TDD for the next day and two models which determine the personalized transition method A and compute noise covariance Q. In addition, to upgrade the value of A, it is essential to determine the BG average.

4. Results and discussion
4.1 Data set used

The proposed work was tested using a Pima Indian diabetes database from the UCI archive of the machine learning database. This data set originally belonged to the National Institute of Diabetes and Digestive and Kidney Diseases. The attribute information was as follows:

- Type: Diabetes mellitus status (positive or negative);
- Age: Age in years (1−100 years);

- Diabetes pedigree function: Family diabetes history;
- BMI: Body mass index (less than 18.5 kg/m^2 is underweight, 18.5–25 kg/m^2 is normal, 25–30 kg/m^2 and greater than 30 kg/m^2 is overweight);
- Insulin: 2-hour serum insulin in mL;
- Skin thickness: Triceps skinfold thickness in mm;
- Blood pressure: Diastolic blood pressure in mmHg (lesser than 80 is normal, 80–120 is medium, and greater than 120 is high);
- Blood glucose levels: Plasma glucose concentration levels in mg/dL (90–130 mg/dL is before meals, and greater than 180 mg/dL is 2 hours after meals);
- Pregnancies: Number of times pregnant.

4.2 Performance validation

Here, we have demonstrated the performance of the proposed AKF-TSA model using a data set of diabetes mellitus on Python (Python Software Foundation, Wilmington, DE, USA). The proposed method was implemented on a computer system using CPU Intel Pentium 1.9 GHz, 64-bit operating system, Microsoft Windows 10, and Java JDK 1.8. The outcomes were achieved with a core i5 processor with 128 GB RAM for about 50 Epochs.

The basal RS was analyzed using a UVa/PADOVA T1DM simulator with five virtual subjects to represent the variability among real adults with T1DM. The FDA for testing animal diseases as an initial sampling model was approved by the T1DM simulator. Also, it was operated based on glucose-insulin dynamics, which is consumed from meals where glucose kinetics in hypoglycemia allow enhanced insulin at low glucose levels; and the process of glucagon kinetics, secretion, and action reproduces endogenous glucose. Hence, glucose dynamics shows the distribution of insulin-adjusting factors, and retardation of glucose in T1DM suffers from numerous challenges. Therefore, the newly projected approach was examined using BC with static variables as well as CBR-related BC. The working principle of basal RS is correlated with the constant basal dosage. In insulin treatment, a constant BC variable and basal dose are provided by default as this is regarded as the best treatment. Consequently, the simulation outcomes are determined using a glycemic range with a minimal duration of BG.

Fig. 9.3 and Table 9.1 depict the average and SD of the time in the target glycemic range to all subjects after the initialization period of 6 weeks.

On comparing the results attained by the proposed model on virtual subject 1, the default BC and basal recommender model failed to obtain a better performance by attaining the time on target of 71.24%, whereas the default BC and basal model resulted in a slightly higher time on target of 73.10%. In the same way, the CBR BC and default basal model led to a moderate performance with the time on target of 78.28%. In addition, CBR BC and basal recommender techniques have showcased competitive performance with a time on target of 83.26%, whereas the proposed AKF-TSA model resulted in a higher time on target of 84.02%. On evaluating the outcomes achieved by the presented method on virtual subject 2, the default BC and basal models failed to achieve better performance by obtaining a time on target of 83.67%, while the default BC and basal recommender methods resulted in a somewhat superior time on target of 86.98%. Likewise, the CBR BC and default basal models led to a moderate performance with a time on target of 87.19%. Also, CBR BC and the basal recommender methods exhibited competitive performance with a time on target of 91.34%, but the proposed AKF-TSA model resulted in a higher time on target of 92.53%.

On measuring the results obtaining by the proposed method on the virtual subject 3, the default BC and basal recommender method failed to attain optimal performance by achieving a time on target of

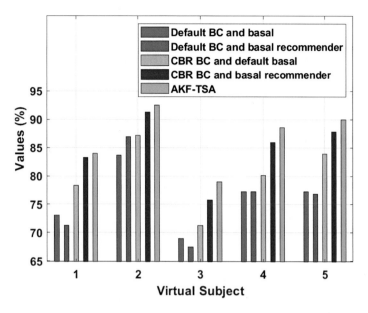

FIGURE 9.3

Result analysis of the AKF-TSA model in terms of time on target.

Table 9.1 Results of the analysis of the existing and proposed methods in terms of time on target.

Methods	Virtual subject				
	1	**2**	**3**	**4**	**5**
Default BC and basal	73.10	83.67	68.96	77.25	77.25
Default BC and basal recommender	71.24	86.98	67.51	77.25	76.83
CBR BC and default basal	78.28	87.19	71.24	80.15	83.88
CBR BC and basal recommender	83.26	91.34	75.80	85.95	87.81
AKF-TSA	84.02	92.53	78.97	88.62	90.01

67.51%, but the default BC and basal model resulted in a slightly better time on target of 68.96%. In line with this result, the CBR BC and default basal method led to a moderate performance with a time on target of 71.24%. In addition, the CBR BC and basal recommender model demonstrated competitive performance with a time on target of 75.8%, while the presented AKF-TSA model resulted in a maximum time on target of 78.97%. On evaluating the results achieved by the proposed method on virtual subject 4, the default BC and basal recommender and default BC and basal methods failed to attain better performance by obtaining a time on target of 77.25%. Similarly, the CBR BC and default basal method led to a moderate performance with a time on target of 80.15%. Also, the CBR

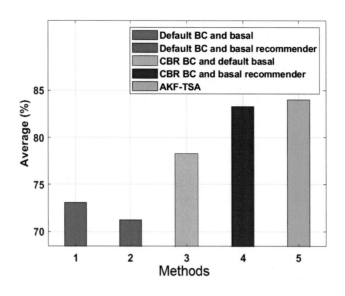

FIGURE 9.4

Average results analysis of the AKF-TSA model with existing models.

BC and basal recommender method showed a competitive performance with a time on target of 85.95%, whereas the presented AKF-TSA model resulted in a higher time on target of 88.62%.

On comparing the outcomes achieved by the presented model on virtual subject 5, the default BC and basal recommender model failed to obtain the optimal performance by attaining a time on target of 76.83%, while the default BC and basal model resulted in a somewhat higher time on target of 77.25%. In the same way, the CBR BC and default basal model led to a moderate performance with a time on target of 83.88%. Also, the CBR BC and basal recommender technique showcased a competitive performance with a time on target of 87.81%, but the proposed AKF-TSA method resulted in a maximum time on target of 90.01%.

Fig. 9.4 analyzes the results obtained by the proposed model on the average, default BC, and basal recommender method that failed to attain a better performance by achieving a time on target of 75.962%, but the default BC and basal model resulted in a slightly superior time on target of 76.046%. Likewise, the CBR BC and default basal models led to a moderate performance with a time on target of 80.148%. In addition, the CBR BC and basal recommender methods exhibited competitive performance with a time on target of 84.832%, while the presented AKF-TSA model resulted in a maximum time on target of 86.83%.

5. Conclusion

This chapter presented a bilevel performance improvement strategy for insulin recommendation to diabetes patients. The major goal is to develop an effective AKF-TSA model to recommend basal insulin for diabetic patients. The proposed AKF-TSA model involves two major processes, namely AKF-based predict/recommend and the TSA tuning process. A bilevel performance improvement strategy, such as AKF and the use of TSA makes the proposed method a robust one in the field of diabetes recommendations. An elaborative simulation analysis was carried out to determine the superior performance of the proposed model. The obtained simulation outcome verified the success of the AKF-TSA model over the earlier methods by a considerable degree.

References

[1] S.A. Brown, B.P. Kovatchev, D. Raghinaru, J.W. Lum, B.A. Buckingham, Y.C. Kudva, L.M. Laffel, C.J. Levy, J.E. Pinsker, R.P. Wadwa, et al., Six-month randomized, multicenter trial of closed-loop control in type 1 diabetes, N. Engl. J. Med. 381 (2019) 1707–1717.

[2] A.J. Ahola, S. Makimattila, M. Saraheimo, V. Mikkila, C. Forsblom, R. Freese, P.H. Groop, D.S.G. Finn, Many patients with Type 1 diabetes estimate their prandial insulin need inappropriately, J. Diabetes 2 (2010) 194–202.

[3] L. Mertz, Automated insulin delivery: taking the guesswork out of diabetes management, IEEE Pulse 9 (1) (2018) 8–9.

[4] S. Alian, J. Li, V. Pandey, A personalized recommendation system to support diabetes self-management for American Indians, IEEE Access 6 (2018) 73041–73051.

[5] F. Zheng, S. Liu, Y. Liu, L. Deng, Effects of an outpatient diabetes self-management education on patients with type 2 diabetes in China: a randomized controlled trial, J. Diabetes Res. 2019 (2019) 1–7, article 1073131.

[6] J.-X. Kong, L. Zhu, H.-M. Wang, et al., Effectiveness of the chronic care model in type 2 diabetes management in a community health service center in China: a group randomized experimental study, J. Diabetes Res. 2019 (2019) 1–12, article 6516581.

[7] L. Yang, C.-K. Hsieh, H. Yang, et al., Yum-Me: a personalized nutrient-based meal recommender system, ACM Trans. Inf. Syst. 36 (1) (2017) 1–31.

[8] R.Y. Toledo, A.A. Alzahrani, L. Martinez, A food recommender system considering nutritional information and user preferences, IEEE Access 7 (2019) 96695–96711.

[9] W. Gu, Y. Zhou, Z. Zhou, et al., SugarMate, Proc. ACM Interact. Mob. Wearable Ubiquitous Technol. 1 (3) (2017) 1–27.

[10] T. Mokdara, P. Pusawiro, J. Harnsomburana, Personalized food recommendation using deep neural network, in: Proceeding of 2018 7th ICT International Student Project Conference, ICT-ISPC, Nakhonpathom, Thailand, 2018.

[11] D. Bianchini, V. De Antonellis, N. De Franceschi, M. Melchiori, PREFer: a prescription-based food recommender system, Comput. Stand. Interfac. 54 (2017) 64–75.

[12] W. Xie, R. Ding, J. Yan, Y. Qu, A mobile-based question answering and early warning system for assisting diabetes management, Wireless Commun. Mobile Comput. 2018 (2018). Article ID 9163160, 14 pages.

[13] S. Mishra, H.K. Tripathy, P.K. Mallick, A.K. Bhoi, P. Barsocchi, EAGA-MLP—an enhanced and adaptive hybrid classification model for diabetes diagnosis, Sensors 20 (14) (2020) 4036.

[14] S. Mishra, P.K. Mallick, H.K. Tripathy, A.K. Bhoi, A. González-Briones, Performance evaluation of a proposed machine learning model for chronic disease datasets using an integrated attribute evaluator and an improved decision tree classifier, Appl. Sci. 10 (22) (2020) 8137.

[15] S. Oniani, G. Marques, S. Barnovi, I.M. Pires, A.K. Bhoi, Artificial intelligence for internet of things and enhanced medical systems, in: Bio-inspired Neurocomputing, Springer, Singapore, 2020, pp. 43–59.

[16] A.M. Vamsi, P. Deepalakshmi, P. Nagaraj, A. Awasthi, A. Raj, IOT based autonomous inventory management for warehouses, in: EAI International Conference on Big Data Innovation for Sustainable Cognitive Computing, Springer, Cham, 2020, pp. 371–376.

[17] P. Nagaraj, V. Muneeswaran, L.V. Reddy, P. Upendra, M.V.V. Reddy, Programmed multi-classification of brain tumor images using deep neural network, in: 2020 4th International Conference on Intelligent Computing and Control Systems (ICICCS), IEEE, 2020, pp. 865–870.

[18] P. Nagaraj, P. Deepalakshmi, A framework for e-healthcare management service using recommender system, Electr. Gov. Int. J. 16 (1–2) (2020) 84–100.

[19] F. Torrent-Fontbona, Adaptive basal insulin recommender system based on Kalman filter for type 1 diabetes, Expert Syst. Appl. 101 (2018) 1–7.

[20] P. Nagaraj, V. Muneeswaran, A.S. Kumar, Competent ultra data compression by enhanced features excerption using deep learning techniques, in: 2020 4th International Conference on Intelligent Computing and Control Systems (ICICCS), IEEE, 2020, pp. 1061–1066.

[21] V. Muneeswaran, B. BenSujitha, S. Ben, P. Nagaraj, A compendious study on security challenges in big data and approaches of feature selection, Int. J. Contr. Automat. 13 (03) (2020) 23–31.

[22] H. Wang, T. Lei, Y. Rong, W. Shao, Y. Huang, Y, Arc length stable method of GTAW based on adaptive Kalman filter, J. Manuf. Process. 63 (2021) 130–138.

[23] P. Nagaraj, M.P. Rajasekaran, V. Muneeswaran, K.M. Sudar, K. Gokul, VLSI implementation of image compression using TSA optimized discrete wavelet transform techniques, in: 2020 Third International Conference on Smart Systems and Inventive Technology (ICSSIT), IEEE, 2020, pp. 667–670.

[24] M.S. Kiran, TSA: tree-seed algorithm for continuous optimization, Expert Syst. Appl. 42 (19) (2015) 6686–6698.

[25] V. Muneeswaran, M. Pallikonda Rajasekaran, Gallbladder Shape Estimation Using Tree-Seed Optimization Tuned Radial Basis Function Network for Assessment of Acute cholecystitis." Intelligent Engineering Informatics, Springer, Singapore, 2018, pp. 229–239.

[26] V. Muneeswaran, M. Pallikonda Rajasekaran, Beltrami-regularized Denoising Filter Based on Tree Seed Optimization Algorithm: An Ultrasound Image application." International Conference on Information and Communication Technology for Intelligent Systems, Springer, Cham, 2017.

Unsupervised deep learning-based disease diagnosis using medical images

M. Ganeshkumar, V. Sowmya, E.A. Gopalakrishnan and K.P. Soman

Center for Computational Engineering and Networking (CEN), Amrita School of Engineering, Amrita Vishwa
Vidyapeetham, Coimbatore, Tamil Nadu, India

1. Introduction

Recently, deep learning algorithms have been very successful in solving various computer vision problems like image classification [1], object detection [2], image segmentation [3], etc. Unlike the traditional machine learning algorithms which require the task of feature engineering, deep learning algorithms can extract meaningful features from raw data automatically. The convolutional neural networks (CNNs) are the most widely used deep learning architecture. CNNs are capable of extracting location-invariant features. Due to the success of CNNs in computer vision tasks, they are also widely applied in various biomedical image classification tasks like disease diagnosis from microscopic images [4], breast cancer identification [5], classification of musculoskeletal radiographs [6], detection of diabetic retinopathy [7], tuberculosis detection [8], etc.

Although CNNs are very successful in disease diagnosis using medical images, often, the labeled data available are not adequate for CNN to learn its filters. It is not possible to train CNN and learn discriminative features when the labeled training data are insufficient. Therefore, in this work, we concentrate on the problem of inadequate labeled data in medical applications and propose a completely unsupervised deep learning framework for medical image classification. Also, we apply the framework to diagnose intracranial hemorrhage (ICH) in a completely unsupervised fashion, without making use of any labels while training. ICH occurs when a blood vessel inside the skull is ruptured. It can occur due to physical trauma to the brain, and also due to nontraumatic causes like hypertension. The diagnostic procedure for ICH involves an expert radiologist analyzing each slice of the computed tomography (CT) image of the patient, so the process of annotating CT slices into ICH and normal is a difficult and tedious task. This makes the data collection process extremely difficult for diseases like ICH. Therefore, to overcome this challenge and also to study the efficacy of our proposed unsupervised framework, we applied it to the task of ICH identification in CT images. The proposed framework works in two stages: first, to achieve the feature learning on CT images, PCANet is employed [9]. PCANet is a completely unsupervised CNN architecture. Second, after feature extraction, the unsupervised classification is done using the K-means clustering algorithm leading to ICH identification. The major advantage of PCANet is that it does not involve any loss function optimization using methods like the stochastic gradient descent (SGD) for its training, which requires a large number of labeled data. Also, when compared to regular CNN architecture available for supervised classifications, the number of hyperparameters that have to be tuned is less for PCANet.

A CT scan is a much preferred diagnostic tool for ICH, due to its wider availability than magnetic resonance imaging (MRI). A CT scanner utilizes a revolving X-ray source to obtain a 3D scan of the relevant part of a human body [10]. While recording a CT scan, the patient moves horizontally through a ring-like structure called the gantry. The revolving X-ray source then shoots narrow X-ray beams through the part of interest of the patient's body. The X-ray beams which pass through the patient's body are captured by special X-ray detectors. These X-ray detectors are connected to a computer, which constructs a 3D CT scan. The X-ray beams with different intensities reach the detector capturing different brain tissues. Based on the quantity of X-ray absorbed [Hounsfield units (HU)] by the tissue, these HU values are converted into grayscale values ([0, 255]) giving us the CT scan of brain tissues [11]. CT scans use a method called windowing, which is a technique in which the grayscale values of a CT image are adjusted via the CT numbers: window level and window width. The brightness of the CT image is adjusted via the window level, the contrast is adjusted via the window width [12]. This helps to highlight the different parts of interest in CT images. There are preconfigured window parameters (window level and window width) available for highlighting different brain tissues in CT images like brain window, stroke window, and bone window [12].

The rest of this chapter is organized as follows: Section 2 describes some of the existing methods for ICH identification. Section 3 describes our methodology, Section 4 the experiment we conducted for ICH identification, and Section 5 the evaluation metrics used in our study. Section 6 is a discussion of the results obtained. Section 7 concludes the chapter, and Section 8 is a discussion on the future works possible related to this current work.

2. Related works

Esther L. Yuh et al. developed a method using a rule-based classifier to diagnose ICH. The authors first identified the blood and cerebrospinal fluid pixels by applying an appropriate threshold on CT density (Hounsfield units) in CT images. Once pixels containing blood are identified, based on various parameters like location relative to the skull, biconvexity, size, and shape, they are further classified into various ICH subtypes using a rule-based classifier [13]. The authors found the optimal value of the threshold using 33 CT scans and tested the model on 250 CT scans.

In another work, Yonghong Li et al. developed an automated method for detecting the existence of subarachnoid hemorrhage (SAH) in CT images using support vector machines (SVM) [14]. First, preprocessing was done on the CT images to remove noise and also to remove any gantry tilt (a technique used while scanning to reduce the effect of radiation on sensitive organs). The angle of the gantry tilt was obtained from the header of DICOM files. The gantry tilt is compensated by applying shear transform on the CT images. Noises are removed from CT images using a median filter. Further, only the brain regions are segmented from the CT images using fuzzy c-means (FCM) clustering. Then, the brain segmented 3D CT volumes are registered against a standard atlas to extract regions of interest in the brain, from which various parameters like mean gray value, variance, entropy, and energy are extracted and fed as the feature to the SVM classifier to detect SAH. The model is trained with 60 CT volumes (30 with SAH and 30 normal) and evaluated on 30 CT volumes with SAH and 39 normal CT volumes.

Kamal Jnawali et al. [15] used a 3D CNN for the identification of ICH in CT images. Their CNN took the whole 3D CT volume as its input and used a logistic function as its last layer to predict the presence of ICH. They further constructed an ensemble of 3D CNN architecture leading to an improvement in ICH identification accuracy. They used a data set consisting of 40,367 head CT scans for their study.

Monika Grewal et al. [16] proposed a novel CNN architecture called RADnet for the automated identification of hemorrhage in CT scans. The working of Recurrent Attention DenseNet (RADnet) is very similar to the way radiologists identify the hemorrhage, that is, the RADnet model incorporates individual predictions on 2D CT slices and also utilizes the 3D context from the neighboring slices to improve the predictions. For slice-wise predictions, RADnet uses DenseNet architecture added with an attention mechanism. For incorporating the 3D context from the neighboring slices, RADnet uses a recurrent neural network layer. The DenseNet used had three dense blocks. The output from the last layer of each of these blocks is taken and upsampled using a deconvolution layer to generate binary segmentations. The weighted sum of the loss of these three intermediate segmentations along with the loss of the final classification task is used for training the DenseNet, thereby allowing the network to pay attention to the hemorrhagic regions of CT slices. The authors trained their model with 185 CT scans.

Hai Ye et al. [17] proposed a classification framework that incorporates both CNN and RNN architecture for the identification of ICH. CNN extracts important features from the individual CT slices and the RNN captures the sequential information from successive slices, thereby adding interslice information to improve the accuracy of ICH identification. The classification is done in two stages; the first stage identifies whether there is any bleeding (thereby detecting whether the ICH is present or not). If there is ICH, the second classification stage classifies the CT slices into five subtypes of ICH. The authors used VGG-16 architecture for their CNN and bidirectional gated recurrent units (GRU) architecture for their RNN. Their model was trained with 10,159 CT scans.

Hyunkwang Lee et al. [18] used multiple deep learning models pretrained on the ImageNet data set and further retrained them for the identification of ICH and also to classify them into their subtypes, thereby analyzing the effect of the transfer learning method in ICH identification. The authors used four CNN architectures: VGG16, ResNet-50, Inception-v3, and Inception-ResNet-v2. Their model was trained with 904 CT scans.

Prevedello et al. [19] used a convolutional neural network (CNN) for identifying ICH in CT images. The authors also detected mass effect, hydrocephalus, and suspected acute infarct (SAI). The authors experimented with the two different window configurations (brain window and stroke window) in the CT images. Their experiments showed that the brain window worked better for the detection of ICH. The authors trained their model with 246 CT scans.

Chang et al. [20] proposed an architecture combining the mask R−CNN and the hybrid 3D/2D variant of the feature pyramid network for identification of ICH in CT images. The mask R−CNN acts as a region proposal network, and recommends different bounding boxes on the input CT image according to a preconfigured distribution, where the presence of abnormality is tested. Further, regions that have a high probability of abnormality are selected and fed to the classifier to identify the hemorrhage, thereby providing an attention mechanism to the model. The mask R−CNN is trained with features extracted from the backbone hybrid 3D/2D variant of the feature pyramid network. The authors used around 10,000 CT scans for training their model.

Arbabshirani et al. [21] used a simple CNN with five convolutional layers and two fully connected layers, and also max-pooling and normalization layers between them for the identification of ICH in CT images. The authors initialized the convolutional network with random numbers from a normal distribution centered at zero. Further, to improve the accuracy the authors trained an ensemble of four networks. The average of predictions made by the ensemble of four networks was taken as the final prediction. The authors used 37,084 CT scans for training their model.

Chilamkurthy et al. [22] trained ResNet18 with five parallel fully connected layers as the output layers. The output from these five parallel layers was given as the input to a random forest algorithm to identify the presence of an ICH. The authors used around 290,000 CT scans for training.

Table 10.1 summarizes the existing methods available in the literature for ICH identification. All the existing methods in the literature for ICH identification make use of a substantial amount of labeled data during their training process [13−22].

Table 10.1 Summary of existing methods in the literature for ICH identification.

Reference	Method	Number of training samples used	Supervised/ unsupervised	Limitations
[13]	Rule-based classifier	33 CT scans	Supervised	• Handcrafted features • Rule-based classifier
[14]	SVM classifier	60 CT scans	Supervised	• Handcrafted features • Deals only with the identification of subarachnoid hemorrhage (SAH) (a particular subtype of ICH)
[15]	Ensemble of 3D CNN architecture	40,367 CT scans	Supervised	• Requires huge labeled training data
[16]	RADnet incorporating DenseNet and RNN	185 CT scans	Supervised	• Requires huge labeled training data
[17]	VGG-16 combined with bidirectional gated recurrent units (GRU)	10,159 CT scans	Supervised	• Requires huge labeled training data
[18]	Transfer learning using ResNet-50, Inception-v3, and Inception-ResNet-v2	904 CT scans	Supervised	• Requires huge labeled training data
[19]	CNN with different window configurations	246 CT scans	Supervised	• Requires huge labeled training data

Table 10.1 Summary of existing methods in the literature for ICH identification.—cont'd

Reference	Method	Number of training samples used	Supervised/ unsupervised	Limitations
[20]	Mask R−CNN trained with extracted features from a hybrid 3D/2D variant of the feature pyramid network	10,000 CT scans	Supervised	• Requires huge labeled training data
[21]	A simple CNN and an ensemble of four networks	37,084 CT scans	Supervised	• Requires huge labeled training data
[22]	ResNet18 combined with random forest algorithm	290,000 CT scans	Supervised	• Requires huge labeled training data

Especially, deep learning methods in the literature use hundreds and even thousands of labeled CT scans for their training [15−22]. Also, the methods in Refs. [13,14] use traditional machine learning algorithms (not deep learning algorithms) and require the difficult and time-consuming task of extracting handcrafted features from the CT images. To the best of our knowledge, our current work is the first attempt to solve the problem of ICH detection in a fully unsupervised fashion.

3. Methodology

Fig. 10.1 describes the methodology we adopted for the unsupervised classification of medical images. Also, we applied the same methodology for the identification of ICH in CT images. As shown in Fig. 10.1, our methodology employs an unsupervised feature extractor PCA-Net [9] for the extraction of features from medical images. Further, the extracted features are used to train an unsupervised K-means algorithm, leading to the classification of medical images. The working of PCA-Net as a feature extractor for medical images and how PCA operation extracts the principal components from the data matrix and also the working of K-means classifier are described below.

3.1 Feature extraction using PCA-Net

As shown in Fig. 10.1, the PCA-Net has two convolutional stages and an output stage. Let the number of filters in the first convolution stage and the second convolution stage be F_1 and F_2, respectively, each of size $s_1 \times s_2$. Once these filters are learned, we pass the input medical images through the first and second convolution stages, and then, in the output stage, we apply some basic processing to the output of the second convolution stage and obtain the final feature vectors of our medical images. The steps followed in the first and second convolution stages to learn its filters and the steps followed in the output stage are described below.

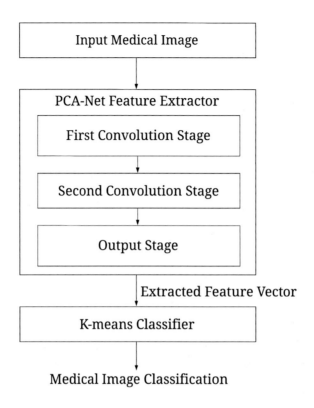

FIGURE 10.1

Flow diagram of the proposed method for the unsupervised classification of medical images.

3.1.1 First convolution stage

In this, each input image first goes through the process of patch mean removal. Assuming each of our input images is of size $m \times n$, we take a patch of size $s_1 \times s_2$ around each pixel of our input image and extract all such intersecting patches and vectorize them. Further, all the extracted vectors are arranged column-wise into a matrix X_i with $s_1 \times s_2$ rows and $(m - s_1 + 1) \times (n - s_2 + 1)$ columns. We then take each column (patch vector) in X_i and subtract their mean from them and get $\overline{X}_i$. We construct the same matrix $\overline{X}_i$ for all the images in the data set and stack them column-wise and get

$$X = \left[\overline{X}_1, \overline{X}_2, ..., \overline{X}_N \right] \tag{10.1}$$

where N denotes the number of input images in the data set. Further, the model performs PCA on XX^T to learn the F_1 convolution filters in the first convolution stage. Using PCA we extract F_1 principal vectors of XX^T corresponding to larger eigenvalues and initialize our convolution filters according to the expression:

$$W_l^1 = \text{mat}_{s_1, s_2} \left(q_l (XX^T) \right), l = 1, 2, ..., F_1 \tag{10.2}$$

where $\text{mat}_{s_1, s_1}(v)$ is the function that maps the eigenvectors to the matrix W by reshaping them. $q_l (XX^T)$ is the l-th principal eigenvector of XX^T.

3.1.2 Second convolution stage

The second convolution stage repeats the same steps as those of the first convolution stage. However, instead of raw input images, it takes the output of convolution between input images and filters in the first convolution stage and does the same process as that of the first convolution stage. The output obtained from any l-th filter in the first convolutional stage I_i^l will be

$$I_i^l = I_i * W_l^1, i \in [1, N] \tag{10.3}$$

where W_l^1 is the weight matrix of any l-th filter in the first convolution stage, I_i is the input image, $*$ denotes the convolution operation. I_i will be zero-padded before convolution to make both I_i^l and I_i have the same size. Repeating the same steps as that of the first stage, the overlapping patches are collected from each of I_i^l and vectorized. Further, the mean is subtracted from each of these vectors and the vectors are stacked column-wise to obtain:

$$Y^l = \left[\overline{Y}_1^l, \overline{Y}_2^l, ..., \overline{Y}_N^l \right] \tag{10.4}$$

further, we obtain the Y^l matrix for all the F_1 filters of the first convolution stage and concatenate them to obtain

$$Y = \left[Y^1, Y^2, ..., Y^{F_1} \right] \tag{10.5}$$

The model learns the F_2 convolution filters of the second stage by doing a PCA on YY^T.

$$W_l^2 = \mathrm{mat}_{s_1 \times s_2} \left(q_l \left(YY^T \right) \right), l = 1, 2, ..., F_2 \tag{10.6}$$

where W_l^2 is the weight matrix of any l-th filter in the second convolution stage. Thus, the F_1 number of filters W_l^1 in the first layer and F_2 number of filters W_l^2 in the second layer are learned. Once the filters are learned, we can pass any input medical image through the first and second convolution stages and extract features, which are further passed through the output stage to obtain the final feature vector.

3.1.3 The output stage

As shown in Fig. 10.1, the output stage has two steps: hashing and histogram generation. In hashing, the F_2 output of the second stage convolution will be converted into a single matrix according to the equation:

$$T_i^l = \sum_{l=1}^{F_2} 2^{l-1} H \left(I_i^l * W_l^2 \right) \tag{10.7}$$

where $H(\cdot)$ is the Heaviside step function. Heaviside step function outputs 1 for any positive input value or 0 for any negative input value. I_i^l, $l \in [1, F_1]$ are input matrices to the second convolution stage and W_l^2, $l \in [1, F_2]$ are weight matrices of the second convolution stage. All the elements of the matrix T_i^l will be of integers in the range $[0, 2^{F_2} - 1]$. After hashing we take each of the F_1 matrices T_i^l, $l \in [1, F_1]$ and we partition them into various blocks. Partitioning is done by taking $p \times p$ overlapping patches around each pixel of T_i^l matrix and further vectorizing them. Let us assume that each of T_i^l is partitioned into B blocks. Then, we compute the histogram of each block with 2^{F_2} bins. This histogram generation step is equivalent to the max-pooling operation in traditional CNNs, used for reducing the dimensions of feature vectors. We further concatenate all the B histograms computed into a single vector Bhist $\left(T_i^l\right)$. Finally, PCA-Net concatenates all the F_1 number of Bhist $\left(T_i^l\right)$ vectors and constructs the final feature vector f_i for any input medical image.

$$f_i = \left[\text{Bhist}\left(T_i^1\right), ..., \text{Bhist}\left(T_i^{F_1}\right)\right]^T \tag{10.8}$$

3.2 Working of principal component analysis (PCA) operation

PCA is a widely used tool for dimensionality reduction [23]. Assume that the input matrix to PCA operation is X. First, PCA computes the covariance matrix of X by taking the transpose of it and multiplying it with itself (XX^T). Further, eigenvectors and their corresponding eigenvalues of XX^T are calculated using the eigenvalue decomposition. The eigenvalue decomposition decomposes the matrix XX^T into VDV^{-1}, where V is the matrix of eigenvectors and D is the diagonal matrix with eigenvalues on the diagonal and zero everywhere else. Let us assume the eigenvalues of the matrix XX^T are $\lambda_1, \lambda_2, ..., \lambda_v$. Each eigenvalue in the matrix D will be associated with the corresponding column (eigenvector) in the matrix V. That is, if the first eigenvalue in the diagonal of D is λ_1, then its corresponding eigenvector is the first column in the matrix V. Now the columns of the matrix V (eigenvectors) are rearranged in accordance with its corresponding eigenvalues from largest to smallest. Let us assume this rearranged matrix to be V^*. Picking n principal components corresponding to large eigenvalues from the input X by applying PCA is by picking n columns (n eigenvectors) from the matrix V^*. Eigenvalues and eigenvectors are critically important for any data. The eigenvectors indicate the different directions in which our data are dispersed. The associated eigenvalues indicate the relative importance of each of these directions, that is, the variance of the data in that particular direction. A good amount of variability usually indicates the presence of important information, whereas little variability usually means unimportant information like noise.

3.3 K-means classifier

K-means is an unsupervised classifier, which partitions the given input data points into K clusters [24]. The steps followed by the K-means classifier are as follows:

(1) First K-means randomly selects K data points for initializing the centroids of the K clusters;
(2) For every data point in the data set, it computes the sum of squared distance between that data point and all the centroids;
(3) Then it assigns each data point to the nearest centroid (cluster) based on the distance obtained in the previous step;
(4) After assigning all the data points to the clusters they belong to, it recomputes the value of every centroid by assigning it with the average of all the data points that belong to that particular cluster;
(5) Steps 2–4 are repeated until the value of centroids does not change significantly.

The final allocation of data points to centroids when the algorithm terminates is taken as the classification of the data points into K clusters.

4. Experiments

This section describes the experiment we conducted for analyzing the efficacy of our proposed framework, by applying it to solve the problem of unsupervised identification of ICH in CT images.

4.1 Data set

We used the "Computed Tomography Images for Intracranial Hemorrhage Detection and segmentation" data set publicly available at PhysioNet [25]. The data set had 82 CT scans, of which, 36 were of patients diagnosed with intracranial hemorrhage. Each CT scan had around 30 2D CT slices. The data set had CT scans of patients with all the subtypes of ICH: intraventricular, intraparenchymal, subarachnoid, epidural, and subdural. Each subtype of ICH differs based on the location in which it occurs in the brain. Since our data set had the CT scans of all five subtypes of ICH, our model would be better generalized and robust in detecting all the different ICH subtypes. Fig. 10.2 shows some of the sample CT slices from the data set. A normal CT slice with no ICH is given in the top row of Fig. 10.2. Four CT slices with ICH at varied locations are given in the bottom row of Fig. 10.2, with a red ellipse marking the regions where the ICH is present.

Normal CT slice

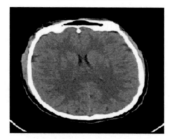

CT slices with ICH

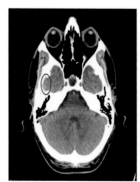 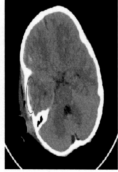 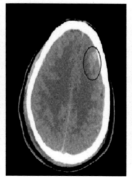 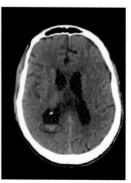

FIGURE 10.2

Sample CT slices from the data set.

We had no preprocessing applied to our data set. All the 2D CT slices used in our experiment were resized to a dimension of 512×512, to reduce memory consumption and also for faster processing.

4.2 Hyperparameters

Fig. 10.3 shows the architecture of our proposed unsupervised deep learning framework. The only hyperparameters that we need to set during our experiment are the following. The filter size in both convolution stages $s_1 \times s_2$ is set to 5×5. The number of filters in both the first convolution stage F_1 and the second convolution stage F_2 is set to eight. In the histogram step, we extracted 2×2 patches for partitioning the output from the hashing step into different blocks. From this, we can see that the number of hyperparameters that have to be set while training our proposed model is much less when compared to standard CNN architecture.

4.3 Incremental training of K-means

The diagnostic procedure for ICH involves a radiologist analyzing the individual slices of a CT scan and identifying the ICH. Therefore, we went for slice-wise training and evaluation of our proposed model for ICH identification. We trained our model with 1750 CT slices (around 57 CT scans) and tested our model with 751 slices (around 25 CT scans) following a 70/30 split. The size of the extracted feature vectors from the PCA-Net was huge in our experiment. K-means is an incremental model, that is, the input data can be continuously used to further train the model, extending the model's knowledge. Therefore, we incrementally trained our K-means classifier by extracting feature vectors from only five CT slices at a time. This led to the possibility of training our proposed method with the limited hardware resources we had. We trained our model with Google Collab's free cloud services offering 25 Gigabytes of RAM.

5. Evaluation metrics

This section describes the evaluation metrics we calculated while testing our model for the task of ICH identification. The CT slices with ICH are considered to be the positive class and the normal CT slices are considered to be the negative class. TP (true positives) is the count of correct identification of the test points belonging to the positive class (the ICH class). TN (true negatives) is the count of correct identification of test points belonging to the negative class (the normal class). FP (false positives) is the count of test points that are wrongly identified as positive points, but actually belong to the negative class. FN (false negatives) is the count of test points that are wrongly identified as negative points, but actually belong to the positive class.

5.1 Accuracy

This is the ratio of the number of correct identifications made by the model to the total number of samples in the test set.

$$\text{Accuracy} = \frac{\text{Number of correct predictions}}{\text{Total number of predictions made}} \tag{10.9}$$

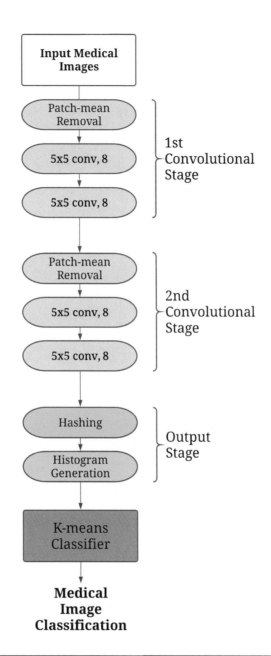

FIGURE 10.3

The architecture of the proposed method for the unsupervised classification of medical images.

5.2 Precision

This is the number of correct positive predictions made by the model divided by the total number of positive predictions by the model.

$$\text{Precision} = \frac{TP}{TP + FP} \tag{10.10}$$

5.3 Recall/sensitivity

this is a measure of what fraction of actual positive points in the test set were identified correctly.

$$\text{Recall/Sensitivity} = \frac{TP}{TP + FN} \tag{10.11}$$

5.4 F1-score

F1-score is the harmonic mean between precision and recall

$$F1 = 2 * \frac{1}{\dfrac{1}{\text{Precision}} + \dfrac{1}{\text{Recall}}} \tag{10.12}$$

5.5 Specificity

This is the measure of what proportion of actual negative points in the test set were identified correctly by the model.

$$\text{Specificity} = \frac{TN}{TN + FP} \tag{10.13}$$

5.6 Matthews correlation coefficient

Matthews correlation coefficient is also another way to estimate the quality of binary classifications.

$$\text{Matthews correlation coefficient} = \frac{TP \times TN - FP \times FN}{\sqrt{(TP + FP)(TP + FN)(TN + FP)(TN + FN)}} \tag{10.14}$$

It is a correlation coefficient between the original ground-truth value and the predictions made by the model. The value of the Matthews correlation coefficient will be between -1 and $+1$. When Matthews correlation coefficient equals $+1$ it means an ideal prediction and -1 means a total disagreement between the original ground-truth value and the predictions made by the model.

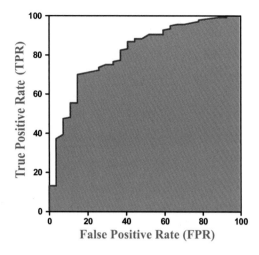

FIGURE 10.4

Area under the ROC curve (AUC).

5.7 Receiver operating characteristic (ROC) curve

The ROC curve conveys the performance of a model at different classification thresholds. The ROC curve plots two parameters: (1) true positive rate and (2) false positive rate. The true positive rate (TPR) is the same as that of recall. The false positive rate (FPR) is given by:

$$FPR = \frac{FP}{FP + TN} \tag{10.15}$$

An ROC curve plots TPR versus FPR at different classification thresholds.

5.8 Area under the ROC curve (AUC)

The AUC is the value of the whole area under the ROC curve. The AUC combines the TPR and FPR values, providing a consolidated measure of performance of the model over different possible classification thresholds. Fig. 10.4 represents a sample ROC curve, with the gray-colored area indicating its area under the ROC curve (AUC).

6. Experimental results and discussions

Our proposed model for ICH identification was tested on 751 CT slices (88 slices with ICH and 663 slices without ICH). Table 10.2 describes the values of various evaluation metrics like accuracy, precision, recall, and F1-score achieved by our proposed method for the task of ICH identification in CT images in a fully unsupervised way. Table 10.3 is the confusion matrix of our proposed method. Fig. 10.5 presents the ROC curve of our proposed method. As discussed in Sections 5.7 and 5.8, the ROC curve plots the values of true positive rate (TPR) and false positive rate (FPR) at different classification thresholds. The area under the ROC curve (AUC), provides a single consolidated

Table 10.2 Scores achieved by the proposed method in various evaluation metrics.

Averaging method	Accuracy	Precision	Recall	F1-score
Macro average	0.67	0.51	0.51	0.48
Weighted average	0.67	0.80	0.67	0.72

Table 10.3 Confusion matrix of the proposed method.

Total number of data points = 751	Predicted ICH	Predicted Non-ICH
Actual ICH	61	27
Actual non-ICH	189	474

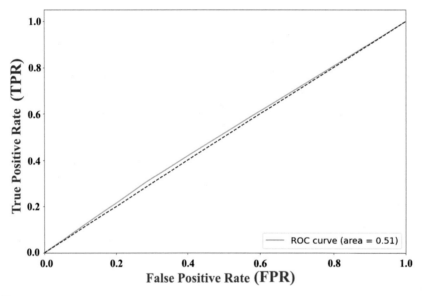

FIGURE 10.5

ROC curve of the proposed method.

performance score of the model by combining the values of *TPR* and *FPR* at different classification thresholds. As shown in Fig. 10.5, the AUC achieved by our model is 0.51. Table 10.4 indicates the performance of our model in other evaluation metrics like specificity, recall, and Matthews correlation coefficient.

For all the evaluation metrics we considered, we calculated both their macroaverage as well as their weighted average. From Table 10.2 we can see that the weighted average of all the metrics is comparatively higher than the macroaverage values. This is due to the huge imbalance between the

Table 10.4 Performance of the proposed method on other metrics.

Specificity	Sensitivity/recall	Matthews correlation coefficient
0.71	0.30	0.015

ICH class and non-ICH class data points in our test set (88 slices with ICH and 663 slices without ICH). Also, from the confusion matrix of our proposed method given in Table 10.3, we can see that the performance of our proposed method is biased toward the normal class. This is due to the huge class imbalance present in our data set, that is, there is a lower number of CT slices that belong to the ICH class compared to that of the non-ICH class (out of 86 scans only 36 were scans of patients with ICH, and in each of those 36 scans, only a few slices have ICH). The F1-score indicates the overall performance of a model, and our model achieved a weighted average F1-score of 0.72.

Despite the small size of the training data set we used (1750 CT slices) and also the huge class imbalance present between the ICH and non-ICH classes, our proposed framework has performed considerably well in identifying the ICH in CT images in a fully unsupervised way. Further, some more CT scans of patients with ICH could be collected for the training process and used to improve our model. The difficult and time-consuming process of manually annotating each CT slice of the scan with the help of a radiologist is not needed.

Fig. 10.6 presents the centroids we obtained from the K-means algorithm for our ICH and normal classes reduced to three-dimensional space using t-SNE [26]. The blue-colored point represents the centroid of the normal class and the red-colored point represents the centroid of the ICH class. From Fig. 10.6, we can see that the centroids are well separated in three-dimensional space.

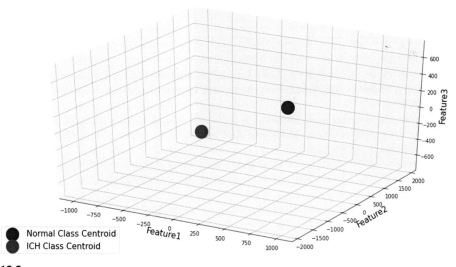

FIGURE 10.6

Centroids obtained from the K-means algorithm for ICH and normal classes reduced to three-dimensional space using t-SNE.

7. Conclusion

In this chapter, we propose a completely unsupervised deep learning framework for the classification of medical images. We also applied our proposed framework to solve the problem of ICH identification in a fully unsupervised way, and gave a detailed literature review on the existing methods available for ICH identification. During our experiments, we demonstrated how incremental training of the K-means algorithm can be used for classifying the large extracted feature vectors when the hardware resources are limited. Despite the small size of the data set used, our proposed framework has performed considerably well in ICH identification in CT images. The bias in the performance of our model toward the normal class is due to the huge class imbalance present in our data set. That is, we had a much lower number of data points that belong to the ICH class in comparison to the non-ICH class. Therefore, the performance of our proposed model could be further improved by adding more CT scans of patients with ICH during training. Since our proposed framework is fully unsupervised, it greatly simplifies the data collection process for any medical image classification task by eliminating the need for manual annotations of images with the help of an expert. Our proposed framework could be very helpful when there is a lack of labeled training data for disease diagnosis using data-driven models.

8. Future work

In the future, the PCA-Net feature extractor could be further improved by making it deeper, that is, by experimenting with the addition of a few more convolution layers. Also, the unsupervised classification stage could be improved by experimenting with other unsupervised classifiers like Gaussian mixture modeling. The K-means algorithm tends to give a circular fit to the points in a particular cluster, whereas Gaussian mixture modeling gives an elliptical fit to the data points in a particular cluster, which tends to work better for some data distributions.

References

[1] N. Jmour, S. Zayen, A. Abdelkrim, Convolutional neural networks for image classification, in: 2018 International Conference on Advanced Systems and Electric Technologies (IC_ASET), IEEE, 2018, pp. 397–402.

[2] R.L. Galvez, A.A. Bandala, E.P. Dadios, R.R.P. Vicerra, J.M.Z. Maningo, Object detection using convolutional neural networks, in: TENCON 2018–2018 IEEE Region 10 Conference, IEEE, 2018, pp. 2023–2027.

[3] S.B. Nemade, S.P. Sonavane, Image segmentation using convolutional neural network for image annotation, in: 2019 International Conference on Communication and Electronics Systems (ICCES), IEEE, 2019, pp. 838–843.

[4] A. Simon, R. Vinayakumar, V. Sowmya, K.P. Soman, E.A.A. Gopalakrishnan, A deep learning approach for patch-based disease diagnosis from microscopic images, in: Classification Techniques for Medical Image Analysis and Computer Aided Diagnosis, Academic Press, 2019, pp. 109–127.

[5] M.A. Anupama, V. Sowmya, K.P. Soman, Breast cancer classification using capsule network with pre-processed histology images, in: 2019 International Conference on Communication and Signal Processing (ICCSP), IEEE, 2019, pp. 0143–0147.

[6] N. Harini, B. Ramji, S. Sriram, V. Sowmya, K.P. Soman, Musculoskeletal radiographs classification using deep learning, in: Deep Learning for Data Analytics, Academic Press, 2020, pp. 79−98.

[7] C. Lam, D. Yi, M. Guo, T. Lindsey, Automated detection of diabetic retinopathy using deep learning, AMIA Summits Transl. Sci. Proc. 2018 (2018) 147.

[8] A. Simon, R. Vinayakumar, Sowmya, K.P. Soman, Shallow Cnn with Lstm layer for tuberculosis detection in microscopic image, Int. J. Recent Technol. Eng. 7 (2019) 56−60.

[9] T.H. Chan, K. Jia, S. Gao, J. Lu, Z. Zeng, Y. Ma, PCANet: a simple deep learning baseline for image classification? IEEE Transac. Image Proc. 24 (12) (2015) 5017−5032.

[10] National Institute of Biomedical Imaging and Bioengineering (NIBIB) 2013, Computed Tomography (CT), https://www.nibib.nih.gov/sites/default/files/CT%20Fact%20Sheet%20508.pdf.

[11] M.D. Hssayeni, M.S. Croock, A.D. Salman, H.F. Al-khafaji, Z.A. Yahya, B. Ghoraani, Intracranial hemorrhage segmentation using A deep convolutional model, Data 5 (1) (2020) 14.

[12] Z. Xue, S. Antani, L.R. Long, D. Demner-Fushman, G.R. Thoma, Window classification of brain CT images in biomedical articles, AMIA Annu. Symp. Proc. 2012 (2012) 1023. American Medical Informatics Association.

[13] E.L. Yuh, A.D. Gean, G.T. Manley, A.L. Callen, M. Wintermark, Computer-aided assessment of head computed tomography (CT) studies in patients with suspected traumatic brain injury, J. Neurotrauma 25 (10) (2008) 1163−1172.

[14] Y. Li, J. Wu, H. Li, et al., Automatic detection of the existence of subarachnoid hemorrhage from clinical CT images, J. Med. Syst. 36 (2012) 1259−1270, https://doi.org/10.1007/s10916-010-9587-8.

[15] K. Jnawali, M.R. Arbabshirani, N. Rao, A.A. Patel, Deep 3D convolution neural network for CT brain hemorrhage classification. Medical Imaging 2018: computer-Aided Diagnosis, Int. Soc. Opt. Phot. 10575 (2018) 105751C.

[16] M. Grewal, M.M. Srivastava, P. Kumar, S. Varadarajan, RADnet: radiologist level accuracy using deep learning for hemorrhage detection in CT scans. Biomedical Imaging (ISBI 2018), in: 2018 IEEE 15th International Symposium on. IEEE, 2018, pp. 281−284.

[17] H. Ye, F. Gao, Y. Yin, D. Guo, P. Zhao, Y. Lu, X. Wang, J. Bai, K. Cao, Q. Song, et al., Precise diagnosis of intracranial hemorrhage and subtypes using a three-dimensional joint convolutional and recurrent neural network, Eur. Radiol. (2019) 1−11.

[18] H. Lee, S. Yune, M. Mansouri, M. Kim, S.H. Tajmir, C.E. Guerrier, S.A. Ebert, S.R. Pomerantz, J.M. Romero, S. Kamalian, R.G. Gonzalez, M.H. Lev, S. Do, An explainable deep-learning algorithm for the detection of acute intracranial haemorrhage from small datasets, Nat. Biomed. Eng. 3 (3) (2019) 173−182, https://doi.org/10.1038/s41551-018-0324-9. Epub 2018 Dec 17. PMID: 30948806.

[19] L.M. Prevedello, B.S. Erdal, J.L. Ryu, K.J. Little, M. Demirer, S. Qian, R.D. White, Automated critical test findings identification and online notification system using artificial intelligence in imaging, Radiology 285 (3) (2017) 923−931.

[20] P.D. Chang, E. Kuoy, J. Grinband, B.D. Weinberg, M. Thompson, R. Homo, J. Chen, H. Abcede, M. Shafie, L. Sugrue, C.G. Filippi, Hybrid 3D/2D convolutional neural network for hemorrhage evaluation on head CT, Am. J. Neuroradiol. 39 (9) (2018) 1609−1616.

[21] M.R. Arbabshirani, B.K. Fornwalt, G.J. Mongelluzzo, J.D. Suever, B.D. Geise, A.A. Patel, G.J. Moore, Advanced machine learning in action: identification of intracranial hemorrhage on computed tomography scans of the head with clinical workflow integration, NPJ Dig. Med. 1 (1) (2018) 1−7.

[22] S. Chilamkurthy, R. Ghosh, S. Tanamala, M. Biviji, N.G. Campeau, V.K. Venugopal, V. Mahajan, P. Rao, P. Warier, Deep learning algorithms for detection of critical findings in head CT scans: a retrospective study, Lancet 392 (10162) (2018) 2388−2396.

[23] S. Wold, K. Esbensen, P. Geladi, Principal component analysis, Chemometr. Intell. Lab. Syst. 2 (1–3) (1987) 37–52.

[24] N. Dhanachandra, K. Manglem, Y.J. Chanu, Image Segmentation using K-means clustering algorithm and subtractive clustering algorithm, Proc. Comput. Sci. 54 (2015) 764–771.

[25] M. Hssayeni, 'Computed tomography images for intracranial hemorrhage detection and segmentation' (version 1.0.0), PhysioNet (2019), https://doi.org/10.13026/w8q8-ky94. Availablae at:.

[26] L.V.D. Maaten, G. Hinton, Visualizing data using t-SNE, J. Mach. Learn. Res. 9 (2008) 2579–2605.

Probabilistic approaches for minimizing the healthcare diagnosis cost through data-centric operations

Akhilesh Kumar Sharma[1], Sachit Bhardwaj[1], Devesh Kumar Srivastava[1], Nguyen Ha Huy Cuong[2] and Shamik Tiwari[3]

[1]*Manipal University Jaipur, Jaipur, Rajasthan, India;* [2]*University of Danang, College of Information Technology, Hai Chau, Da Nang, Vietnam;* [3]*UPES, Dehradun, Uttarakhand, India*

1. Introduction

Reflex and sequential testing, and cost savings analysis for quality improvement, etc. have significant impacts individuals', various healthcare industries', and nations' economies. Over treatment also not sufficiently enough to provide relief to the patients which is costly. Thus its recommended to use selective diagnostic testing to reduce cost. For this kind of specialized treatment commercial laboratories have been created, but again the costs of these can be are very high, however they can be reduced by data-driven diagnosis, such as the use of IBM Watson, etc.

Healthcare costs can increase rapidly and become unaffordable. Health care has become extremely expensive all around the world, and the cost has continued to increase for several years. Health care also can harm people, through medical mistakes, or overprescription, but the damage caused to people's lives from its very costs is most harmful. The costs of health care can lead to long-term poverty and rising income inequality [6]. There is a complete absence of understanding of how much it costs to deliver health care to patients, let alone understand how the cost balances with the outcome of the care given. The whole process is supposed to be transparent but is very rough and expensive [5]. The expeditiously expanding field of data analytics is playing a crucial role in healthcare research [18] today by opening doors to remarkable advancements while reducing costs at the same time. It provides us with tools to collect, control, study, and obtain results from large volumes of unstructured data produced by the healthcare systems around the world, with the enormous amounts of unstructured data that healthcare data analytics provides [7]. Healthcare officials now can create better medical and financial recommendations while also delivering improved quality of patient care. Big data and machine learning are effectively used today for disease exploration, detection, etc. [16–18].

2. Bayesian neural networks

Bayesian neural networks are the recapitulation of the neural network and statistical model [1]. Bayesian neural networks are basically an augmented version of the neural network with the addition of posterior interference. Posterior inference which is also known as Bayesian inference is a modus operandi of statistics in which Bayes' theorem is used iteratively. Bayes' theorem is shown in Eq. (11.1) [4]. BNN training is optimized [19,20] using maximum likelihood estimation (MLE) considering the weights [3].

$$p(\theta_{i+1} \mid \theta_i, x_i, y_i) = \frac{p(y_i \mid x_i, \theta_i)p(\theta_i)}{p(x_i, y_i)} \tag{11.1}$$

where $p(\theta_{i+1} \mid \theta_i, x_i, y_i)$ is posterior distribution, $p(y_i \mid x_i, \theta_i)$ is likelihood, and $p(\theta_i)$ is prior distribution.

The selection of prior distribution is the deciding factor of regularization addition to the model. The selection of prior distribution is described as conjugate for the likelihood through which analytical formulas toward the reformation of parameters is accessible as shown in Eq. (11.2). However, if incompatibility between prior distribution and likelihood is observed, then this problem is resolved using approximation methods like MCMC and variational inference [8]. Most distributions are conjugate to at least one other distribution.

$$p(\theta_{i+1} \mid \theta_i, x_i, y_i) \propto p(y_i \mid x_i, \theta_i)p(\theta_i) \tag{11.2}$$

The predictive distribution is the combination of likelihood and current distribution of the weights as shown in Eq. (11.3).

$$p(y_i \mid x_i) \propto p(y_i \mid x_i, \theta_i)p(\theta_i) \tag{11.3}$$

By marginalizing over parameters θ_i, predictive distribution is computed as shown in Eq. (11.4), (Fig. 11.1). The fig. 11.1 shows the probabilistic estimates with their likelihood.

$$p(y_i \mid x_i) = \int p(y_i \mid w, \ x_i)p(w)dw. \tag{11.4}$$

3. Markov chain Monte Carlo (MCMC)

The technique through which posterior distribution of parameters is computed by random sampling in likelihood space is known as Markov chain Monte Carlo (MCMC). The MCMC technique attempts to generate samples in a way that weights $\left\{ \widetilde{w_1}, \ldots, \widetilde{w_n} \right\}$ indulged with each sample remains constant.

Innumerable statistics like mean, variance, and in addition approximating the likelihood by kernel density estimation are regulated through these samples [9]. This is well illustrated in Fig. 11.2, which is demonstrating the statistical estimations and distributions.

The basic objective of the Markov chain Monte Carlo algorithm is to engender samples from a stated probability likelihood. Samples generated from the cumulative probability distribution are defined up to an augmentative factor, as shown in Fig. 11.3.

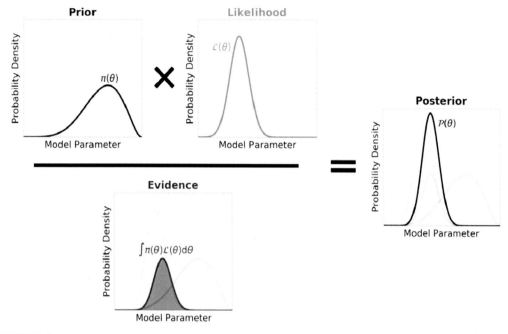

FIGURE 11.1

Bayes' theorem, where posterior probability is $P(\Theta)$, model parameters Θ upon the mixture of prior belief $\pi(\Theta)$ and the likelihood $\mathcal{L}(\Theta)$ normalized to $\mathcal{Z} = \int \pi(\Theta)\mathcal{L}(\Theta)d$ [3].

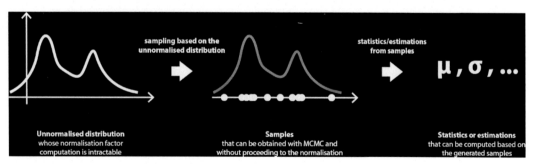

FIGURE 11.2

Sampling approach demonstration [14].

The Markov chain as shown in Eq. (11.5) denotes probabilities around a state space E which is hypothesized to be reversible if a probability likelihood γ prevails as expressed in Eq. (11.6).

$$k(\alpha, \beta) \equiv p(X_{n+1} = \beta \,|\, X_n = \alpha) \tag{11.5}$$

$$k(\alpha, \beta)\gamma(\alpha) = k(\beta, \alpha)\gamma(\beta) \quad \forall \alpha, \beta \in E \tag{11.6}$$

Build a Markov Chain
whose stationary distribution is the
distribution we want to sample from

Generate a sequence from
that Markov Chain long enough
to reach the steady state

Keep some well chosen states
from that sequence as samples
to be returned

FIGURE 11.3

MCMC footsteps for samples generated from cumulative probability distribution [14].

The resulting expression is shown in Eq. (11.7).

$$\int_{\beta \in E} k(\beta, \alpha)\gamma(\beta)d\beta = \int_{\beta \in E} k(\alpha, \beta)\gamma(\alpha)d\beta = \gamma(\alpha) \tag{11.7}$$

where γ is a stationary distribution. States which are adequate from the beginning of the generated sequences are considered, hence the first imitated states cannot be used and usually this juncture in time which is required to reach stationarity is known as the burn-in time. All the successive states after the burn-in time cannot be used altogether in order to obtain independent samples.

There should be a significant difference between the states in order to be defined as almost in-dependent. Hence the engendered sequences are separated from each other by a lag L. The successive states are denoted as shown in Eq. (11.8), while the burn-in time B is demonstrated in Eq. (11.9) (Fig. 11.4). The fig. 11.4 states the lag and the burn in time.

$$(X_n)_{n \geq 0} = X_0, X_1, X_2, \tag{11.8}$$

$$X_B, X_{B+L}, X_{B+2L}, X_{B+3L} \tag{11.9}$$

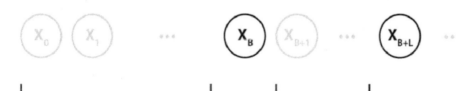

Burn-in time

The chain is not considered to have reached the
steady state yet and, so, these states do not
follow the target probability distribution

Lag

These states are too correlated with $X_{g'}$
so they can't be kept as we want to
generate (almost) independent samples

FIGURE 11.4

MCMC sampling depicting the lag and burn-in time [14].

3.1 Variational inference (VI)

Variational inference (VI) is another method through which we can overcome computational difficulties. This method incorporates the best estimation of a distribution among parametric figures. An optimization-based process is carried out to acquire the targeted distribution up to an explicated factor. The main objective of this technique is to obtain the adjoining element to the target with reference to a well-known error measure.

$$\pi(.) = C \times g(.) \propto g(.) \tag{11.10}$$

where π is the probability distribution and C is the normalization factor.

$$\mathscr{F}_\Omega = \{f_\omega;\ \omega \in \Omega\} \tag{11.11}$$

where Ω is a set of possible parameters.

General variational inference techniques are less accurate, but faster than Markov chain Monte Carlo methods. These methods are best for industry-based statistical problems [9] (Fig. 11.5).

3.2 Applications

Libraries associated with the implementation of BNNs include Stan, PYMC3, Edward, and Pyro. Bayesian neural networks are used in almost two-thirds of all healthcare aiming to four types of complications, that is, cardiac, cancer, psychological, and lung disorders [2]. With the help of this chapter, the scope of BNNs can be limitless to this field. Herein, breast cancer prediction is carried out using a Bayesian neural network, and also single probabilistic models. The number of infected cases over a period of time can be predicted using probabilistic models like the Bayesian spatiotemporal interaction model (BSTI) [12]. The BSTI model is a combination of various features like seasonality and trends with the addition of a linear model based on probability [13].

An hhh4 model is a chequered time series model mainly used to discover the future trend of spread of a disease. This model is also used as a reference to new approaches like the BSTI model. In a study

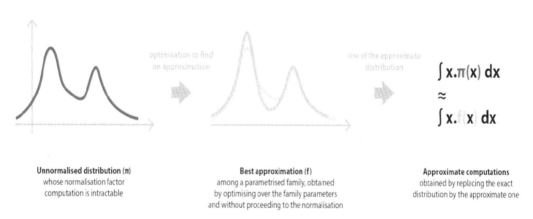

Unnormalised distribution (π)
whose normalisation factor
computation is intractable

Best approximation (f)
among a parametrised family, obtained
by optimising over the family parameters
and without proceeding to the normalisation

Approximate computations
obtained by replacing the exact
distribution by the approximate one

FIGURE 11.5

Variational inference steps [14].

by Stojanovic et al. they used the BSTI model to predict the future spread of three main infectious diseases in Germany, that is, Lyme borreliosis, campylobacteriosis, and rotaviral enteritis [12]. Methods like these are very prone to uncertainties like aleatoric and epistemic variables, which are later dealt with using various techniques. Monte Carlo methods are among the main types these executions as they use randomness to approach a problem.

Applications of models are not just limited to probabilistic-based techniques but also various descent and backpropagation techniques are available. Time series models like the ARIMA model, Holt's linear model, Holt's winter model, etc. can be used to predict future cases of virus outbreaks, including COVID [11]. Through speech, features can be extracted and passed through a backpropagation-based neural network to predict emotions which can help in predicting diseases like dyslexia [10].

4. Breast cancer prediction using a Bayesian neural network

Breast cancer is one of the most common forms of cancer. According to a survey, 2.1 million individuals are diagnosed with this form of cancer annually. The condition is observed when cells starts to grow at an exponential rate, resulting in the production of more cells than are required. Hence a lump is formed and the cells may spread throughout the entire body over a period of time. Lifestyle, hormonal, and environmental factors may contribute to an increased risk of this form of cancer, while 5%−10% of the cancers have genetic causes. *BRCA1* and *BRCA2* are the two genes responsible for the majority of the genetic-related cases. To predict this common and dangerous form of cancer, a Bayesian neural network is proposed in this chapter.

A Bayesian neural network-inspired model has been sculptured in PyMC3, which uses ADVI as an optimizer for the parameters. The basic objective of this model is to forecast whether a cell is benign or malignant. A tumor which does not spread throughout the body is described as benign, whereas a tumor that spreads to the whole body through blood is described as malignant, as demonstrated in Fig. 11.6 [15].

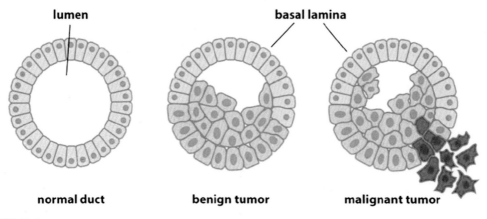

FIGURE 11.6

Types of tumor [15,16].

The crucial obstacles to this model are false positives and false negatives. A false-positive result shows as a benign tumor labeled as malignant, which basically means high-intensity medicines are prescribed to the patient resulting in overtreatment and extra cost, whereas a false-negative result shows as a malignant tumor labeled as benign, which can be fatal. While creating this model, the goal has been to minimize the number of false negatives. A confusion matrix is demonstrated in Fig. 11.7 [16].

The University of California produced the data set used in this example, which is widely available on UCI Machine Learning Repository. The images of tumor cells have been transformed into nine matrices, that is, radius, texture, perimeter, area, smoothness, compactness, concavity, concave points, and symmetry, as shown in Fig. 11.8.

The overall methodology of the model is proposed in Fig. 11.9.

The raw data are converted into NumPy arrays as data cleaning in which, basically, strings are converted to values and blank columns are dealt with. 0 represents benign cancer, while 1 represents malignant cancer in the target. A graphical portrayal of data in which statistical representation is obtained through colors is known as a heatmap. A heatmap is produced by masking the upper triangle of the correlation matrix from the data set. A heatmap was created using the Seaborn library. The correlation heatmap is demonstrated in Fig. 11.10.

An excessive correlation which defined around 80% is observed over nondiagonal elements among variables. In Fig. 11.6, a high correlation between parameter and texture can be observed, which play a crucial role in diagnosing the tumor. Therefore they cannot be removed or edited as that could greatly affect the model negatively. The concavity feature is removed in data cleaning as it proved to be improving performance of the model. The updated heatmap is shown in Fig. 11.11.

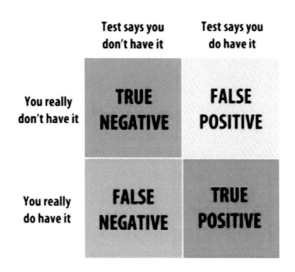

FIGURE 11.7

Confusion matrix [16].

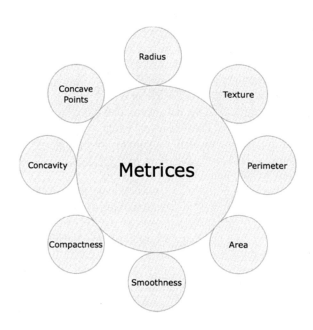

FIGURE 11.8

Matrices

The data are normalized in order to illustrate a new distribution with 0 mean and 1 standard deviation using a standard scaler function. The normalized data are now processed with a technique which helps in dimensional reduction. This process is widely known principal component analysis (PCA). PCA helps to reduce the number of false negatives and improve the accuracy of the model. The plot of the PCA is shown in Fig. 11.12.

The challenges that are faced during the creation of this model are: prediction uncertainty, weights uncertainty, prior on weights, and hierarchical modeling. Variational inference (VI) has been used to overcome the computational difficulties in this model. A version of VI known as automated differentiation variational inference (ADVI) has been used in this example. Coordinate descent is used to optimize parameter updates or to acquire a parameter updates equation. The ELBO (evidence lower bound) is maximized using an ADVI approach which is a gradient-based method, as shown in Eq. (11.12).

$$\nabla_{\phi}\mathrm{ELBO}(\phi) \approx \log p\left(\mathrm{data}, T^{-1}\left(\tilde{\zeta}\right)\right) + \log\left|\det J_{T^{-1}}\left(\tilde{\zeta}\right)\right| - \log q\left(\tilde{\zeta};\phi\right) \qquad (11.12)$$

Every layer takes inputs and provides outputs. Output dimensionality is reduced by one after each successive layer, which means layer 1 is provided with nine inputs but produces eight outputs. Therefore, layer 2 is provided with eight inputs but produces seven outputs. After the second layer output, it is processed as a base layer of logistic regression.

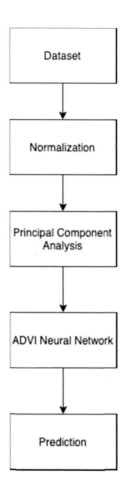

FIGURE 11.9

Methodology.

The final output is obtained through Bernoulli likelihood, which provides a binary outcome. Each node has a tanh activation function. For distribution of neural network weights, ADVI is used. The mean field inference function is mainly used in ADVI, which makes it dependent on it. The ADVI is plotted on an ELBO graph as shown in Fig. 11.13.

A total of 19 s were spent on the above execution of ELBO. Noise has been perceived succeeding 500 iterations along with the ELBO convergence. Due to the scarcity of data points in the data set, that is, 342, the ELBO optimization process has had tremendous success. Therefore, fine tuning has been performed to ensure ELBO does not diverge. There are two key concepts through which we can fine

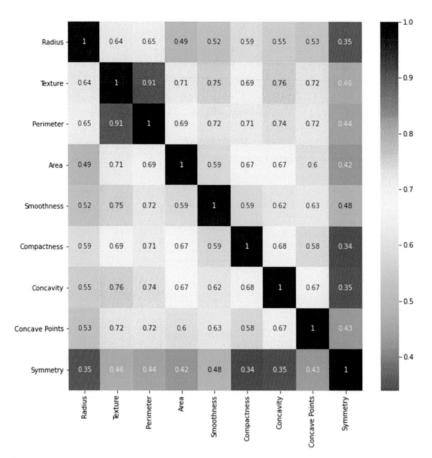

FIGURE 11.10

Correlation heatmap of breast cancer data.

tune the model: The first is through controlling and modifying the numerosity of hidden layers in the neural network, and the other is through controlling and modifying the number of neurons in the neural network.

A function for predicting the output has been made using samples generated from the posterior. Through the function, the numbers of overall false positives, total errors, and total false negatives have been obtained. The outcome probability, that is, classification as not benign and as malignant, are predicted through a decision boundary, as shown in Fig. 11.14.

The number of false positives is very high for a very low decision boundary, whereas when the decision boundary increases, at 0.3 few false negatives are seen. A 2% false-negative rate has been observed at 0.6, which also increases further. A flawless decision boundary sits in the middle of 0.3 and 0.6; and 97.3% accuracy has been obtained for a decision boundary of 0.4.

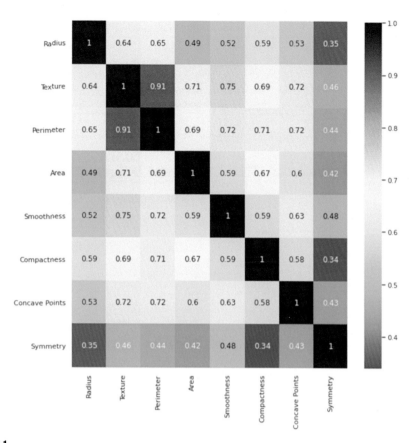

FIGURE 11.11

Refurbished Heatmap.

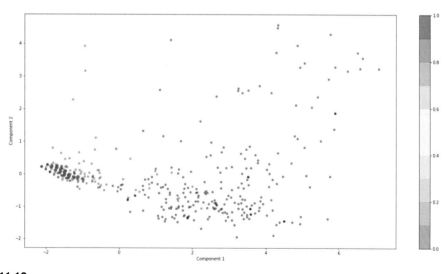

FIGURE 11.12

Principal component analysis (PCA).

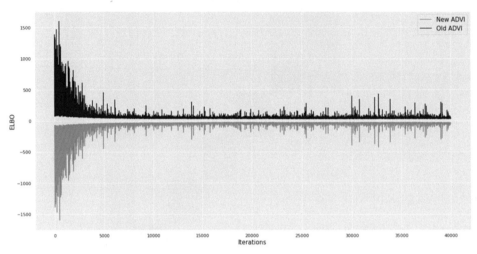

FIGURE 11.13

ELBO plot.

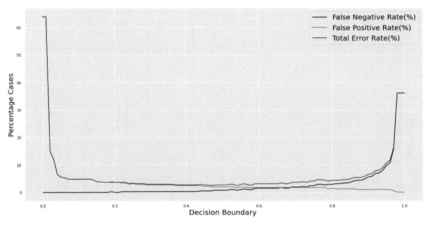

FIGURE 11.14

Outcome probability.

Elucidating the weights for each node in the first mapping is shown in Fig. 11.15. The fig. 11.15 shows the distribution of weights from features, the chart representation shown clearly address the effect of weights and the distribution.

When the mean is close to 0, these weights are known as statistically insignificant weights [19,20]. Statistically insignificant weights do not supply the variance of the model, hence resulting in positive

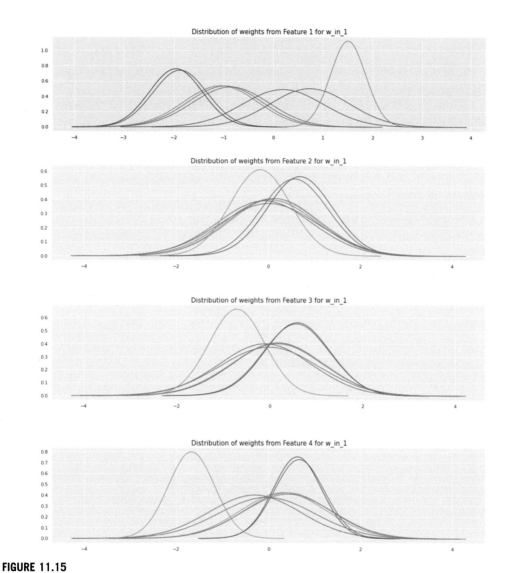

FIGURE 11.15

Dissection of model weights for mapping to the first layer.

effects in some cases while they are negative in others. Features 2 and 7 are observed to be statistically insignificant weights. Less insignificant weights and more variability are observed in features 3 and 4. This gives variance of the model with more consistency, hence resulting in more being on either the positive or negative side.

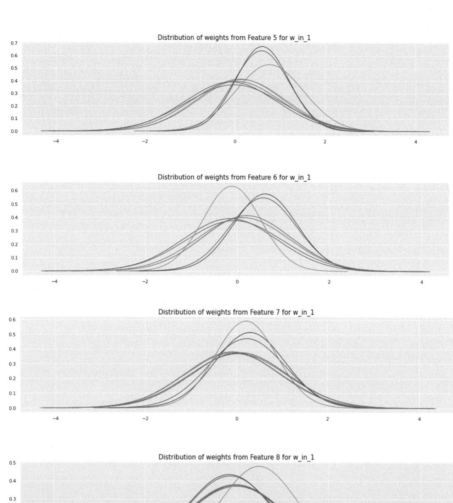

FIGURE 11.15 Cont'd

Elucidating the weights for each node in the second mapping is shown in Fig. 11.16. The Fig. 11.16 shows the distribution of weights and their effect on featureswith the varying weights.

Node 5, 6, and 8 are observed to be statistically insignificant weights. Statistically insignificant weights do not supply the variance of the model, hence resulting in positive effects in some cases while

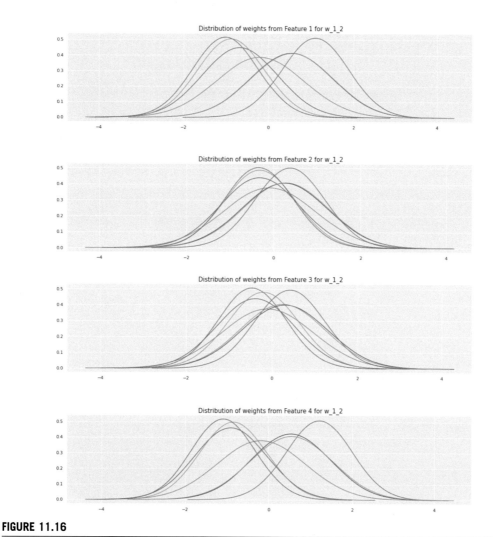

FIGURE 11.16

Dissection of model weights for mapping from the first layer to the second layer.

they are negative in others. Less insignificant weights and more variability are observed in nodes 2, 3, 4, and 7. This gives variance of the model with more consistency, hence resulting in more being on either the positive or negative side.

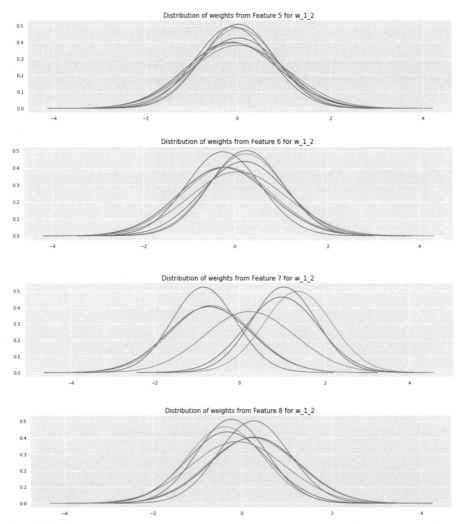

FIGURE 11.16 Cont'd

5. Conclusion

In chapter, we have discussed in depth the probabilistic approach to minimize diagnosis costs. We have proposed a prototype model for minimizing the cost of breast cancer diagnosis. We discussed the foundations of a probabilistic model [19,20] through which we created a model and also discussed some more approaches to these foundations to minimize other diagnosis problems. We have also discussed one of the most important topics in probabilistic statistics, that is, the Bayesian neural network, along with Markov chain Monte Carlo and variational inference. Around 97.3% accuracy has been observed using our model with 0.4 as the decision boundary. We have discussed also the problems faced while creating a probabilistic-based model and how to overcome these issues using numerous techniques. Therefore, in this chapter a knowledge-based predictive system is outlined that can assist medical practitioners in forecasting disease status on the basis of the existing clinical data of patients with good accuracy as a clinical analytical method which can further help to minimize the cost of healthcare diagnosis [20] and make it more economical.

References

[1] V. Mullachery, A. Khera, A. Husain, Bayesian Neural Networks (1), 18, ArXiv, abs/1801.07710, 2018, pp. 01–16.

[2] S. McLachlan, K. Dube, G. Hitman, N. Fenton, E. Kyrimi, Bayesian networks in healthcare: distribution by medical condition, Artif. Intell. Med. 107 (2020).

[3] J. Speagle, A Conceptual Introduction to Markov Chain Monte Carlo Methods, 2019.

[4] R. Kulshrestha, P. Ramani, A.K. Sharma, A hybrid of scheduling and probabilistic approach to decrease the effect of idle listening in WSN, in: S.L. Peng, L. Son, G. Suseendran, D. Balaganesh (Eds.), Intelligent Computing and Innovation on Data Science, Lecture Notes in Networks and Systems, vol. 118, Springer, Singapore, 2020.

[5] A.K. Waljee, et al., A primer on predictive models, Clin. Transl. Gastroenterol. 5 (1) (January 2, 2014) e44.

[6] M. Arabi, R.S. Govindaraju, M.M. Hantush, A probabilistic approach for analysis of uncertainty in the evaluation of watershed management practices, J. Hydrol. 333 (2–4) (2007) 459–471.

[7] M.W. Vanik, J.L. Beck, S. Au, Bayesian probabilistic approach to structural health monitoring, J. Eng. Mech. 126 (7) (2000) 738–745.

[8] A.G. De Brevern, C. Etchebest, S. Hazout, Bayesian probabilistic approach for predicting backbone structures in terms of protein blocks, Proteins Struct. Func. & Bioinf. 41 (3) (2000) 271–287.

[9] C.F. Chiu, W.M. Yan, K.V. Yuen, Estimation of water retention curve of granular soils from particle-size distribution—a Bayesian probabilistic approach, Can. Geotech. J. 49 (9) (2012) 1024–1035.

[10] S. Bhardwaj, A.K. Sharma, Speech audio cardinal emotion sentiment detection and prediction using deep learning approach, in: 3rd International Conference on Recent Trends in Advanced Computing — Artificial Intelligence and Technology (ICRTAC-AIT, 2020), Springer, 2020.

[11] D.K. Srivastava, A.K. Sharma, S. Bhardwaj, Prediction of COVID-19 outbreak by using ML based time series forecasting approach, in: Innovations in Information and Communication Technologies (IICT-2020), Springer, 2020.

[12] O. Stojanović, J. Leugering, G. Pipa, S. Ghozzi, A. Ullrich, A Bayesian Monte Carlo approach for predicting the spread of infectious diseases, Plos One (2019), https://doi.org/10.1371/journal.pone.0225838.

[13] P. McCullagh, J.A. Nelder, Generalized linear models, in: Chapman & Hall/CRC Monographs on Statistics and Applied Probability, second ed., Chapman & Hall/CRC, 1989.

[14] J. Rocca, Bayesian Inference Problem, MCMC and Variational Inference, 2019. https://towardsdatascience.com/bayesian-inference-problem-mcmc-and-variational-inference-25a8aa9bce29.

[15] Alberts, et al., Molecular Biology of the Cell, sixth ed., Gon.

[16] D. Radecic, A Non-Confusing Guide to Confusion Matrix. https://www.betterdatascience.com/a-non-confusing-guide-to-confusion-matrix/.

[17] N. Gomanie, Z. Day, N. Weaver, A. Roy, S. Moros, K. Mehta, Data-Centric Operations Design for Disseminating a Biomedical Screening Technology: A Case Study, 2020.

[18] R. Ekambaram, N. Gomanie, K. Mehta, Analysis of Failure Modes: Case Study of Ruggedizing a Low-Cost Screening Technology in Sub-saharan Africa, 2019.

[19] A. Sharma, D. Shrivastava, Statistical approach to detect Alzheimer's disease and autism spectrum related neurological disorder using machine learning, in: SMARTCOM 2020, Advances in Intelligent Systems and Computing, vol. 182, 2020 (ISSN: 2190-3018).

[20] A.K. Sharma, S. Kumar Vishwakarma, S.S. Verma, On neurological disorders for schizophrenic and AD patients prediction using AI approach, International Conference on Artificial Intelligence and Sustainable Engineering (AISE 2020).

Effects of EEG-sleep irregularities and its behavioral aspects: review and analysis

12

Santosh Satapathy[1], D. Loganathan[1], Akash Kumar Bhoi[2,3] and Paolo Barsocchi[3]

[1]*Department of Computer Science and Engineering, Pondicherry Engineering College, Puducherry, India;* [2]*Department of Computer Science and Engineering, Sikkim Manipal Institute of Technology, Sikkim Manipal University, Majitar, Sikkim, India;* [3]*Institute of Information Science and Technologies, National Research Council, Pisa, Italy*

1. Introduction

Sleep is a basic requirement of human life for the functioning of different internal and external parts of the body. It plays an important role in properly maintaining an individual's memory concentration, immunity system performance, learning ability, and physical movement [1–9]. In general, sleep is an active and regulated process, and it is majorly responsible for performing an essential restorative function. It helps to create a proper balance between physical and mental health [10]. Sleep is a universally recurring and dynamic state for the human body, and its physiological changes reflect our daily lifestyles in diverse ways. According to the different scientific views, humans can spend one-third of their life sleeping [11]. It has been reported from different sleep studies that proper sleep helps to strengthen the mind, motor functioning, and it directly improves the performance at workplaces [12]. According to Institute of Medicine statistics, it was found that 50–70 million Americans were affected by various types of sleep problems. It has been reported by the Center for Disease Control and Prevention that the people of the United States of America have an average of less than 7 h sleep per night. Sleep deprivation sleep causes other health issues in the human body, such as heart disease, obesity, diabetes, and other neurological disorders. Sometimes, it has also reflected that sleep disturbances affect the balance between memory consolidation, mental restoration, and behavior [14]. The major boost reached in this sleep research was with the invention of electroencephalography in 1930. For the first time, from an EEG signal in 1937, the sleep behavior was seen to not be a homogeneous procedure, but it consists of different sleep stages [15]. According to sleep experts, sleep is linked to metabolic function and obesity [16]. Its negative impact is on our health, subject to cognition processes such as vigilant attention and public health [17,18]. Sleep deprivation can causes people to feel drowsy and unable to concentrate on their job appropriately. The term drowsiness is considered to be sleepiness, where the subject needs to asleep. It has been seen in recent years that drowsiness causes a huge losses in society through loss of life. It has been observed that, due to drowsiness, road accidents have increased globally. According to a report from the US National Highway Traffic Safety Administration, deaths are often caused by drowsiness, and also as a result,

Cognitive and Soft Computing Techniques for the Analysis of Healthcare Data. https://doi.org/10.1016/B978-0-323-85751-2.00009-8

there are 100,000 vehicle collisions annually. It has also been seen that, due to drowsiness, most of these collisions were caused by "drift-out-of-lane" accidents [19]. Sleep is an important part of human health function. As per the National Institute of Health report, sleep plays an important role in the human daily routine, and its importance is equal to food and water for survival. The proper sleep staging is directly connected to maintaining good health physically and mentally, and also it is strongly associated with proper cognitive and physiological well-being. On the other hand, it is also seen that poor and/or disordered sleep patterns may cause serious health issues such as impairments of cognitive function, resulting in the degradation of health [20]. These reasons demand proper analysis of the sleep stages, changes in sleep behavior regarding the individual sleep stages, and investigation into the possible treatment solutions. Some of the existing studies have also observed that continuous changes in lifestyles and stress at work may also be important causes of poor sleep patterns, which directly affect the work capacity of the subjects and threatens their daily routine and public safety [21]. Apart from all these direct risks, traumatic childhood experiences may also sometimes increase sleep disorders in adulthood [22]. From the Willemen et al. study, it has found that around 27.6% of the Italian population had sleep problems [23]. This public health issue also links directly with the economic state of the country. Wickwire et al. [24] reported that around $100 billion per year is spent on the diagnosis of different sleep-related disorders. It has been observed from the sleep study that the direct and indirect investment for diagnosing sleep-related disorders is $1000 in 6 months, which is incomparable with the subjects without sleep problem patient's treatments [25]. It has been reported from a number of summaries that different types of sleep-related disorders result in a significantly increasing public health risk that requires medical attention [26]. In late 1950, polysomnography (PSG) was originated and regarded as one of the gold standards to analyze sleep patterns and detect the different sleep-related disorders. The changes in physiological activities during REM and non-REM

Table 12.1 Changes in physiological behavior.

Physiological behavior	NREM	REM
Brain behavior	Decreases, incomparable to wakefulness	Increases
Heart rhythm	Stable	Fluctuating
Blood pressure	Stable	Fluctuating
Nerve functioning	Stable	Increases
Movements of muscles	Absent	Present
Respiration	Stable	Fluctuating
Blood circulation	Decreases	Increases, incomparable to NREM
Body temperature	Stable	Fluctuating
Dreams	Absent	Present
Swallowing	Decreases	Decreases
Cerebral blood flow	Decreases	Increases
Muscle tone	Mild	Absent

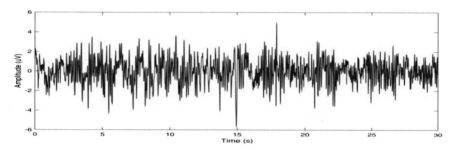

FIGURE 12.1

Typical EEG signal behavior in wake stage (W).

(NREM) sleep stages are presented in Table 12.1. The behavior of each sleep stages is described as follows:

1. **Wake stage (W):** During this stage, the subject is completely awake and can carry out his/her daily activities. Generally, the time period for this sleep stage is about 14–16 h [27] (Fig. 12.1).
2. **NREM stage 1 (N1):** This is the transitional stage between wake and sleep. It is also called the light sleep stage, where the person can easily awaken from sleep. During this stage, eye movements are slow, muscles are relaxed, and the heart rhythms gradually slow down [27] (Fig. 12.2).
3. **NREM stage 2 (N2):** This sleep stage is a deeper sleep stage than the N1 sleep stage, where the brain activities slow down, body temperature drops, and the movements of the eyes cease. However, occasional bursts of brain waves appear [27] (Fig. 12.3).
4. **NREM stage 3 (N3):** During this stage, the individual goes into a much deeper sleep, and the brain waves are completely dominated by slow delta waves, which are smaller in size. The major dysfunctional symptoms of a person in this stage are sleepwalking and night terrors [27] (Fig. 12.4).
5. **REM stage (R):** During this sleep stage, the movements of the eyes are rapid and maximum arousal times occur. The brain behavior of this sleep stage is quite similar to the wake–sleep stage [28] (Fig. 12.5).

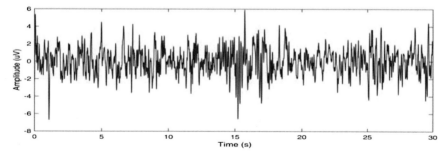

FIGURE 12.2

Typical EEG signal behavior in NREM sleep stage 1 (N1).

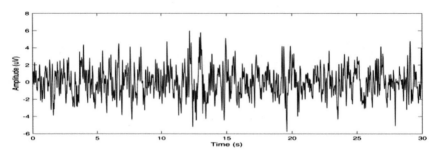

FIGURE 12.3

Typical EEG signal behavior in NREM sleep stage 2 (N2).

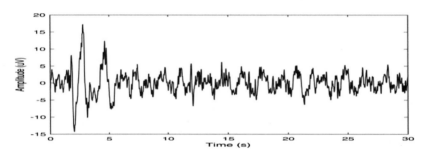

FIGURE 12.4

Typical EEG signal behavior in NREM sleep stage 3 (N3).

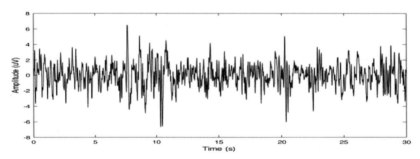

FIGURE 12.5

Typical EEG signal behavior in REM sleep stage (R).

2. Medical background

Sleep state scoring is one of the primary steps toward diagnosing any type of sleep-related problems and different mental diseases. In a clinical system, sleep analysis takes greater importance for the identification of sleep irregularities during sleep. During sleep stage analysis, various physiological

Table 12.2 Causes of sleep disruption/deprivation.

Category	Factors
Lifestyle	Habitual alcohol consumption
	Shift working
	Drug abuse
Environmental	Excessive noise
Psychosocial	Anxieties, worries, parents of young children, family members with chronic disorders, serious illness
Sleep-related disorders	Insomnia
	Periodic limb movement disorder
	Obstructive sleep apnea
	Narcolepsy
	Parasomnias
Health conditions	Diabetes
	Certain medications
	Chronic neurological disorders

signals are considered, such as electroencephalogram, electrooculogram, electromyogram, and electrocardiogram. Sleep staging is one of the essential parts of the diagnosis related to sleep-related disorders such as sleep apnea syndrome [29]. One of the most important points of research work is the proper evaluation of sleep-related diseases. Therefore, proper monitoring, screening, and analysis of sleep behavior changes throughout the night is an important issue in this respect. The various causes of sleep disruption/deprivation are described in Table 12.2.

Sleep stage scoring has been processed according to two sleep standards, which were edited and published by Rechtschaffen and Kales (R&K) [30] and the American Academy of Sleep Medicine [31]. According to the R&K rules, each sleep epoch is segmented into 30 s and classified as awake (W), nonrapid eye movement sleep stages (NREM1, NREM2, NREM3, and N-FREM4) and rapid eye movement. In 2007, the AASM released new sleep standards with minor revisions on existing R&K sleep rules; according to the AASM rules, the NREM sleep stages are segmented into three sleep stages that are NREM1, NREM2, and NREM3. Among all physiological signals, EEG signals are considered for most cases because they are directly derived from the brain behavior of the subject, which helps in the diagnosis process [32]. With the help of EEG recordings, different sleep behavior characteristics have been identified from different sleep stages during sleep. EEG waves distinguish brain activities with the help of subbands such as delta, theta, alpha, and beta. Each sleep stage is characterized by certain EEG sleep patterns, such as in the REM sleep stage, maximum waveforms are in nature of low-amplitude, mixed-EEG frequency, saw-tooth wave-like patterns, low-EMG patterns, highly fluctuated EOG behavior from both eyes. Similarly, in the NREM1 sleep stage, alpha patterns are found, with frequency ranges of 2−7 Hz. In this stage, the EMG level is lower than in the awake stages. In the NREM stage 2, in general, two different types of events occur, including sleep spindles, which occur within the frequency range of 12−14 Hz, and k-complexes. NREM stage 3 and NREM stage 4 are considered deep sleep, where low-frequency waves are seen, ranging from less than 2 Hz. Sometimes, in this part, sleep spindles are seen. Generally, the PSG signals contain combinations of the signal information such as brain activation through an EEG signal, eye movement information through an EOG signal, muscle-skeletal information through an EMG signal, heart rhythms using an ECG signal, and breathing information using respiratory airflow and oxygen saturation. The PSG test's general procedure is for patients to be admitted overnight into the hospital; during that period, biophysiological signals are recorded. This entire process is called sleep scoring or sleep staging. During sleep scoring, the main objective is to analyze the complete information from the different electrophysiological signals. The focus is to analyze the sleep stages properly, and the arousals, respiratory events, cardiac events have to be correctly identified. Three main bio-signals, EEG, EOG, and EMG signals, are used to analyze the sleep characteristics. The existing sleep stages process with manual visual monitoring is quite tedious. Sometimes, this process may produce the wrong sleep scoring analysis due to inaccurate human interpretation of the sleep recordings. Another important factor is that variations by sleep experts may also produce different sleep scoring results. There should be a requirement for the automated sleep staging system to use a computer-aided system to overcome these differences. The different researchers proposed different techniques and methods for automated sleep staging systems, reported excellent sleep staging accuracy. It has been seen that AI plays a crucial role in developing and upgrading for the diagnosis of various types of sleep-related disorders. Artificial intelligence and its subset techniques have recently attracted more attention and performed well in several fields such as engineering [33–35], healthcare [36–39], and psychology [40].

3. Visual scoring procedure

This is one of the approaches for monitoring sleep behavior and its characteristics. The obtained polysomnography record of sleep is generally segmented into 30-s epochs. During the visual inspection, each epoch is annotated with a sleep stage. Sometimes, it has been seen that two or more sleep stages can coexist within a single epoch; in that case, that epoch is aligned to that particular sleep stage which covers the major portions of the 30-s epoch. R&K sleep scoring rules followed the entire sleep scoring procedure, and these rules were widely adopted worldwide until 2007. After that, the AASM updated the existing sleep manuals, which R&K edited in terms of sleep scoring rules and PSG results interpretation. According to the AASM manual, the stages of sleep were restricted to up to five sleep stages: wake stage, N1 stage, N2 stage, N3 stage, and REM stage, and the movement time (MT) stage was abolished. Most of the time, sleep experts recommended EEG signals for monitoring sleep behavior because EEG provides meaningful information directly from the brain activities, which helps to analyze the sleep irregularities during sleep.

The EEG signal is generally represented in terms of its frequency components. Each frequency subband presents different characteristic waveforms. These are δ rhythms (0.5–4 Hz), θ rhythms (4–8 Hz), α rhythms (8–12 Hz), and β rhythms (12–35 Hz). The waveform in the frequency range 0.5–2 Hz and peak-to-peak amplitude $>75\mu v$ are considered as slow-wave activity. Sometimes, during the N2 and N3 sleep stages, sleep spindles (distinct wave patterns in the range of 12–14 Hz that continue for more than 0.5 s), k-complexes (sharp negative waves followed by positive waves, which continue for up to 0.5 s), and all these wave-patterns can be seen during the different stages of sleep. The main intention of sleep stages is to recognize the EEG frequency components and analyze the sleep patterns. Still, sometimes it is also observed that applying these rules may create unnecessary complexity. In general, sleep progresses from the wake stages through the REM stage, then begins again with the wake stages. The process takes 90–110 min for each iteration. The human sleep cycles

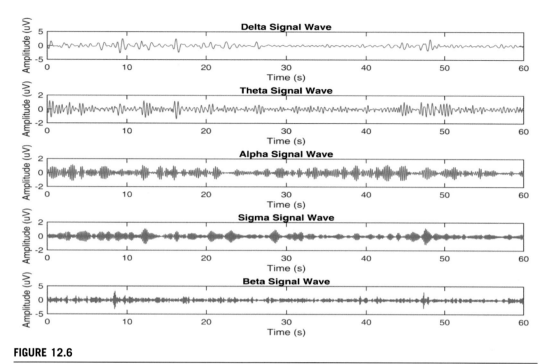

FIGURE 12.6

Changes in sleep behavior: healthy subject.

show REM sleep and a longer period of NREM sleep. The sleep stage characteristics according to the AASM sleep scoring rules are briefly summarized in the following. The changes in sleep behavior in the different signal subbands for healthy controlled and sleep-disordered subjects are shown in Figs. 12.6 and 12.7, respectively.

4. AI and sleep staging

This section discusses some existing applicable methods of diagnosis and various types of sleep-related disorders and the globe. This section's main purpose is to explore the different strategies and effectiveness of techniques for sleep staging and focuses upon the latest updates on the different sleep disorders. This section presents different ideas, which can speed up the treatment and diagnosis process. The effectiveness of AI tools depends on the proper analysis and classification of the sleep stage patterns. The different approaches and steps taken during sleep staging analysis through AI-based methods to overcome the risk of sleep-related disorders are presented in the structural framework shown in Fig. 12.8. The first and most important step in preparing the data is essential for popularly understanding sleep behavior. In this phase, we briefly discuss his/her medical information, daily routine activities, professional and social lifestyles, and various information to be transformed into the data, which can be understood by the machine easily. The main objectives of understanding sleep recordings includes understanding the sleep characteristics. Before the sleep records can be

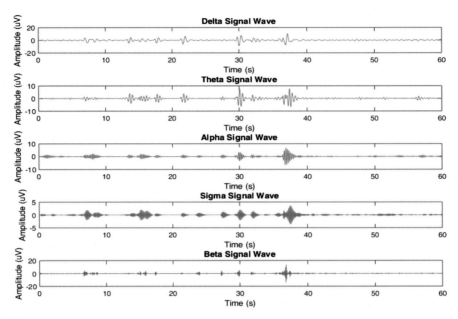

FIGURE 12.7

Changes in sleep behavior: sleep-disordered subject.

processed further, the contained signal compositions need to be separated from the raw data. On the other hand, this is a process where we are acquiring, analyzing, and preprocessing data. During this process, human intervention takes place, and experts analyze sleep behavior and its patterns.

Sleep expert interpretations highly impact this section because their knowledge and experiences concerning monitoring sleep behavior are not available in ML solutions. Generally, ML techniques depend upon structured data. Another common challenge during handling a huge record like PSG signals is that it can cause the model to overfit [41]. Therefore, the feature extraction step is more helpful in the traditional ML algorithms for overcoming overfitting issues when handling huge amounts of sleep records [42]. Human interpretation is required during the extraction of hand-crafted features from the sleep record in ML techniques. The extracted features are fed into classification models such as the SVM or RF classifiers. Sometimes it has been seen that all the extracted features may not be effective for all the subject cases [42]. ML techniques are limited to classifying multiclass sleep stages with high accuracy and precision for all these mentioned reasons.

However, deep learning techniques are well suited for managing enormous or complicated recordings. DL is a subset of ML, and consists of several layers of the algorithm, which interprets the data. The main function of DL methods is training the PSG signals without any feature reduction techniques [43]. It automatically extracts the features from the input PSG signals without any inter-pretation. DL models handle large volumes of data and make accurate predictions. They also consider which features are more helpful during the inference and neglect the other features. Therefore, DL techniques are more effective rather than ML techniques while dealing with a high volume of PSG signals.

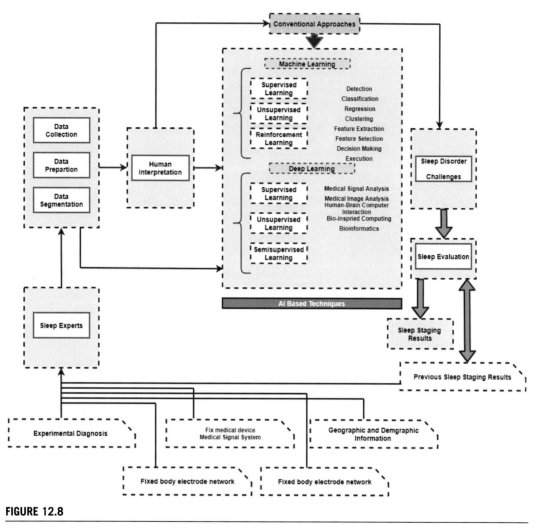

FIGURE 12.8

AI-based structural framework.

AI and its supporting tools are widely applied in sleep staging. Accordingly, these solutions are categorized into two parts: recognizing and diagnosis. The AI-based sleep staging system is presented in Fig. 12.9, and is specifically desired for analysis and classification of sleep-related disorders.

The entire procedure is presented in five layers. The initial layer is called the input layer, which is used to associate the database, and this layer is specifically designed for collecting sleep recordings. A high-configuration system is used during the data preparation for further processing. The next layer is the selection layer, which is specifically designed by AI-based techniques for discontinuing sleep stage characteristics. If clinicians confirm the obtained techniques, the recommended suggestions are taken in the third layer by obtaining the required signals. For each subject, the biosignals are recorded for

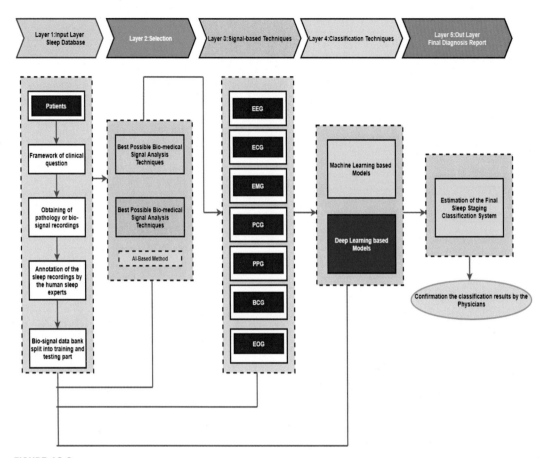

FIGURE 12.9

AI-based structural framework.

some time. Generally, the most widely used biosignals during the sleep staging classification are ECG, EMG, phonocardiography (PCG), photoplethysmography (PPG), ballistocardiography (BCG), and other biosignals like EOG, respiratory signals, blood pressure, and skin temperature. The fourth layer is specifically focused on preprocessing the signals by the remaining irrelevant artifacts and segmentation of the recorded signals to analyze sleep characteristics better. Finally, in the fifth layer, the learning algorithms are used for classifying the sleep stage patterns using ML and DL models. Finally, the evaluation results may be decided for the treatment process. It has been discussed [44–46] that, sometimes, subjects complain about their sleep quality. However, for noncomplementary subjects, we must discuss their sleep-onset latency (S_{OL}), wake after sleep onset (W_{ASO}), total sleep time (T_{ST}), and sleep efficiency (S_E) to analyze the sleep behavior. Some additional parameters are also considered together, such as the distribution of sleep epochs per individual sleep stage, the time and quality of sleep, and the pathological events like PLMD and SDB. It can be seen from the existing contributions that several parameters have been used to assess sleep quality.

4.1 Analysis of human sleep behavior using sleep variables

Each person has their own internal physiological process, which is repeated approximately every 24 hours. It can be seen that over the last 60 years, sleep studies have involved a huge amount of sleep technicians, physiologists, and sleep experts. The two sleep standards, R&K and AASM standards, were widely used for sleep scoring rules. Finally, the required sleep parameters during the investigation of sleep quality are described in Table 12.3. For characterizing the sleep behavior, both sleep manuals followed certain variables. According to the R&K sleep standards, four conventional parameters were used: S_{OL}, T_{ST}, W_{ASO}, and S_E. The different possibilities with regards to assessment of sleep quality are shown in Fig. 12.10.

S_{OL}: The time taken from the wake stage to sleep stage.

W_{ASO}: This is the total awakening periods in minutes during the sleep hours. It can be computed as

$$W_{ASO} = \sum_{i=1}^{N_A} D_{AW}$$

where N_A = Number of awakening periods between sleep onset and sleep offset.

D_{AW} = The duration of the i-th awakenings.

T_{ST}: The total sleep time from sleep onset to the wake stage. This represents the actual sleeping time.

$$T_{ST} = T_B - (S_{OL} + W_{ASO})$$

where T_B = Total sleep time in bed.

S_E: This is the ratio between T_{ST} and T_B

$$S_E = \frac{T_{ST}}{T_B}$$

Table 12.3 Required sleep parameters during sleep staging.

Variable	Definition
Total sleep time	The time between starting and ending sleep
Total in bed	The total time in bed
First in bed time	The time when the subject first went to bed
Final out in bed time	The time when the subject finally leaves the bed
Sleep onset	The first time the subject falls asleep
Sleep offset	The time which the subject is awake
Number of awakenings	The total number of awake episodes per night
Number of arousals	The total number of arousals per night
Total sleep time in bed	The total time in bed
Total recording time	Total time between light on and light off
Sleep interval	The time between first sleep and last sleep
N1 (%)	The ratio of time spent between the N1 sleep and TST
N2 (%)	The ratio of time spent between N2 and TST
N3 (%)	The ratio of time spent between N3 and TST
REM (%)	The ratio of time spent between REM and TST

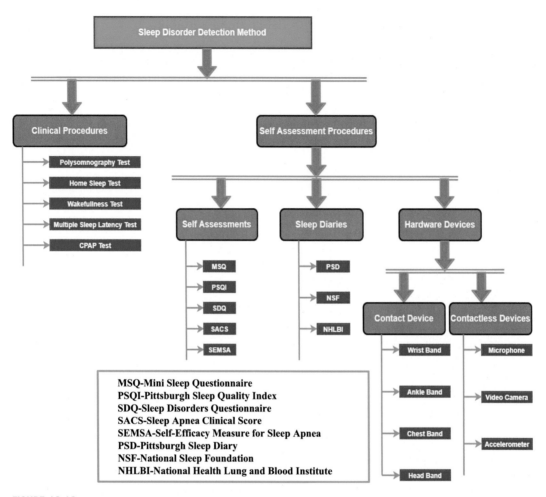

FIGURE 12.10

Sleep detection procedures.

4.2 Characteristics of biosignals

The required biomedical signals are recorded for a central period of time. The physiological biosignals are highly nonstationary and heterogeneous [47,48].

4.2.1 Technical characteristics

Generally, the human body uses a complex cognitive, physiological processes. The biosignals are dynamic changes over time and reflect the different behaviors during each stage of sleep. All the biosignals with electrical activities and conductance also measure their temperature, pressure, sound, and acceleration [49,50]. The characteristics of the different biosignals are described in Table 12.4.

Table 12.4 Biosignal parameter characteristics.

Biosignals	Channels	Frequency range (Hz)	Amplitude	Electrode placement
EEG	1–6	0.5–100	2 to 200 μv	Scalp
ECG	1–12	0.05–150	0.1 to 5 μv	Surface
EMG	1–32	5–2000	0.1 to 5 μv	Needle
EOG	1–2	1–100	10 to 3500 μv	Contact
PPG	1	0.25–40	−10 to 10 μv	Fingerttips
PCG	1	10–400	−2 to 2 μv	Surface
BCG	3	1–20	−0.05 to 0.05 μv	Surface
Skin temperature	1	1–200	−50 to 50 μv	Surface

4.2.2 Clinical characteristics

According to the existing findings, most of the outcomes used three biosignals (EEG, ECG, and EMG signals) for analyzing the sleep behavior of subjects. Despite observing these existing statistics, some recent studies based on EEG signals were also required. The different clinical procedures for diagnosing the different sleep-related disorders are presented in Table 12.5. The clinical properties of the different biosignals are briefly described below.

EEG: This helps to measure brain activities during sleep by measuring the electrical activity of the brain. During the monitoring of the brain's behavior, electrodes that are cup- or disc-shaped are placed on the scalp. These fixed electrodes pick up the brain's electrical signals, which are recorded on an electroencephalogram. Generally, the EEG signals are widely used to diagnose different types of neurological disorders, sleep-related disorders, epilepsy, brain tumors, and brain hemorrhage. The brain's recording details are obtained by either fixing the electrodes to the scalp or mounting a special band on the head. Three different EEG recordings are acquired, the first being a routine EEG, where the recordings from the 20 electrodes fixed on the scalp are received. The second type is sleep EEG, where the EEG is recorded with the heart rate, airflow, oxygen saturation, and limb movement. The final type is ambulatory EEG, in which the recording details from the subject are collected throughout

Table 12.5 Laboratory tests for the diagnosis of sleep-related diseases.

Clinical procedures to assess sleep-related diseases
Polysomnography test
Primary diagnostic workshop due to the initial causes of the sleep disturbances
Sleep latency test
Standard EEG test and video-EEG monitoring system
Actigraphy test
PSG test using video monitoring
Electromyogram test for analysis of restless leg syndrome
Upper airway imaging techniques for obstructive sleep apnea
Wakefulness test
A clinical test for the diagnosis of the various types of sleep-related disorders

the whole day by fixing a small portable EEG recorder. The EEG signal's main advantage is that it supports noninvasive techniques; hardware implementation is also very low in comparison to the other techniques, and this allows for better analysis of the auditory stimuli [42].

ECG: This is recorded in a noninvasive manner. Primarily it helps to provide information regarding changes to heart rhythms and the heart rate. This information makes it easier clinically to analyze sleep behavior changes in relation to an abnormal heart rate [51,52]. Sometimes, subjects are also affected by different heart-related dreams; they may not complete their proper sleep cycle because of an irregular heartbeat and irregular pattern changes.

EMG: The importance of this signal is to obtain information about muscle movement, which directly helps to analyze abnormal body movements during sleep, which is also one of the methods to study sleep patterns. It is also recorded from subjects noninvasively [53].

EOG: This helps to capture information about the eyes' movements, which also helps to analyze the behavior of different sleep-related disorders. This information is obtained from both eyes using a fixed electrode on each eye [42].

PCG: In general, this signal captures information about the different sounds produced during the sleep. It is one of the best and most significant methods to analyze various sleep problems [52].

PPG: This is recorded in a noninvasive manner using an oximeter device. The recorded PPG data are highly complex, due to the skin thickness. It also helps during sleep staging by obtaining the heart's information making it one of the best detection methods during the sleep staging process [54].

Some of the existing contributions to sleep studies using different biosignals are discussed with concern to the used data set, feature extraction, and classification model, and this information is presented in Table 12.6.

Table 12.6 Sleep studies using different biosignals.

Existing study	Input	Feature extraction	Classification model
Selected recent existing sleep studies based on EEG signal			
Mousavi et al. [55], 2019 Michielli et al. [56], 2019	Sleep—European Data Format (S-EDF) dataset S-EDF	Time and frequency domain features	DL
Sharma et al. [57], 2018		Time—frequency localized wavelet filter bank	SVM
Seifpour et al. [58], 2018		Statistical behavior	Multiclass SVM
Chriskos et al. [59], 2018	23 healthy male adults	Synchronization likelihood and wavelet entropy	SVM,NN,KNN
Memar and faradji et al. [60], 2018	S-EDF UCDDB XESEDF DREAMS	Nested fivefold cross-validation and subject-wise cross-validation	RF
Pillay et al. [61], 2018	16 preterms and newborns	Multiple time and frequency domain features	HMMs and GMMs

Table 12.6 Sleep studies using different biosignals.—cont'd

Existing study	Input	Feature extraction	Classification model
Hassan and Subasi et al. [62], 2017	S-EDF DREAMS	Tunable-Q wavelet transform	Bagging
Based on ECG signal			
Yucelbas et al. [63], 2018	Sleep Center, Erbakan University, and PhysioNet	Morphological methods	RF
Yoon et al. [64], 2017	21 healthy subjects and 30 subjects with obstructive sleep apnea	Statistical parameters, spectral power	
Liu et al. [65], 2017	75 sleep apnea subjects obtained from Shandong Province of Traditional Chinese Medicine Hospital	Time-domain statistical parameters	Statistical analysis
Based on the EOG signal			
Rahman et al. [66], 2018	EOG, PhysioNet database	Discrete wavelet transform	SVM, RUSBoost, and RF
Based on PSG signal			
Tripathy et al. [67], 2018	MIT-BIH polysomnography	Variance, entropy	DNN
Takatani et al. [68], 2018	16 adults and 74 newborn	EEG spectral power	Statistical analysis
Lerman et al. [69], 2017	125 women under medication of joint disorder	Sleep parameters	Multiple regression analysis
Rosipal et al. [70] 2015	148 subjects, healthy controlled		Probabilistic sleep model
Orff et al. [71], 2012	137 women subjects with different medical conditions		Multivariate analysis of variance

From Table 12.5, it has been found that the different approaches taken on the sleep staging methods also highlight the different sleep parameters with regard to medical and psychology backgrounds. During sleep staging, the sleep parameters are derived in two ways: the sleep stages and the other derived variables. The sleep stages part includes the information collected from stages 1, 2, 3, and 4, slow-wave sleep, and REM sleep. On the other hand, the derived variables contain the information with regards to total sleep time (h), sleep period times (h), sleep onset latency (epoch), sleep efficiency, number of awakenings, and sleep offset.

4.3 Non-REM sleep

EEG signal is more effective in the analysis of sleep behavior in the NREM sleep stages. For a better analysis of the individual sleep stages characteristics during NREM sleep, the best method is spectral analysis of the EEG signal. EEG signals are analyzed by decomposing the entire signal into the different frequency subbands (from 0.5 to 45 Hz). The recorded EEG signals are segmented into different frequency bands with different frequency levels for better discrimination of the sleep stages. We divided them into two different waveforms, $\beta 1(13-20$ Hz$)$ and $\beta 2(20-30$ Hz$)$, for better discrimination between the wake and REM sleep stages. It has been reported that waveforms significantly impact the classification of sleep stages, so that we divided them into $\gamma 1(30-40$ Hz$)$ and $\gamma 2(40-49.5$ Hz$)$ waveforms.

4.4 Sleep diaries and questions

Previously, to understand sleep-related problems, subjective analysis was conducted to gather information on sleep and its quality. Till now, the debate is still on-going to discover the best method of sleep behavior monitoring. The main difference found in the subjective way of analysis from the PSG test is obtaining the different self-report questions to analyze sleep behavior. These should be followed by several mechanisms to understand and validate the self-report assessment. The two approaches, sleep diaries and PSQI, are used for maintaining the day-to-day information on sleep behavior but sometimes it has been seen that this method of sleep behavior monitoring for elderly subjects may lead to errors due to poor memory cognition. The general format of the self-assessment and daily sleep diaries includes information about the different sleep parameters. Sleep diaries provide information about the sleep schedule and awakening in the nighttime. Sleep diaries mainly are used for clinical reasons, and for maintaining intervention effects and the actigraphy data. On the other hand, sleep questions are low cost-effective approaches for collecting information about sleep and sleep patterns, sleep problems, and behaviors. These discussions are mainly used during the subjective self-assessment process and analysis of their strengths and weaknesses.

5. Sleep patterns and clinical age

Sleep behavior, in general, changes with age, with sleep requirements being different from infancy to adulthood. It has been observed that sleep patterns are also quite different with regard to the initiation and maintenance of sleep efficiency. It has been seen that the quality of sleep degrades with increasing age. Age can also have an impact on understanding sleep characteristics.

5.1 Newborns

For newborn children, sleeping time is significantly longer across the day and/or night. Sleep experts identify two stages, REM and NREM, for the first 2−3 weeks, and by the age of 3 months old, four sleep stages are seen. Two main sleep phases appear, these are quiet sleep and active sleep. During active (REM) sleep, the baby makes noises and cries, with small limb movements. On the other hand, during quiet (NREM) sleep, the baby is still and does not move [73]. Sometimes the sleep patterns can change with great demand from social cues. Once the baby reaches the age of 3 months, its sleep cycles become similar to those of adults, and all four stages (N1, N2, N3, and REM) are present. With the age of 3 months, the sleep cycle has entered the normal process, begins with NREM sleep stage, and the REM sleep stage decreasing [74]. By the age of 1 year, the infant typically sleeps 14–15 h per day, with the majority of the sleep happening in the night, with one or two naps during the daytime [75].

5.2 Young children

As there are few studies conducted with regards to young children and their sleep behavior, it has been found that the sleep amount decreases significantly for young children as they age. The major reasons behind the decrease in sleeping time are due to social and cultural environments [72]. Several social and cultural factors may alter sleep patterns in the daytime, such as the school schedule [76].

5.3 Adolescents

According to the different sleep studies, adolescents' sleep requirements are 9–10 h each night. The US 8th standard students sleep around 7–9 h per day [77]. It has also been found that high school or college students were sleep-deprived. Due to the development of pubertal activity, the subject's SWS and sleep efficiency decreases [78]. Most of the subjects in this category spent more time in sleep stage 2. These changes happened due to the hormonal changes in the body. In this group, with increasing age, the sleep period decreased [78].

5.4 Adults

In general, the sleep architecture for adults continuously changes with increases in age adulthood. Two major things to be observed during sleep for adult subjects are early wake time and reduced sleep time [79]. According to the subject's age, older adults with an age range from 60 to 70 typically wake before 2 h of sleep incomparble to the young adults having age ranges from 20 to 30 [80].

5.5 Gender differences

Some research studies have been systematically based on gender-based changes in sleep behavior and circadian rhythms. Changes in sleep characteristics have also been found in infants [81], children [82], and adolescents [83]. In general, adults spend more time in the N1 sleep stage and experience more awakenings [84]. It has been seen that women have longer slow-wave sleep patterns compared to men. Sometimes they also complain about difficulty falling asleep and awakening midsleep. On the other hand, the general complaint with regards to men is excess daytime sleepiness. During menstruation, the sleep cycle is influenced [85]. Some good findings already exist with regards to difficult sleep problems during pregnancy and the postpartum period [86].

5.6 Elderly people

Sleep problems directly affect most individuals, irrespective of age; however, this is somewhat increased for older subjects. Generally, the older population's sleep patterns are broken continuously [87]. The SWS segments continuously change with the subject's age. It has been found that changes in sleep behavior affect males and females differently. At age 70 women spend around 20% of their time asleep in N3 and N4, however for men it was around 5%.

6. Case study of an automated sleep staging system

6.1 Experimental data

This research used two public sleep data sets, the sleep-EDF data set (S-EDF), Sleep-EDF expanded data set (SE-EDF) dataset, for method evaluation.

6.1.1 Sleep-EDF (S-EDF) database

In this data set, a total of eight Caucasian subjects' full PSG recordings are collected with age ranges from 21 to 35, who were not associated with any types of medication during the recordings. These recordings are grouped into two major subcategories: sc* and st*. The sc* contained four (sc4002e0, sc4012e0, sc4102e0, and sc4112e0) recordings from healthy controlled subjects, which were recorded over a 24-h period. The st* category contained four subjects (st7022j0, st7052j0, st7121j0, and st7132j0), who were affected with mild difficulty maintaining sleep. For both categories, the recordings of two EEG signals (Fpz-Oz, Pz-Oz) and one horizontal EOG signal were recorded. The recorded signals were sampled with a sampling rate of 100 Hz. The sleep stages' annotation was carried by a group of sleep experts manually as per the R&K sleep study, and were labeled as W, N1, N2, N3, N4, and REM. The complete description of the data set is described in Ref. [88]. Table 12.7 show the distribution of the number of sleep stages.

Table 12.7 Ddetailed explanation of the sleep data set obtained in this proposed research study.

Sleep scoring standards	Rechtschaffen and Hales (R&K) manuals
Database	Sleep-EDF *(S-EDF)* (scored by one sleep expert)
Number of subjects	8
Gender (male/female)	04/04
Age (years)	21–35
Epoch length (s)	30
Sampling frequency (Hz)	100
Total sleep periods length (h)	~126.5
EEG montage	Bipolar
Channel	Fpz-Cz
Sleep stages	
Wake (W)	8006 (53%)
S1 (N1)	604 (4%)
S2 (N2)	3621 (24%)
S3 (N3)	672 (4%)
S4	627 (4%)
REM	1609 (11%)
Total epochs	15,139

6.2 Proposed ensemble learning stacking model

Ensemble techniques are one of the machine learning approaches for improving the model by combining several models. The main advantage of ensemble learning is to reduce the variance and bias factors. It helps to increase the accuracy of the model and reduces the variability of prediction. The major advantage of the proposed stacking over the alternatives is that the parallel ensembling approach can analyze in the meta-model. It also helps to identify the mispredicted samples continuously from the base-layer classifiers' feature space due to inconsistent learning. Ensemble techniques can be approached in two ways, namely, the sequential manner and parallel manner. In the sequential methods, the model considers the previous model performance in the sequence manner to improve the system's performance. This approach encompasses most machine learning models such as AdaBoost, XGBoost, etc. On the other hand, in a parallel approach, the models are allowed to perform independently, which helps them handle the data better. This approach includes machine learning models such as random forest and gradient boosting. Fig. 12.11 presents the proposed ensemble learning stacking model for classification of the sleep stages.

The same problem is easily recognized through the meta-model and using suitable base models suited for that specific feature space. The same challenges may not be possible for identifying through voting or simple aggregation of bagging approaches. Additionally, we also obtained cross-validation techniques to overcome the overfitting problem. In this work, we have used a fivefold cross-validation approach. During this approach, the training data set is split randomly into five equal-sized folds. Of those five folds, four are fit for the training, and the remaining one is used for testing purposes.

6.3 Sleep staging results in the S-EDF database

The reported confusion matrix and performance evaluation results are described in Tables 12.8 and 12.9. It was observed from Table 12.8 that the Fpz-Cz channel of the EEG signal with inclusion of age (49) features, overall accuracy, F1 score, and kappa score of the proposed model are 91.10%, 85.42%, and 0.87, respectively. Similarly the same model achieved overall accuracy (90.68%), F1 score (84.86%), and kappa score (0.86) with the exclusion of the age (48) features (Table 12.9).

On the other hand, the S-EDF data set using Pz-Oz EEG channel was based on with or without age features. The confusion matrix and the performance metrics results for the Pz-Oz channel of the EEG signal are presented in Tables 12.10 and 12.11.

It has been observed from Tables 12.10 and 12.11 that the overall accuracy performance decreases from 90.56% to 90.11%. Further, the F1 score decreases from 84.53% to 83.91%, and the kappa score remains the same with regards to the inclusion and exclusion of the age features.

7. Chapter outcome and conclusion

Monitoring the different sleep-related disorders is highly important research for both the health and industrial sectors. Millions of people suffered from different types of sleep-related diseases, which often remain neglected in terms of proper diagnosis and treatments. Most developing countries do not have sufficient health resources to fulfill the clinical setting demands to diagnose such disorders. Based on different reports, millions suffer from different types of sleep disorders, which affect their professional and social lives. It has been observed that a lack of concentration is one of the major

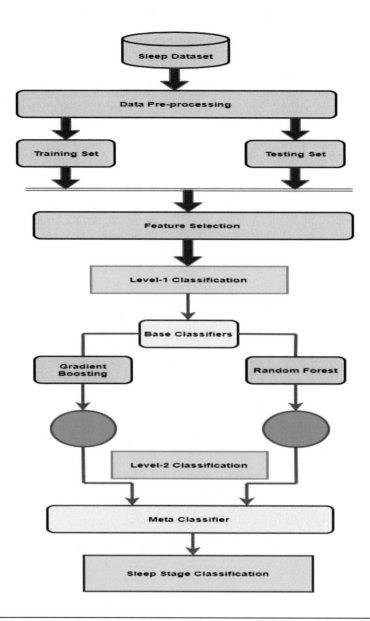

FIGURE 12.11

Proposed ensemble learning stacking model structure.

challenges caused by sleep deprivation. The current major concern is the requirement for proper technology and diagnostic tools for good management of the diagnosis. Advanced techniques and procedures may help to reduce the gap between traditional and automated sleep staging processes. An automated sleep monitoring system would be able to enhance the changes in sleep characteristics

Table 12.8 The confusion matrix and classification performance of six sleep states classification on the S-EDF data set using the EEG Fpz-Cz channel with the inclusion of age features under the R&K standards.

Automatic classification		Expert classification						SEN (%)	PRE (%)	F1Score (%)
		W	S1	S2	S3	S4	REM			
	W	6671	37	25	8	10	55	95.65	98.01	96.81
	S1	100	1095	51	3	1	54	86.22	83.97	85.08
	S2	53	35	3273	101	25	134	92.51	90.38	91.43
	S3	34	6	94	1269	168	1	90.32	80.72	85.25
	S4	14	11	40	18	834	10	79.65	84.96	82.21
	REM	102	86	55	6	9	651	71.93	71.61	71.76
	Overall							ACC:91.10%	F1Sc:85.42%	Kappa Sc:0.87

Table 12.9 The confusion matrix and classification performance of six sleep states classification on the S-EDF data set using the EEG Fpz-Cz channel with exclusion of age features under the R&K standards.

Automatic classification	Expert classification						SEN (%)	PRE (%)	F1Score (%)
	W	S1	S2	S3	S4	REM			
W	6651	57	25	8	10	55	95.72	97.72	96.71
S1	109	1082	51	3	5	54	84.13	82.97	83.55
S2	33	35	3253	131	35	134	93.90	89.83	91.82
S3	34	10	69	1289	161	8	87.92	82.05	84.88
S4	19	21	31	18	803	25	76.62	87.56	81.73
REM	102	81	35	17	34	651	70.22	70.76	70.49
Overall							ACC:90.68%	F1Sc:84.86%	Kappa Sc:0.86

Table 12.10 The confusion matrix and classification performance of six sleep states classification on the S-EDF data set using the EEG Pz-Oz channel with inclusion of age features under the R&K standards.

Automatic classification	Expert classification							SEN (%)	PRE (%)	F1Score (%)
		W	S1	S2	S3	S4	REM			
	W	6714	95	49	11	45	12	98.17	96.39	97.27
	S1	48	1412	47	15	6	70	76.57	88.36	82.04
	S2	27	110	3033	55	127	69	91.71	88.65	90.15
	S3	16	12	115	1051	85	10	90.68	81.53	85.86
	S4	10	15	48	10	515	29	63.26	82.13	71.47
	REM	24	200	15	17	36	986	83.84	77.15	80.36
	Overall							ACC:90.56%	F1Sc:84.53%	Kappa Sc:0.86

Table 12.11 The confusion matrix and classification performance of six sleep states classification on the S-EDF data set using the EEG Pz-Oz channel with exclusion of age features under the R&K standards.

Automatic classification	Expert classification						SEN (%)	PRE (%)	F1Score (%)
	W	S1	S2	S3	S4	REM			
W	6690	92	53	24	43	14	98.02	96.73	97.37
S1	41	1409	47	22	11	68	75.75	88.17	81.49
S2	37	110	3013	55	132	74	91.60	88.07	89.80
S3	16	33	114	1031	85	10	88.19	79.98	83.88
S4	17	21	42	13	512	22	62.51	81.65	70.81
REM	24	195	20	24	36	979	83.89	76.60	80.08
Overall							ACC:90.11%	F1Sc:83.91%	Kappa Sc:0.86

during different stages of sleep. Recently, this process has made it easier due to emerging biomedical signal processing techniques and devices that can accurately identify sleep irregularities and measure sleep quality.

In this chapter, we have discussed how sleep plays an important role in our lives. This chapter provides information about how sleep problems affect individuals' social and professional lives. Some statistics have been provided to show readers how sleep problems are now considered to be one of the global health challenges. Further, we also provided information about how the different physiological signals are the most important for the analysis of brain behaviors and activities. This chapter gave basic outlines regarding changes in sleep characteristics during different sleep stages and briefly discussed sleep deprivation with regard to the age of the subjects.

References

[1] E. Estrada, H. Nazeran, P. Nava, K. Behbehani, J. Burk, E. Lucas, Itakura distance: a useful similarity measure between EEG and EOG signals in computer-aided classification of sleep stages, in: Proceedings of the 27th IEEE Annual International Conference of Engineering in Medicine and Biology Society, Shanghai, China, 1—4 September, 2005, pp. 1189—1192.

[2] Y. Li, F. Yingle, L. Gu, T. Qinye, Sleep stage classification based on EEG Hilbert— Huang transform, in: Proceedings of the 4th IEEE Conference on Industrial Electronics and Applications (ICIEA), Xi'an, China, 25—27 May, 2009, pp. 3676—3681.

[3] K.A. Aboalayon, M. Faezipour, Multi-class SVM based on sleep stage identification using EEG signal, in: Proceedings of the IEEE Healthcare Innovation Conference (HIC), Seattle,WA, USA, 8—10 October, 2014, pp. 181—184.

[4] C.-S. Huang, C.-L. Lin, L.-W. Ko, S.-Y. Liu, T.-P. Sua, C.-T. Lin, A hierarchical classification system for sleep stage scoring via forehead EEG signals, in: Proceedings of the IEEE Symposium on Computational Intelligence, Cognitive Algorithms, Mind, and Brain (CCMB), Singapore, 16—19 April, 2013, pp. 1—5 [5].

[5] C.-S. Huang, C.-L. Lin, W.-Y. Yang, L.-W. Ko, S.-Y. Liu, C.-T. Lin, Applying the fuzzy c-means based dimension reduction to improve the sleep classification system, in: Proceedings of the IEEE International Conference on Fuzzy Systems (FUZZ), Hyderabad, India, 7—10 July, 2013, pp. 1—5.

[6] Y.-H. Lee, Y.-S. Chen, L.-F. Chen, Automated sleep staging using single EEG channel for REM sleep deprivation, in: Proceedings of the Ninth IEEE International Conference on Bioinformatics and BioEngineering, Taichung, Taiwan, 22—24 June, 2009, pp. 439—442.

[7] A.R. Hassan, M.I.H. Bhuiyan, Automatic sleep scoring using statistical features in the EMD domain and ensemble methods, Biocybern. Biomed. Eng. 36 (2016) 248—255 [CrossRef].

[8] S. Khalighi, T. Sousa, G. Pires, U. Nunes, Automatic sleep staging: a computer assisted approach for optimal combination of features and polysomnographic channels, Expert Syst. Appl. 40 (2013) 7046—7059 [CrossRef].

[9] B. Sen, M. Peker, A. Çavuşoğlu, F.V. Çelebi, A Comparative Study on Classification of Sleep Stage Based on EEG Signals Using Feature Selection and Classification Algorithms.

[10] L. Zoubek, S. Charbonnier, S. Lesecq, A. Buguet, F. Chapotot, Feature selection for sleep/wake stages classification using data driven methods, Biomed. Signal Process Contr. 2 (2007) 171—179.

[11] C.B. Saper, P.M. Fuller, N.P. Pedersen, J. Lu, T.E. Scammell, Sleep state switching, Neuron 68 (2010) 1023—1042.

[12] R. Stickgold, M.P. Walker, Memory consolidation and reconsolidation: what is the role of sleep? Trends Neurosci. 28 (2005) 408—415.

[13] E. Aserinsky, The discovery of REM sleep, J. Hist. Neurosci. 5(3) (1996) 213–227, https://doi.org/10.1080/09647049609525671, 11618742.

[14] H. Berger, Hans Berger and the discovery of the electroencephalogram, Electroencephalogr. Clin. Neurophysiol. 28 (1969) 1–36, 4188910.

[15] S.L. Worley, The Extraordinary Importance of Sleep: The Detrimental Effects of Inadequate Sleep on Health and Public Safety Drive an Explosion of Sleep Research. PT, 2018.

[16] K.L. Knutson, K. Spiegel, P. Penev, E. VanCauter, The metabolic consequences of sleep deprivation, Sleep Med. Rev. 11 (2007) 163–178, 2007.

[17] J. Lim, D.F. Dinges, Sleep deprivation and vigilant attention, Ann. N. Y. Acad. Sci. 1129 (2008) 305–322.

[18] T.J. Balkin, T. Rupp, D. Picchioni, N.J. Wesensten, Sleep loss and sleepiness: current issues, Chest J. 134 (2008) 653–660.

[19] P. Rau, Drowsy Driver Detection and Warning System for Commercial Vehicle Drivers: Field Operational Test Design, Analysis, and Progress, National Highway Traffic Safety Administration, Washington, DC, USA, 2005.

[20] G.J. Landry, T. Liu-Ambrose, Buying time: a rationale for examining the use of circadian rhythm and sleep interventions to delay progression of mild cognitive impairment to Alzheimer disease, Front. Aging Neurosci. 6 (2014).

[21] M.M. Ohayon, Epidemiology of insomnia: what we know and what we still need to learn, Sleep Med. Rev. 6 (2) (2002) 97–111.

[22] S. Kajeepeta, B. Gelaye, C.L. Jackson, M.A. Williams, Adverse childhood experiences are associated with adult sleep disorders: a systematic review, Sleep Med. 16 (3) (2015) 320–330.

[23] M.M. Ohayon, Smirne, Prevalence and consequences of insomnia disorders in the general population of Italy, Sleep Med. 3 (2) (2002) 115–120.

[24] E.M. Wickwire, F.T. Shaya, S.M. Scharf, Health economics of insomnia treatments:the return on investment for a good night's sleep, Sleep Med. Rev. 30 (2016) 72–82.

[25] R.J. Ozminkowski, S. Wang, J.K. Walsh, The direct and indirect costs of untreated insomnia in adults in the United States, Sleep 30 (3) (2007) 263–273.

[26] D. Leger, B. Poursain, D. Neubauer, M. Uchiyama, An international survey of sleeping problems in the general population, Curr. Med. Res. Opin. 24 (1) (2008) 307–317.

[27] C. Iber, The AASM Manual for the Scoring of Sleep and Associated Events: Rules, Terminology and Technical Specifications, American Academy of Sleep Medicine, 2007.

[28] A. Iranzo, J. Santamaria, E. Tolosa, The clinical and pathophysiological relevance of REM sleep behavior disorder in neurodegenerative diseases, Sleep Med. Rev. 13 (6) (2009) 385–401.

[29] A. Ambrogetti, M.J. Hensley, L.G. Olsen, Sleep Disorders: A Clinical Textbook, Quay Books, London, 2006.

[30] A. Rechtschaffen, A. Kales, A Manual of Standardized Terminology, Techniques and Scoring System for Sleep Stages of Human Subjects, U.S. National Institute of Neurological Diseases and Blindness, Neurol. Inform. Netw, Bethesda, MD, 1968.

[31] C. Iber, S. Ancoli-Israel, A.L. Chesson, S.F. Quan, The AASM Manual for the Scoring of Sleep and Associated Events: Rules, Terminology and Technical Specification, American Academy of Sleep Medicine, Westchester, USA, 2007.

[32] B. Sen, M. Peker, Novel approaches for automated epileptic diagnosis using FCBF feature selection and classification algorithms, Turk. J. Electr. Eng. Comput. Sci. 21 (2013) 2092–2109.

[33] M. Jamshidi, A. Lalbakhsh, S. Lot, H. Siahkamari, B. Mohamadzade, J. Jalilian, A neuro-based approach to designing a Wilkinson power divider, Int. J. RF Microw. Computer-Aided Eng. 30 (3) (2020).

[34] M. Jamshidi, A. Lalbakhsh, B. Mohamadzade, H. Siahkamari, S.M.H. Mousavi, A novel neural-based approach for design of microstrip lters, AEU-Int. J. Electron. Commun. 110 (2019).

[35] M.B. Jamshidi, N. Alibeigi, A. Lalbakhsh, S. Roshani, An ANFIS approach to modeling a small satellite power source of NASA, in: Proc. IEEE 16th Int. Conf. Netw., Sens. Control (ICNSC), 2019, pp. 459−464.

[36] Y. Mintz, R. Brodie, Introduction to artificial intelligence in medicine, Minim Invasive Ther. Allied Technol. 28 (2) (2019) 73−81.

[37] R.B. Parikh, Z. Obermeyer, A.S. Navathe, Regulation of predictive analytics in medicine, Science 363 (6429) (2019) 810−812.

[38] A. Becker, Artificial intelligence in medicine: what is it doing for us today? Health Pol. Technol. 8 (2) (2019) 198−205.

[39] N.J. Schork, Artificial intelligence and personalized medicine, in: Precision Medicine in Cancer Therapy, Springer, Cham, Switzerland, 2019, pp. 265−283.

[40] M.B. Jamshidi, N. Alibeigi, N. Rabbani, B. Oryani, A. Lalbakhsh, Artificial neural networks: a powerful tool for cognitive science, in: Proc. IEEE 9th Annu. Inf. Technol., Electron. Mobile Commun. Conf.(IEMCON), 2018, pp. 674−679.

[41] B. Mirza, W. Wang, J. Wang, H. Choi, N.C. Chung, P. Ping, Machine learning and integrative analysis of biomedical big data, Genes 10 (2019) 87.

[42] O. Faust, H. Razaghi, R. Barika, E.J. Ciaccio, U.R. Acharya, A review of automated sleep stage scoring based on physiological signals for the new millennia, Comput. Methods Progr. Biomed. 176 (2019) 81−91.

[43] O. Faust, Y. Hagiwara, T.J. Hong, O.S. Lih, U.R. Acharya, Deep learning for healthcare applications based on physiological signals: a review, Comput. Methods Progr. Biomed. 161 (2018) 1−13 [CrossRef].

[44] S. Miano, M.C. Paolino, R. Castaldo, M. Villa, Visual scoring of sleep: a comparison between the Rechtschaffen and kales criteria and the American academy of sleep medicine criteria in a pediatric population with obstructive sleep apnea syndrome, Clin. Neurophysiol. 121 (1) (2010) 39−42.

[45] W.H. Spriggs, Essentials of Polysomnography, Jones & Bartlett Publishers, 2014.

[46] A.G. Harvey, K. Stinson, K.L. Whitaker, D. Moskovitz, H. Virk, The subjective meaning of sleep quality: a comparison of individuals with and without insomnia, Sleep 31 (3) (2008) 383−393.

[47] S. Koelstra, C. Muhl, M. Soleymani, Jong-Seok, Lee, A. Yazdani, T. Ebrahimi, DEAP: a database for emotion analysis using physiological signals, IEEE Trans. Affect. Comput. 3 (1) (2012) 18−31.

[48] J. Luo, M. Wu, D. Gopukumar, Y. Zhao, Big data application in biomedical research and healthcare: a literature review, Biomed. Inf. Insights 8 (2016) 1−10.

[49] P. Degoulet, M. Fieschi, Introduction to Clinical Informatics, Springer Publications, New York, 2012.

[50] Q. Zhang, X. Chen, Q. Zhan, T. Yang, S. Xia, Respiration-based emotion recognition with deep learning, Comput. Ind. 92 (2017) 84−90.

[51] S. Kiranyaz, T. Ince, M. Gabbouj, Personalized ECG classification, in: In Multidimensional Particle Swarm Optimization for Machine Learning and Pattern Recognition, Springer, Berlin, 2014, pp. 231−258.

[52] R. Maestri, G.D. Pinna, A. Porta, R. Balocchi, R. Sassi, M.G. Signorini, Assessing nonlinear properties of heart rate variability from short-term recordings: are these measurements reliable? Physiol. Meas. 28 (9) (2007) 1067−1077.

[53] P.A. Karthick, G. Venugopal, S. Ramakrishnan, Analysis of muscle fatigue progression using cyclostationary property of surface electromyography signals, J. Med. Syst. 40 (1) (2016) 28.

[54] J. Allen, Photoplethysmography and its application in clinical physiological measurement, Physiol. Meas. 28 (3) (2007).

[55] S. Mousavi, F. Afghah, U.R. Acharya, Sleepeegnet: Automated Sleep Stage Scoring with Sequence to Sequence Deep Learning Approach, 2019.

[56] N. Michielli, U.R. Acharya, F. Molinari, Cascaded lstm recurrent neural network for automated sleep stage classification using single-channel EEG signals, Comput. Biol. Med. 106 (2019) 71−81, https://doi.org/10.1016/j.compbiomed.2019.01.013, 30685634.

[57] M. Sharma, D. Goyal, P. Achuth, U.R. Acharya, An accurate sleep stages classification system using a new class of optimally time-frequency localized three–band wavelet filter bank, Comput. Biol. Med. 98 (2018) 58–75.

[58] S. Seifpour, H. Niknazar, M. Mikaeili, A.M. Nasrabadi, A new automatic sleep staging system based on statistical behavior of local extrema using single channel EEG signal, Expert Syst. Appl. 104 (2018) 277–293.

[59] P. Chriskos, C.A. Frantzidis, P.T. Gkivogkli, P.D. Bamidis, C. Kourtidou-Papadeli, Achieving accurate automatic sleep staging on manually preprocessed EEG data through synchronization feature extraction and graph metrics, Front. Hum. Neurosci. 12 (2018) 110.

[60] P. Memar, F. Faradji, A novel multi-class EEG-based sleep stage classification system, IEEE Trans. Neural Syst. Rehabil. Eng. 26 (1) (2018) 84–95.

[61] K. Pillay, A. Dereymaeker, K. Jansen, G. Naulaers, S. VanHuffel, M. DeVos, Automated EEG sleep staging in the term-age baby using a generative modelling approach, J. Neural. Eng. 15 (3) (2018).

[62] A.R. Hassan, A. Subasi, A decision support system for automated identification of sleep stages from single-channel EEG signals, Know.-Based Syst. 128 (2017) 115–124.

[63] S. Yücelbas, C. Yücelbas, G.S. Tezel, Automatic sleep staging based on SVD, VMD, HHT and morphological features of single-lead ECG signal, Expert Syst. Appl. 102 (2018) 193–206.

[64] H. Yoon, S.H. Hwang, J.-W. Choi, Y.J. Lee, D.-U. Jeong, K.S. Park, Rem sleep estimation based on autonomic dynamics using r–r intervals, Physiol. Meas. 38 (4) (2017) 631.

[65] S. Liu, J. Teng, X. Qi, S. Wei, C. Liu, Comparison between heart rate variability and pulse rate variability during different sleep stages for sleep apnea patients, Technol. Health Care 25 (3) (2017) 435–445.

[66] M.M. Rahman, M.I.H. Bhuiyan, A.R. Hassan, Sleep stage classification using single-channel EOG, Comput. Biol. Med. 102 (2018) 211–220, https://doi.org/10.1016/j.compbiomed.2018.08.022, 30170769.

[67] R. Tripathy, U.R. Acharya, Use of features from rr-time series and EEG signals for automated classification of sleep stages in deep neural network framework, Biocybernet. Biomed. Eng. 38 (4) (2018) 890–902.

[68] T. Takatani, Y. Takahashi, R. Yoshida, R. Imai, T. Uchiike, M. Yamazaki, M. Shima, T. Nishikubo, Y. Ikada, S. Fujimoto, Relationship between frequency spectrum of heart rate variability and autonomic nervous activities during sleep in newborns, Brain Dev. 40 (3) (2018) 165–171.

[69] S. Lerman, L. Buenaver, P. Finan, M. Medak, T. Amani, H. Tennen, J. Haythornthwaite, M. Smith, 1071 Amount of slow wave sleep is associated with the discrepancies between objective and subjective sleep measures, Sleep 40 (2017) A398.

[70] R. Rosipal, A. Lewandowski, G. Dorffner, In search of objective components for sleep quality indexing in normal sleep, Biol. Psychol. 94 (1) (2013) 210–220.

[71] H.J. Orff, C.J. Meliska, A. Lopez, F. Martinez, D. Sorenson, B.L. Parry, Polysomnographic evaluation of sleep quality and quantitative variables in women as a function of mood, reproductive status, and age, Dialogues Clin. Neurosci. 14 (4) (2012) 413.

[72] H.P. Roffward, J.N. Muzio, W.C. Dement, Ontogenetic development of the human sleepdream cycle, Science 152 (3722) (1966) 604–619.

[73] K.F. Davis, K.P. Parker, G.L. Montgomery, Sleep in infants and young children: part one: normal sleep, J. Pediatr. Health Care 18 (2) (2004) 65–71.

[74] O.G. Jenni, M.A. Carskadon, Normal human sleep at different ages: infants to adolescents, in: Sleep Research Society, Eds. SRS Basics of Sleep Guide, Sleep Research Society., Westchester, IL, 2000, pp. 11–19.

[75] T.F. Anders, A. Sadeh, V. Appareddy, Normal sleep in neonates and children, in: R.K.M. Ferber (Ed.), Principles and Practice of Sleep Medicine in the Child, Saunders, Philadelphia, 1995, pp. 7–18.

[76] O.G. Jenni, B.B. O'Connor, Children's sleep: an interplay between culture and biology, Pediatrics 115 (1 Suppl. l) (2005) 204–216.

[77] P.W. Mercer, S.L. Merritt, J.M. Cowell, Differences in reported sleep need among adolescents, J. Adolesc. Health 23 (5) (1998) 259−263.

[78] M.A. Carskadon, The second decade, in: C. Guilleminault (Ed.), Sleeping and Waking Disorders:Indications and Techniques, Addison-Wesley, Menlo Park, CA, 1982, pp. 99−125.

[79] D.J. Dijk, J.F. Duffy, C.A. Czeisler, Contribution of circadian physiology and sleep homeostasis to age-related changes in human sleep, Chronobiol. Int. 17 (3) (2000) 285−311.

[80] J.F. Duffy, D.J. Dijk, E.B. Klerman, C.A. Czeisler, Later endogenous circadian temperature nadir relative to an earlier wake time in older people, Am. J. Physiol. 275 (1998) 1478−R1487.

[81] V. Bach, F. Telliez, A. Leke, J.P. Libert, Gender-related sleep differences in neonates in thermoneutral and cool environments, J. Sleep Res. 9 (3) (2000) 249−254.

[82] A.M. Meijer, H.T. Habekothe, G.L. Van Den Wittenboer, Time in bed, quality of sleep and school functioning of children, J. Sleep Res. 9 (2) (2000) 145−153.

[83] F. Giannotti, F. Cortesi, T. Sebastiani, S. Ottaviano, Circadian preference, sleep and daytime behaviour in adolescence, J. Sleep Res. 11 (3) (2002) 191−199.

[84] R. Kobayashi, M. Kohsaka, N. Fukuda, H. Honma, S. Sakakibara, T. Koyama, Gender differences in the sleep of middle-aged individuals, Psychiatr. Clin. Neurosci. 52 (2) (1998) 186−187.

[85] M.G. Metcalf, Incidence of ovulation from the menarche to the menopause: observations of 622 New Zealand women, N. Z. Med. J. 96 (738) (1983) 645−648.

[86] K.A. Lee, M.E. Zaffke, K. Baratte-Beebe, Restless legs syndrome and sleep disturbance during pregnancy: the role of folate and iron, J. Wom. Health Gend. Base Med. 10(4) 335−341.

[87] D. Bliwise, Normal aging, in: M.H. Kryger, T. Roth, W.C. Dement (Eds.), Principles and Practice of Sleep Medicine, fourth ed., Saunders, Philadelphia, 2005, pp. 24−38.

[88] B. Kemp, A.H. Zwinderman, B. Tuk, H.A.C. Kamphuisen, J.J.L. Oberye, Analysis of a sleep-dependent neuronal feedback loop: the slow-wave micro continuity of the EEG, IEEE Trans. Biomed. Eng. 47 (9) (2000) 11851194, https://doi.org/10.1109/10.867928.

Index

Note: 'Page numbers followed by "f" indicate figures and "t" indicate tables.'

269

Printed in the United States
by Baker & Taylor Publisher Services